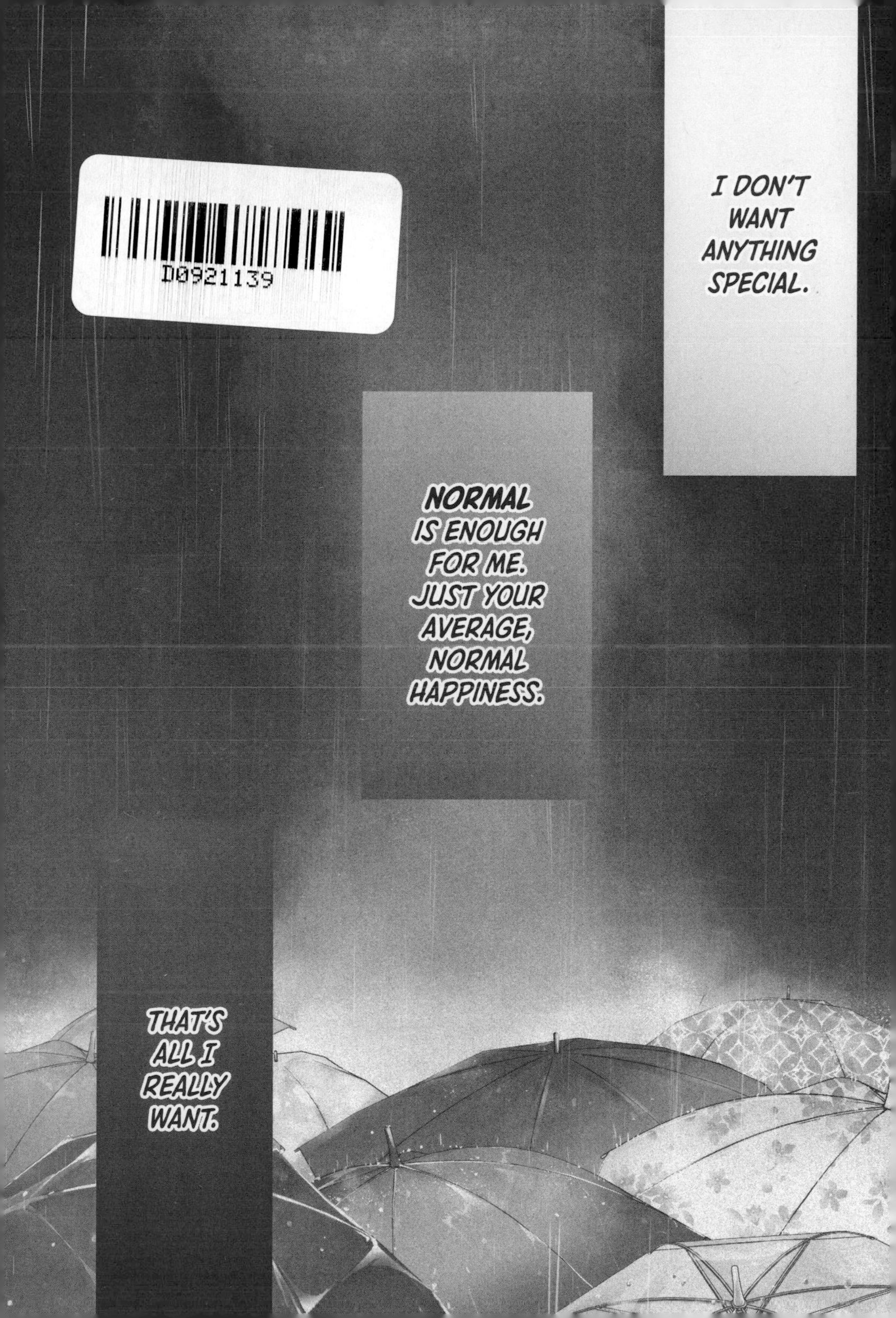
I DON'T WANT ANYTHING SPECIAL.
NORMAL IS ENOUGH FOR ME. JUST YOUR AVERAGE, NORMAL HAPPINESS.
THAT'S ALL I REALLY WANT.

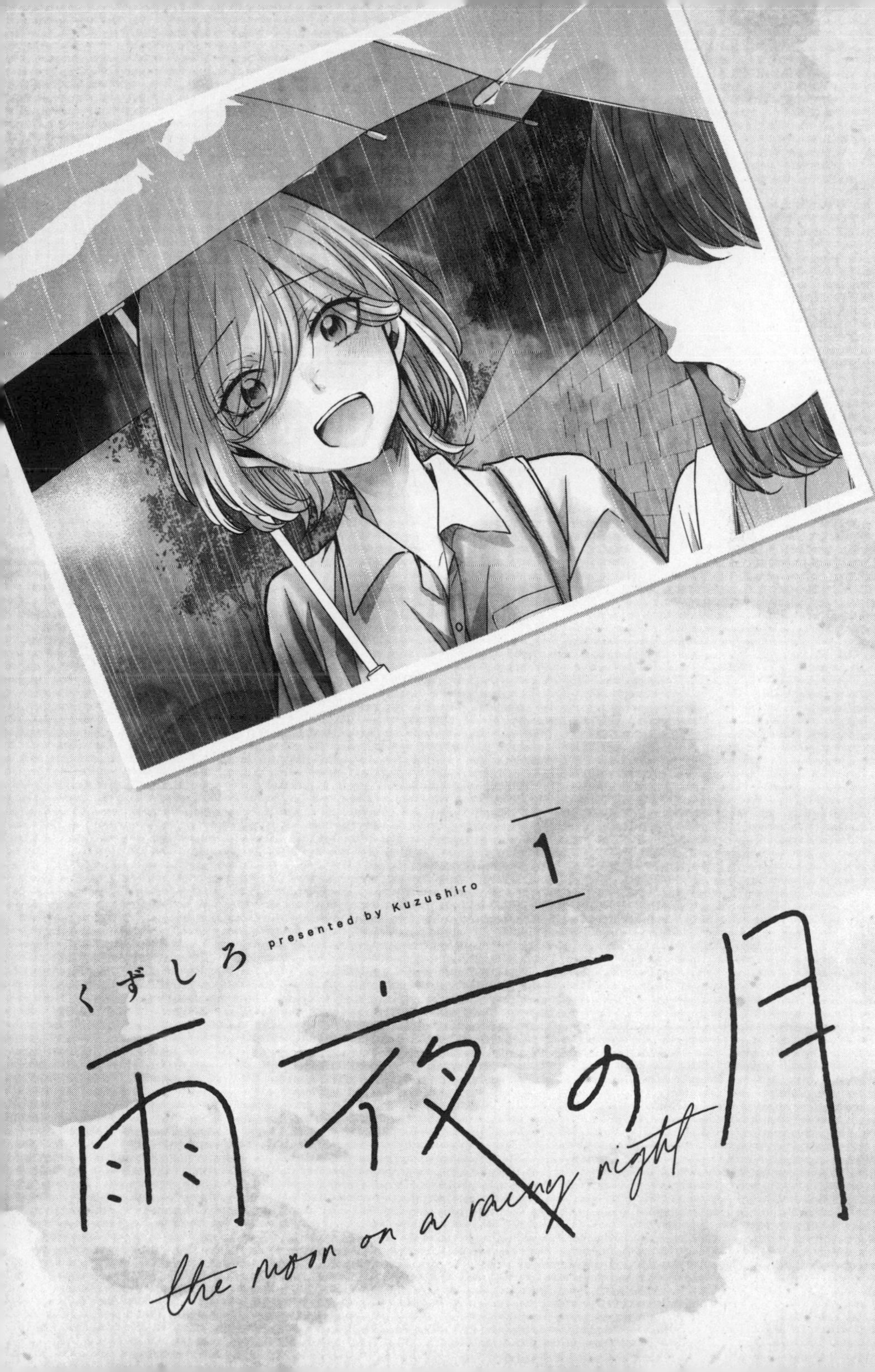

1

くずしろ presented by Kuzushiro

雨夜の月

the moon on a rainy night

Contents

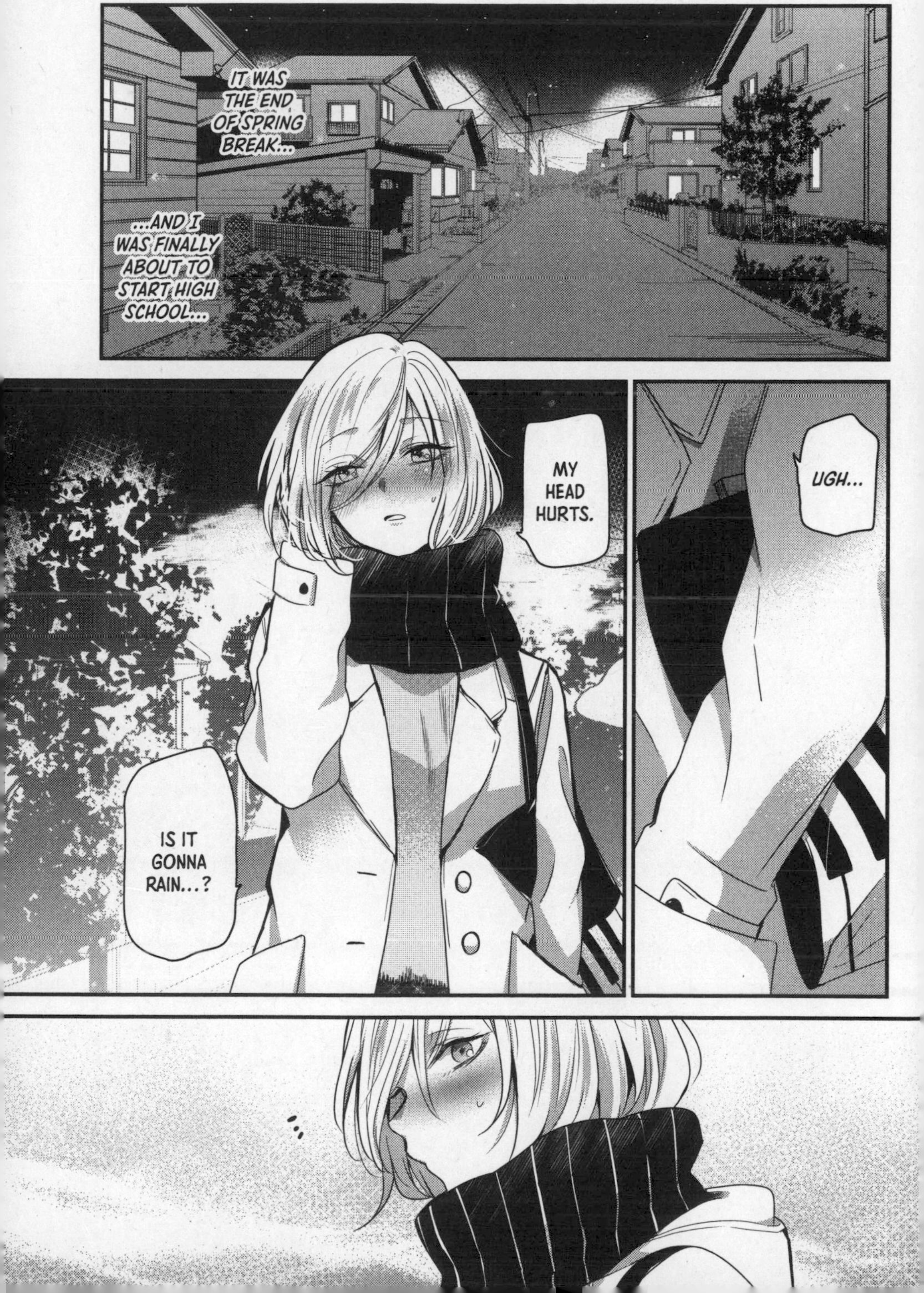
IT WAS THE END OF SPRING BREAK...
...AND I WAS FINALLY ABOUT TO START HIGH SCHOOL...
UGH...
MY HEAD HURTS.
IS IT GONNA RAIN...?
...

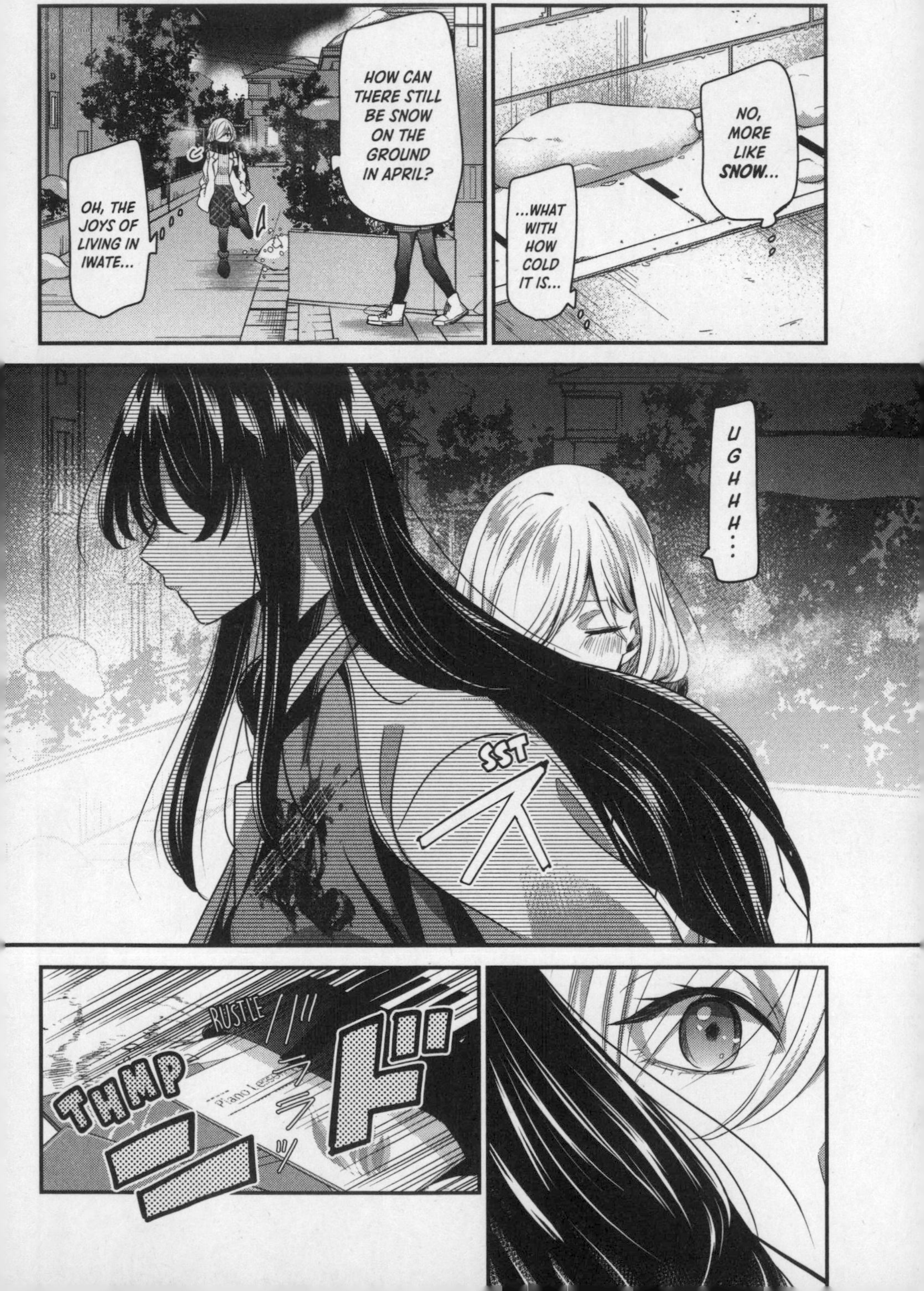
NO, MORE LIKE SNOW...
...WHAT WITH HOW COLD IT IS...
HOW CAN THERE STILL BE SNOW ON THE GROUND IN APRIL?
OH, THE JOYS OF LIVING IN IWATE...
UGHHH...
SST
RUSTLE
THMP

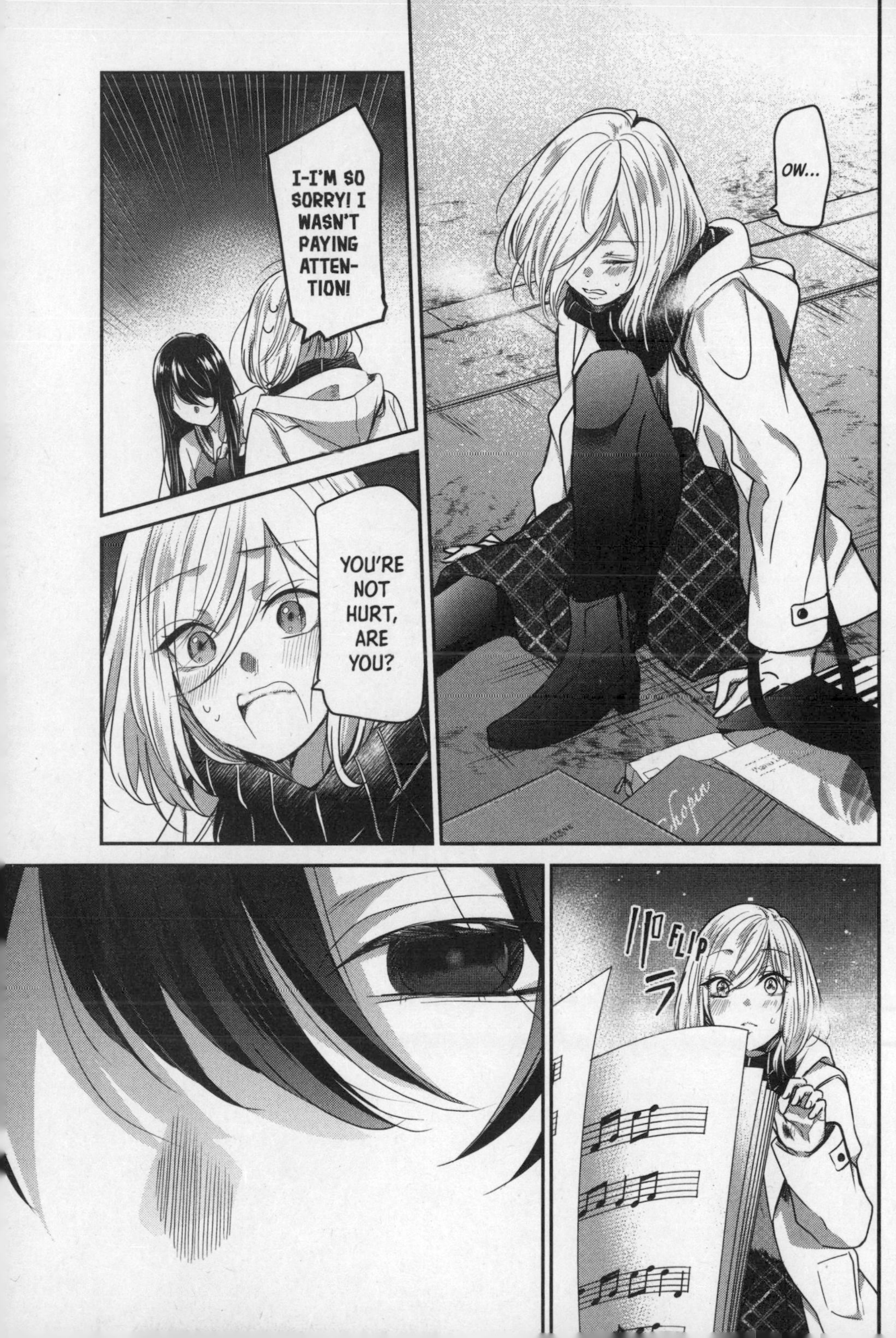
OW...
I-I'M SO SORRY! I WASN'T PAYING ATTEN-TION!
YOU'RE NOT HURT, ARE YOU?
パラ FLIP

Chapter 1: Kanon & Saki

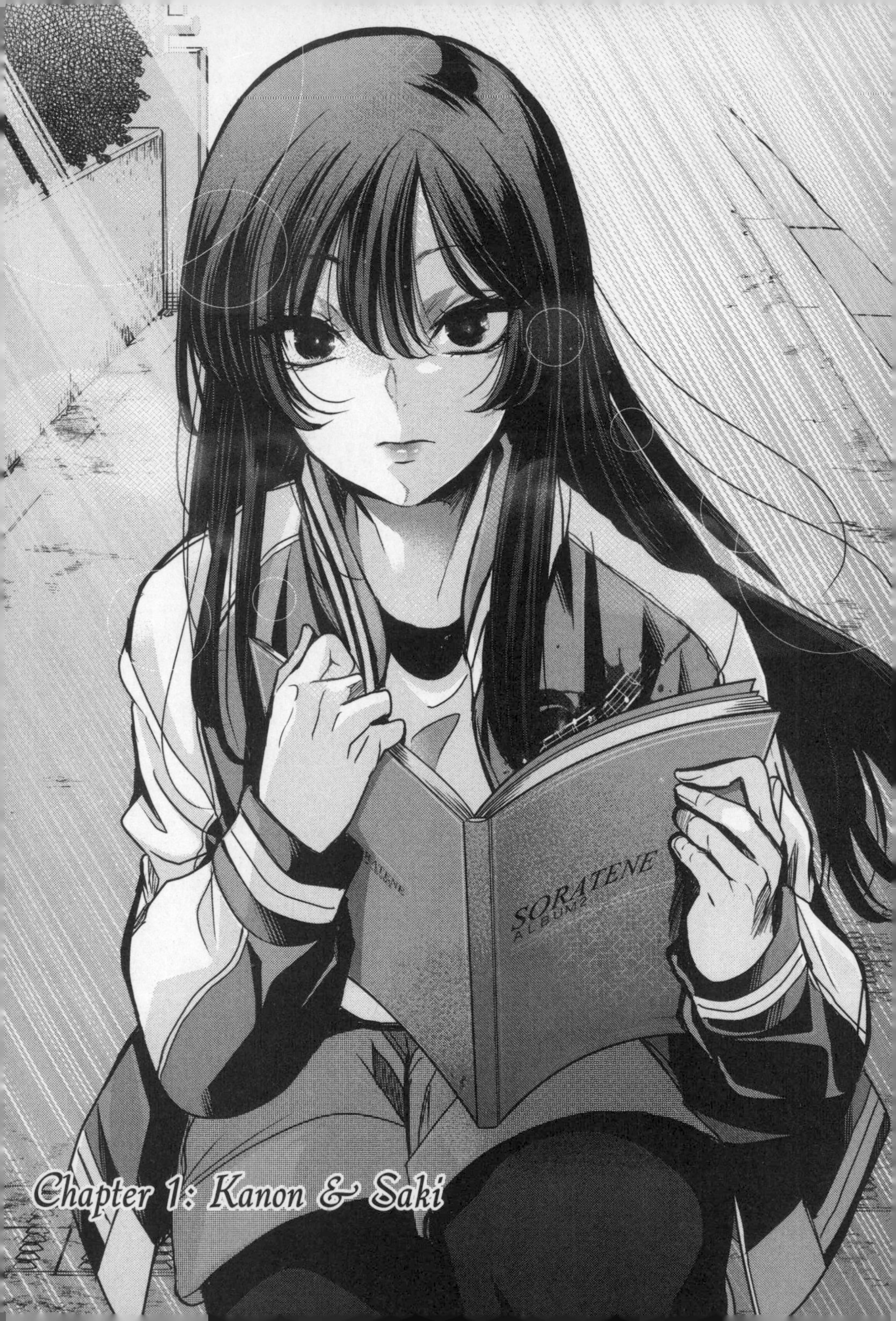
SORATENE
ALBUM2

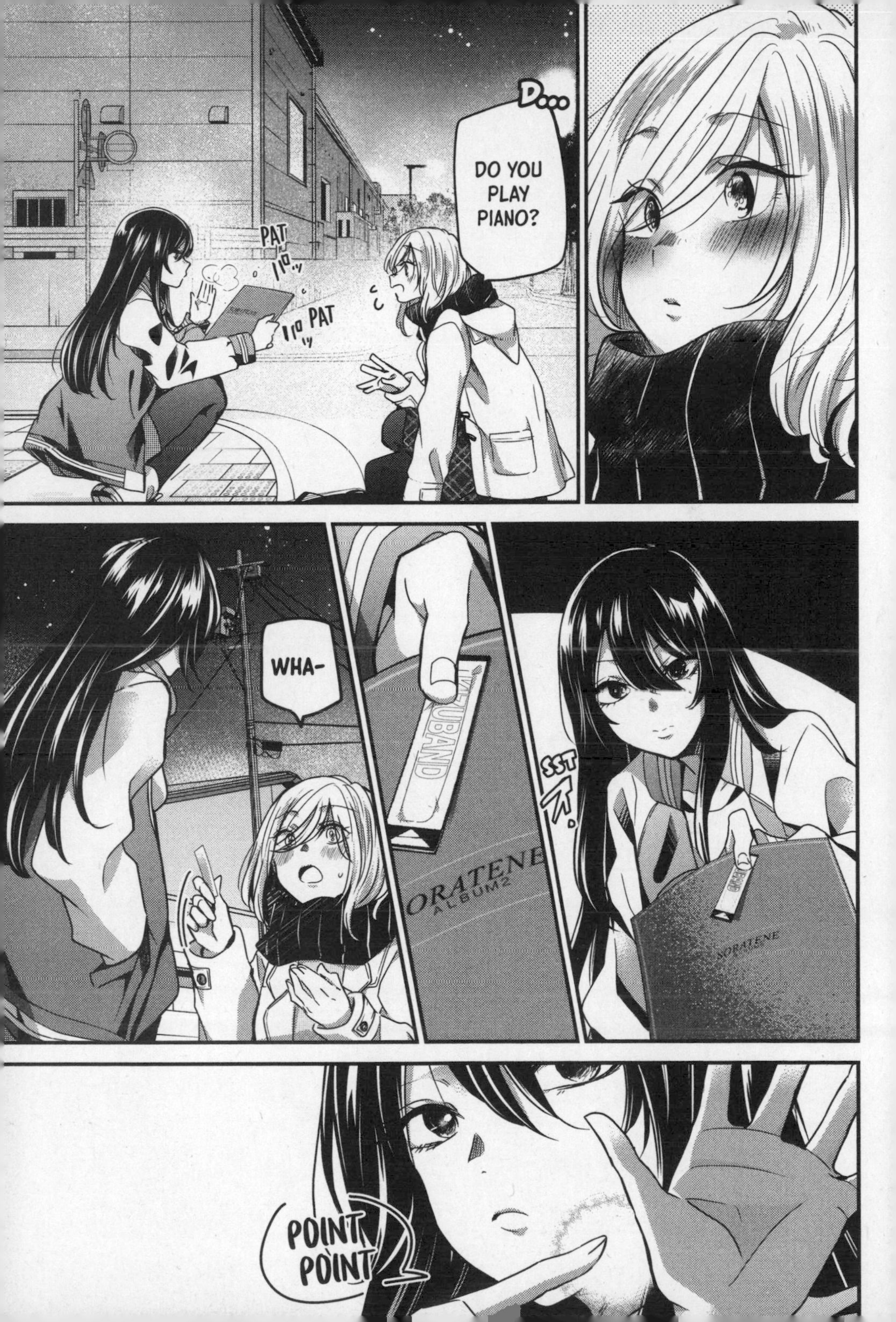
D...
DO YOU PLAY PIANO?
PAT
PAT
SST
WHA-
POINT POINT

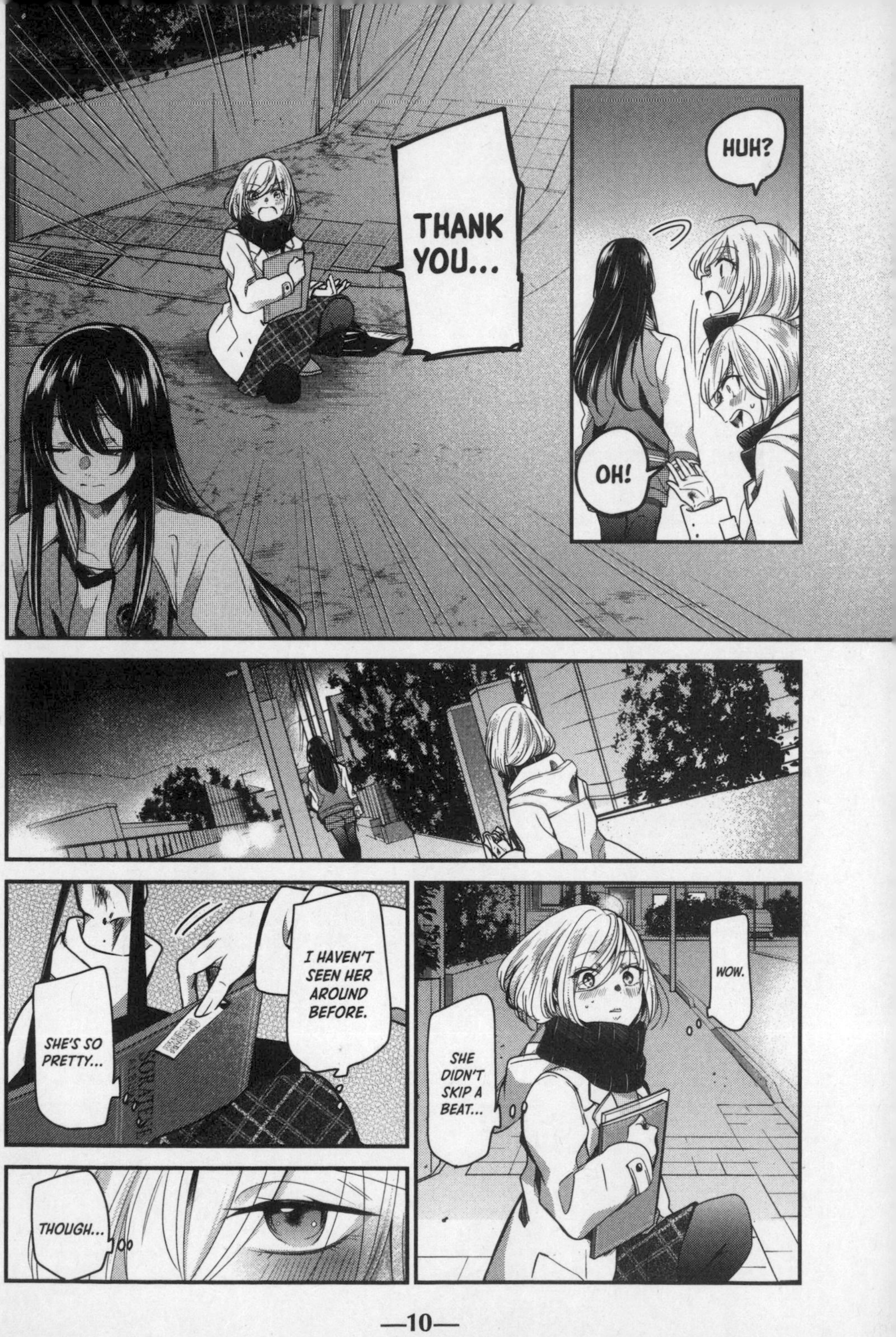
HUH?
OH!
THANK YOU...
WOW.
SHE DIDN'T SKIP A BEAT...
I HAVEN'T SEEN HER AROUND BEFORE.
SHE'S SO PRETTY...
THOUGH...

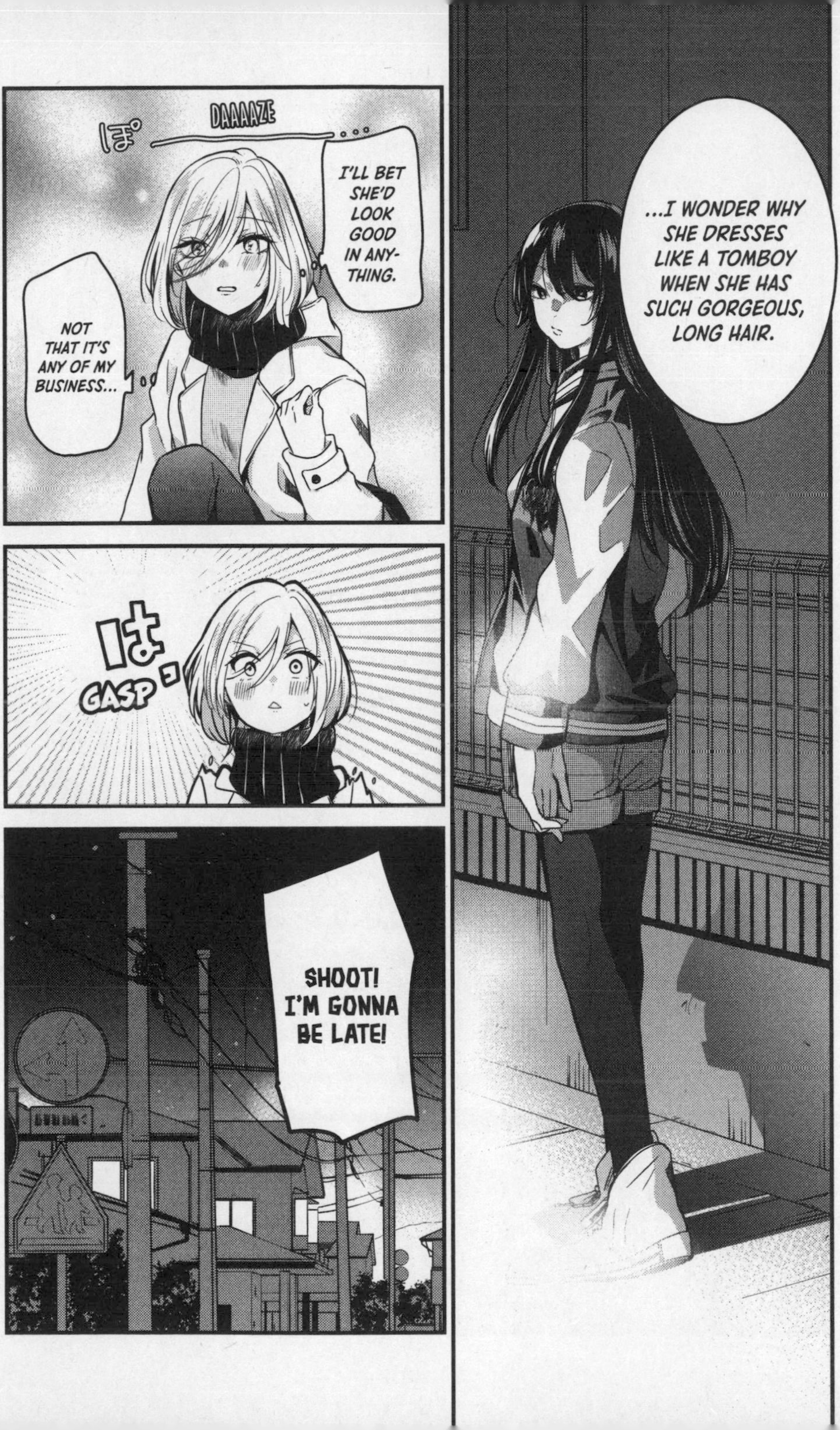
...I WONDER WHY SHE DRESSES LIKE A TOMBOY WHEN SHE HAS SUCH GORGEOUS, LONG HAIR.
ぽ DAAAAZE
I'LL BET SHE'D LOOK GOOD IN ANY-THING.
NOT THAT IT'S ANY OF MY BUSINESS...
は GASP っ
SHOOT! I'M GONNA BE LATE!

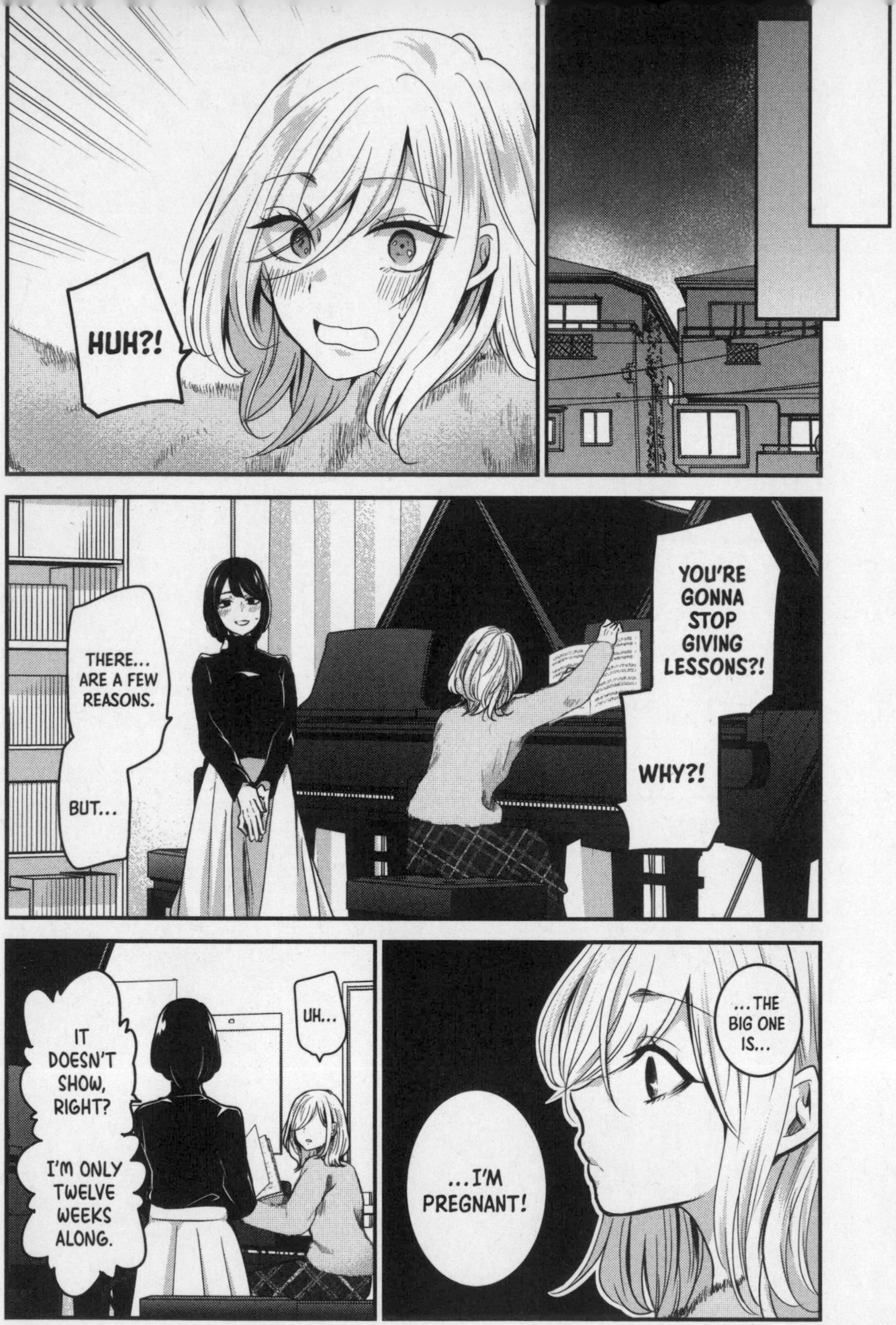
HUH?!
YOU'RE GONNA STOP GIVING LESSONS?!
WHY?!
THERE... ARE A FEW REASONS.
BUT...
...THE BIG ONE IS...
...I'M PREGNANT!
UH...
IT DOESN'T SHOW, RIGHT?
I'M ONLY TWELVE WEEKS ALONG.

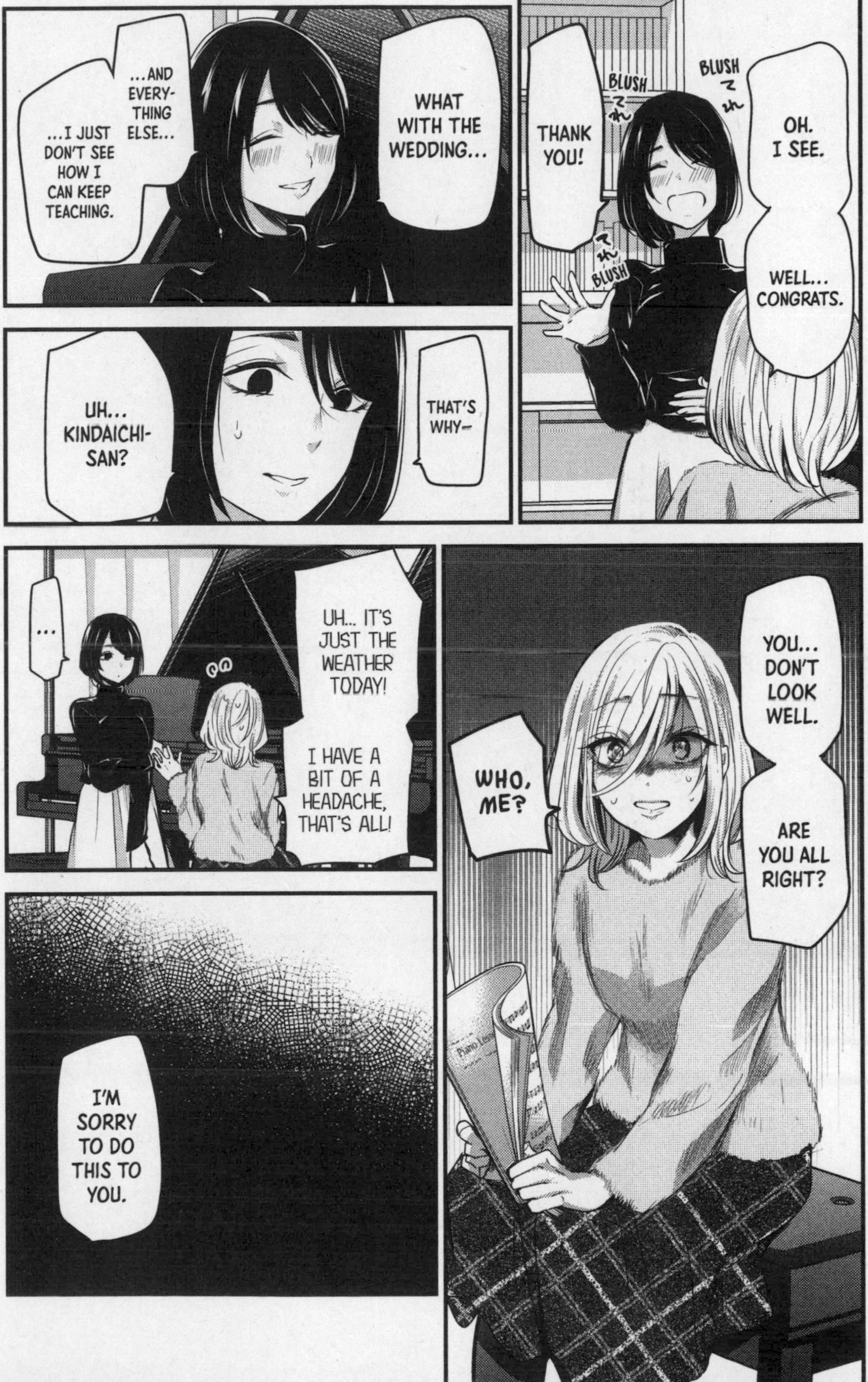
BLUSH てれ
OH. I SEE.
WELL... CONGRATS.
THANK YOU!
BLUSH てれ
BLUSH てれ
WHAT WITH THE WEDDING...
...AND EVERYTHING ELSE...
...I JUST DON'T SEE HOW I CAN KEEP TEACHING.
THAT'S WHY—
UH... KINDAICHI-SAN?
YOU... DON'T LOOK WELL.
ARE YOU ALL RIGHT?
WHO, ME?
UH... IT'S JUST THE WEATHER TODAY!
I HAVE A BIT OF A HEADACHE, THAT'S ALL!
...
I'M SORRY TO DO THIS TO YOU.

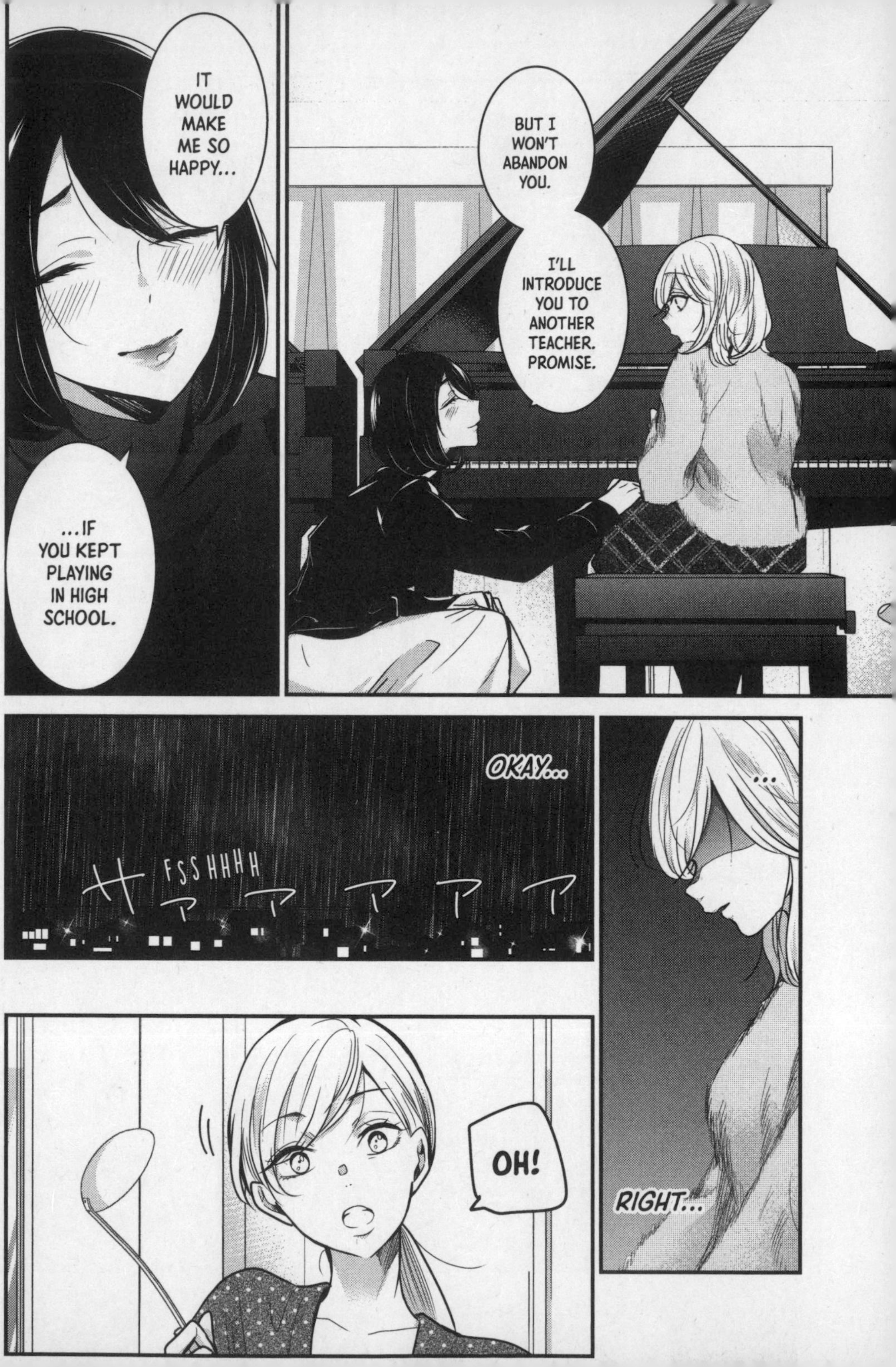
BUT I WON'T ABANDON YOU.
I'LL INTRODUCE YOU TO ANOTHER TEACHER. PROMISE.
IT WOULD MAKE ME SO HAPPY...
...IF YOU KEPT PLAYING IN HIGH SCHOOL.
...
RIGHT...
OKAY...
サァァァァァ
FSSHHHH
OH!

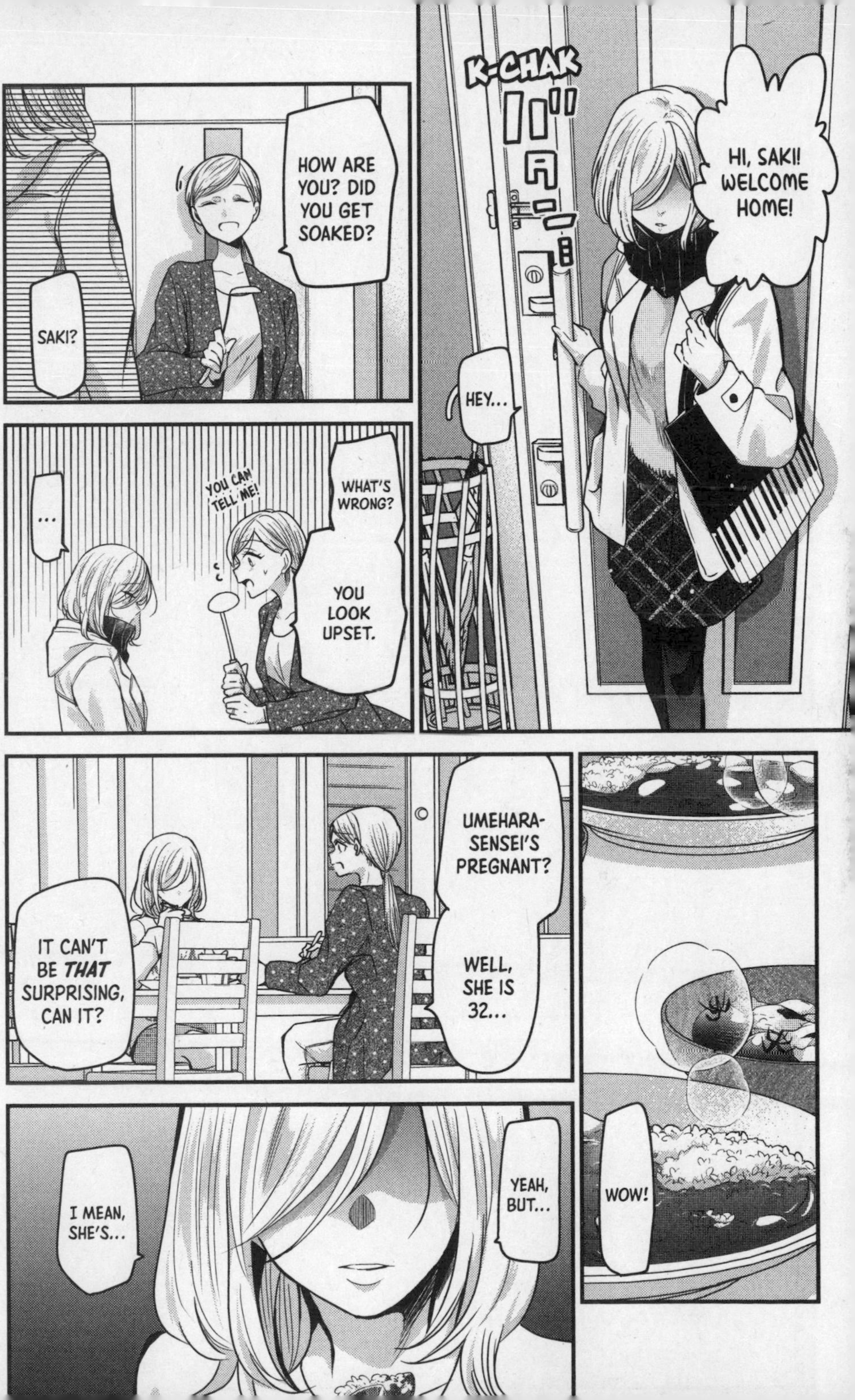
K-CHAK
HI, SAKI! WELCOME HOME!
HEY...
HOW ARE YOU? DID YOU GET SOAKED?
SAKI?
WHAT'S WRONG?
YOU LOOK UPSET.
YOU CAN TELL ME!
...
WOW!
UMEHARA-SENSEI'S PREGNANT?
WELL, SHE IS 32...
IT CAN'T BE *THAT* SURPRISING, CAN IT?
YEAH, BUT...
I MEAN, SHE'S...

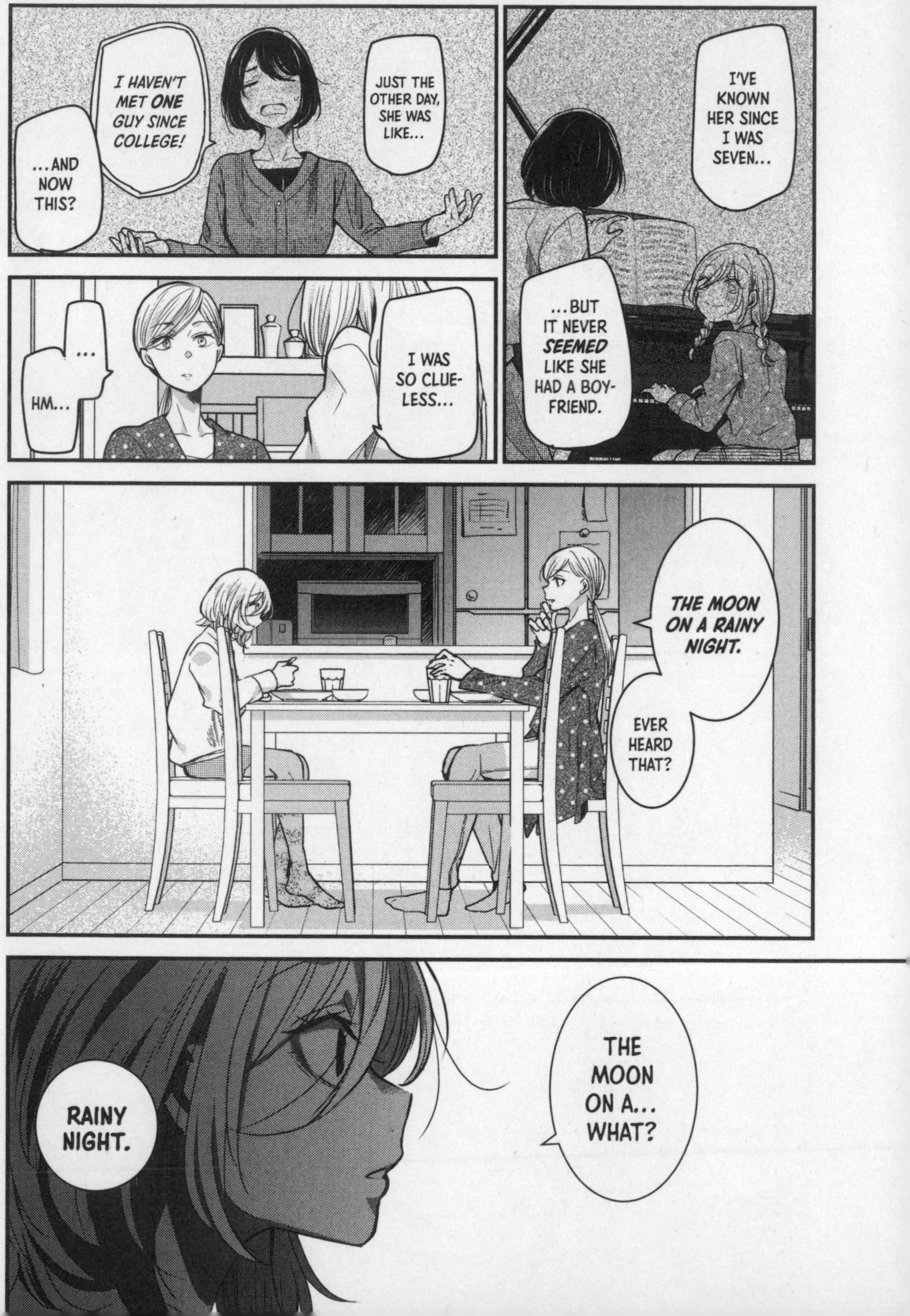
I'VE KNOWN HER SINCE I WAS SEVEN...
...BUT IT NEVER SEEMED LIKE SHE HAD A BOY-FRIEND.
JUST THE OTHER DAY, SHE WAS LIKE...
I HAVEN'T MET ONE GUY SINCE COLLEGE!
...AND NOW THIS?
I WAS SO CLUE-LESS...
...
HM...
THE MOON ON A RAINY NIGHT.
EVER HEARD THAT?
THE MOON ON A... WHAT?
RAINY NIGHT.

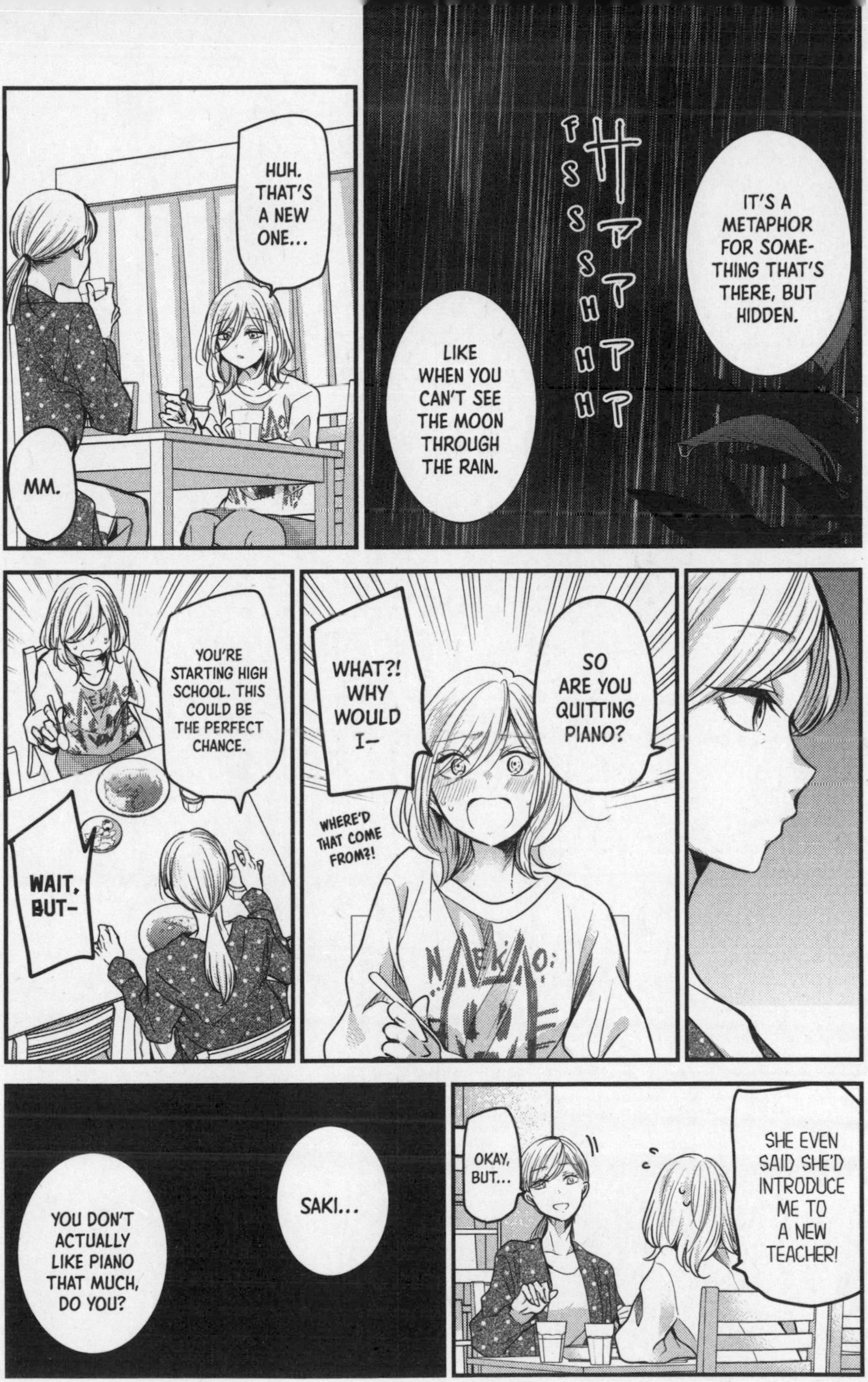
IT'S A METAPHOR FOR SOME- THING THAT'S THERE, BUT HIDDEN.
FSSSHHH
LIKE WHEN YOU CAN'T SEE THE MOON THROUGH THE RAIN.
HUH. THAT'S A NEW ONE...
MM.
SO ARE YOU QUITTING PIANO?
WHAT?! WHY WOULD I–
WHERE'D THAT COME FROM?!
YOU'RE STARTING HIGH SCHOOL. THIS COULD BE THE PERFECT CHANCE.
WAIT, BUT–
SHE EVEN SAID SHE'D INTRODUCE ME TO A NEW TEACHER!
OKAY, BUT...
SAKI...
YOU DON'T ACTUALLY LIKE PIANO THAT MUCH, DO YOU?

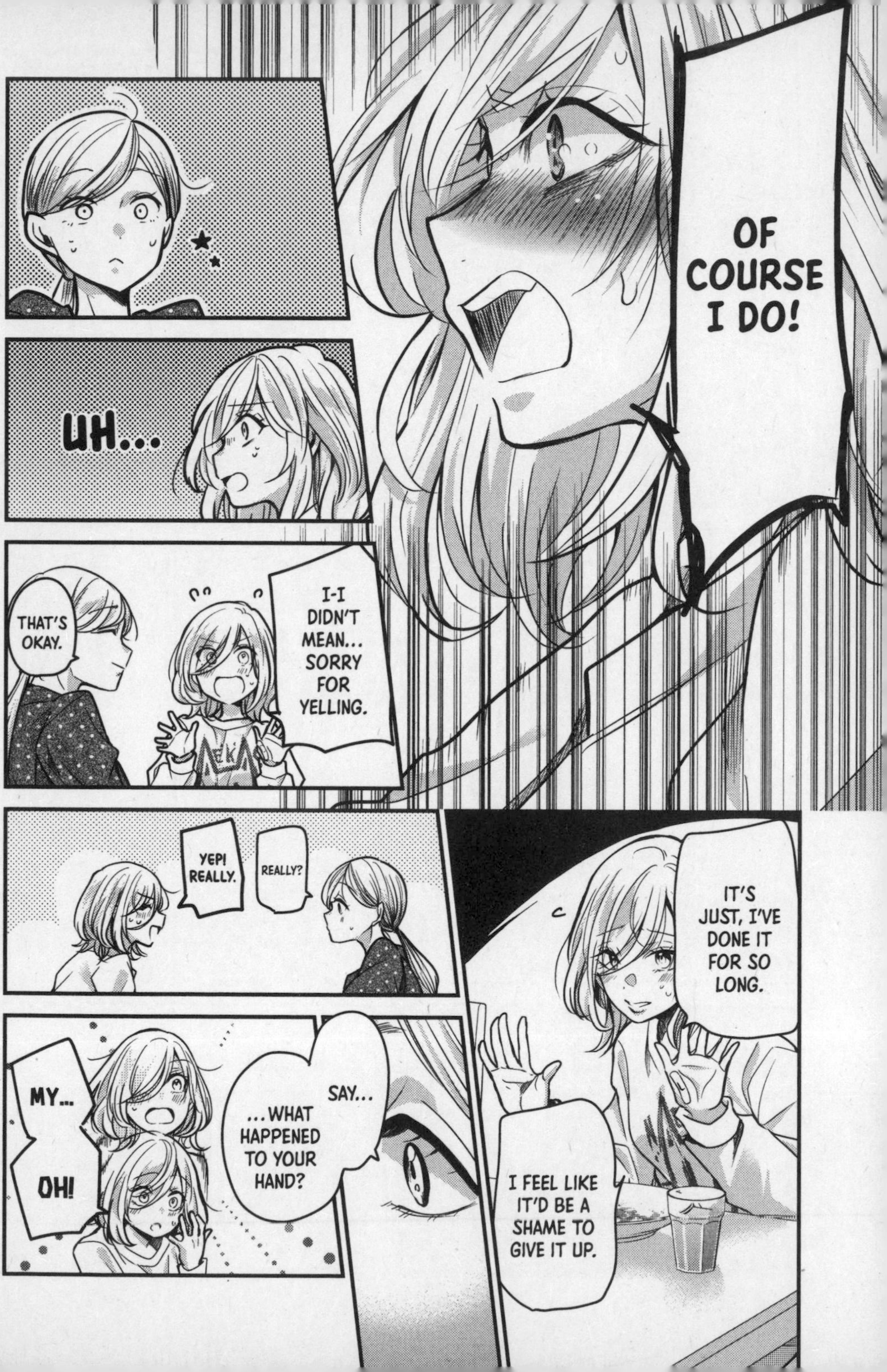
OF COURSE I DO!
UH...
I-I DIDN'T MEAN... SORRY FOR YELLING.
THAT'S OKAY.
IT'S JUST, I'VE DONE IT FOR SO LONG.
I FEEL LIKE IT'D BE A SHAME TO GIVE IT UP.
REALLY?
YEP! REALLY.
SAY...
...WHAT HAPPENED TO YOUR HAND?
MY...
OH!

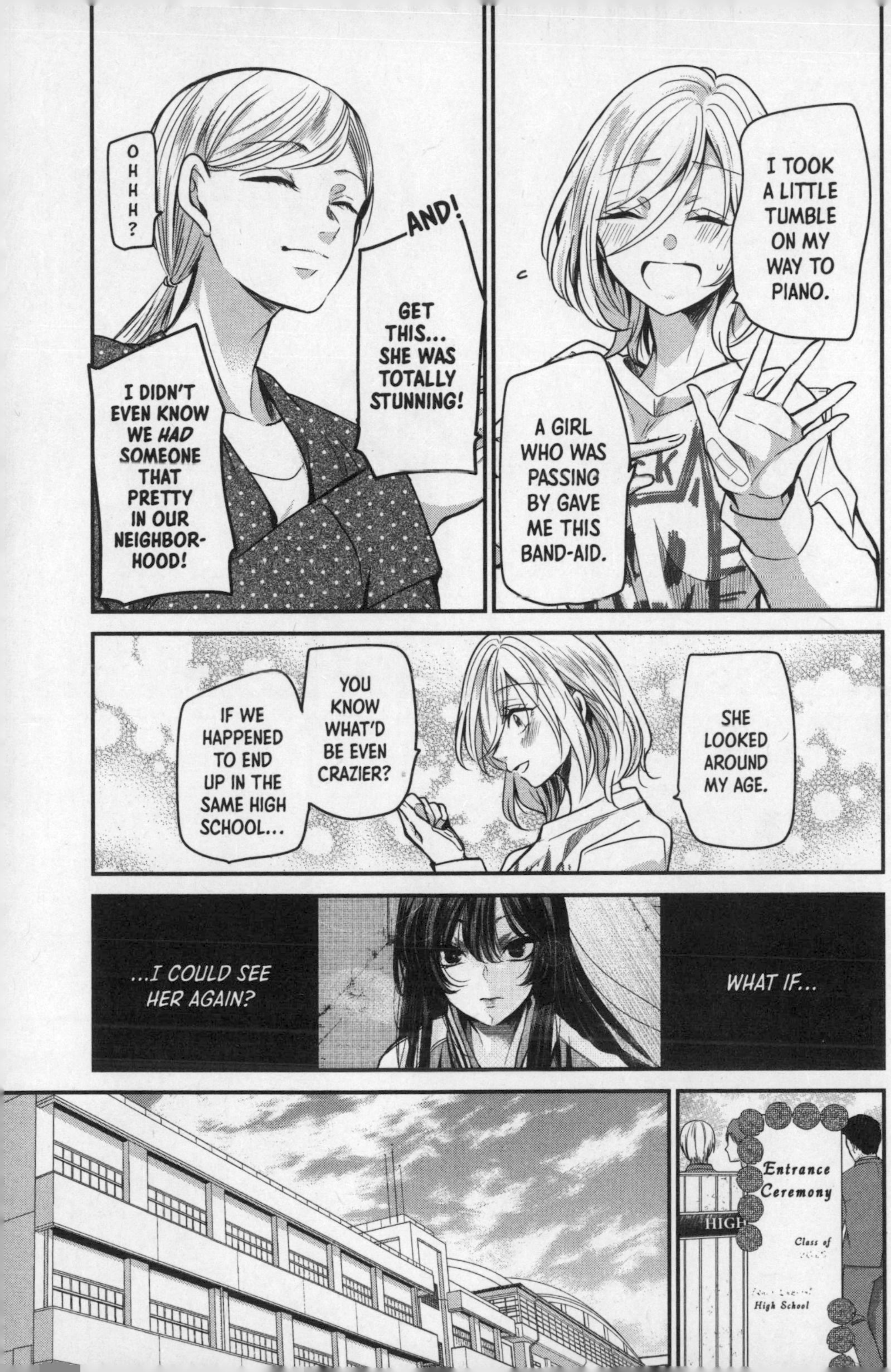
I TOOK A LITTLE TUMBLE ON MY WAY TO PIANO.
A GIRL WHO WAS PASSING BY GAVE ME THIS BAND-AID.
OHHH?
AND!
GET THIS... SHE WAS TOTALLY STUNNING!
I DIDN'T EVEN KNOW WE *HAD* SOMEONE THAT PRETTY IN OUR NEIGHBORHOOD!
SHE LOOKED AROUND MY AGE.
YOU KNOW WHAT'D BE EVEN CRAZIER?
IF WE HAPPENED TO END UP IN THE SAME HIGH SCHOOL...
WHAT IF...
...I COULD SEE HER AGAIN?
HIGH
Entrance Ceremony
Class of
High School

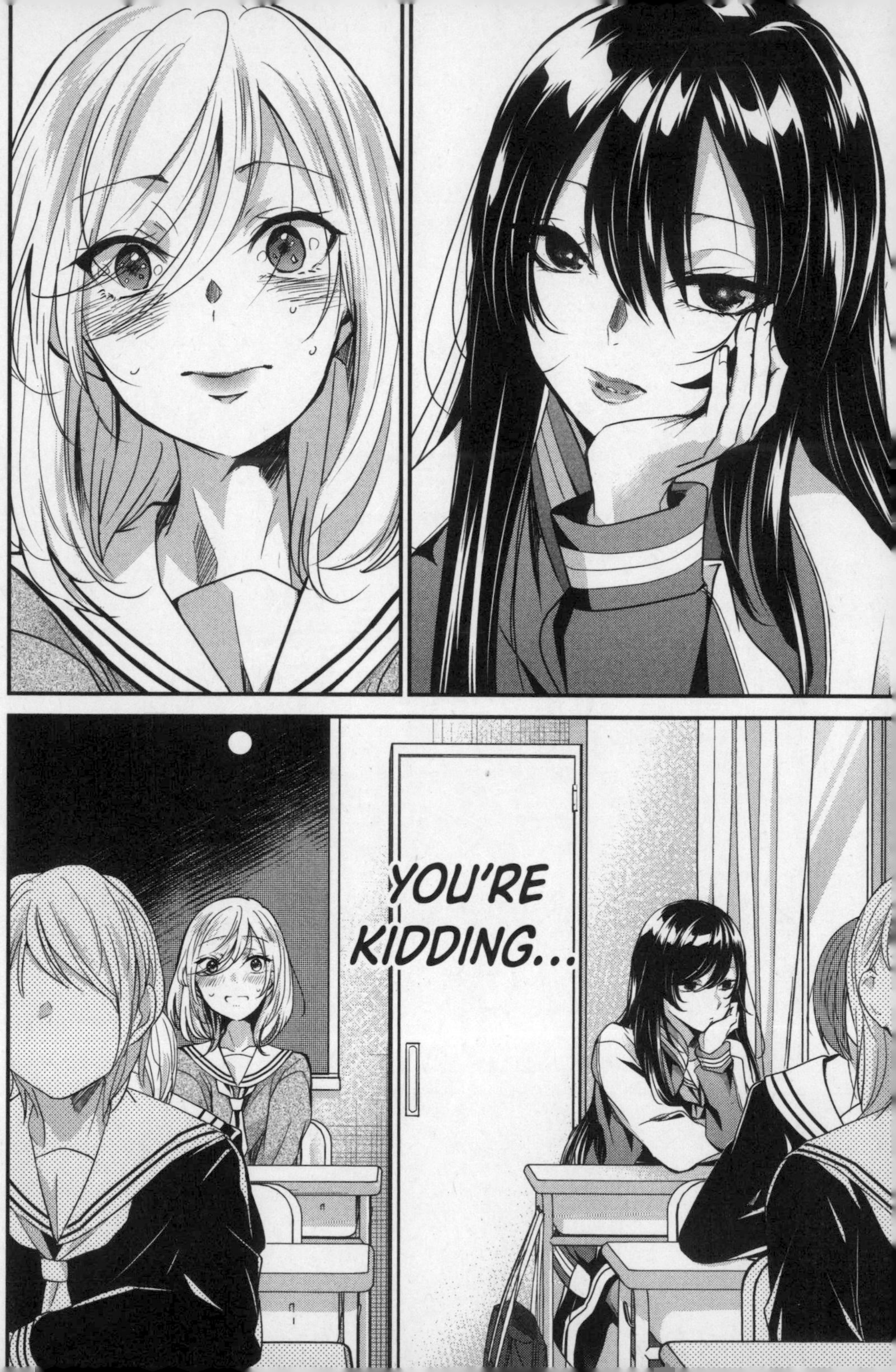
YOU'RE KIDDING...

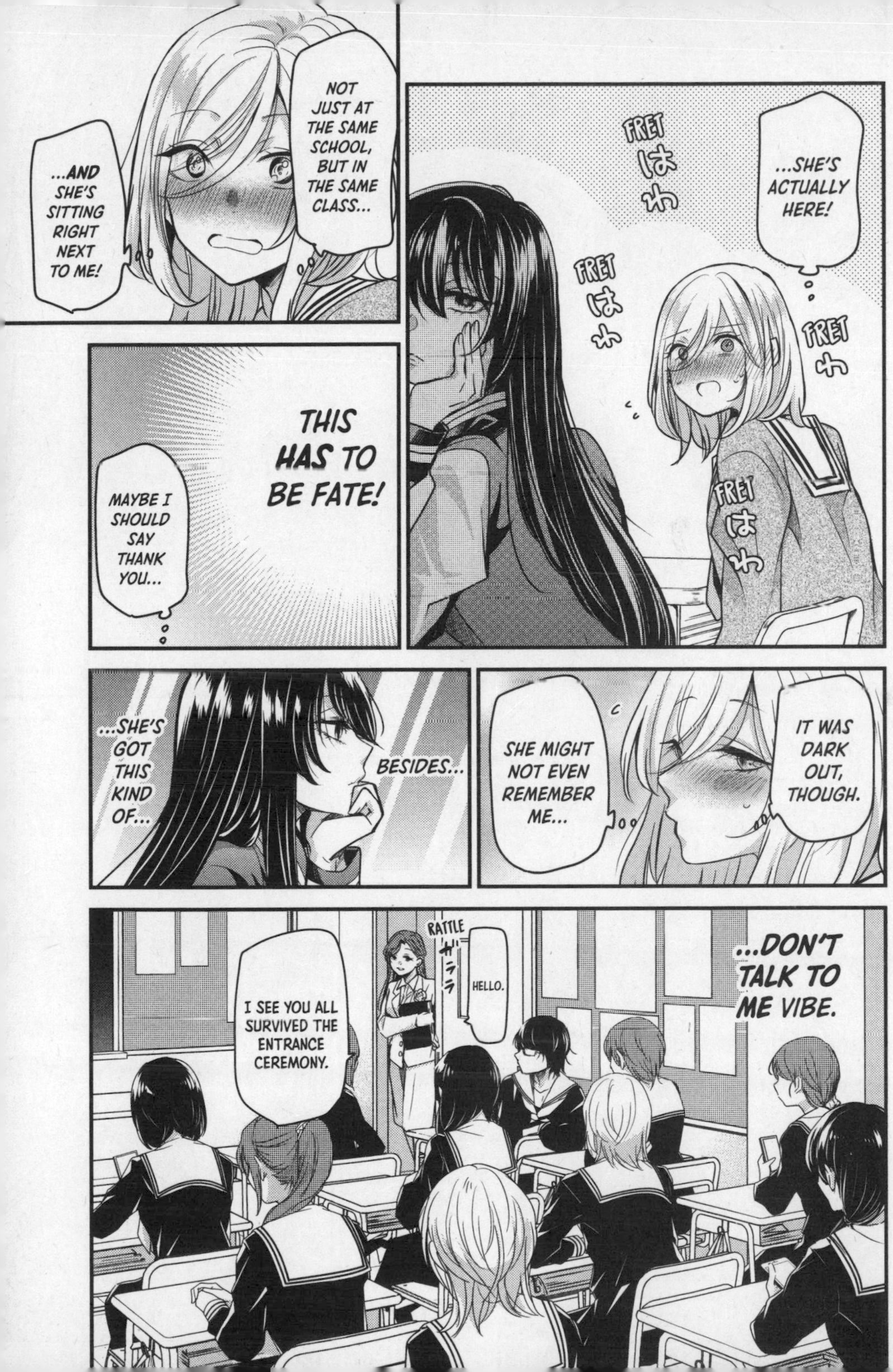
...SHE'S ACTUALLY HERE!
FRET はわ
FRET はわ
FRET わ
FRET はわ
NOT JUST AT THE SAME SCHOOL, BUT IN THE SAME CLASS...
...AND SHE'S SITTING RIGHT NEXT TO ME!
THIS HAS TO BE FATE!
MAYBE I SHOULD SAY THANK YOU...
IT WAS DARK OUT, THOUGH.
SHE MIGHT NOT EVEN REMEMBER ME...
BESIDES...
...SHE'S GOT THIS KIND OF...
...DON'T TALK TO ME VIBE.
RATTLE ガラ
HELLO.
I SEE YOU ALL SURVIVED THE ENTRANCE CEREMONY.

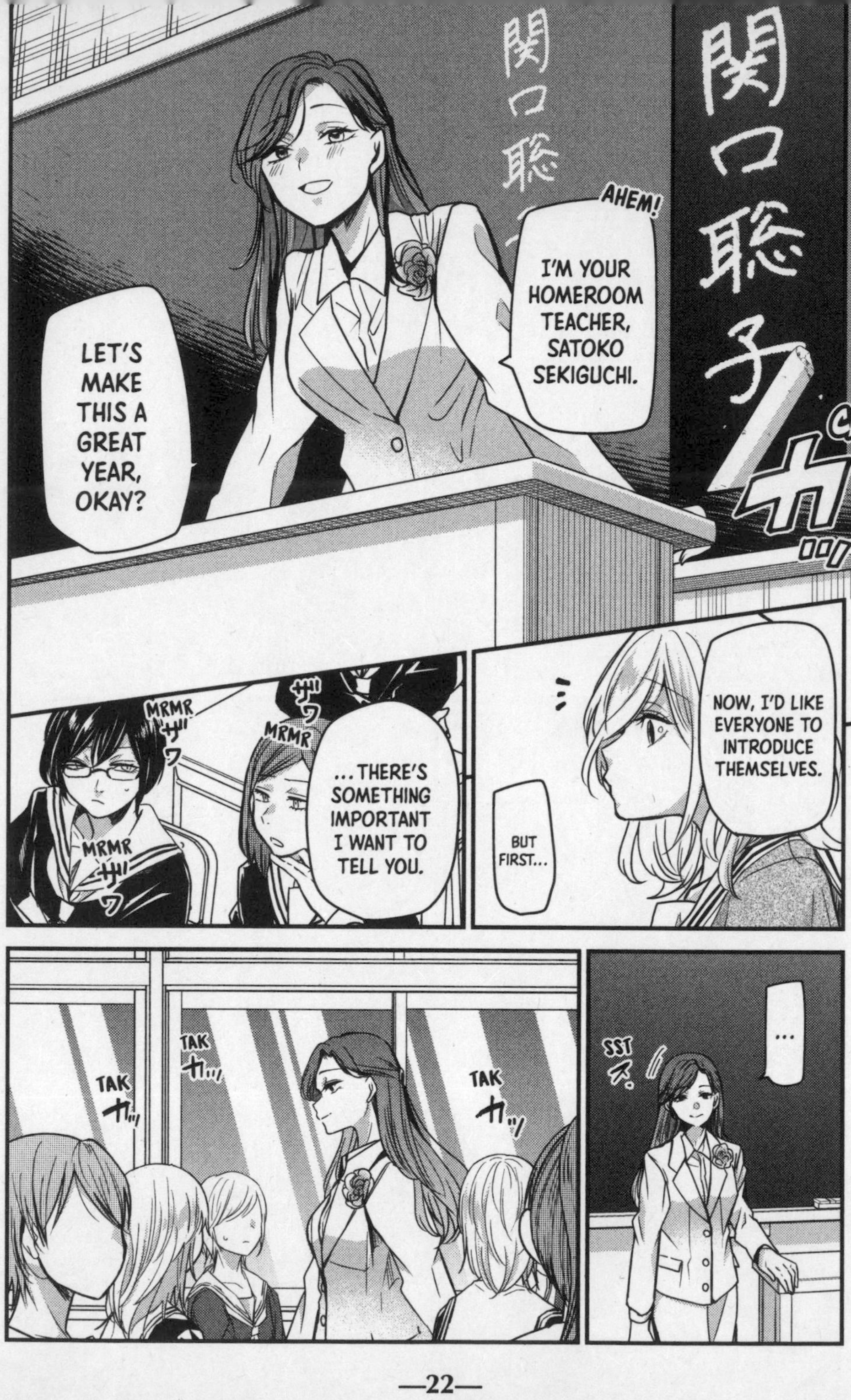
関口聡子
関口聡子
CLACK
カッ
AHEM!
I'M YOUR HOMEROOM TEACHER, SATOKO SEKIGUCHI.
LET'S MAKE THIS A GREAT YEAR, OKAY?
NOW, I'D LIKE EVERYONE TO INTRODUCE THEMSELVES.
BUT FIRST...
...THERE'S SOMETHING IMPORTANT I WANT TO TELL YOU.
MRMR ザワ
MRMR ザワ
MRMR ザワ
...
SST ス
TAK カッ
TAK カッ
TAK カッ

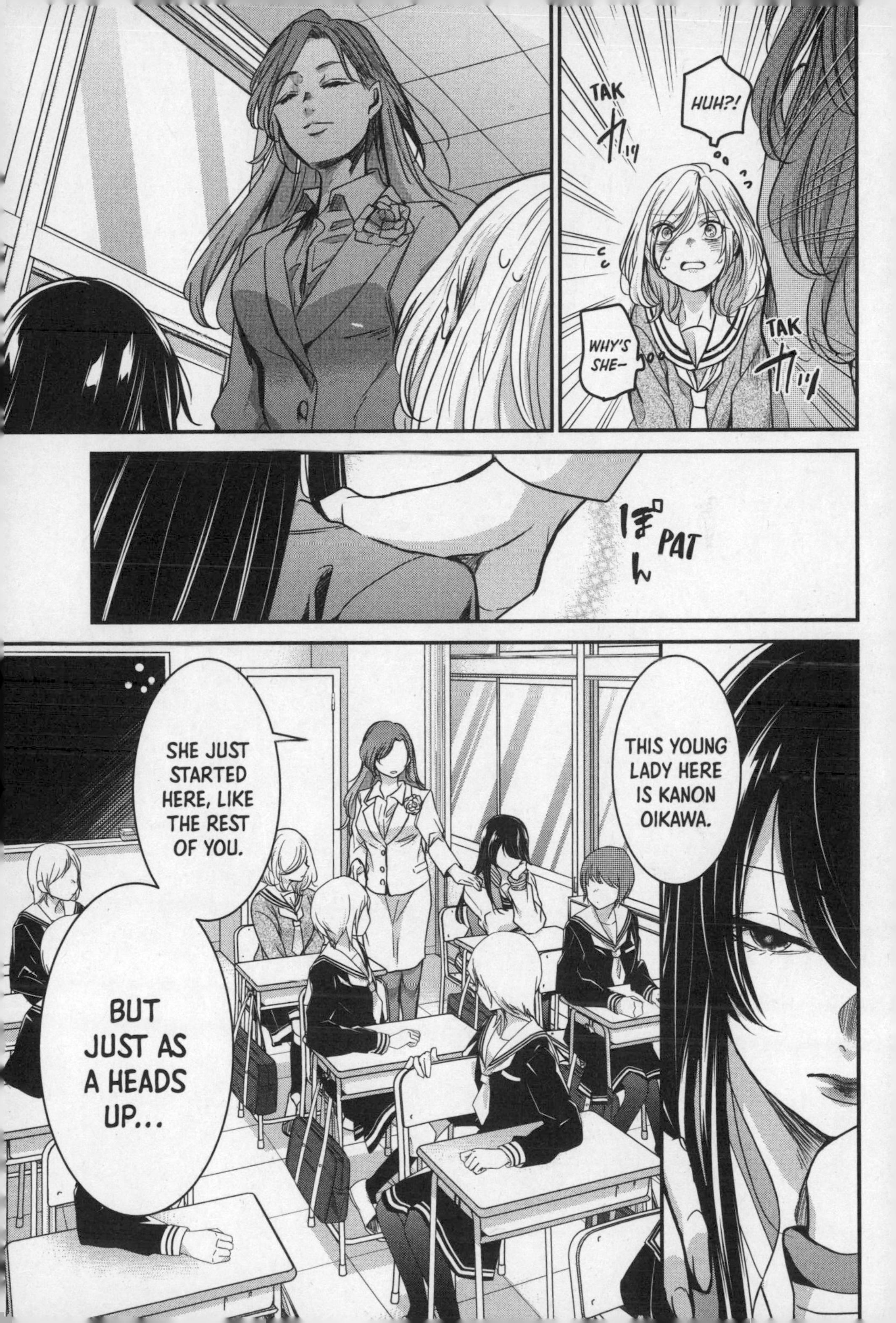
TAK
カッ
HUH?!
WHY'S SHE—
TAK
カッ
ぽん
PAT
THIS YOUNG LADY HERE IS KANON OIKAWA.
SHE JUST STARTED HERE, LIKE THE REST OF YOU.
BUT JUST AS A HEADS UP...

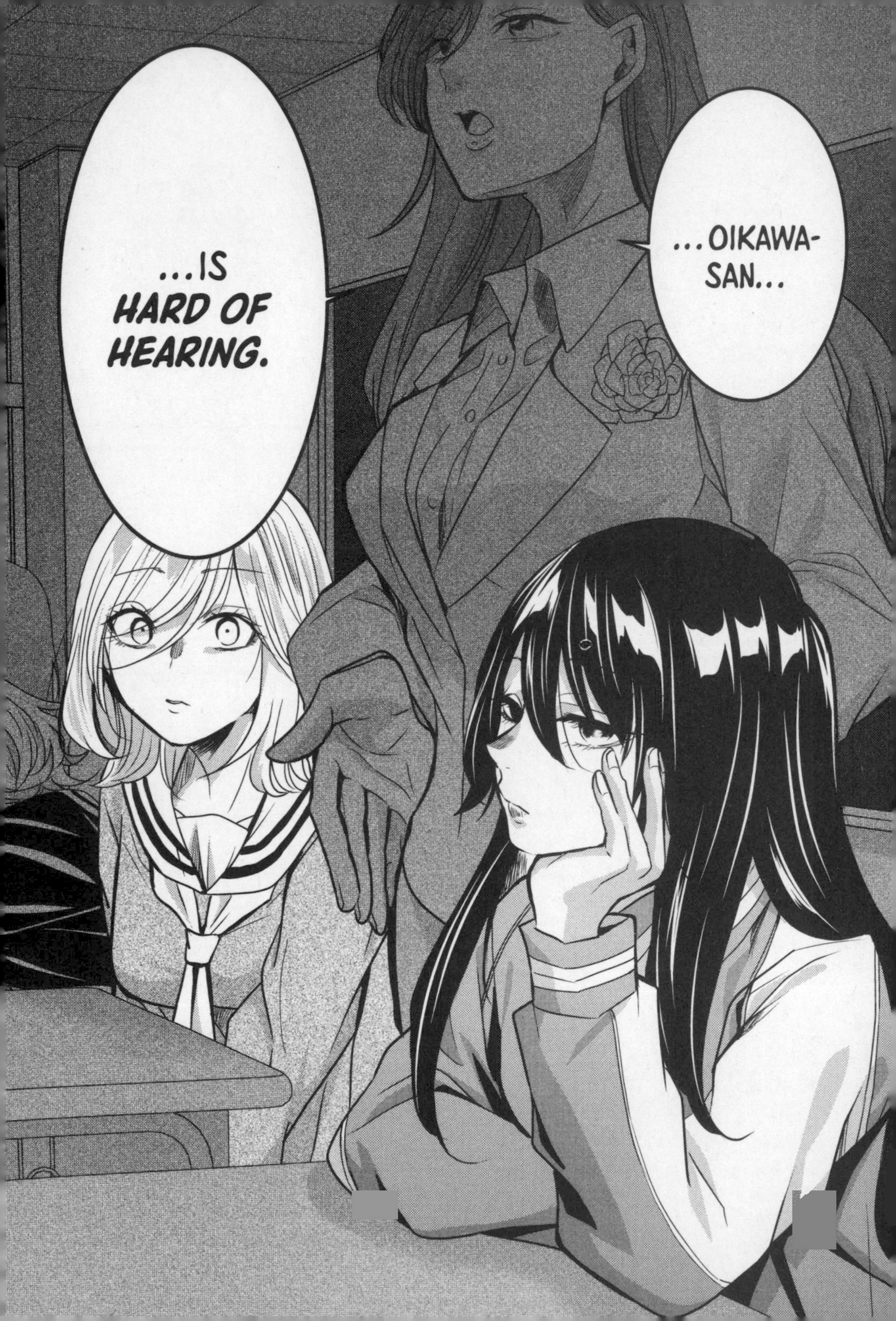
...OIKAWA-SAN...
...IS HARD OF HEARING.

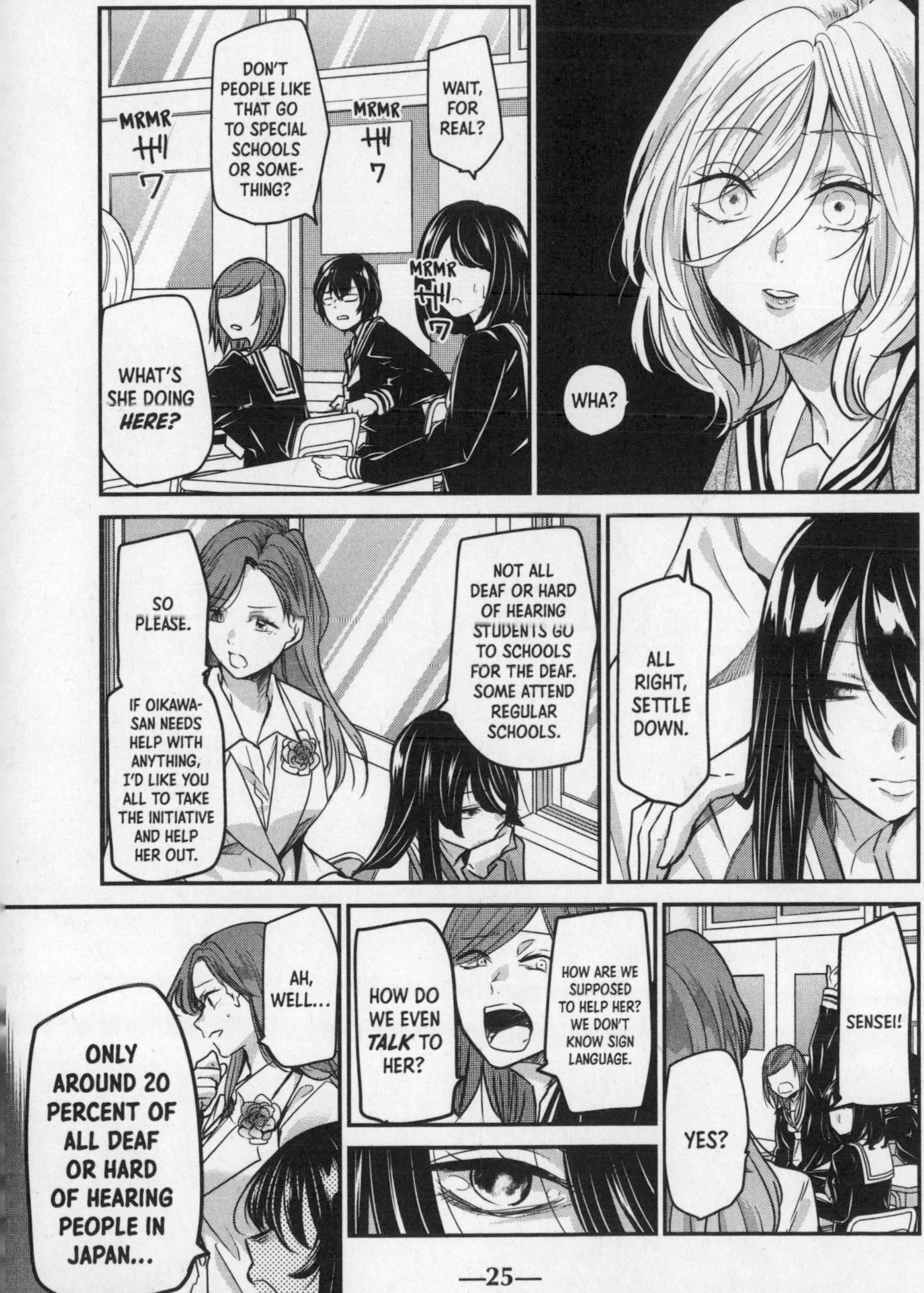
WHA?
WAIT, FOR REAL?
MRMR
DON'T PEOPLE LIKE THAT GO TO SPECIAL SCHOOLS OR SOME-THING?
MRMR
MRMR
WHAT'S SHE DOING *HERE?*
ALL RIGHT, SETTLE DOWN.
NOT ALL DEAF OR HARD OF HEARING STUDENTS GO TO SCHOOLS FOR THE DEAF. SOME ATTEND REGULAR SCHOOLS.
SO PLEASE.
IF OIKAWA-SAN NEEDS HELP WITH ANYTHING, I'D LIKE YOU ALL TO TAKE THE INITIATIVE AND HELP HER OUT.
SENSEI!
YES?
HOW ARE WE SUPPOSED TO HELP HER? WE DON'T KNOW SIGN LANGUAGE.
HOW DO WE EVEN *TALK* TO HER?
AH, WELL...
ONLY AROUND 20 PERCENT OF ALL DEAF OR HARD OF HEARING PEOPLE IN JAPAN...

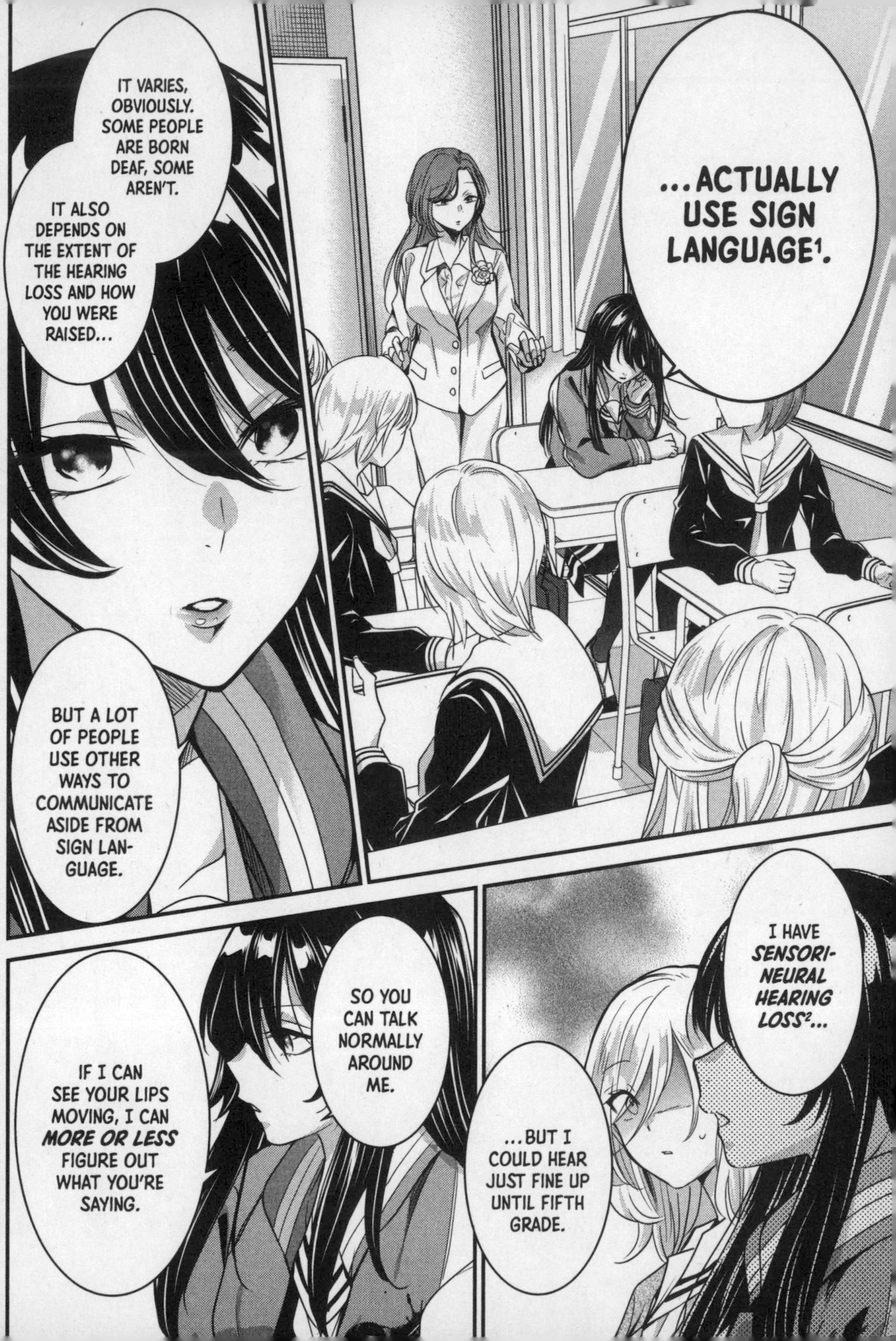
...ACTUALLY USE SIGN LANGUAGE[1].
IT VARIES, OBVIOUSLY. SOME PEOPLE ARE BORN DEAF, SOME AREN'T.
IT ALSO DEPENDS ON THE EXTENT OF THE HEARING LOSS AND HOW YOU WERE RAISED...
BUT A LOT OF PEOPLE USE OTHER WAYS TO COMMUNICATE ASIDE FROM SIGN LAN-GUAGE.
I HAVE *SENSORI-NEURAL HEARING LOSS*[2]...
...BUT I COULD HEAR JUST FINE UP UNTIL FIFTH GRADE.
IF I CAN SEE YOUR LIPS MOVING, I CAN *MORE OR LESS* FIGURE OUT WHAT YOU'RE SAYING.
SO YOU CAN TALK NORMALLY AROUND ME.

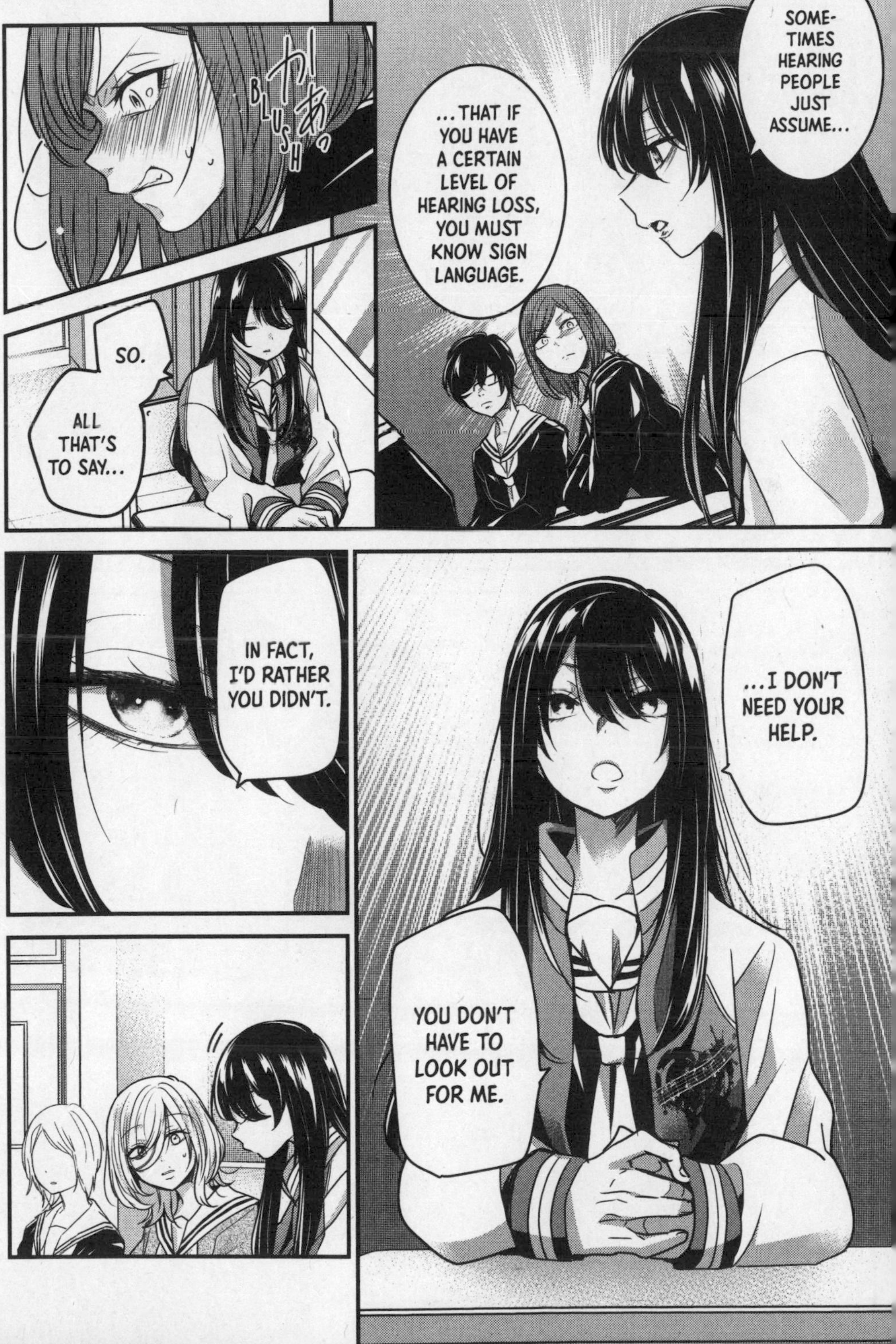

SOME-TIMES HEARING PEOPLE JUST ASSUME...
...THAT IF YOU HAVE A CERTAIN LEVEL OF HEARING LOSS, YOU MUST KNOW SIGN LANGUAGE.
かぁっ
BLUSH
SO.
ALL THAT'S TO SAY...
...I DON'T NEED YOUR HELP.
YOU DON'T HAVE TO LOOK OUT FOR ME.
IN FACT, I'D RATHER YOU DIDN'T.

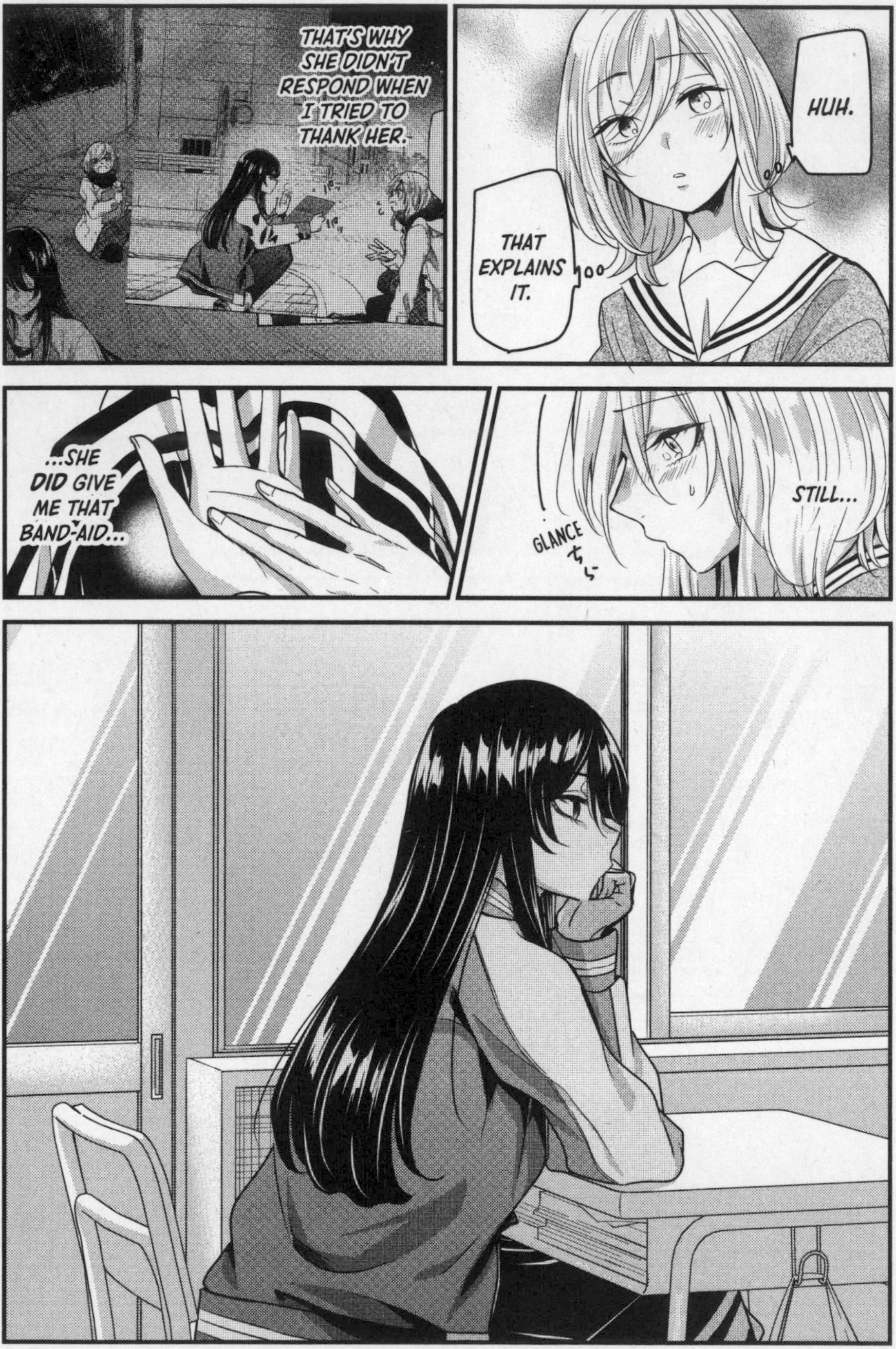
HUH.
THAT EXPLAINS IT.
THAT'S WHY SHE DIDN'T RESPOND WHEN I TRIED TO THANK HER.
STILL...
GLANCE ちら
...SHE DID GIVE ME THAT BAND-AID...

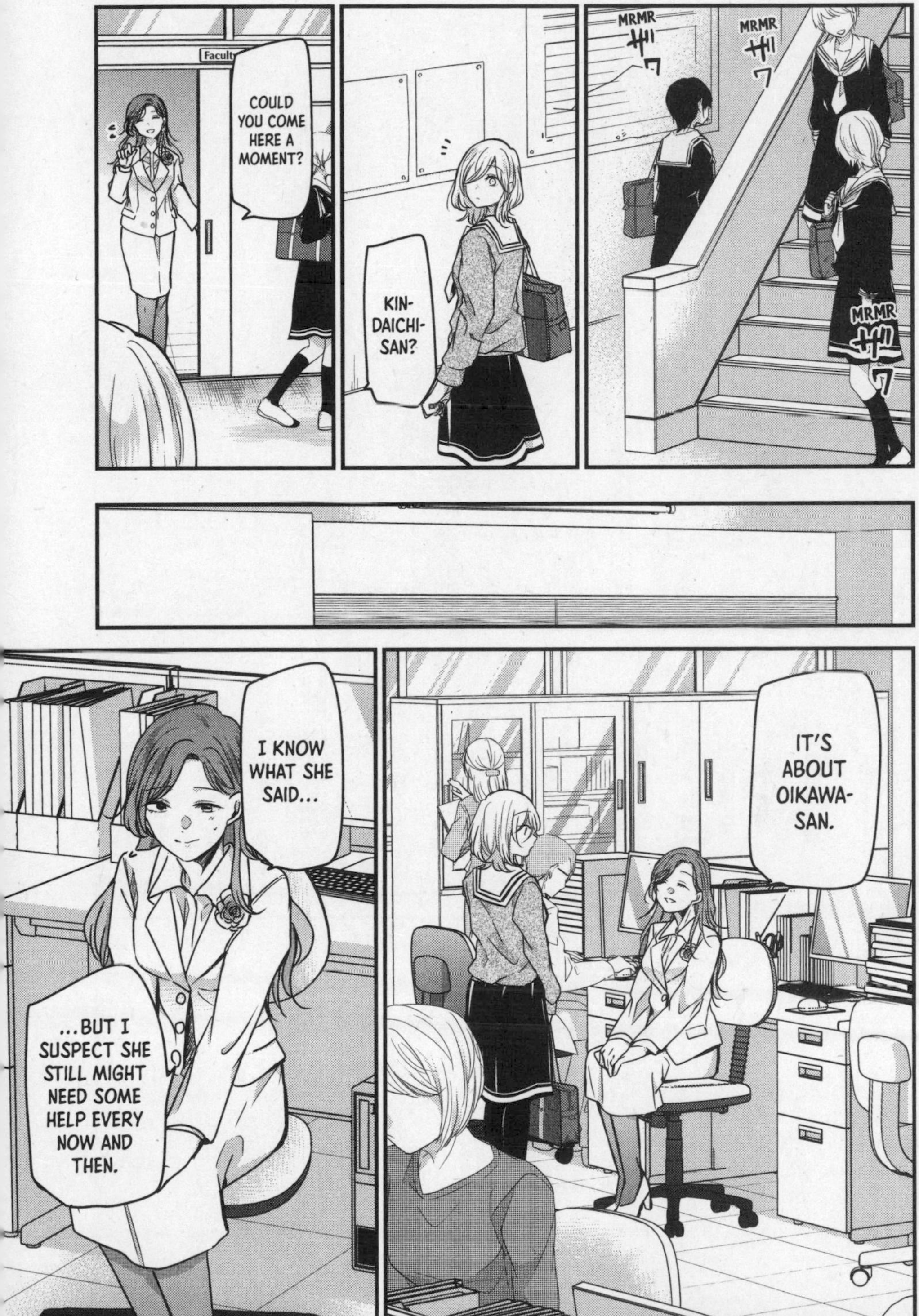

MRMR ザワ
MRMR ザワ
MRMR ザワ
KIN-DAICHI-SAN?
COULD YOU COME HERE A MOMENT?
IT'S ABOUT OIKAWA-SAN.
I KNOW WHAT SHE SAID...
...BUT I SUSPECT SHE STILL MIGHT NEED SOME HELP EVERY NOW AND THEN.

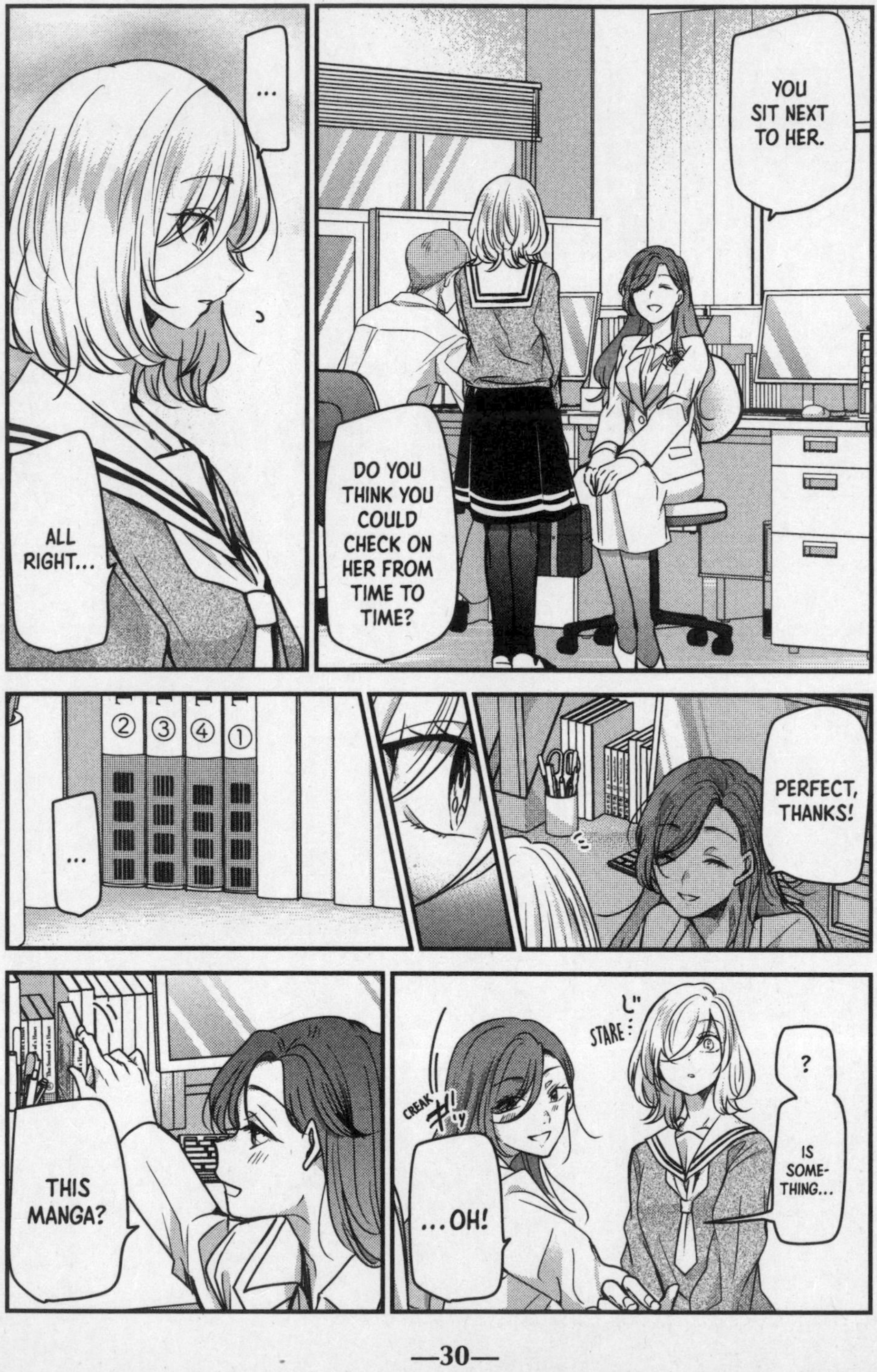
YOU SIT NEXT TO HER.
DO YOU THINK YOU COULD CHECK ON HER FROM TIME TO TIME?
...
ALL RIGHT...
PERFECT, THANKS!
...
STARE
?
IS SOMETHING...
...OH!
CREAK
THIS MANGA?

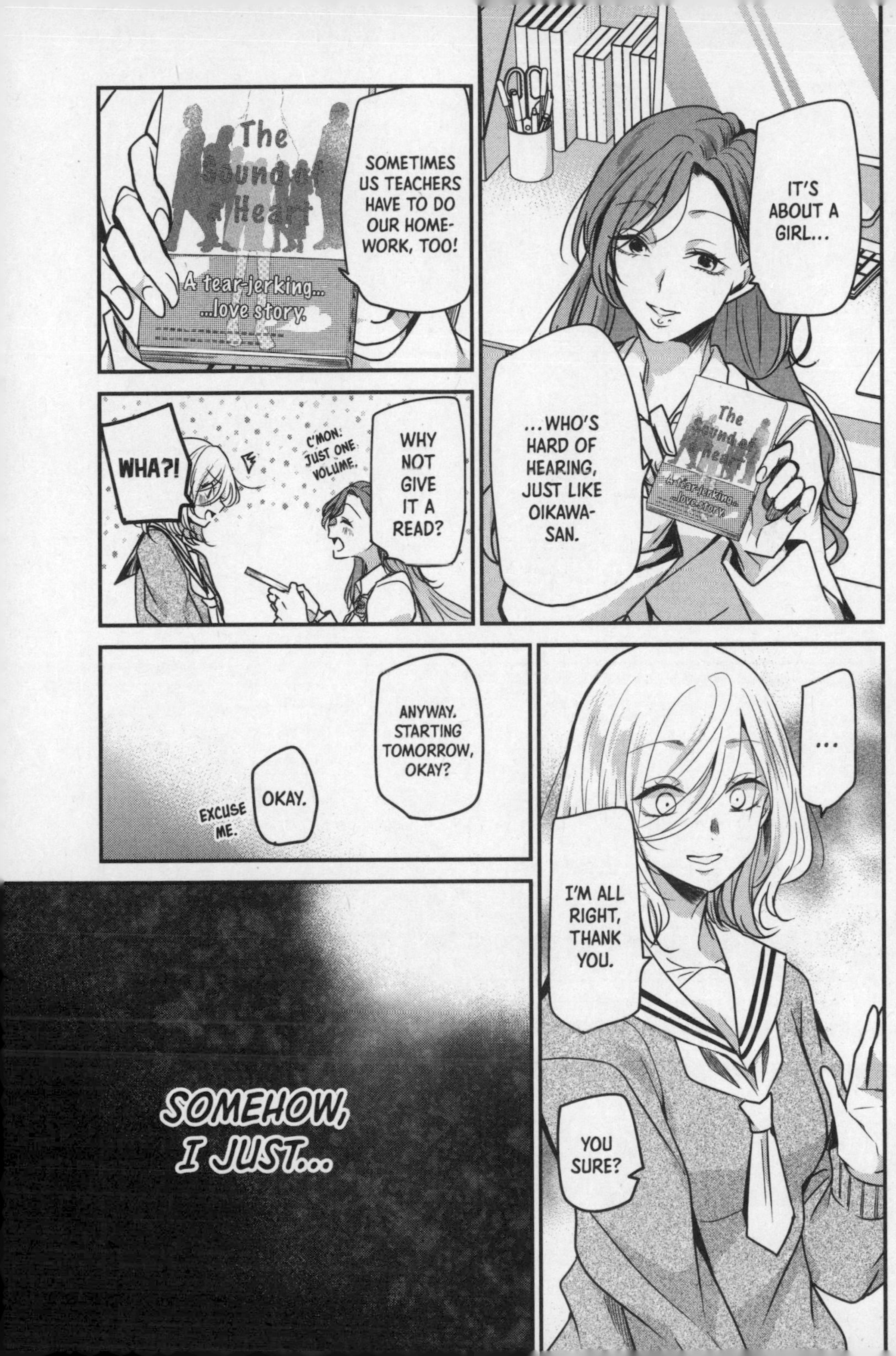
IT'S ABOUT A GIRL...
...WHO'S HARD OF HEARING, JUST LIKE OIKAWA-SAN.
The Sound of a Heart
A tear-jerking... ...love story.
SOMETIMES US TEACHERS HAVE TO DO OUR HOME-WORK, TOO!
WHY NOT GIVE IT A READ?
C'MON: JUST ONE VOLUME.
WHA?!
...
I'M ALL RIGHT, THANK YOU.
YOU SURE?
ANYWAY. STARTING TOMORROW, OKAY?
OKAY.
EXCUSE ME.
SOMEHOW, I JUST...

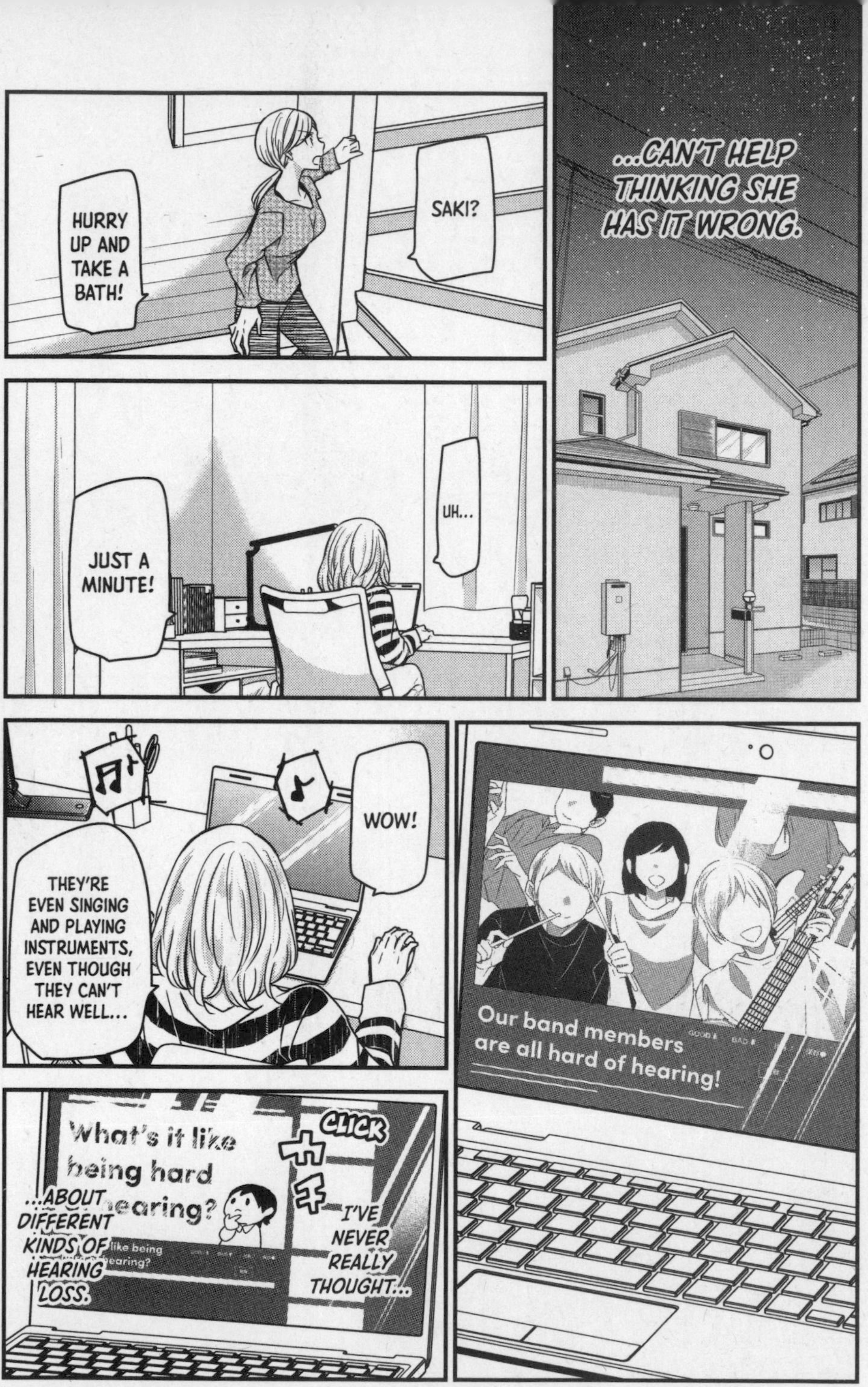
...CAN'T HELP THINKING SHE HAS IT WRONG.
SAKI?
HURRY UP AND TAKE A BATH!
UH...
JUST A MINUTE!
Our band members are all hard of hearing!
WOW!
THEY'RE EVEN SINGING AND PLAYING INSTRUMENTS, EVEN THOUGH THEY CAN'T HEAR WELL...
CLICK
What's it like being hard
I'VE NEVER REALLY THOUGHT...
...ABOUT DIFFERENT KINDS OF HEARING LOSS.

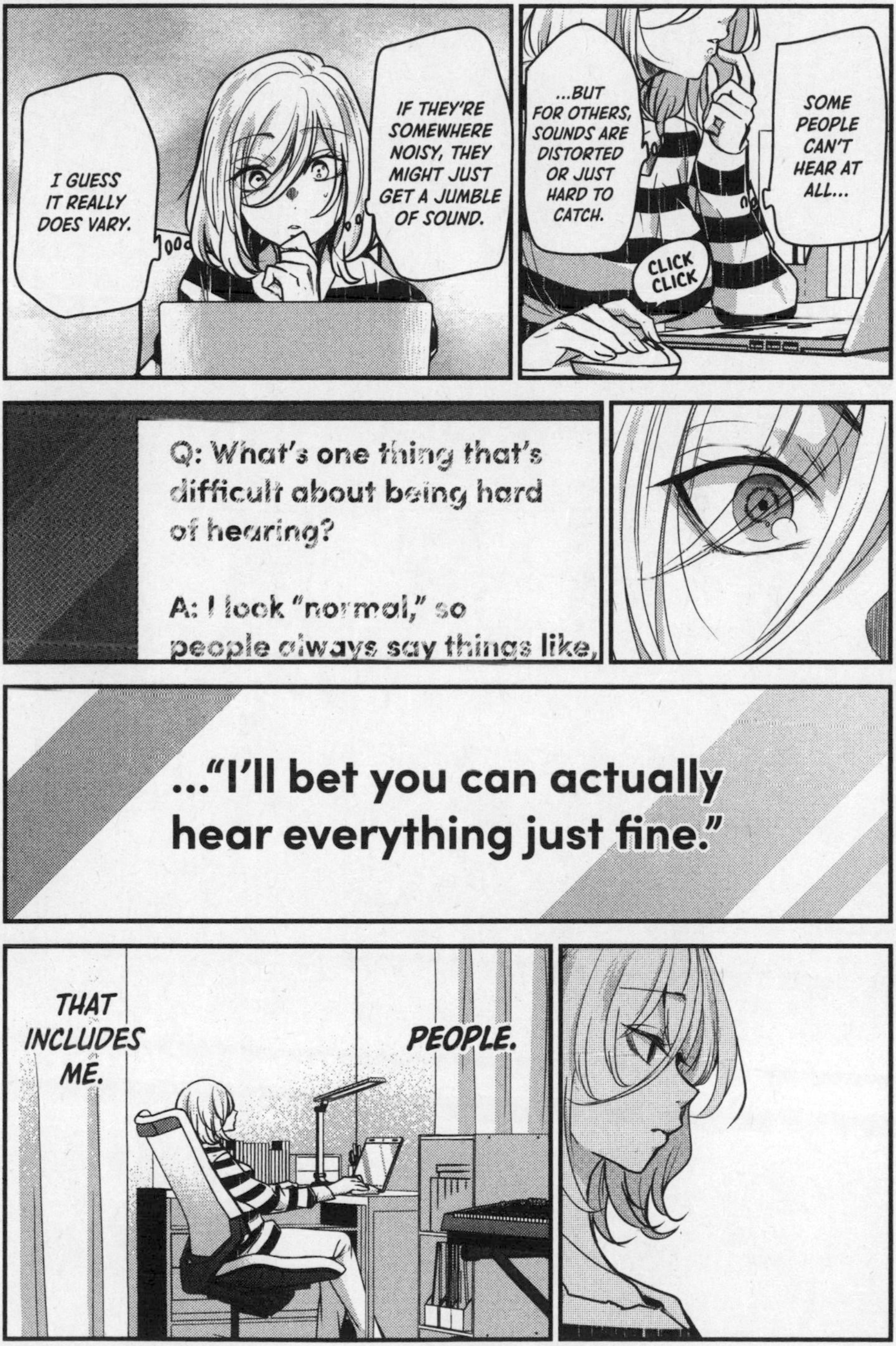
SOME PEOPLE CAN'T HEAR AT ALL...
...BUT FOR OTHERS, SOUNDS ARE DISTORTED OR JUST HARD TO CATCH.
CLICK CLICK
IF THEY'RE SOMEWHERE NOISY, THEY MIGHT JUST GET A JUMBLE OF SOUND.
I GUESS IT REALLY DOES VARY.
Q: What's one thing that's difficult about being hard of hearing?
A: I look "normal," so people always say things like,
..."I'll bet you can actually hear everything just fine."
PEOPLE.
THAT INCLUDES ME.

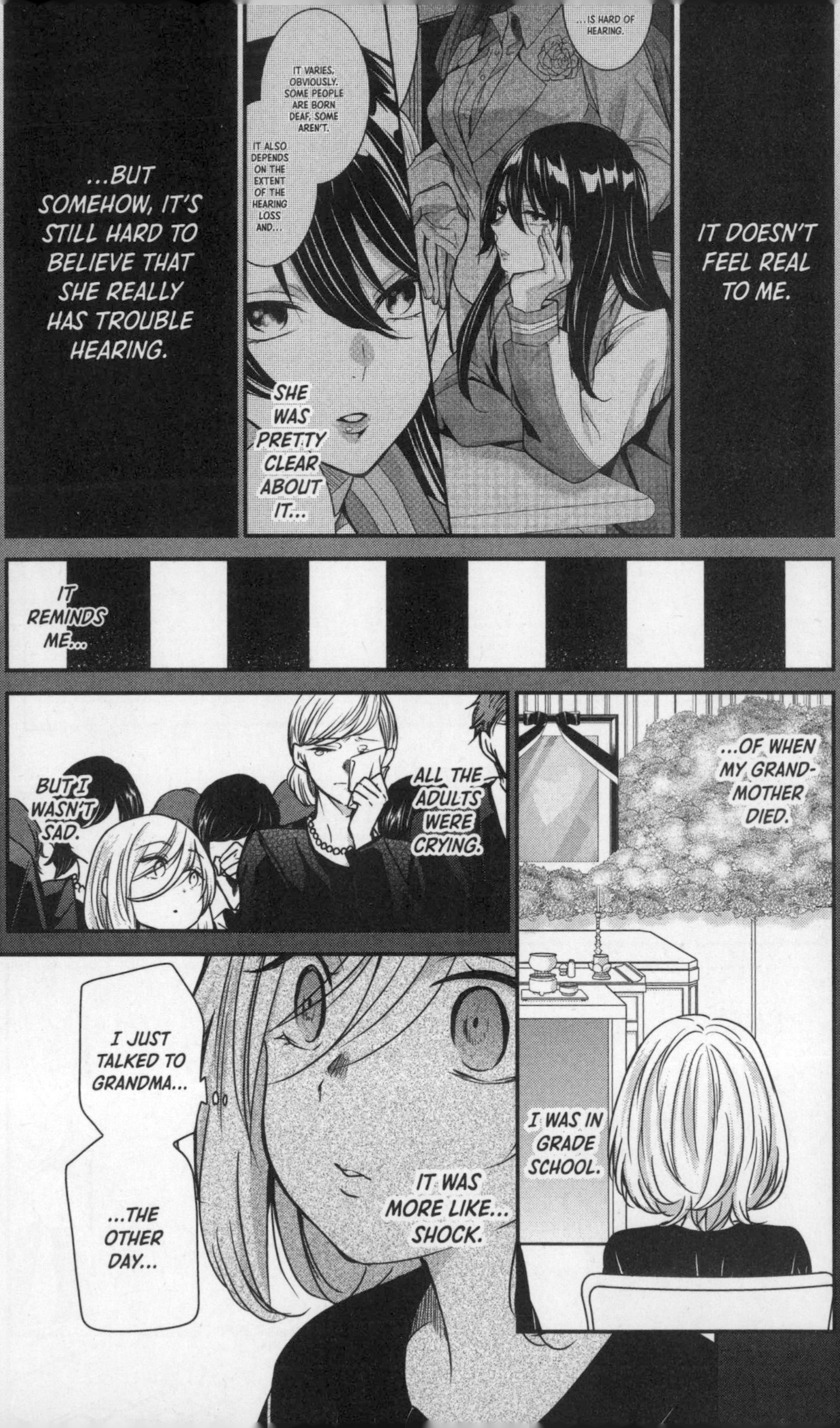
IT DOESN'T FEEL REAL TO ME.
...IS HARD OF HEARING.
IT VARIES, OBVIOUSLY. SOME PEOPLE ARE BORN DEAF, SOME AREN'T.
IT ALSO DEPENDS ON THE EXTENT OF THE HEARING LOSS AND...
SHE WAS PRETTY CLEAR ABOUT IT...
...BUT SOMEHOW, IT'S STILL HARD TO BELIEVE THAT SHE REALLY HAS TROUBLE HEARING.
IT REMINDS ME...
...OF WHEN MY GRAND-MOTHER DIED.
I WAS IN GRADE SCHOOL.
ALL THE ADULTS WERE CRYING.
BUT I WASN'T SAD.
IT WAS MORE LIKE... SHOCK.
I JUST TALKED TO GRANDMA...
...THE OTHER DAY...

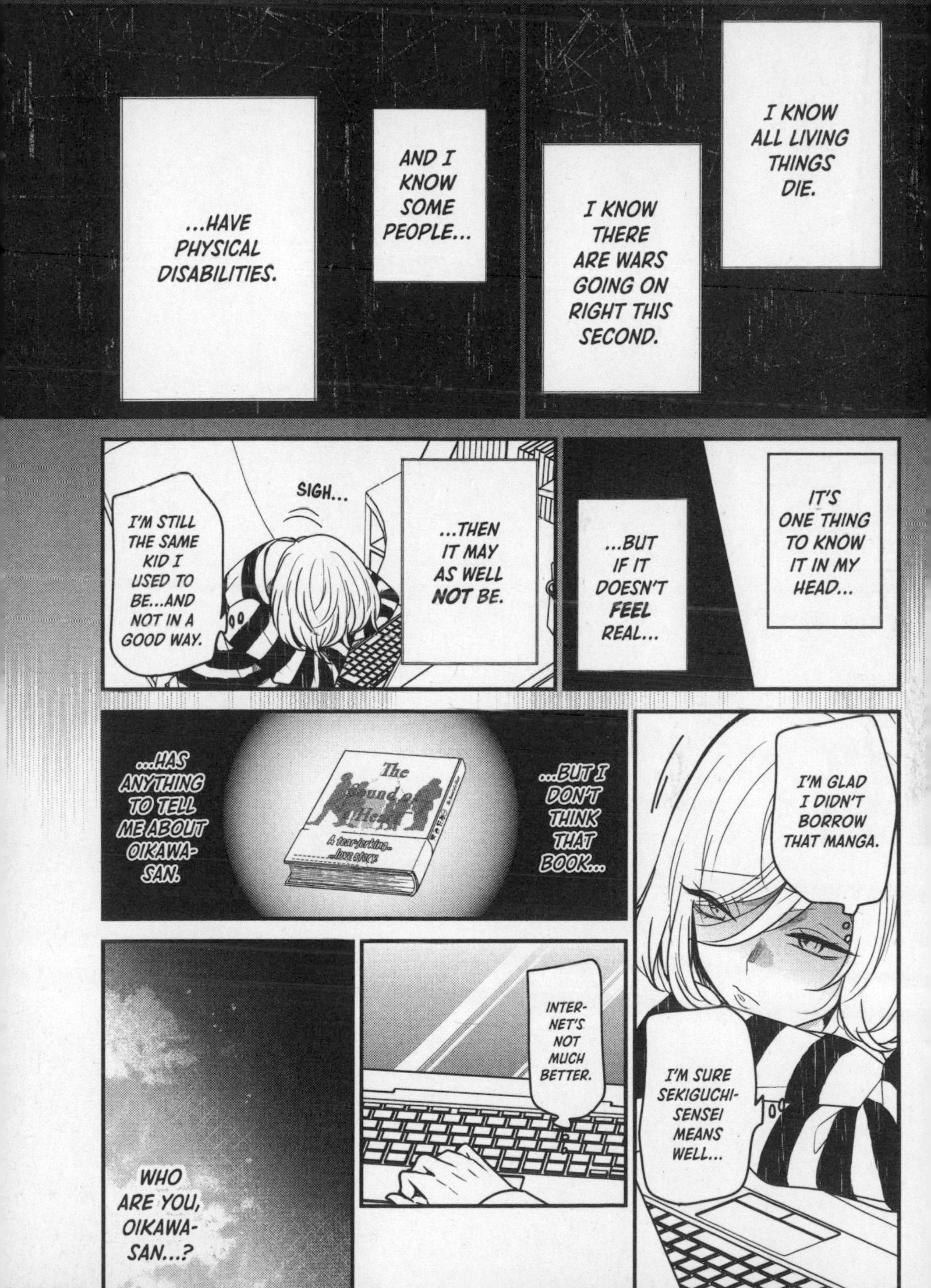
I KNOW ALL LIVING THINGS DIE.
I KNOW THERE ARE WARS GOING ON RIGHT THIS SECOND.
AND I KNOW SOME PEOPLE...
...HAVE PHYSICAL DISABILITIES.
IT'S ONE THING TO KNOW IT IN MY HEAD...
...BUT IF IT DOESN'T FEEL REAL...
...THEN IT MAY AS WELL NOT BE.
SIGH...
I'M STILL THE SAME KID I USED TO BE...AND NOT IN A GOOD WAY.
I'M GLAD I DIDN'T BORROW THAT MANGA.
I'M SURE SEKIGUCHI-SENSEI MEANS WELL...
...BUT I DON'T THINK THAT BOOK...
A tear-jerking... ...love story.
...HAS ANYTHING TO TELL ME ABOUT OIKAWA-SAN.
INTERNET'S NOT MUCH BETTER.
WHO ARE YOU, OIKAWA-SAN...?

CAN YOU HEAR...

...SOME SOUNDS?

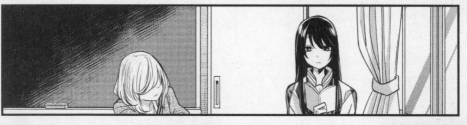

OH. SHE DIDN'T NOTICE.

YEAH?

UM...

TAP TAP

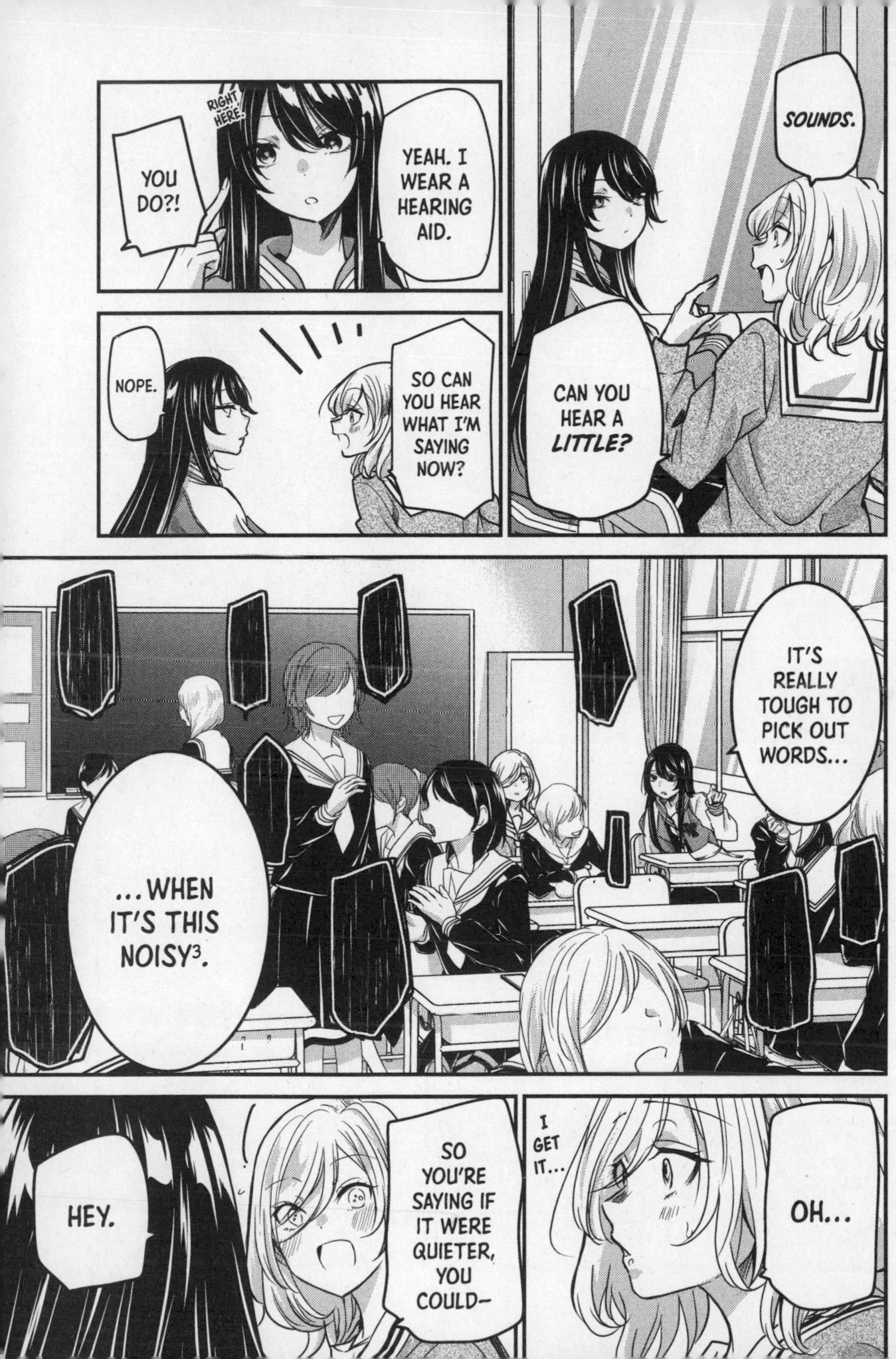
SOUNDS.
CAN YOU HEAR A *LITTLE?*
YEAH. I WEAR A HEARING AID.
RIGHT HERE!
YOU DO?!
SO CAN YOU HEAR WHAT I'M SAYING NOW?
NOPE.
IT'S REALLY TOUGH TO PICK OUT WORDS...
...WHEN IT'S THIS NOISY[3].
OH...
I GET IT...
SO YOU'RE SAYING IF IT WERE QUIETER, YOU COULD–
HEY.

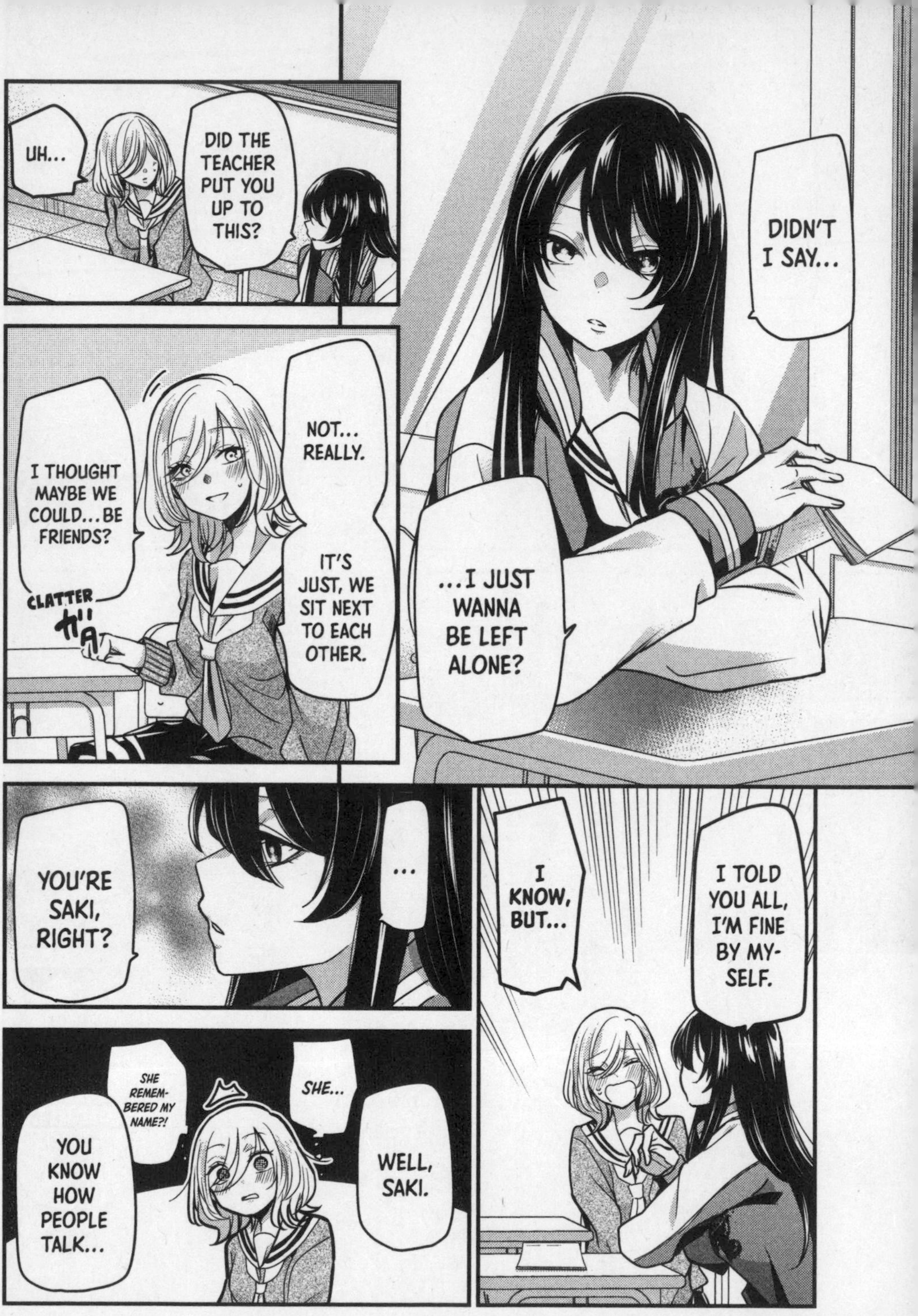
DIDN'T I SAY...
...I JUST WANNA BE LEFT ALONE?
DID THE TEACHER PUT YOU UP TO THIS?
UH...
NOT... REALLY.
IT'S JUST, WE SIT NEXT TO EACH OTHER.
I THOUGHT MAYBE WE COULD...BE FRIENDS?
CLATTER
I TOLD YOU ALL, I'M FINE BY MY-SELF.
I KNOW, BUT...
...
YOU'RE SAKI, RIGHT?
SHE...
WELL, SAKI.
SHE REMEMBERED MY NAME?!
YOU KNOW HOW PEOPLE TALK...

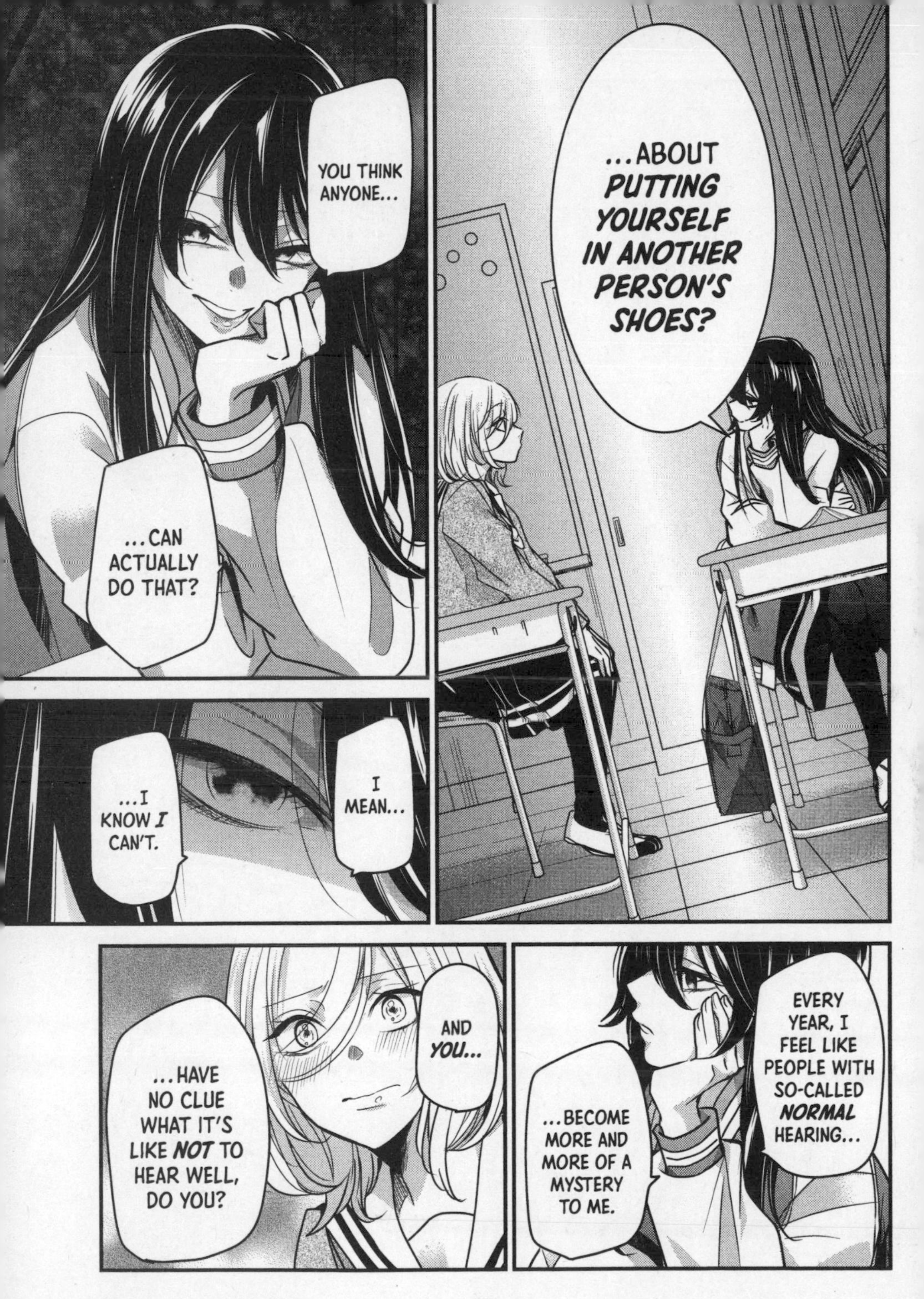
...ABOUT *PUTTING YOURSELF IN ANOTHER PERSON'S SHOES?*
YOU THINK ANYONE...
...CAN ACTUALLY DO THAT?
I MEAN...
...I KNOW *I* CAN'T.
EVERY YEAR, I FEEL LIKE PEOPLE WITH SO-CALLED *NORMAL* HEARING...
...BECOME MORE AND MORE OF A MYSTERY TO ME.
AND *YOU...*
...HAVE NO CLUE WHAT IT'S LIKE *NOT* TO HEAR WELL, DO YOU?

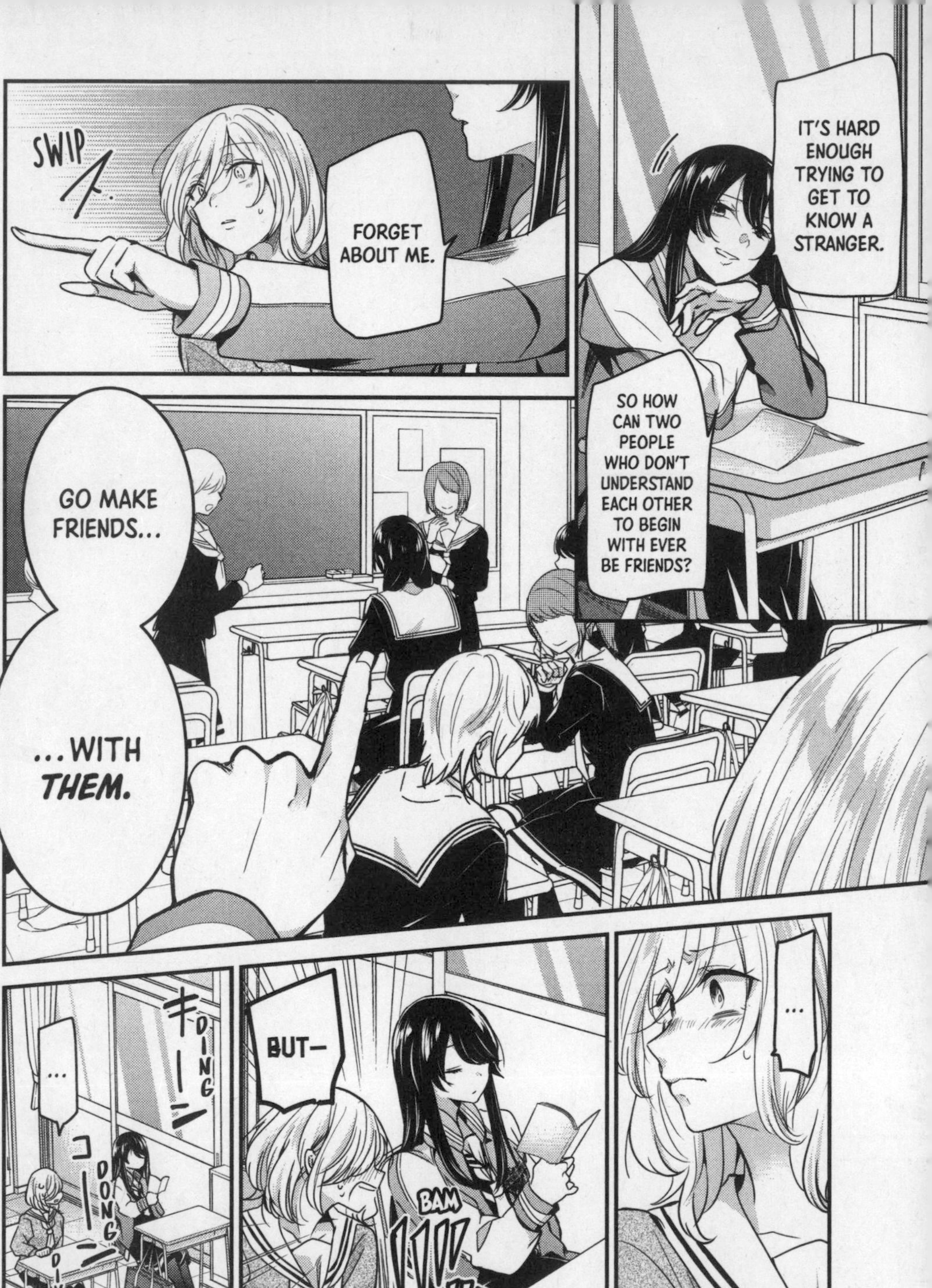
IT'S HARD ENOUGH TRYING TO GET TO KNOW A STRANGER.
SO HOW CAN TWO PEOPLE WHO DON'T UNDERSTAND EACH OTHER TO BEGIN WITH EVER BE FRIENDS?
SWIP
FORGET ABOUT ME.
GO MAKE FRIENDS...
...WITH *THEM.*
...
BUT—
BAM
...
DING
DONG
DING

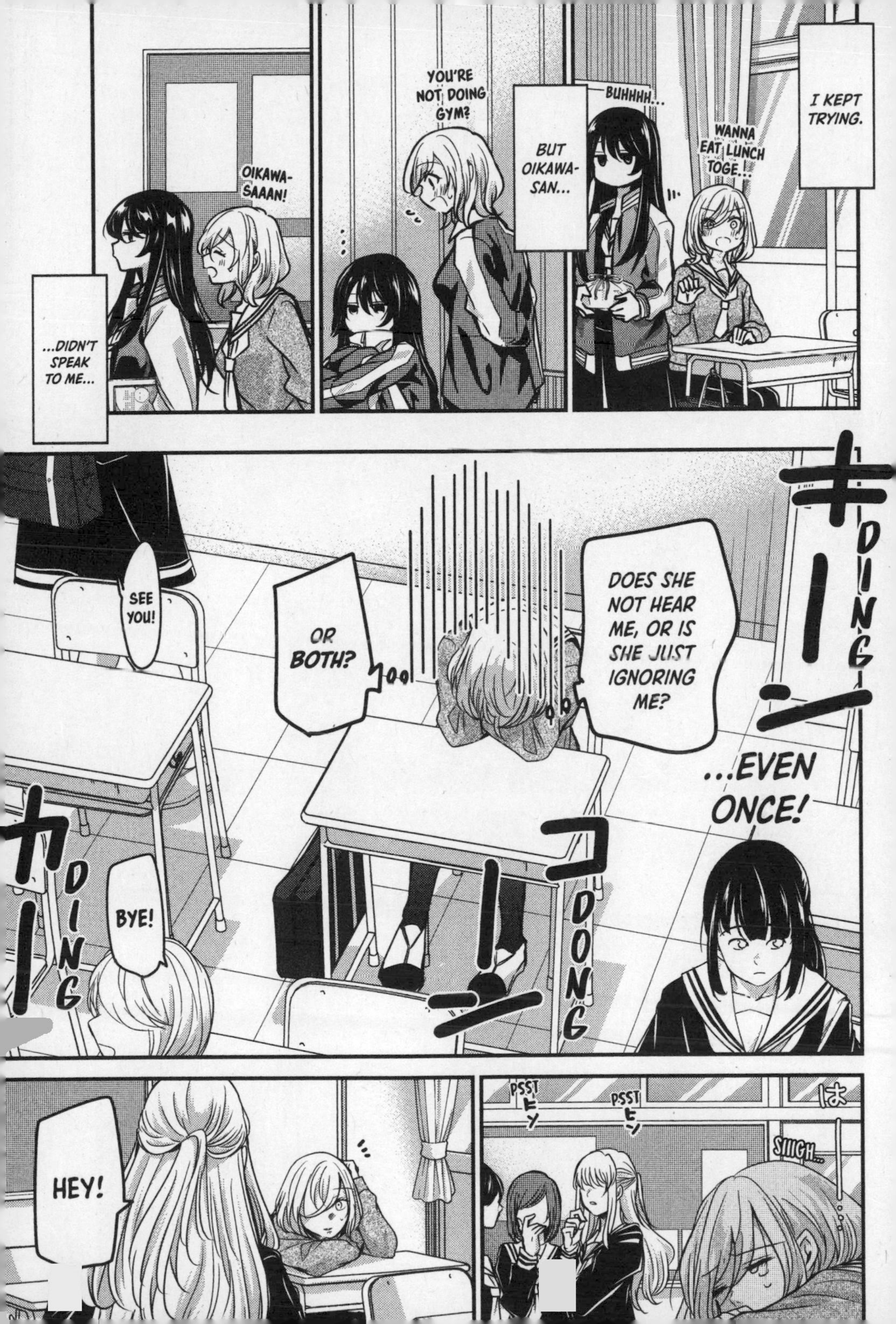
I KEPT TRYING.
BUHHHH...
WANNA EAT LUNCH TOGE...
BUT OIKAWA-SAN...
YOU'RE NOT DOING GYM?
OIKAWA-SAAAN!
...DIDN'T SPEAK TO ME...
DING
DOES SHE NOT HEAR ME, OR IS SHE JUST IGNORING ME?
...EVEN ONCE!
OR BOTH?
DONG
SEE YOU!
BYE!
DING
SIIIGH...
PSST
PSST
HEY!

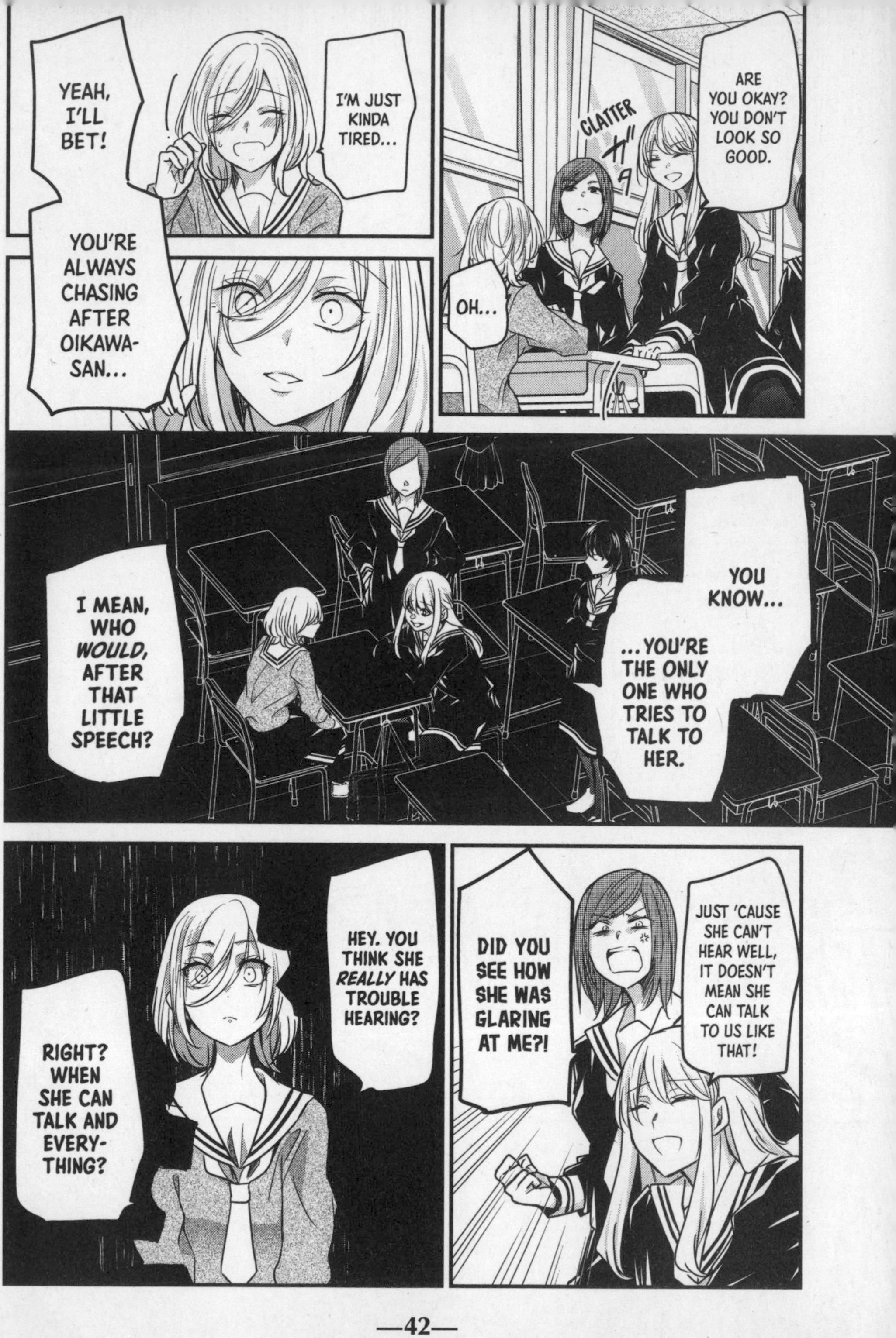
ARE YOU OKAY? YOU DON'T LOOK SO GOOD.
CLATTER
ガタ
OH...
I'M JUST KINDA TIRED...
YEAH, I'LL BET!
YOU'RE ALWAYS CHASING AFTER OIKAWA-SAN...
YOU KNOW...
...YOU'RE THE ONLY ONE WHO TRIES TO TALK TO HER.
I MEAN, WHO *WOULD*, AFTER THAT LITTLE SPEECH?
JUST 'CAUSE SHE CAN'T HEAR WELL, IT DOESN'T MEAN SHE CAN TALK TO US LIKE THAT!
DID YOU SEE HOW SHE WAS GLARING AT ME?!
HEY. YOU THINK SHE *REALLY* HAS TROUBLE HEARING?
RIGHT? WHEN SHE CAN TALK AND EVERY-THING?

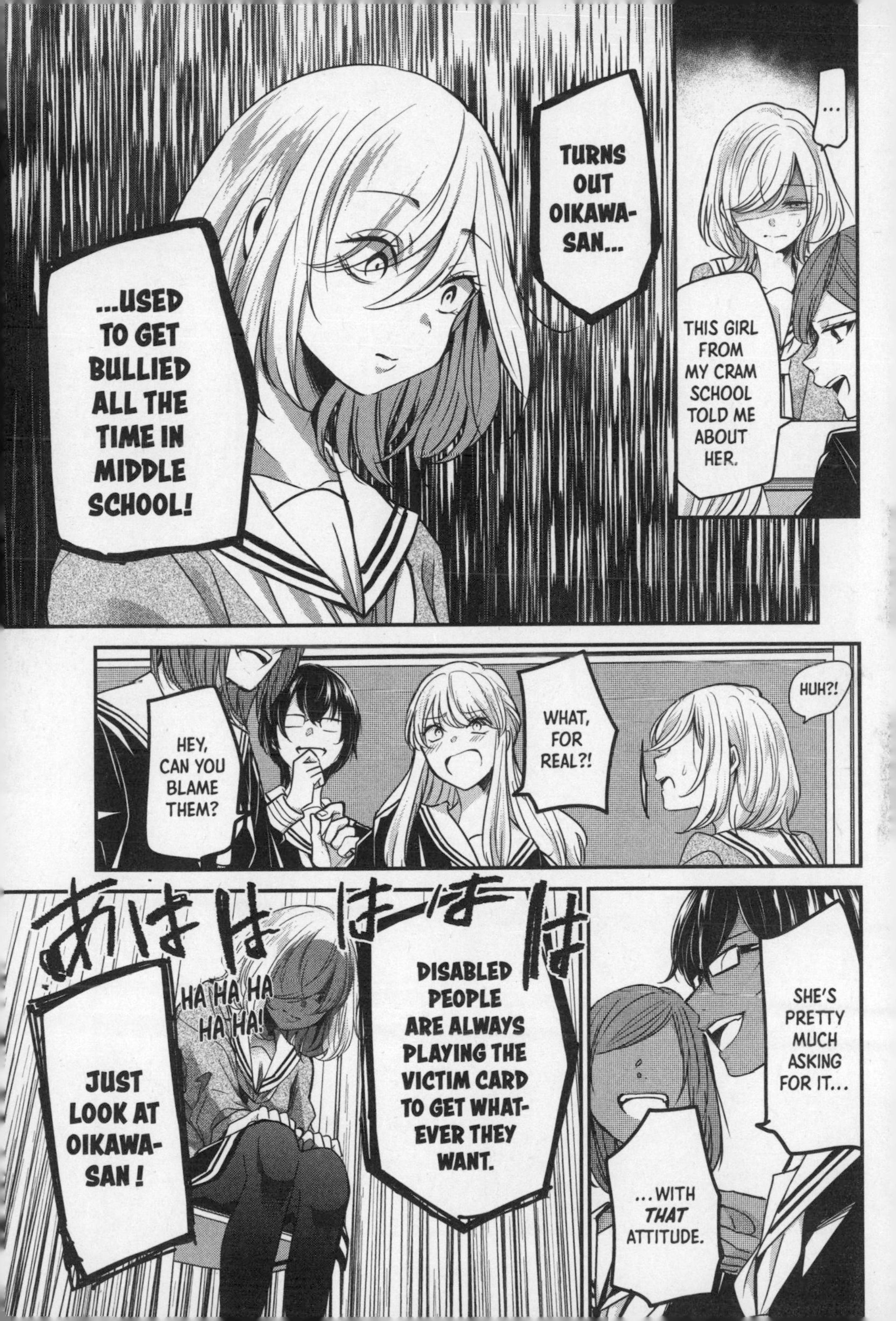
...
THIS GIRL FROM MY CRAM SCHOOL TOLD ME ABOUT HER.
TURNS OUT OIKAWA-SAN...
...USED TO GET BULLIED ALL THE TIME IN MIDDLE SCHOOL!
HUH?!
WHAT, FOR REAL?!
HEY, CAN YOU BLAME THEM?
SHE'S PRETTY MUCH ASKING FOR IT...
...WITH THAT ATTITUDE.
あははは はーはは
DISABLED PEOPLE ARE ALWAYS PLAYING THE VICTIM CARD TO GET WHAT-EVER THEY WANT.
HA HA HA HA HA!
JUST LOOK AT OIKAWA-SAN !

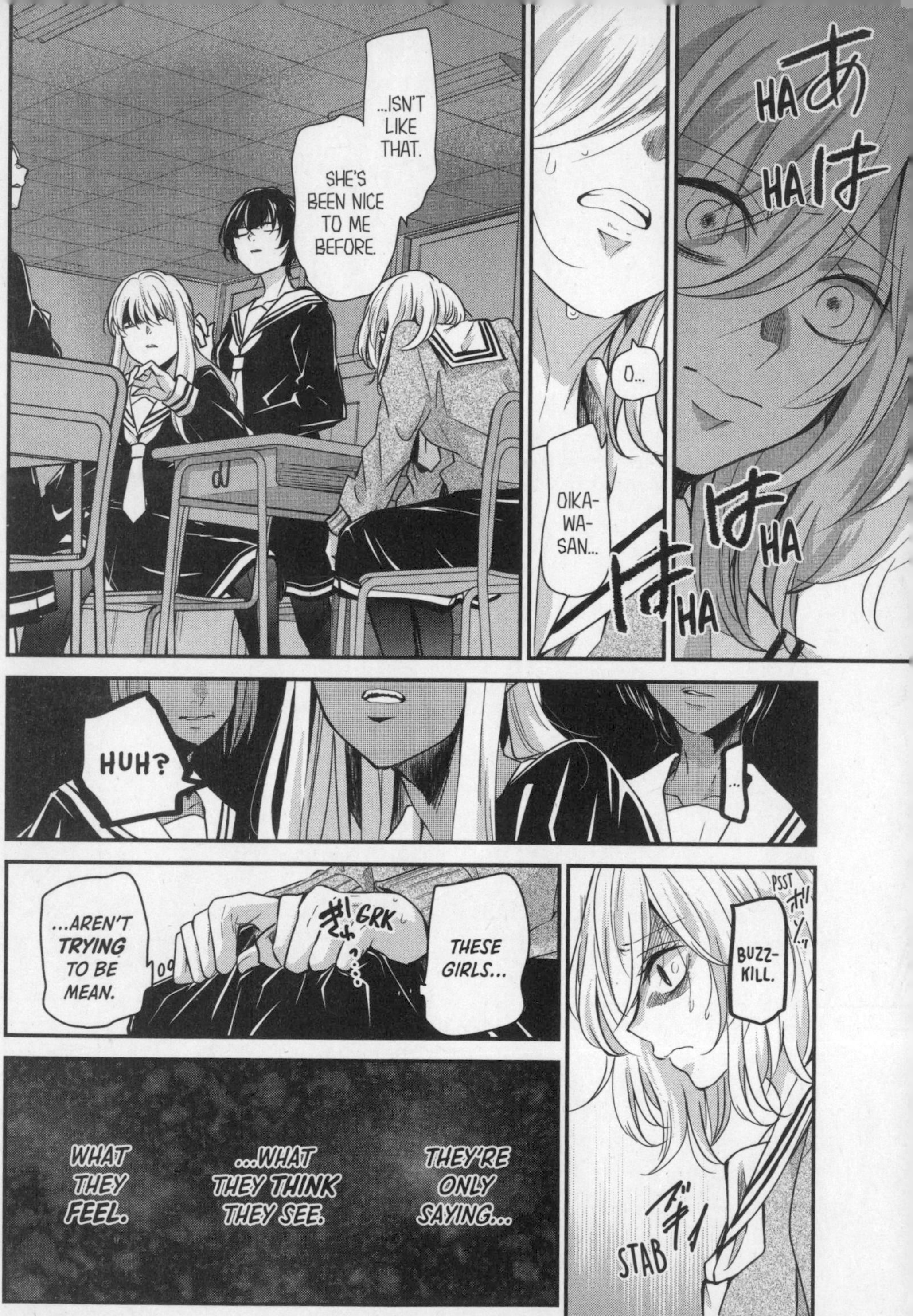
HA あ
HA は
は HA
は HA
O...
OIKAWA-SAN...
...ISN'T LIKE THAT.
SHE'S BEEN NICE TO ME BEFORE.
...
HUH?
PSST ボソッ
BUZZ-KILL.
STAB ズキ
THESE GIRLS...
GRK ぎゅ
...AREN'T TRYING TO BE MEAN.
THEY'RE ONLY SAYING...
...WHAT THEY THINK THEY SEE.
WHAT THEY FEEL.

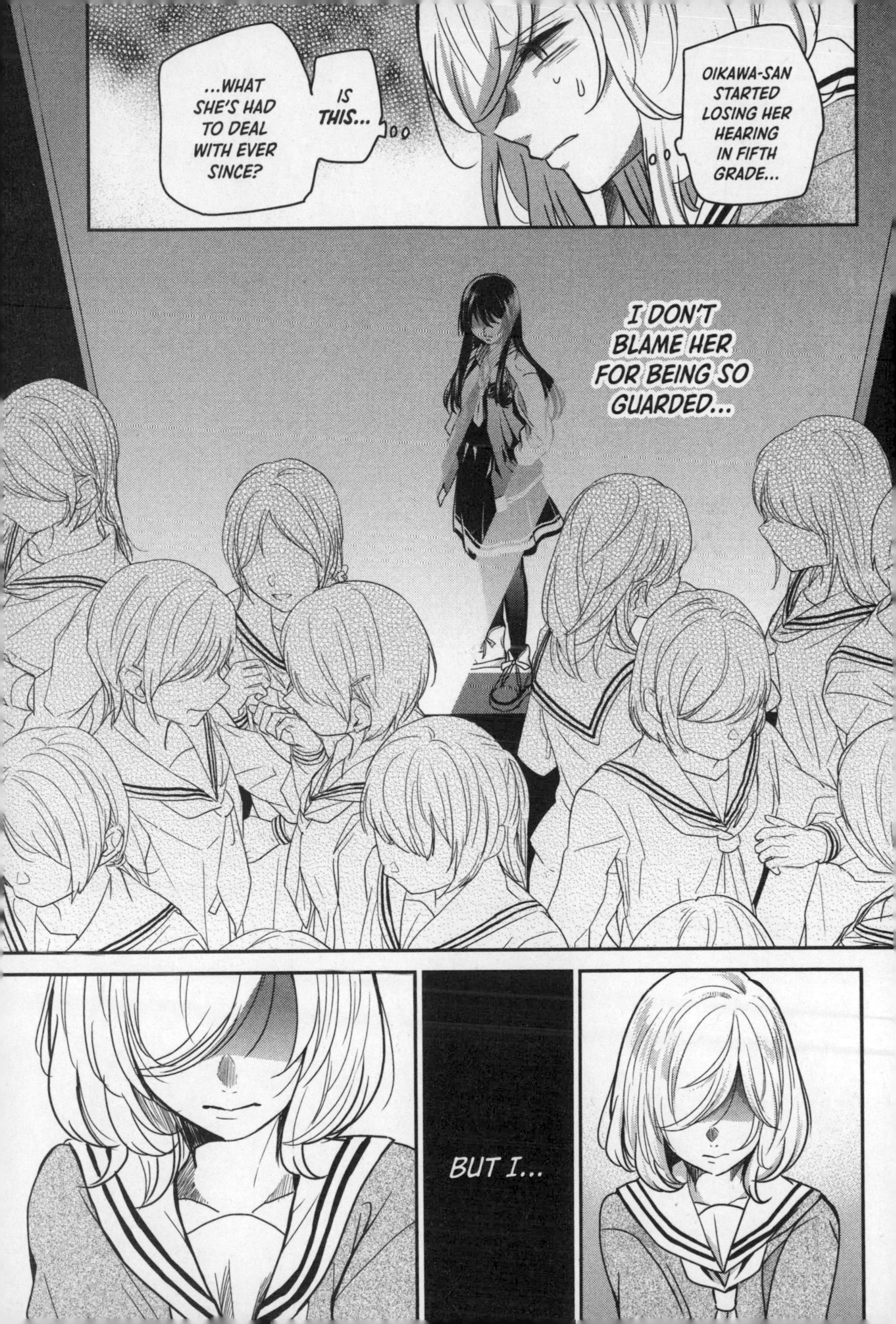
OIKAWA-SAN STARTED LOSING HER HEARING IN FIFTH GRADE...
IS THIS...
...WHAT SHE'S HAD TO DEAL WITH EVER SINCE?
I DON'T BLAME HER FOR BEING SO GUARDED...
BUT I...

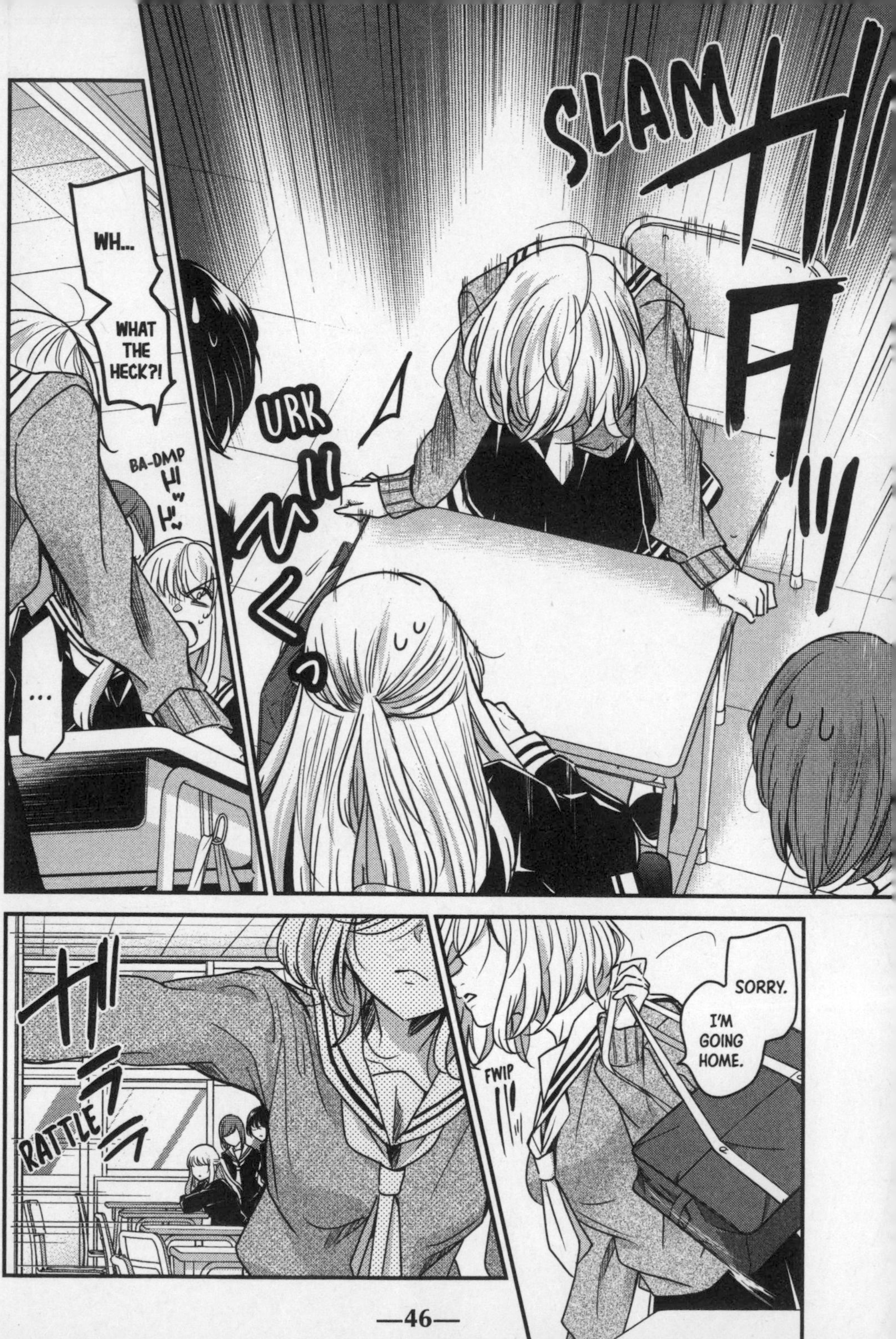
SLAM
URK
WH...
WHAT THE HECK?!
BA-DMP
...
SORRY.
I'M GOING HOME.
FWIP
RATTLE

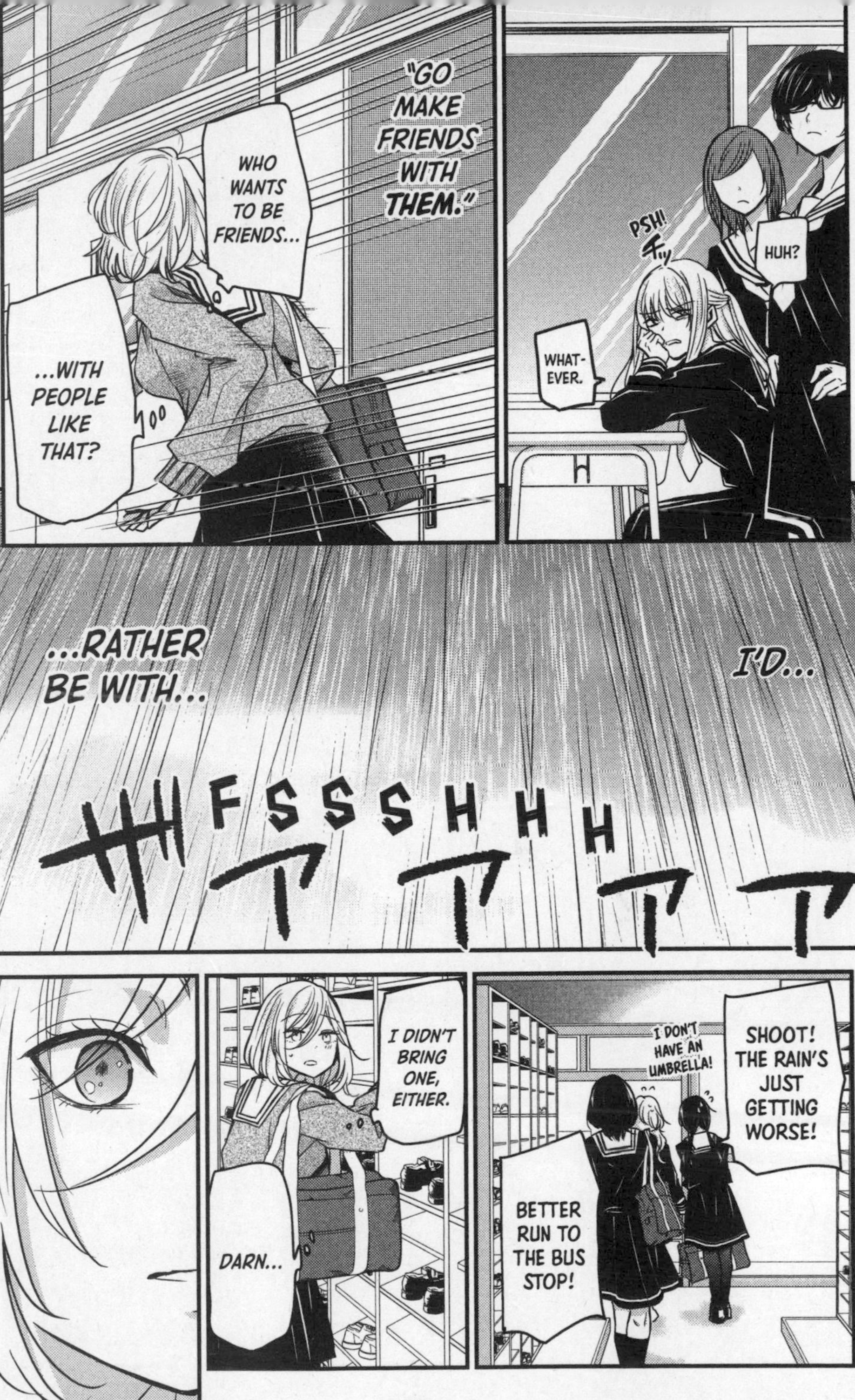
PSH!
チッ
HUH?
WHAT-EVER.
"GO MAKE FRIENDS WITH THEM."
WHO WANTS TO BE FRIENDS...
...WITH PEOPLE LIKE THAT?
I'D...
...RATHER BE WITH...
FSSSHHH
サアアア
SHOOT! THE RAIN'S JUST GETTING WORSE!
I DON'T HAVE AN UMBRELLA!
BETTER RUN TO THE BUS STOP!
I DIDN'T BRING ONE, EITHER.
DARN...

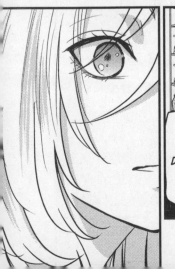

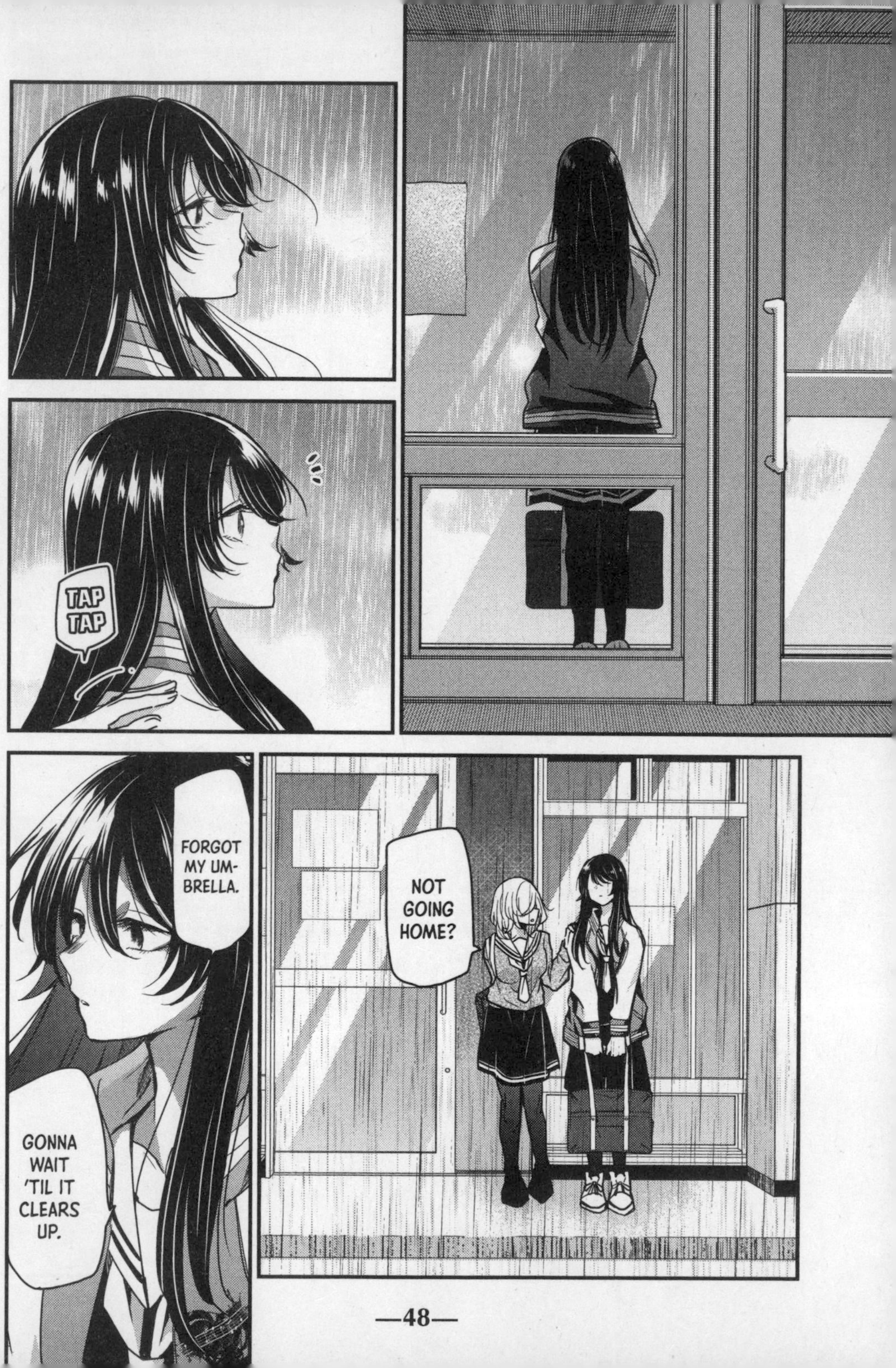
TAP TAP
NOT GOING HOME?
FORGOT MY UM-BRELLA.
GONNA WAIT 'TIL IT CLEARS UP.

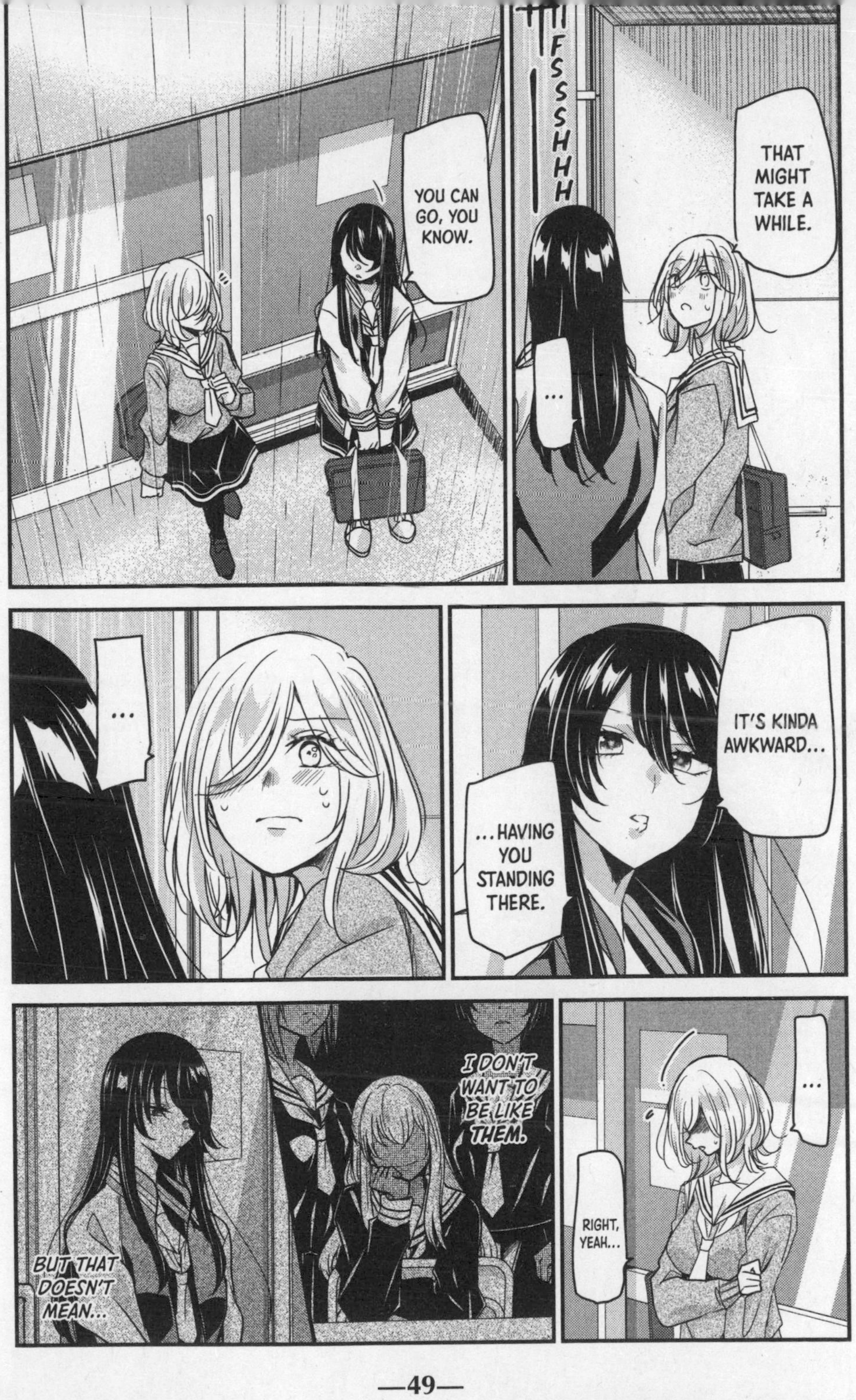
FSSSHHH
THAT MIGHT TAKE A WHILE.
...
YOU CAN GO, YOU KNOW.
IT'S KINDA AWKWARD...
...HAVING YOU STANDING THERE.
...
...
RIGHT, YEAH...
I DON'T WANT TO BE LIKE THEM.
BUT THAT DOESN'T MEAN...

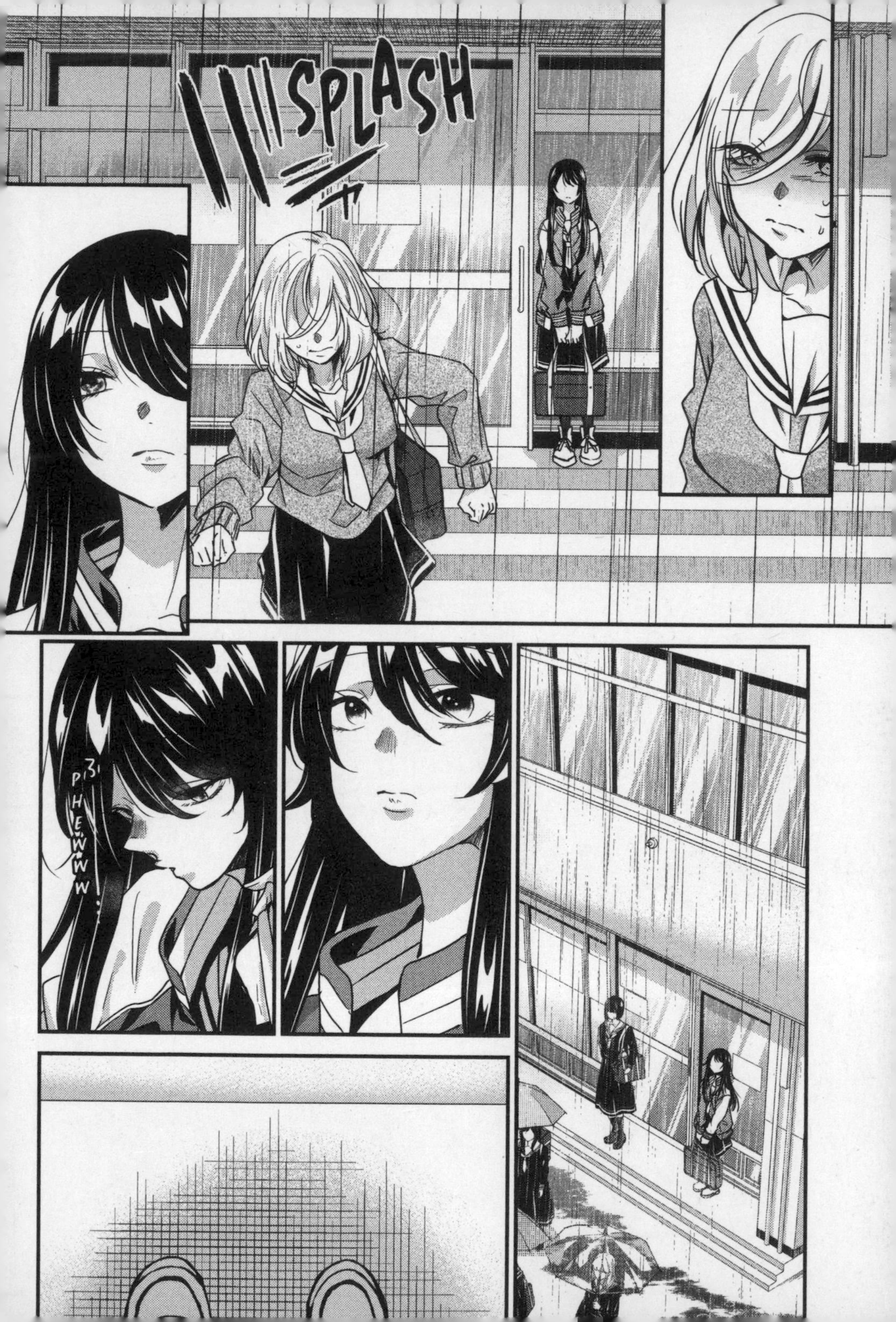
SPLASH
PHEWWW

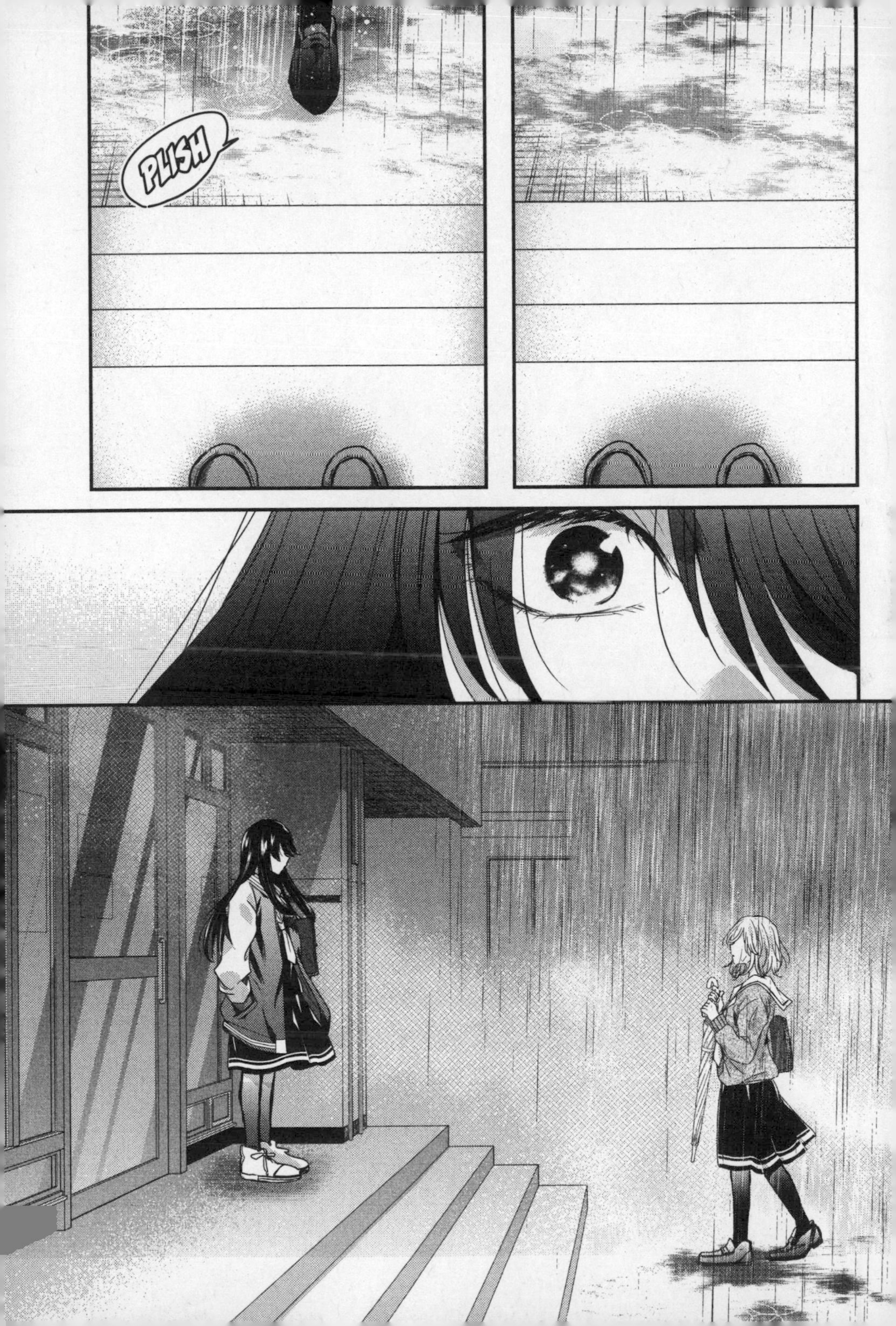
PLISH

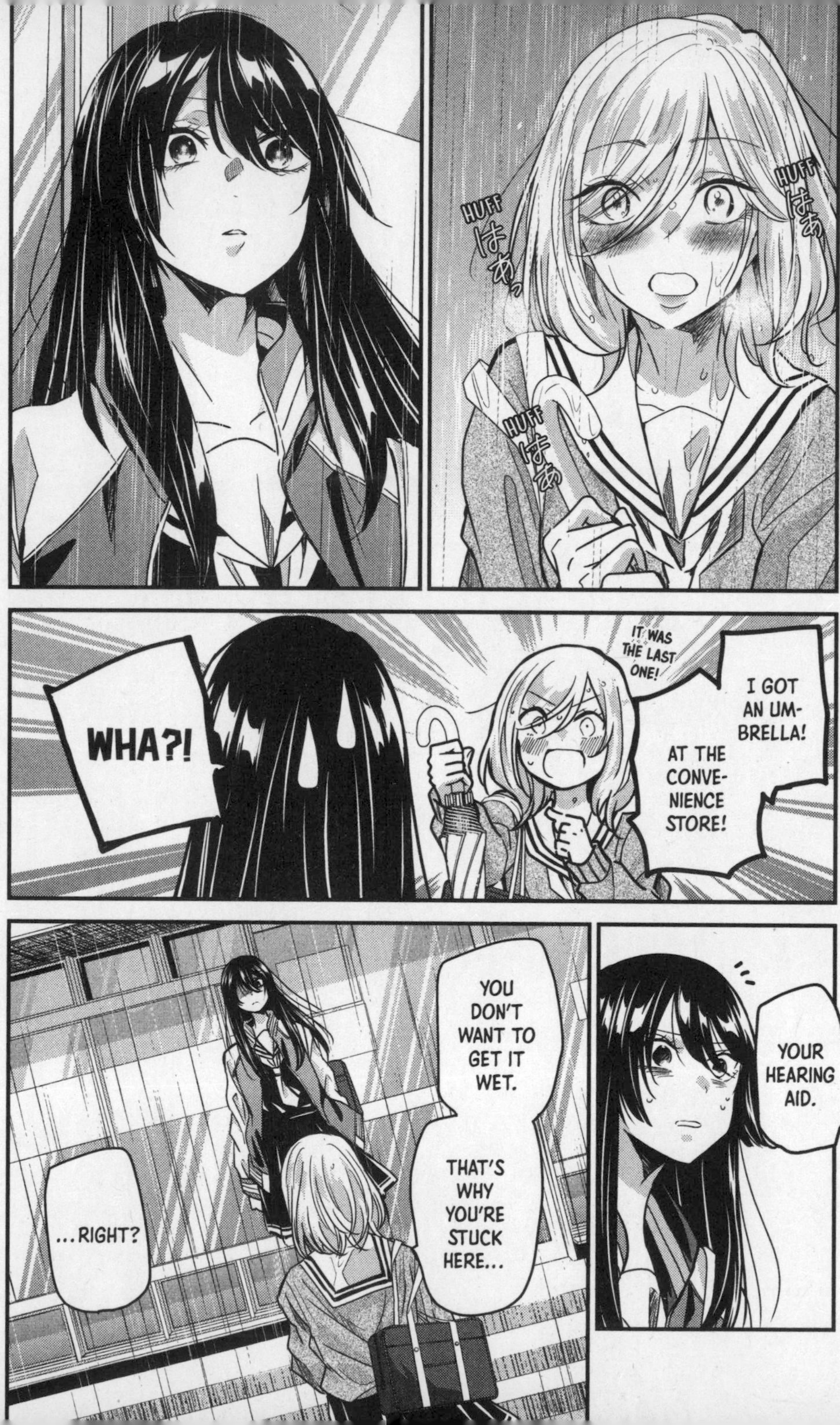
HUFF はぁ
HUFF はあっ
HUFF はぁ
I GOT AN UMBRELLA! AT THE CONVENIENCE STORE!
IT WAS THE LAST ONE!
WHA?!
YOUR HEARING AID.
YOU DON'T WANT TO GET IT WET.
THAT'S WHY YOU'RE STUCK HERE...
...RIGHT?

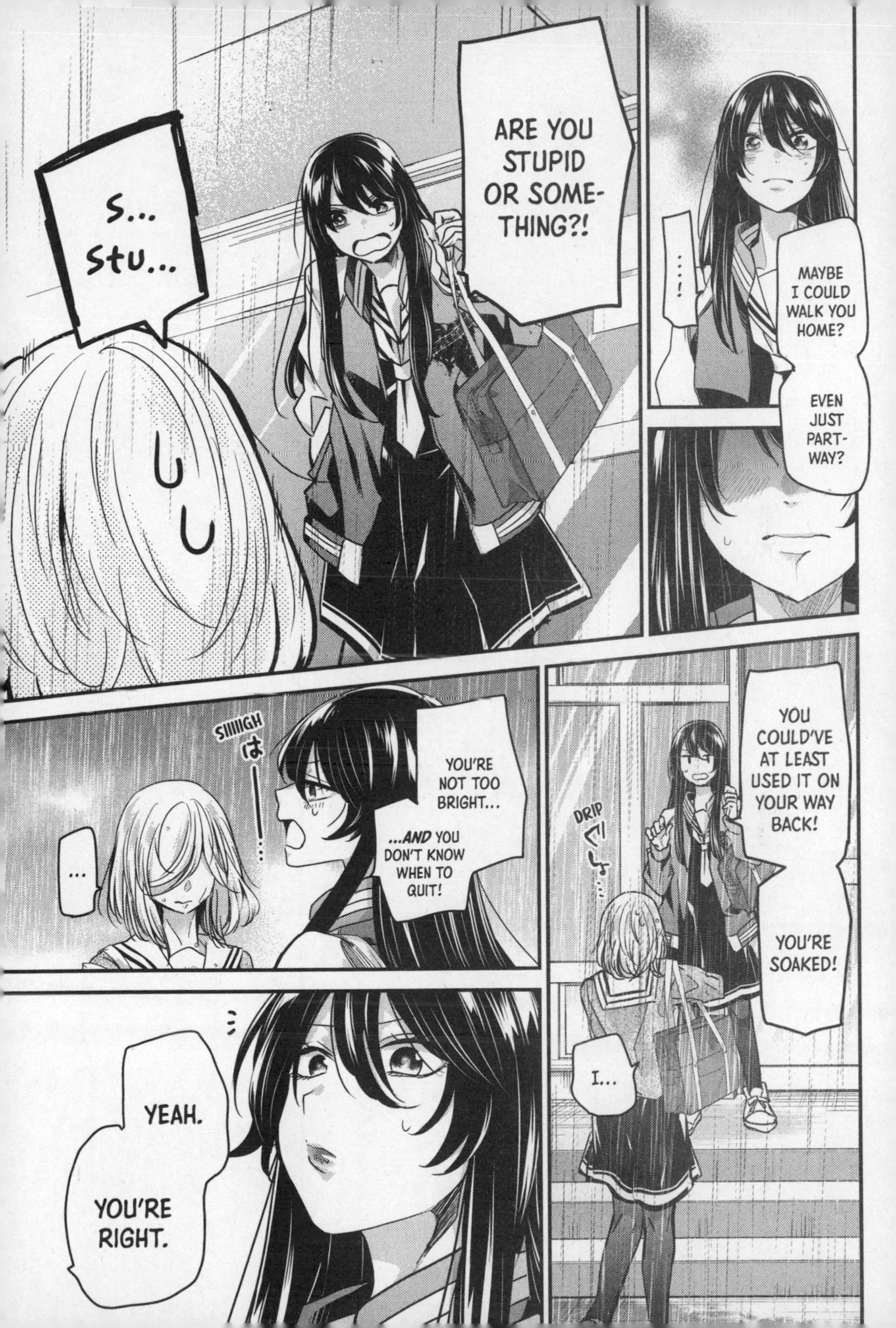
...!
MAYBE I COULD WALK YOU HOME?
EVEN JUST PART-WAY?
ARE YOU STUPID OR SOME-THING?!
S... Stu...
U U
YOU COULD'VE AT LEAST USED IT ON YOUR WAY BACK!
DRIP
YOU'RE SOAKED!
I...
YOU'RE NOT TOO BRIGHT...
...AND YOU DON'T KNOW WHEN TO QUIT!
SIIIIGH
は——…
...
YEAH.
YOU'RE RIGHT.

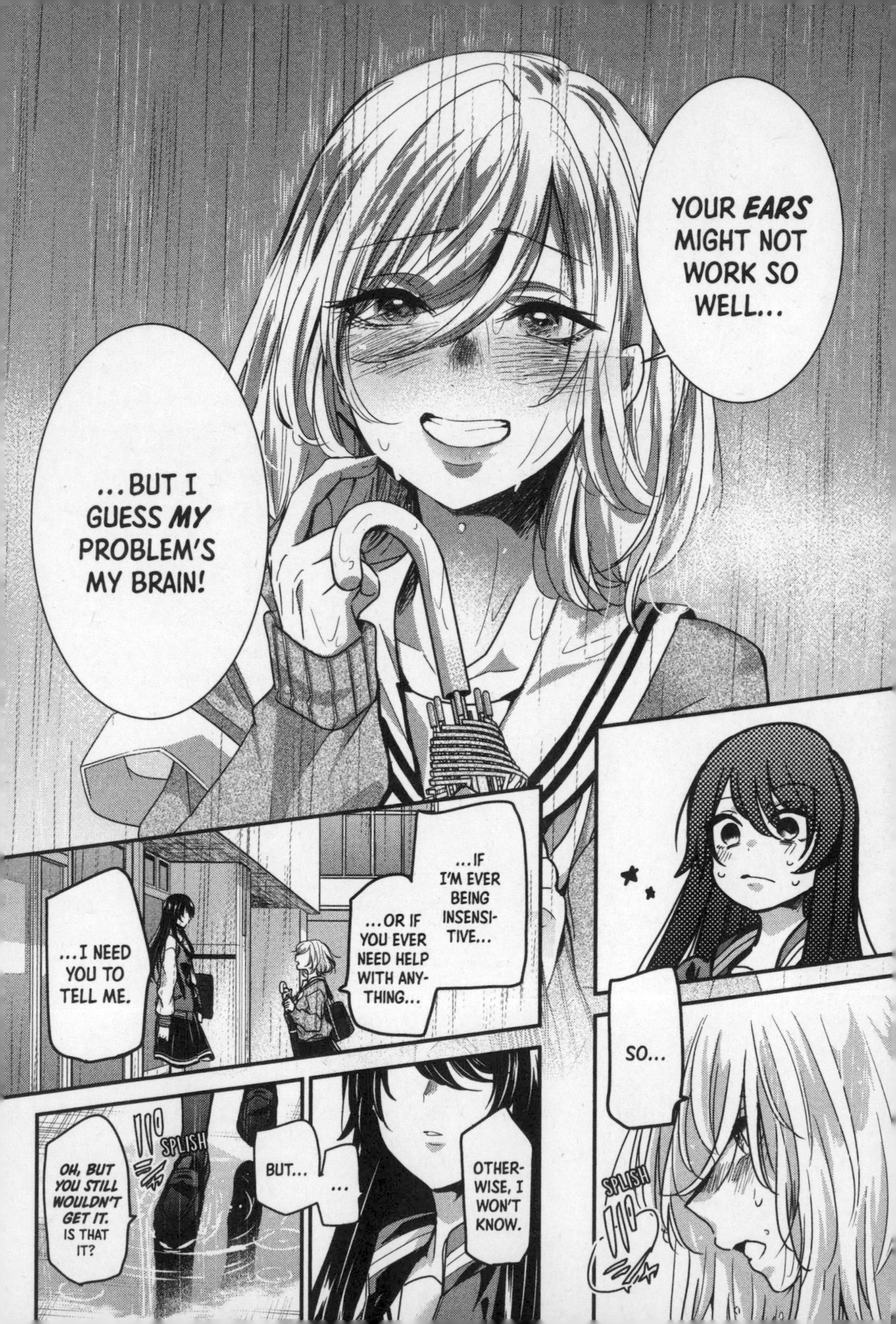
YOUR *EARS* MIGHT NOT WORK SO WELL...
...BUT I GUESS *MY* PROBLEM'S MY BRAIN!
...IF I'M EVER BEING INSENSI-TIVE...
...OR IF YOU EVER NEED HELP WITH ANY-THING...
...I NEED YOU TO TELL ME.
SO...
SPLISH
OTHER-WISE, I WON'T KNOW.
BUT...
...
SPLISH
OH, BUT YOU STILL WOULDN'T GET IT. IS THAT IT?

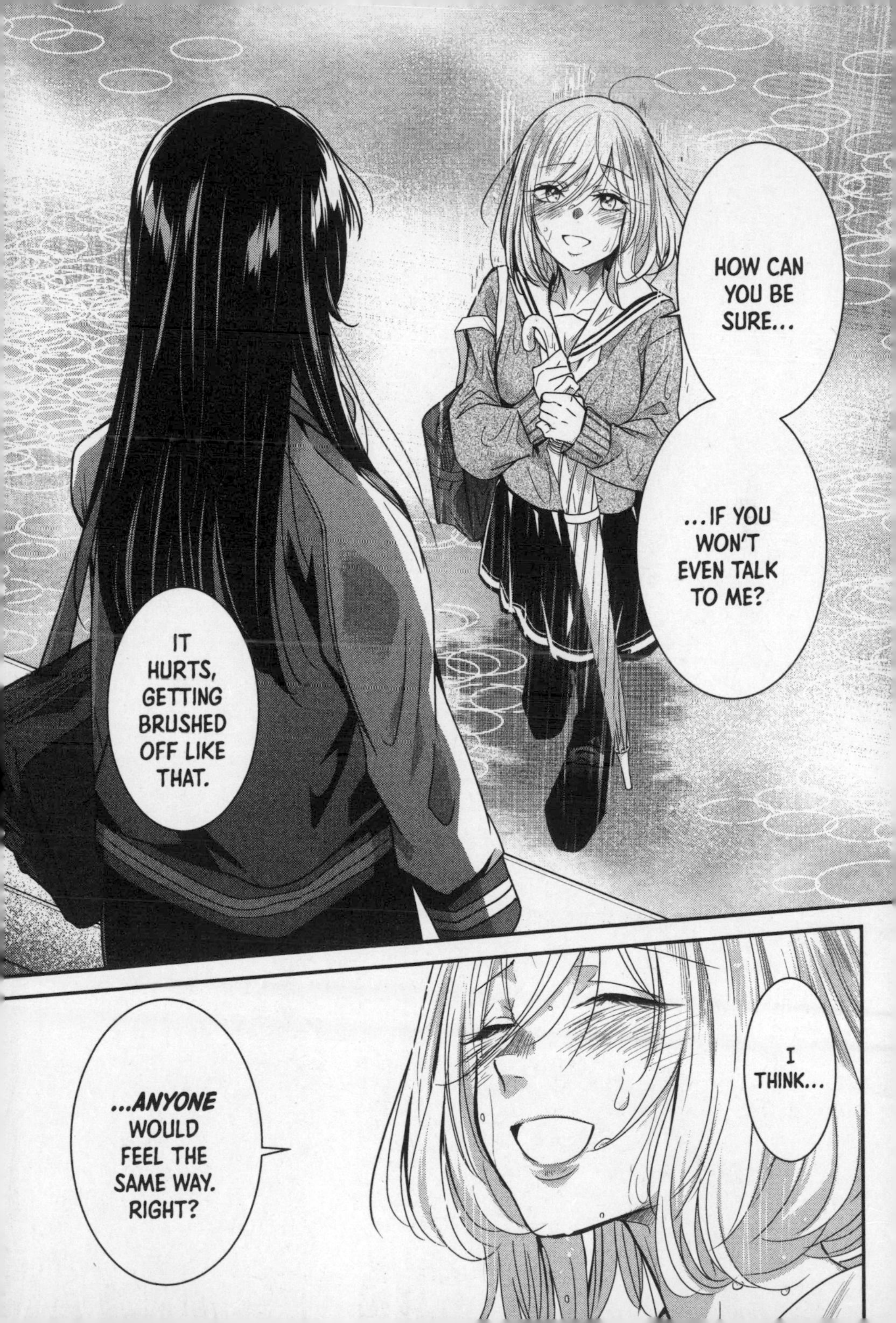
HOW CAN YOU BE SURE...
...IF YOU WON'T EVEN TALK TO ME?
IT HURTS, GETTING BRUSHED OFF LIKE THAT.
I THINK...
...*ANYONE* WOULD FEEL THE SAME WAY. RIGHT?

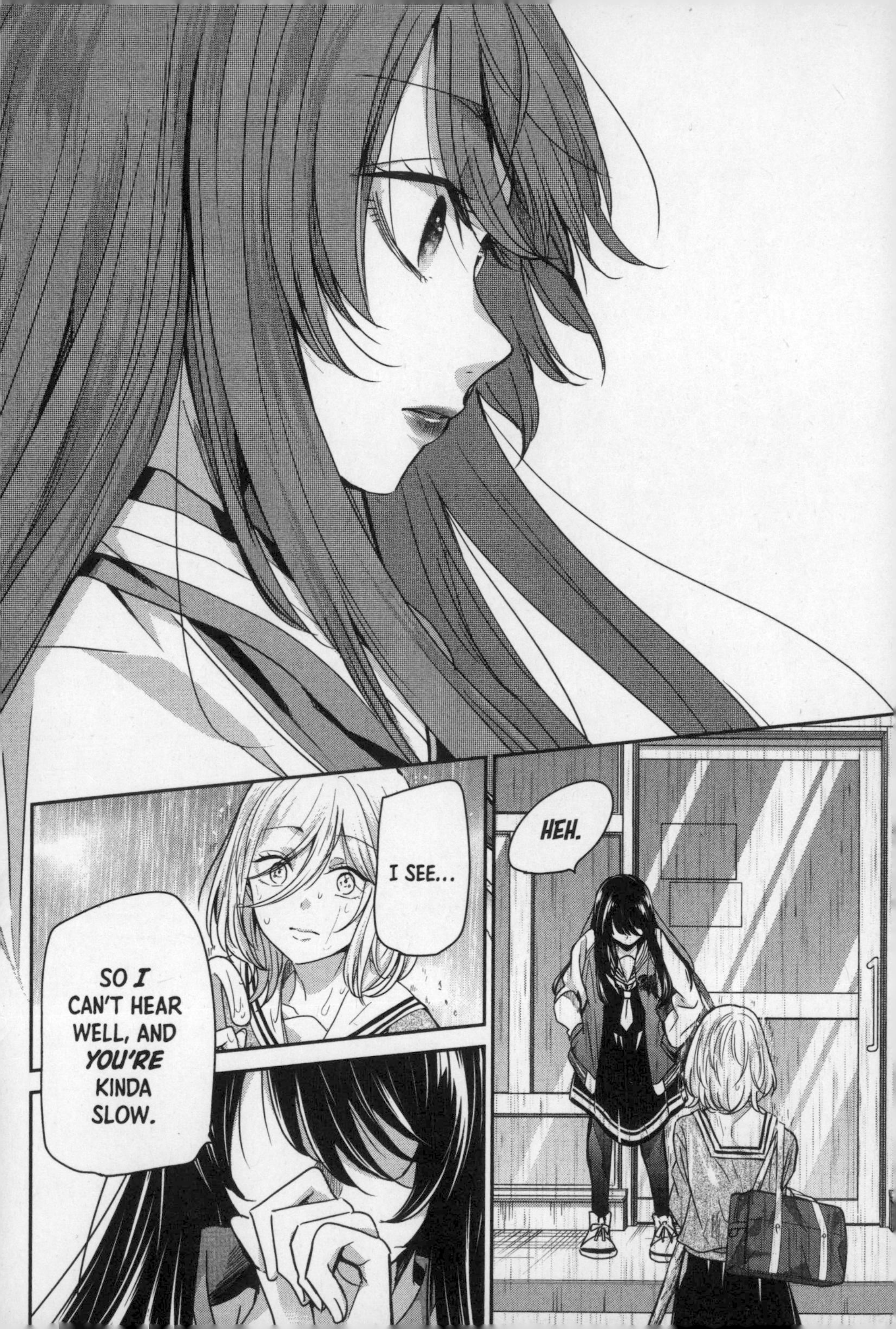
HEH.
I SEE...
SO *I* CAN'T HEAR WELL, AND *YOU'RE* KINDA SLOW.

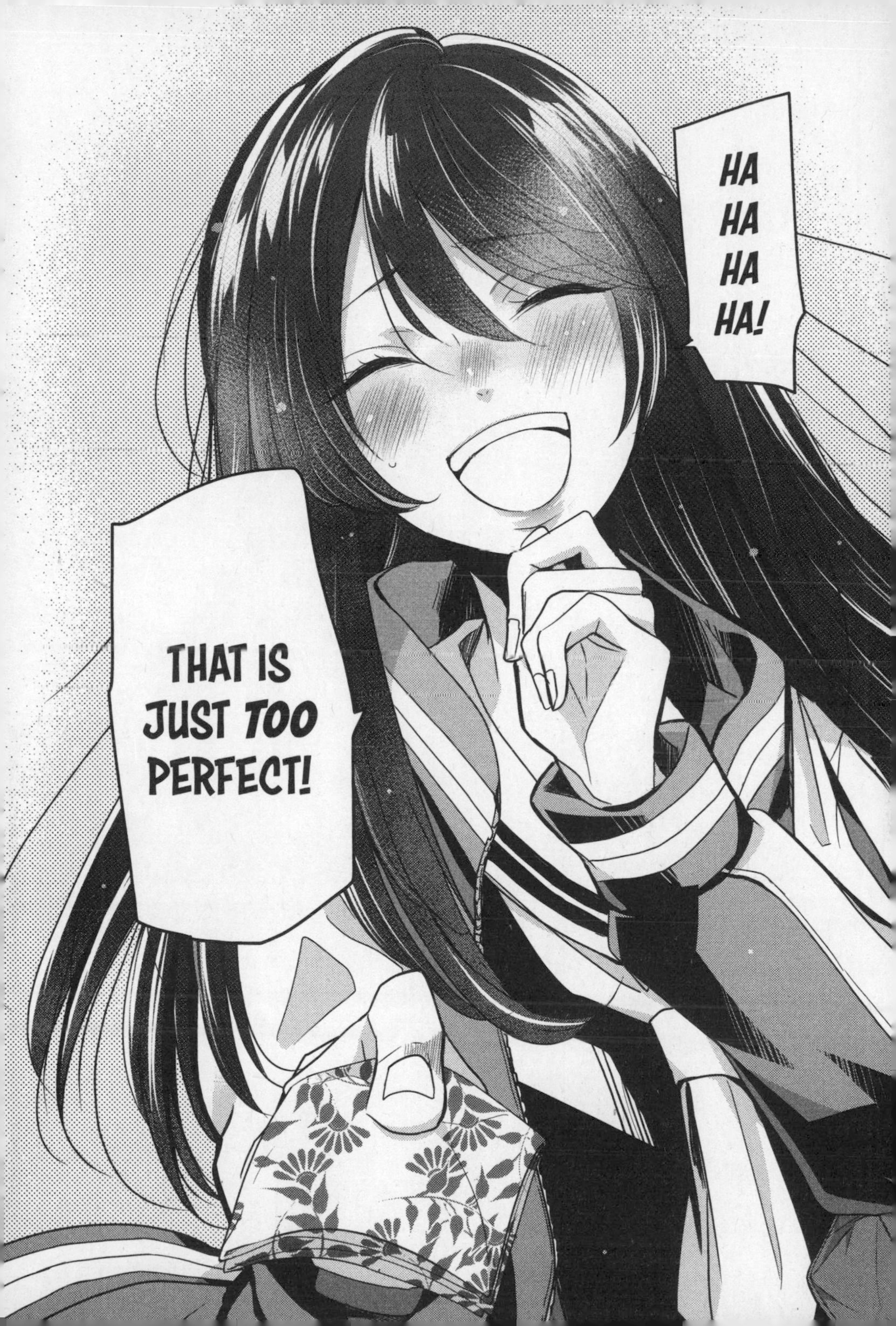

HA HA HA HA!
THAT IS JUST *TOO* PERFECT!

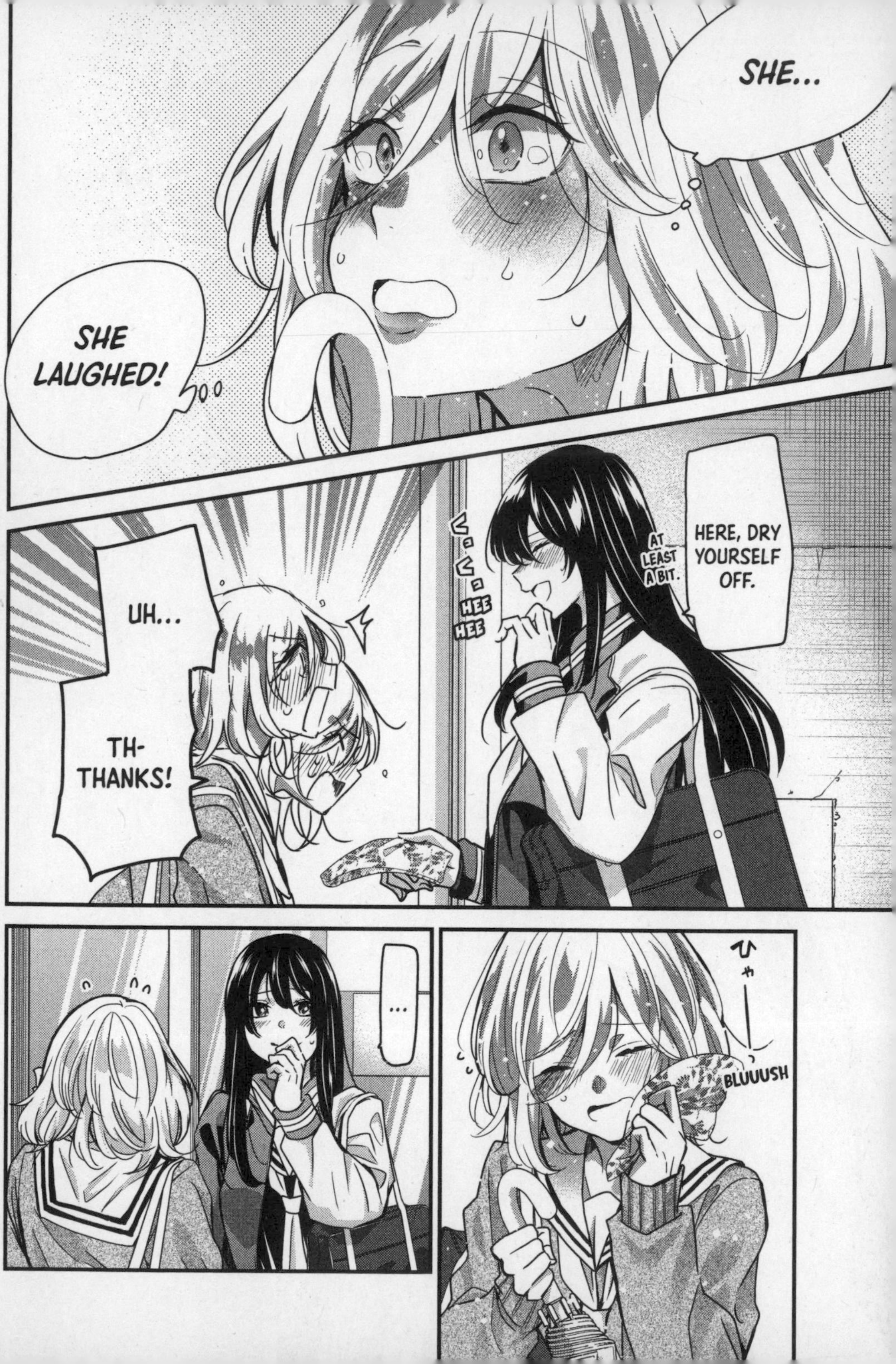
SHE...
SHE LAUGHED!
HERE, DRY YOURSELF OFF.
AT LEAST A BIT.
HEE HEE
UH...
TH- THANKS!
ひゃー
BLUUUSH
...

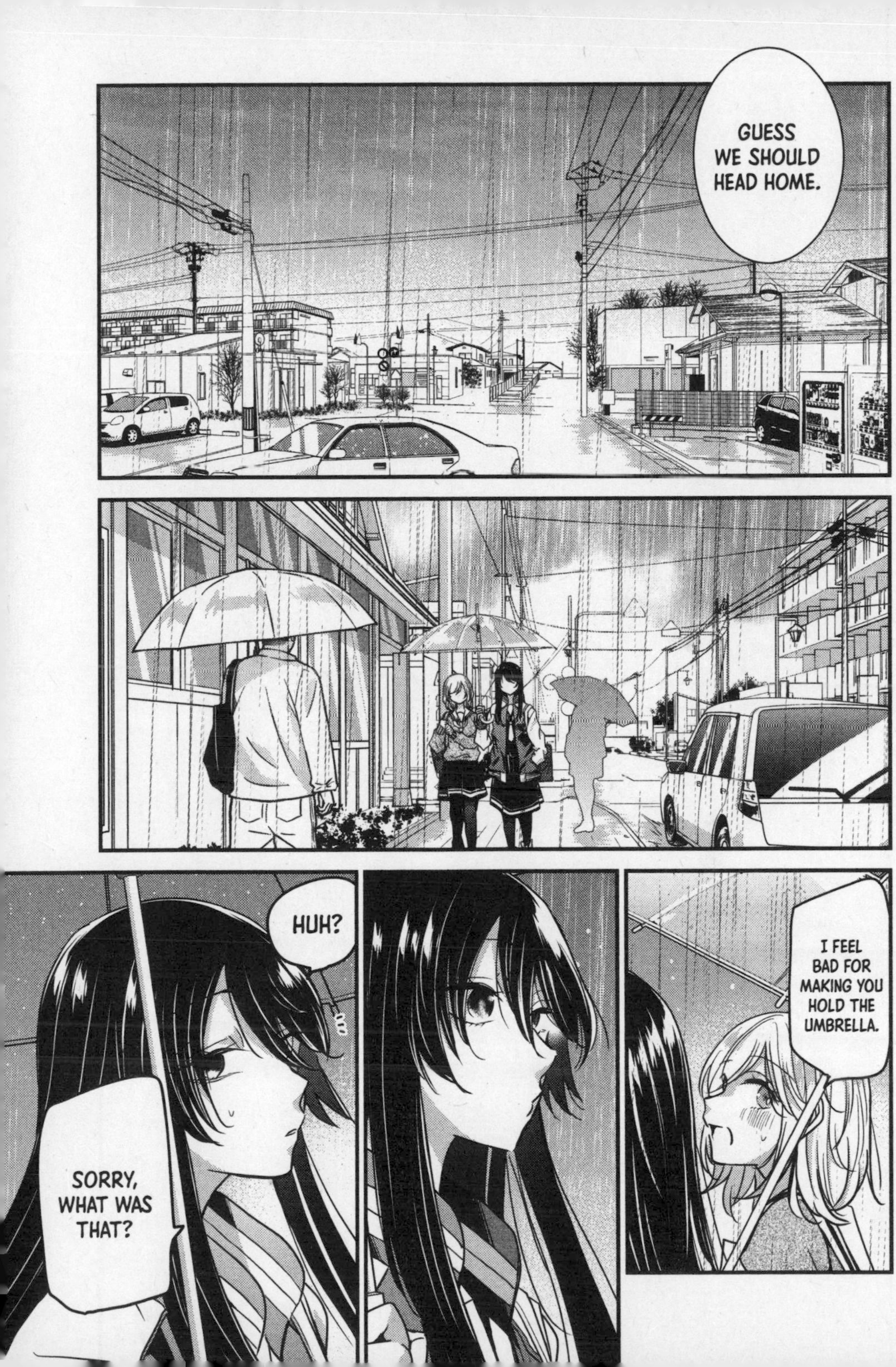
GUESS WE SHOULD HEAD HOME.
I FEEL BAD FOR MAKING YOU HOLD THE UMBRELLA.
HUH?
SORRY, WHAT WAS THAT?

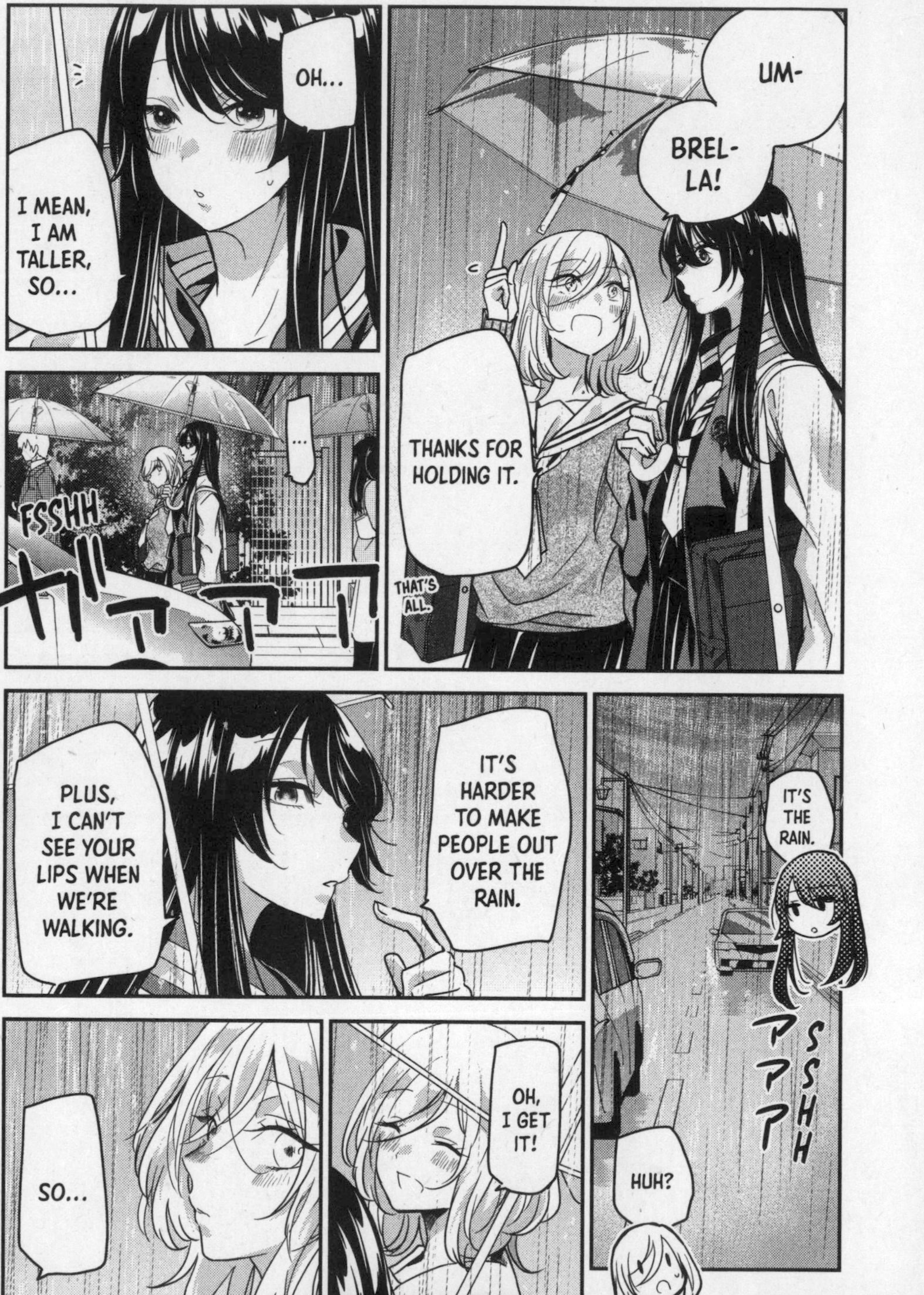
UM-
BREL-
LA!
THANKS FOR HOLDING IT.
THAT'S ALL.
OH...
I MEAN, I AM TALLER, SO...
...
FSSHH
IT'S THE RAIN.
SSHH
HUH?
IT'S HARDER TO MAKE PEOPLE OUT OVER THE RAIN.
PLUS, I CAN'T SEE YOUR LIPS WHEN WE'RE WALKING.
OH, I GET IT!
SO...

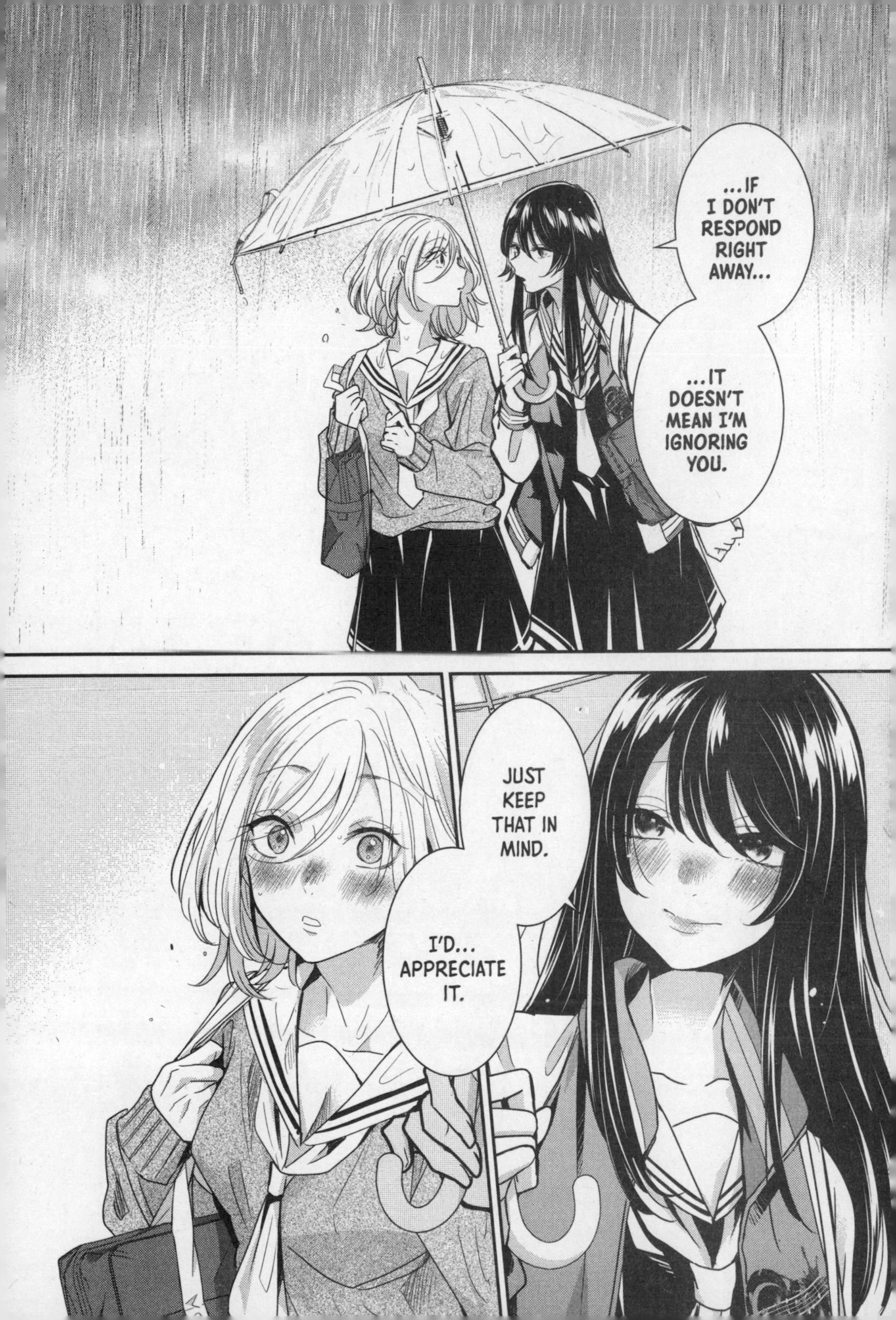
...IF I DON'T RESPOND RIGHT AWAY...
...IT DOESN'T MEAN I'M IGNORING YOU.
JUST KEEP THAT IN MIND.
I'D... APPRECIATE IT.

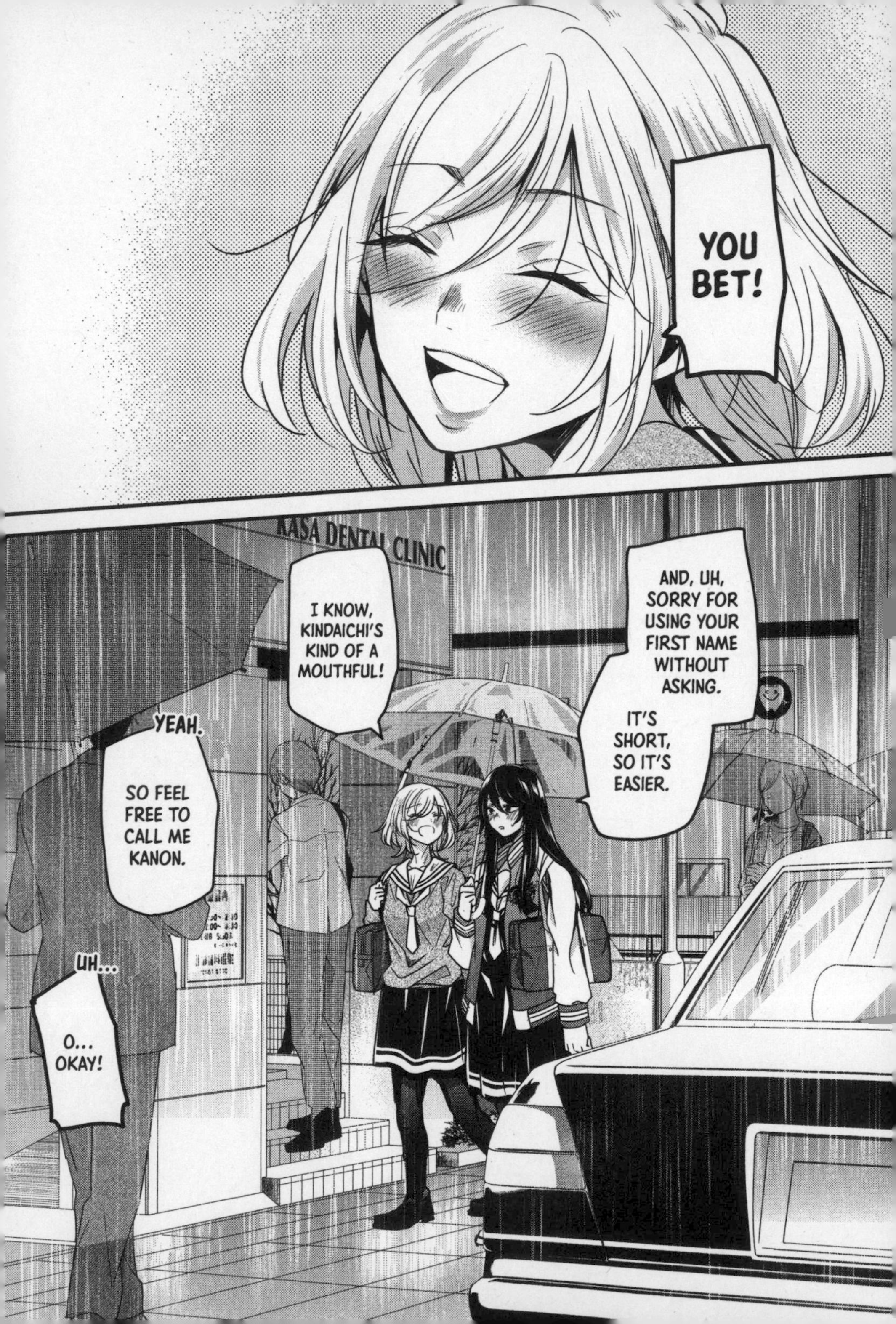
YOU BET!
KASA DENTAL CLINIC
AND, UH, SORRY FOR USING YOUR FIRST NAME WITHOUT ASKING.
IT'S SHORT, SO IT'S EASIER.
I KNOW, KINDAICHI'S KIND OF A MOUTHFUL!
YEAH.
SO FEEL FREE TO CALL ME KANON.
UH...
O... OKAY!

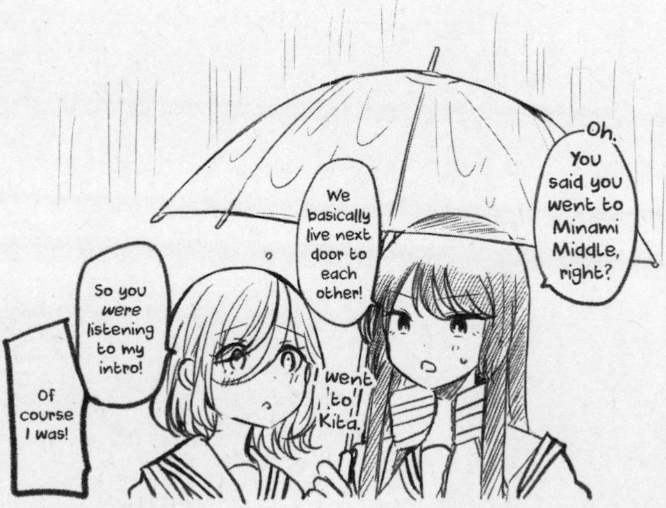
Oh. You said you went to Minami Middle, right?
So you were listening to my intro!
Of course I was!
I went to Kita.
We basically live next door to each other!

the moon on a rainy night

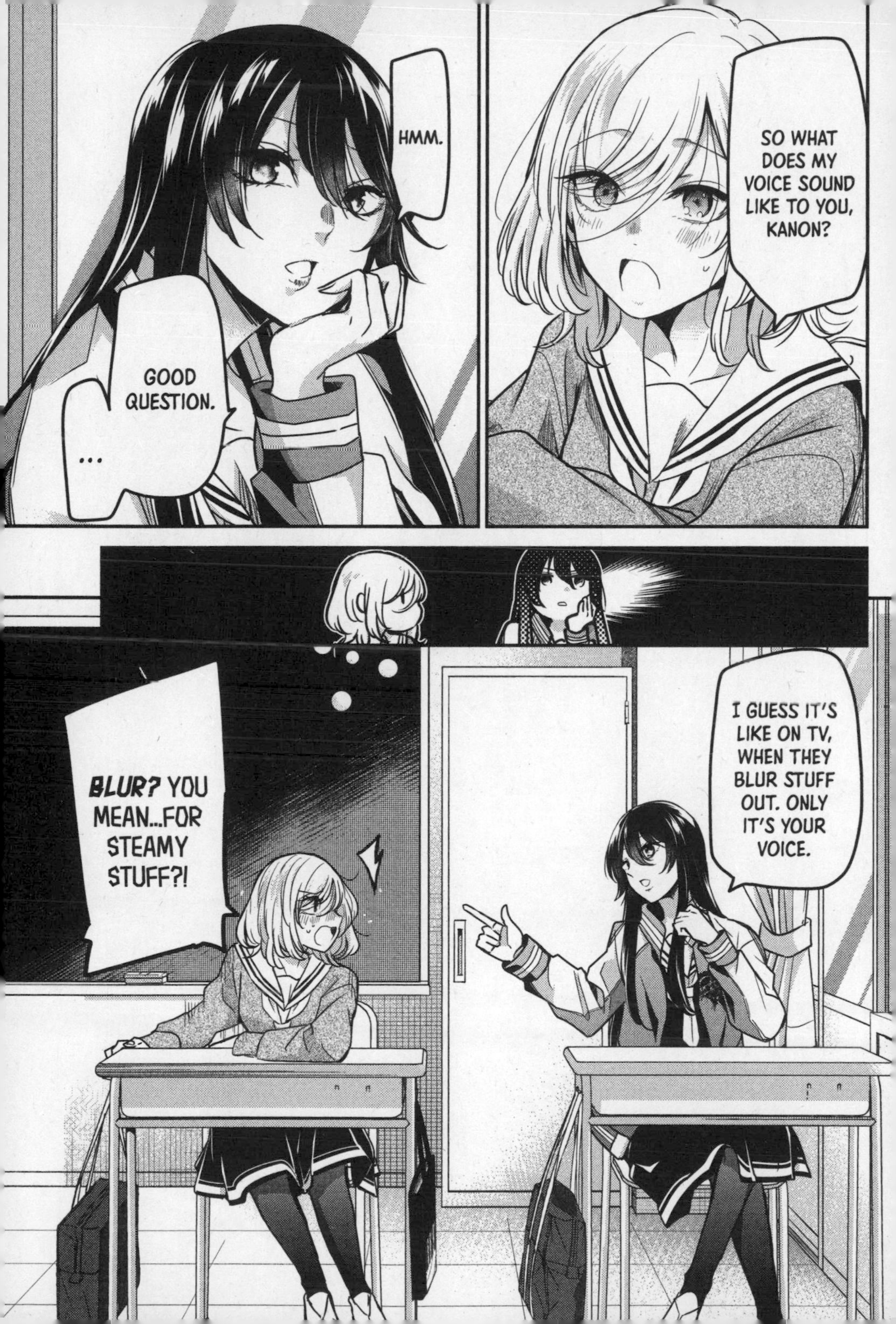
SO WHAT DOES MY VOICE SOUND LIKE TO YOU, KANON?
HMM.
GOOD QUESTION.
...
I GUESS IT'S LIKE ON TV, WHEN THEY BLUR STUFF OUT. ONLY IT'S YOUR VOICE.
BLUR? YOU MEAN...FOR STEAMY STUFF?!

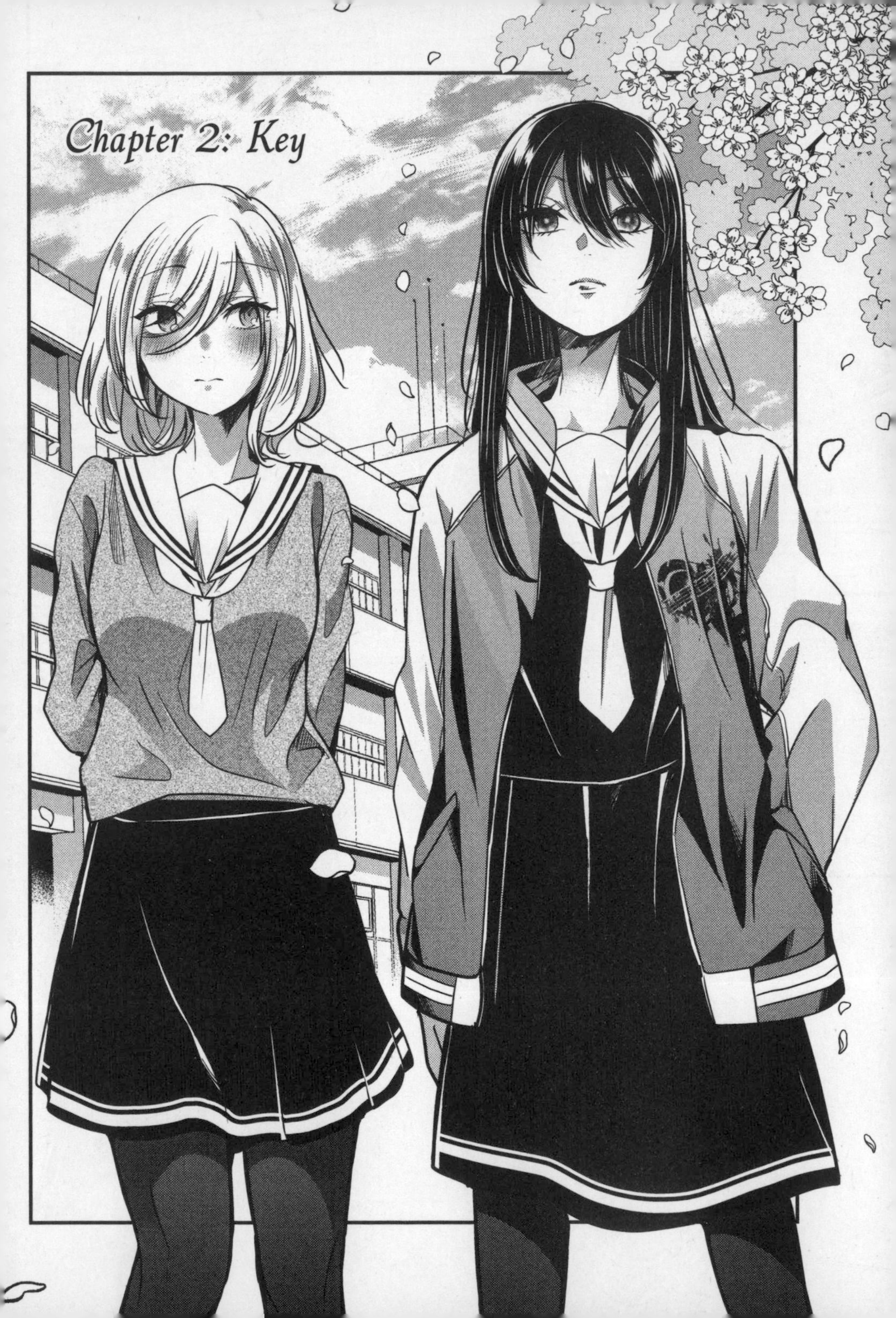
Chapter 2: Key

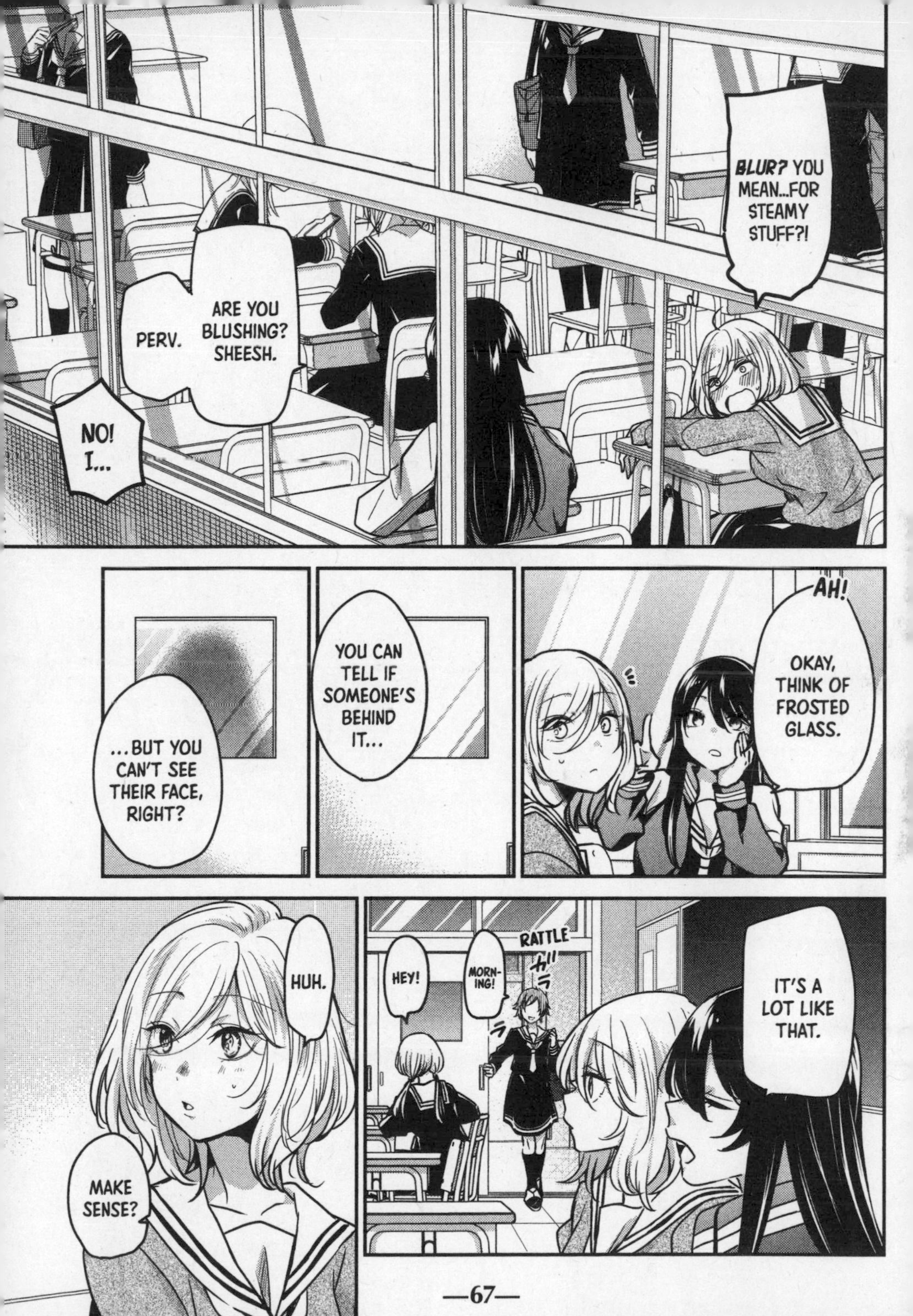
BLUR? YOU MEAN...FOR STEAMY STUFF?!
ARE YOU BLUSHING? SHEESH.
PERV.
NO! I...
AH!
OKAY, THINK OF FROSTED GLASS.
YOU CAN TELL IF SOMEONE'S BEHIND IT...
...BUT YOU CAN'T SEE THEIR FACE, RIGHT?
IT'S A LOT LIKE THAT.
RATTLE
MORN-ING!
HEY!
HUH.
MAKE SENSE?

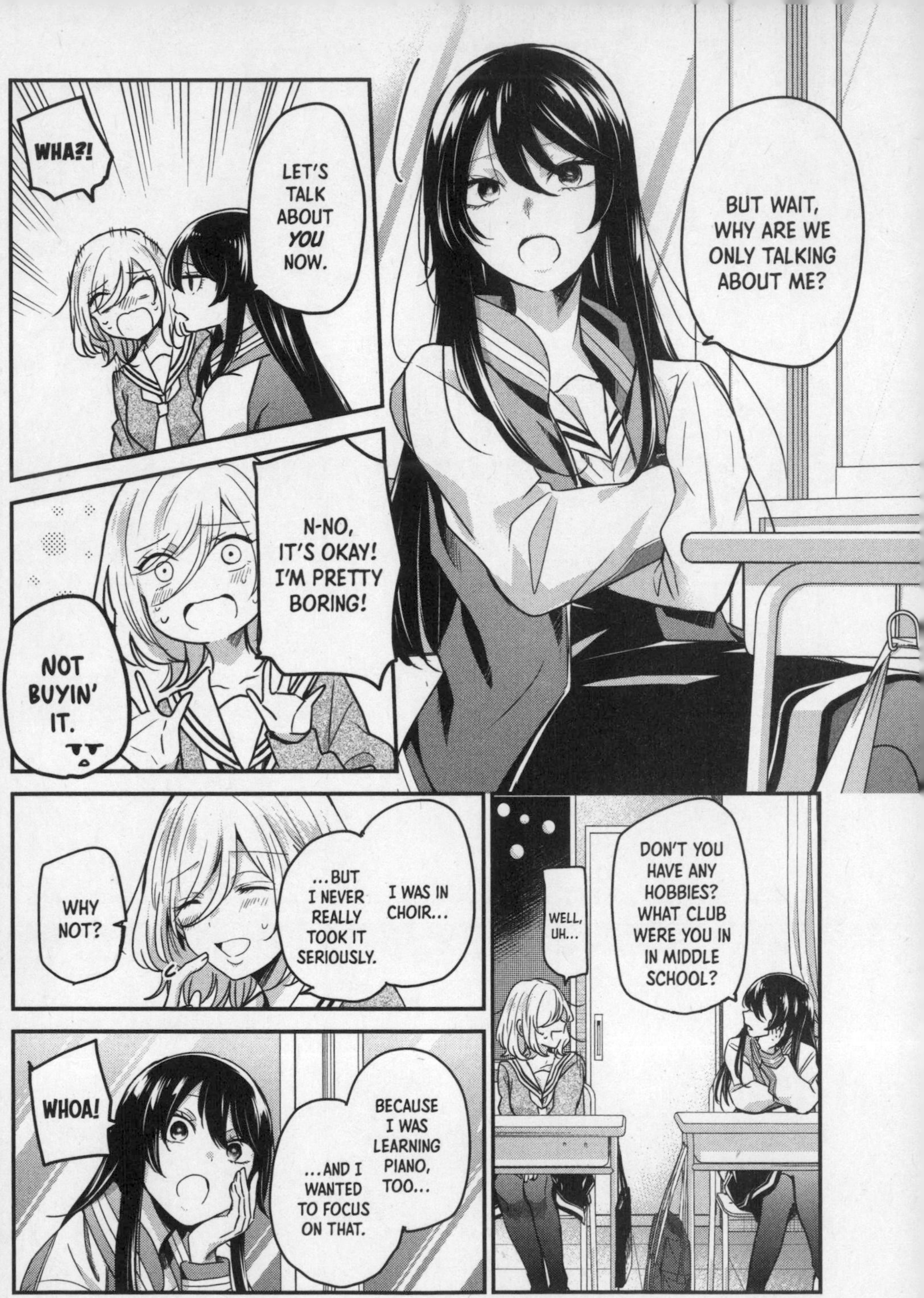
BUT WAIT, WHY ARE WE ONLY TALKING ABOUT ME?
LET'S TALK ABOUT YOU NOW.
WHA?!
N-NO, IT'S OKAY! I'M PRETTY BORING!
NOT BUYIN' IT.
DON'T YOU HAVE ANY HOBBIES? WHAT CLUB WERE YOU IN IN MIDDLE SCHOOL?
WELL, UH...
I WAS IN CHOIR...
...BUT I NEVER REALLY TOOK IT SERIOUSLY.
WHY NOT?
BECAUSE I WAS LEARNING PIANO, TOO...
...AND I WANTED TO FOCUS ON THAT.
WHOA!

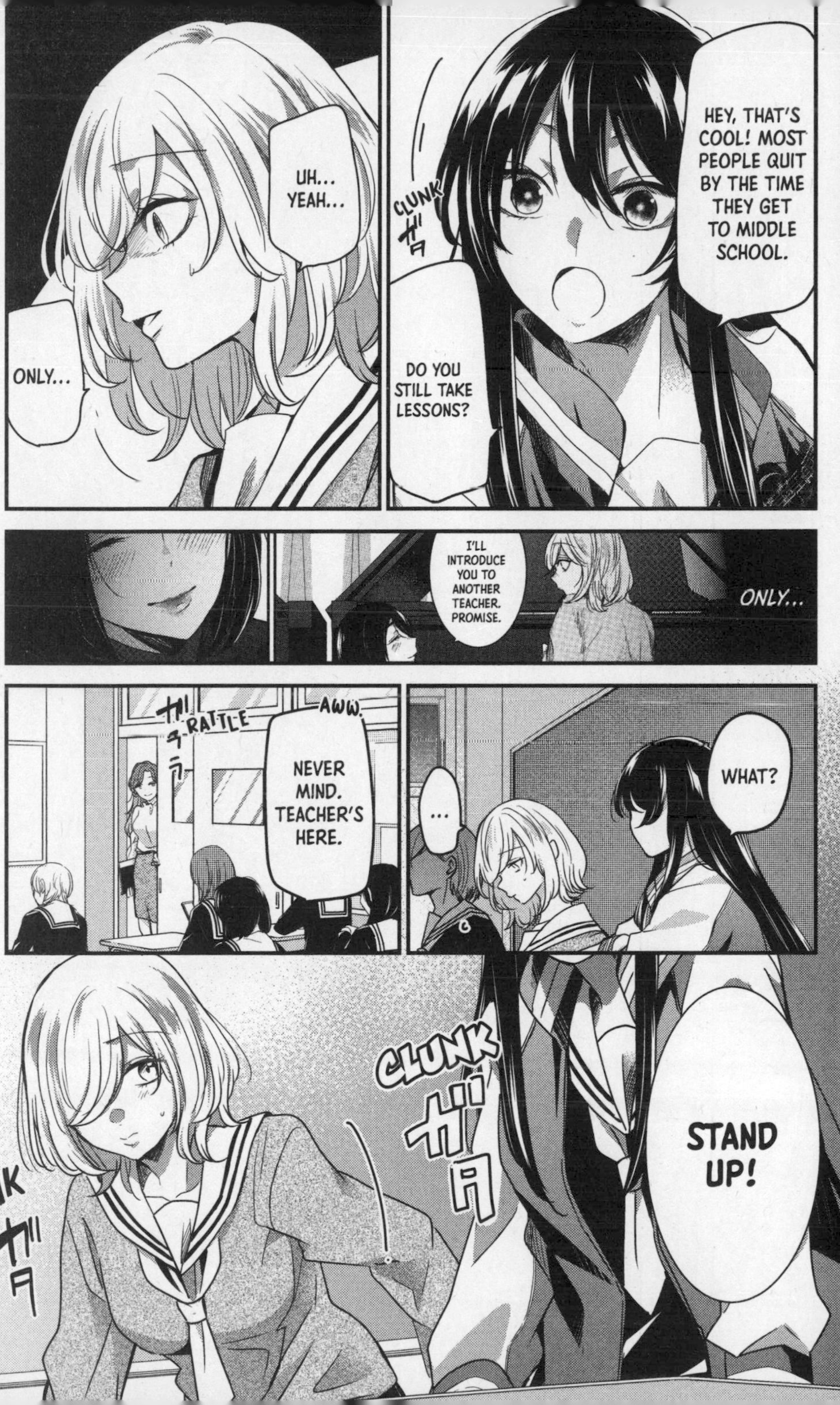
HEY, THAT'S COOL! MOST PEOPLE QUIT BY THE TIME THEY GET TO MIDDLE SCHOOL.
CLUNK
ガタ
DO YOU STILL TAKE LESSONS?
UH... YEAH...
ONLY...
ONLY...
I'LL INTRODUCE YOU TO ANOTHER TEACHER. PROMISE.
WHAT?
...
AWW.
NEVER MIND. TEACHER'S HERE.
RATTLE
ガラ
STAND UP!
CLUNK
ガタ
CLUNK
ガタ

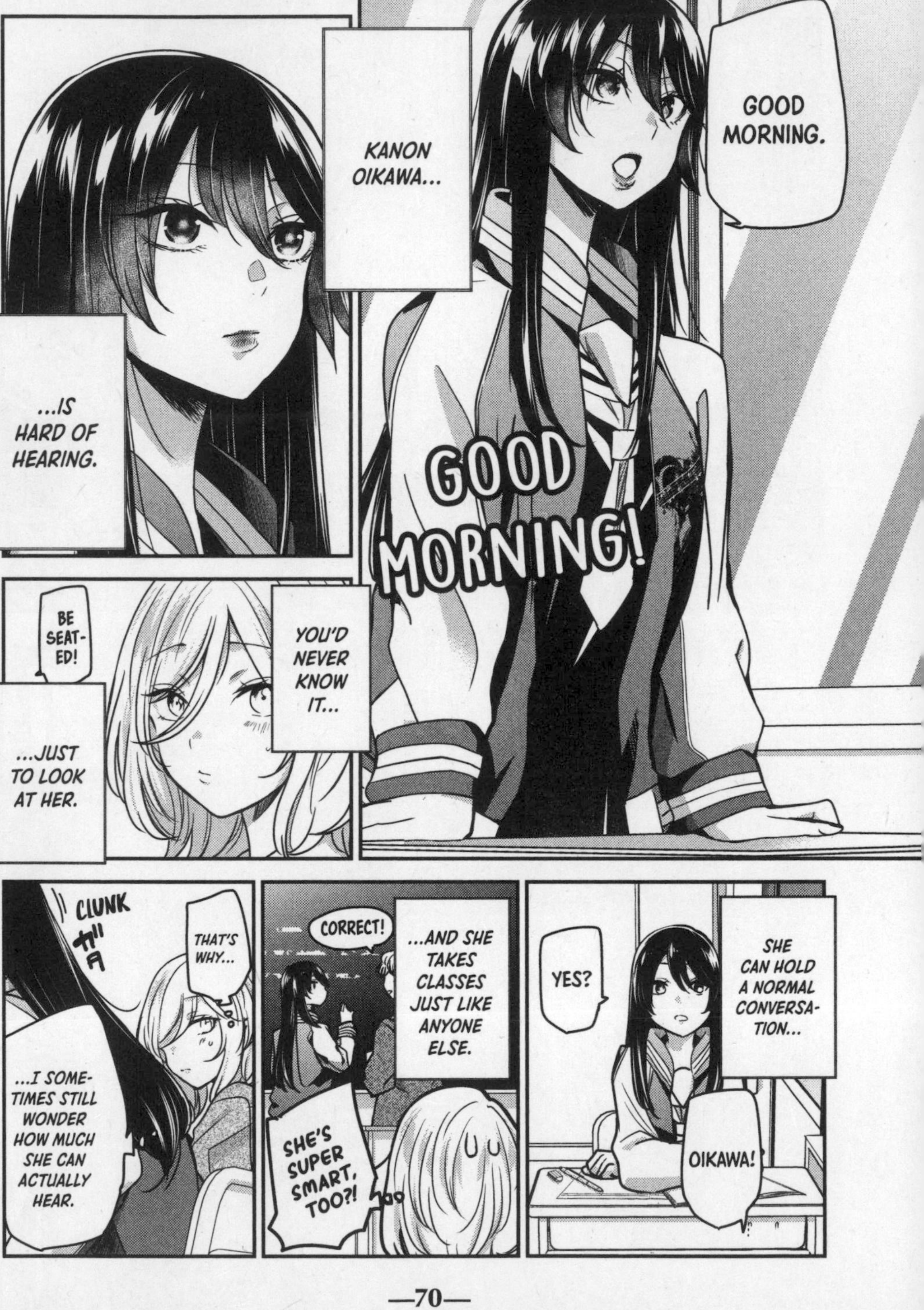
GOOD MORNING.
KANON OIKAWA...
GOOD MORNING!
...IS HARD OF HEARING.
YOU'D NEVER KNOW IT...
BE SEAT-ED!
...JUST TO LOOK AT HER.
SHE CAN HOLD A NORMAL CONVERSA-TION...
YES?
OIKAWA!
...AND SHE TAKES CLASSES JUST LIKE ANYONE ELSE.
CORRECT!
SHE'S SUPER SMART, TOO?!
CLUNK
ガタ
THAT'S WHY...
...I SOME-TIMES STILL WONDER HOW MUCH SHE CAN ACTUALLY HEAR.

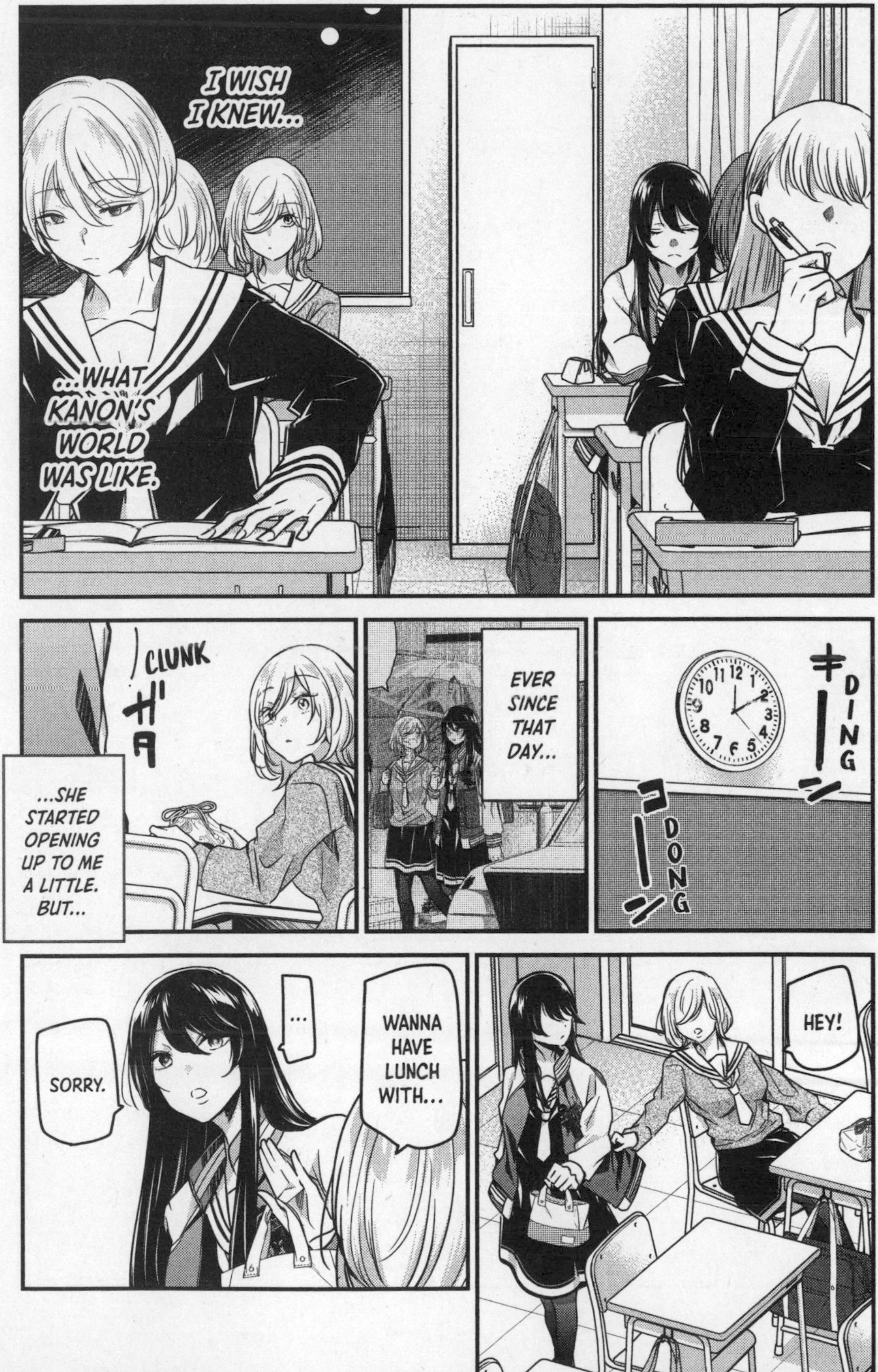
I WISH I KNEW...
...WHAT KANON'S WORLD WAS LIKE.
DING
DONG
EVER SINCE THAT DAY...
CLUNK
ガタ
...SHE STARTED OPENING UP TO ME A LITTLE. BUT...
HEY!
WANNA HAVE LUNCH WITH...
...
SORRY.

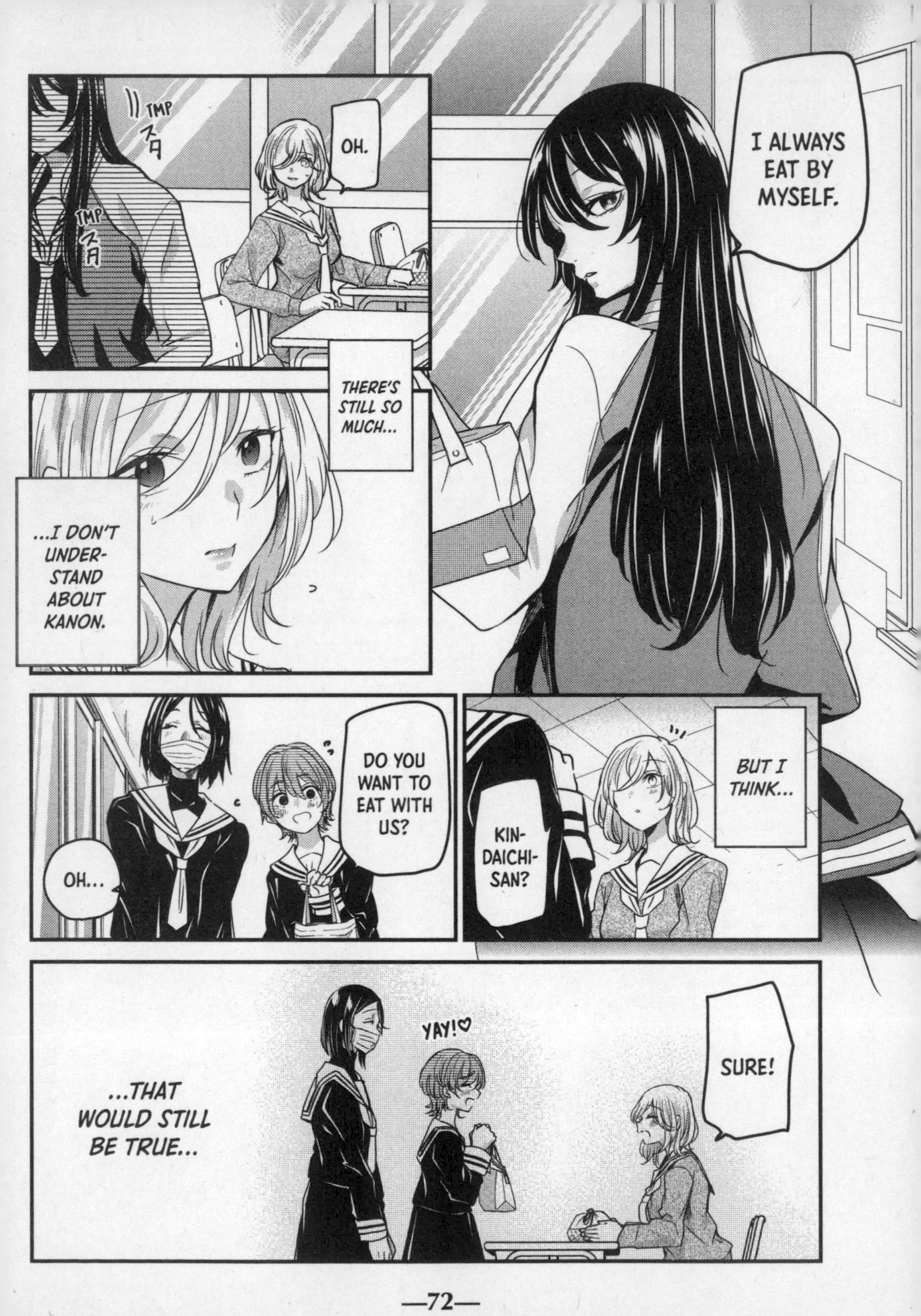
I ALWAYS EAT BY MYSELF.
OH.
TMP スタ
TMP スタ
THERE'S STILL SO MUCH...
...I DON'T UNDERSTAND ABOUT KANON.
BUT I THINK...
KIN-DAICHI-SAN?
DO YOU WANT TO EAT WITH US?
OH...
SURE!
YAY!♡
...THAT WOULD STILL BE TRUE...

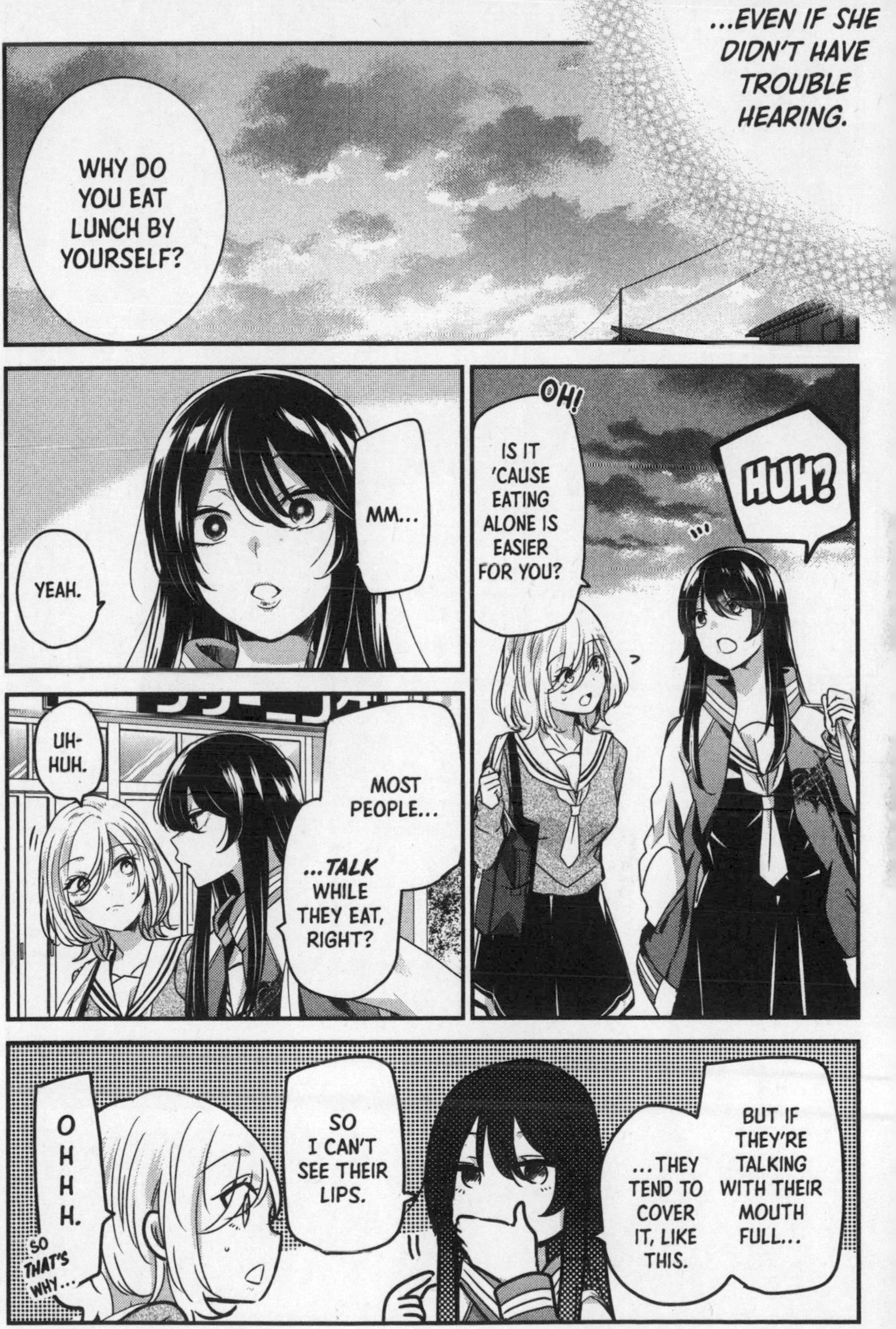
...EVEN IF SHE DIDN'T HAVE TROUBLE HEARING.
WHY DO YOU EAT LUNCH BY YOURSELF?
OH!
IS IT 'CAUSE EATING ALONE IS EASIER FOR YOU?
HUH?
MM...
YEAH.
MOST PEOPLE...
...TALK WHILE THEY EAT, RIGHT?
UH-HUH.
BUT IF THEY'RE TALKING WITH THEIR MOUTH FULL...
...THEY TEND TO COVER IT, LIKE THIS.
SO I CAN'T SEE THEIR LIPS.
OHHH.
SO THAT'S WHY...

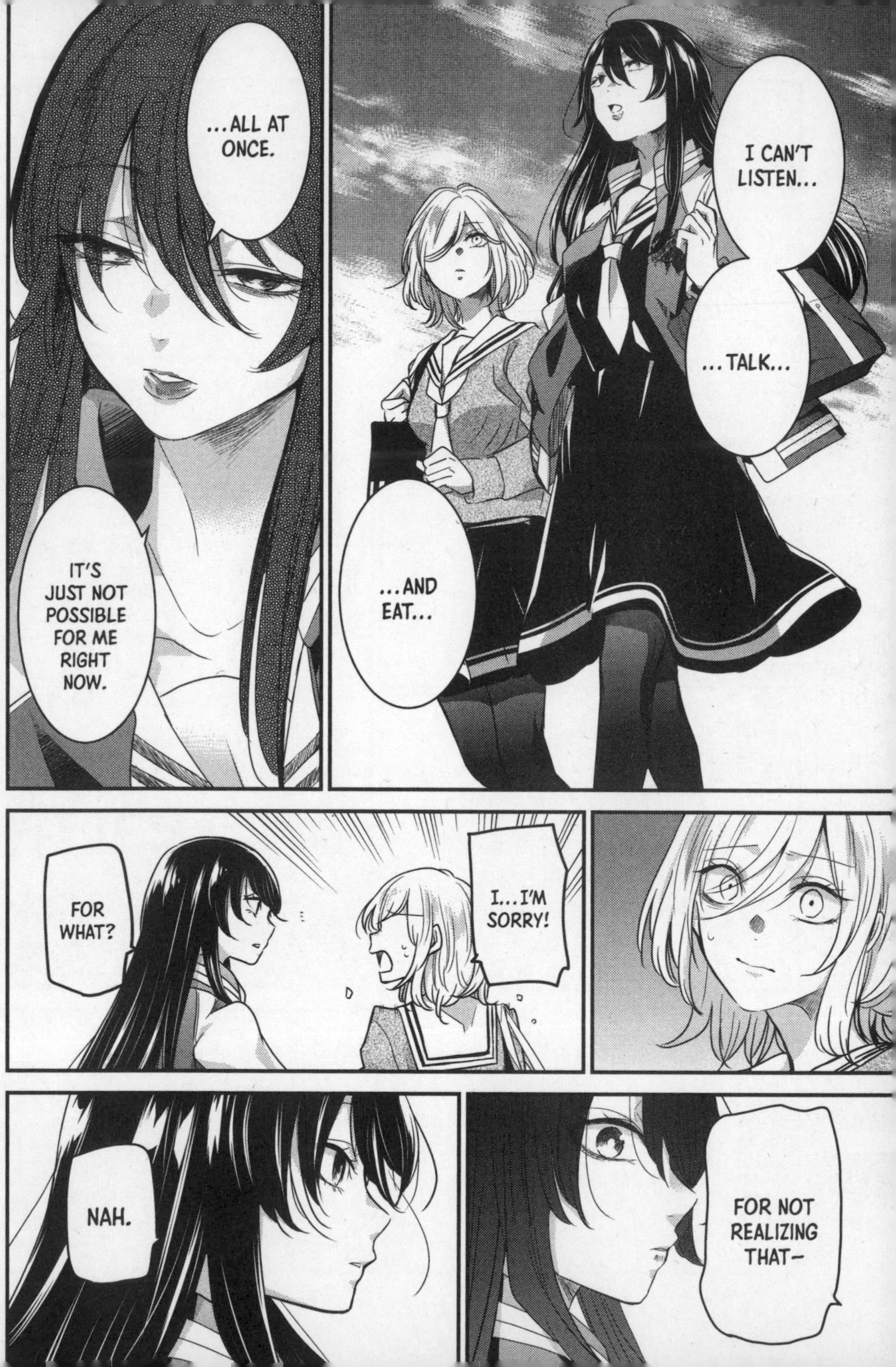
I CAN'T LISTEN...
...TALK...
...AND EAT...
...ALL AT ONCE.
IT'S JUST NOT POSSIBLE FOR ME RIGHT NOW.
I...I'M SORRY!
FOR WHAT?
FOR NOT REALIZING THAT—
NAH.

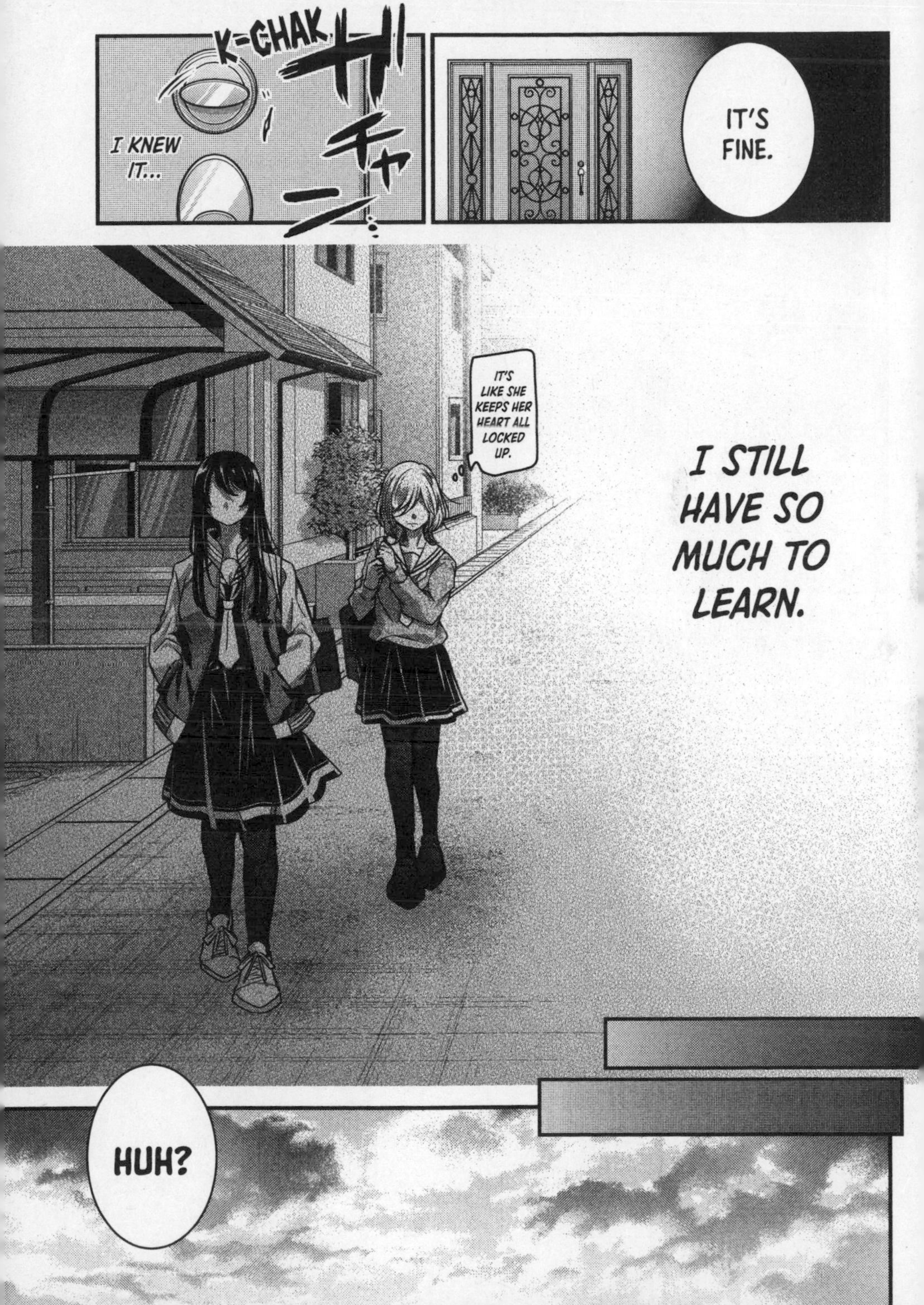
IT'S FINE.
K-CHAK
ガチャン
I KNEW IT...
I STILL HAVE SO MUCH TO LEARN.
IT'S LIKE SHE KEEPS HER HEART ALL LOCKED UP.
HUH?

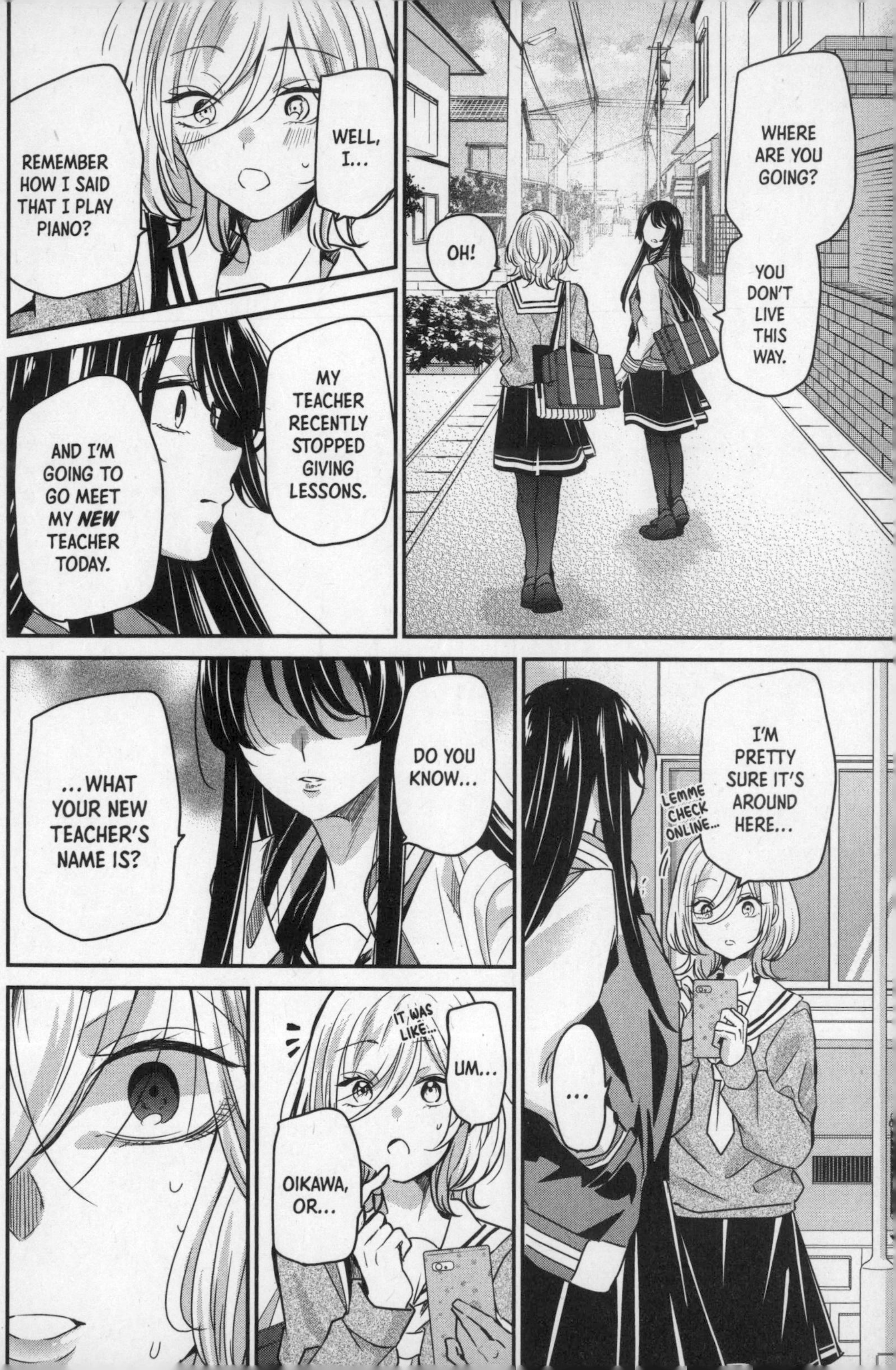
WHERE ARE YOU GOING?
YOU DON'T LIVE THIS WAY.
OH!
WELL, I...
REMEMBER HOW I SAID THAT I PLAY PIANO?
MY TEACHER RECENTLY STOPPED GIVING LESSONS.
AND I'M GOING TO GO MEET MY *NEW* TEACHER TODAY.
I'M PRETTY SURE IT'S AROUND HERE...
LEMME CHECK ONLINE...
...
DO YOU KNOW...
...WHAT YOUR NEW TEACHER'S NAME IS?
IT WAS LIKE...
UM...
OIKAWA, OR...

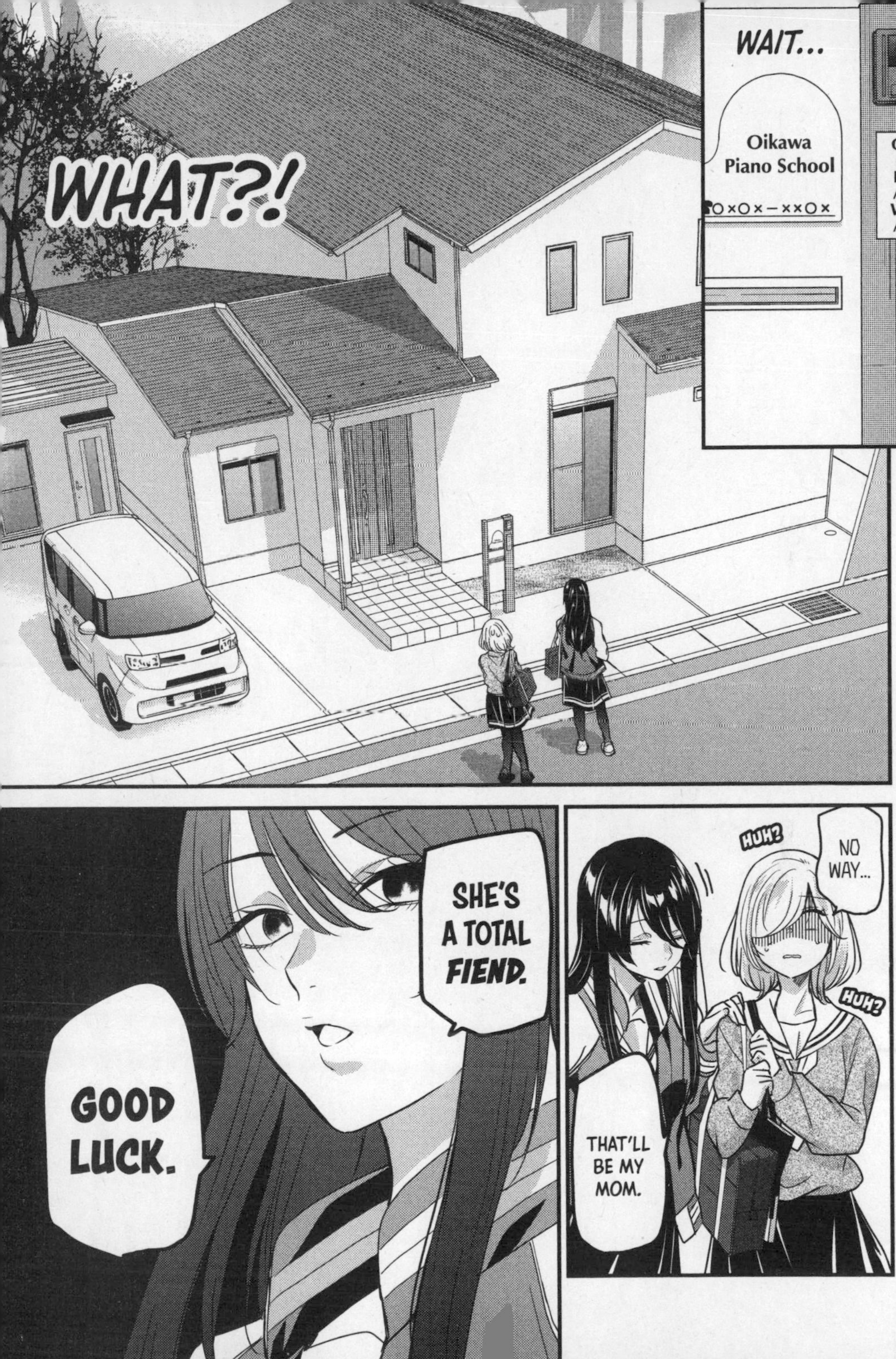
WAIT...
Oikawa Piano School
O×O×−××O×
OIKAWA
WHAT?!
NO WAY...
HUH?
HUH?
THAT'LL BE MY MOM.
SHE'S A TOTAL FIEND.
GOOD LUCK.

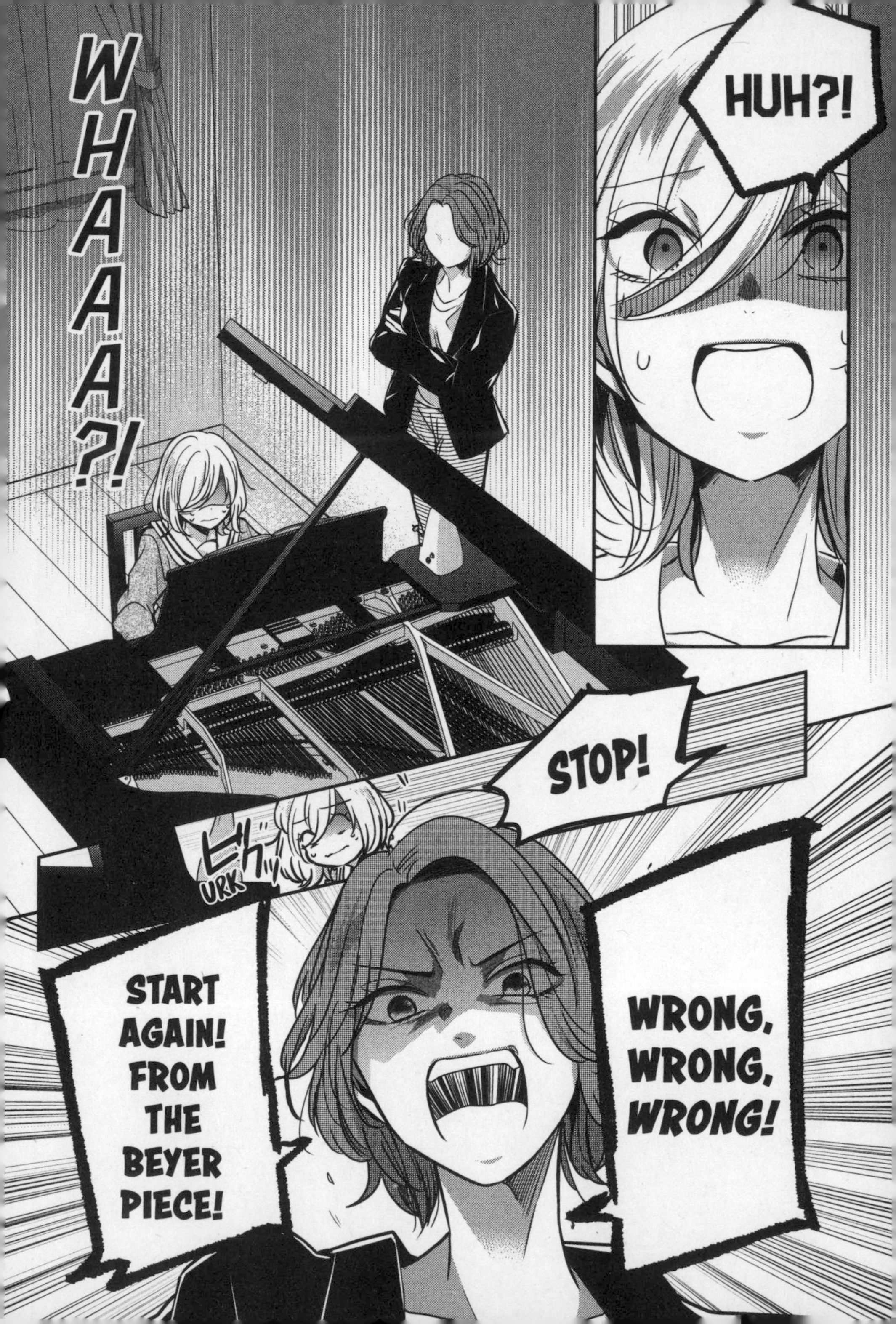
HUH?!
WHAAAA?!
ビクッ
URK
STOP!
WRONG, WRONG, WRONG!
START AGAIN! FROM THE BEYER PIECE!

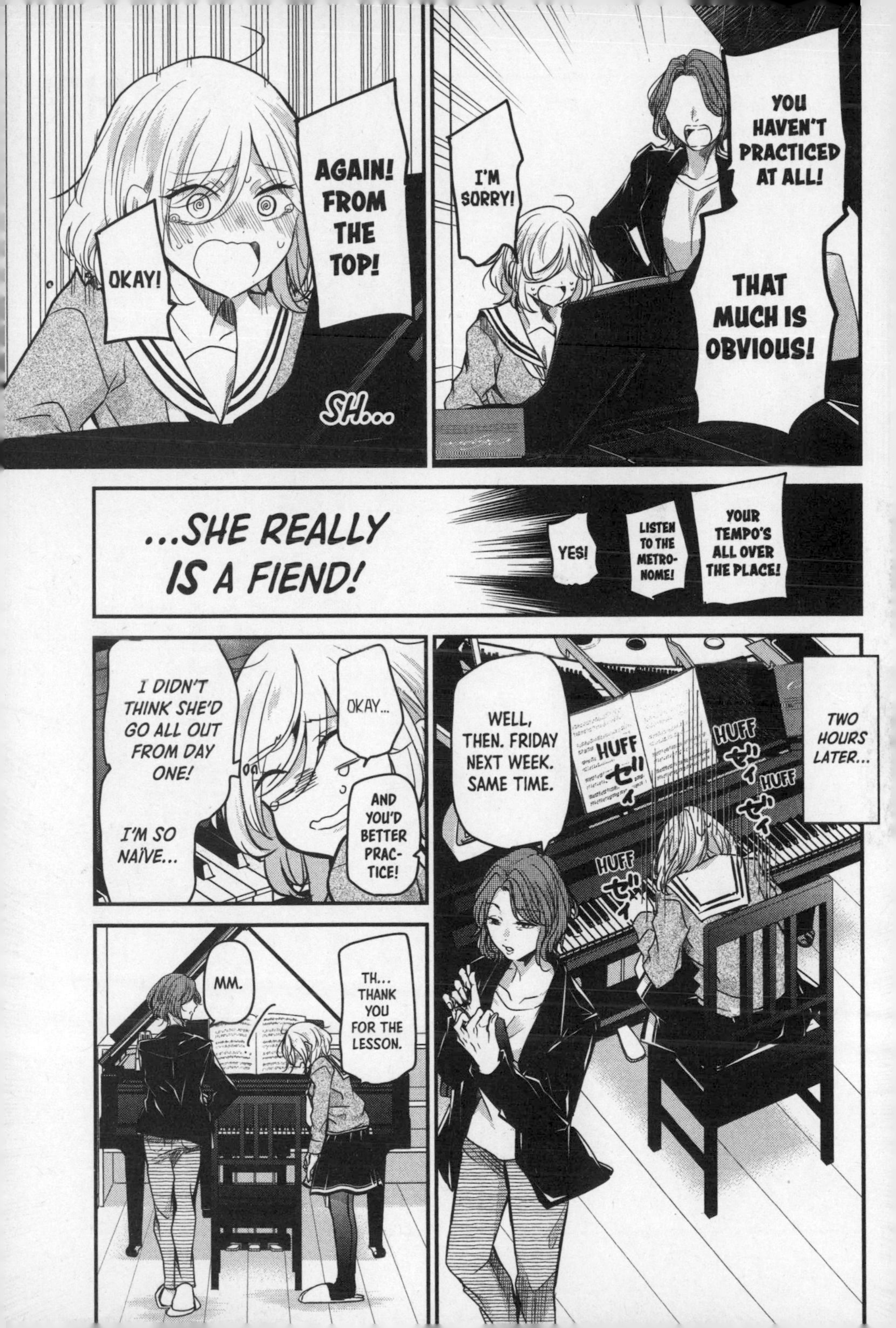
YOU HAVEN'T PRACTICED AT ALL!
THAT MUCH IS OBVIOUS!
I'M SORRY!
AGAIN! FROM THE TOP!
OKAY!
SH...
YOUR TEMPO'S ALL OVER THE PLACE!
LISTEN TO THE METRONOME!
YES!
...SHE REALLY IS A FIEND!
TWO HOURS LATER...
HUFF ゼィ
HUFF ゼィ
HUFF ゼィ
HUFF ゼィ
WELL, THEN. FRIDAY NEXT WEEK. SAME TIME.
OKAY...
AND YOU'D BETTER PRAC-TICE!
I DIDN'T THINK SHE'D GO ALL OUT FROM DAY ONE!
I'M SO NAÏVE...
TH... THANK YOU FOR THE LESSON.
MM.

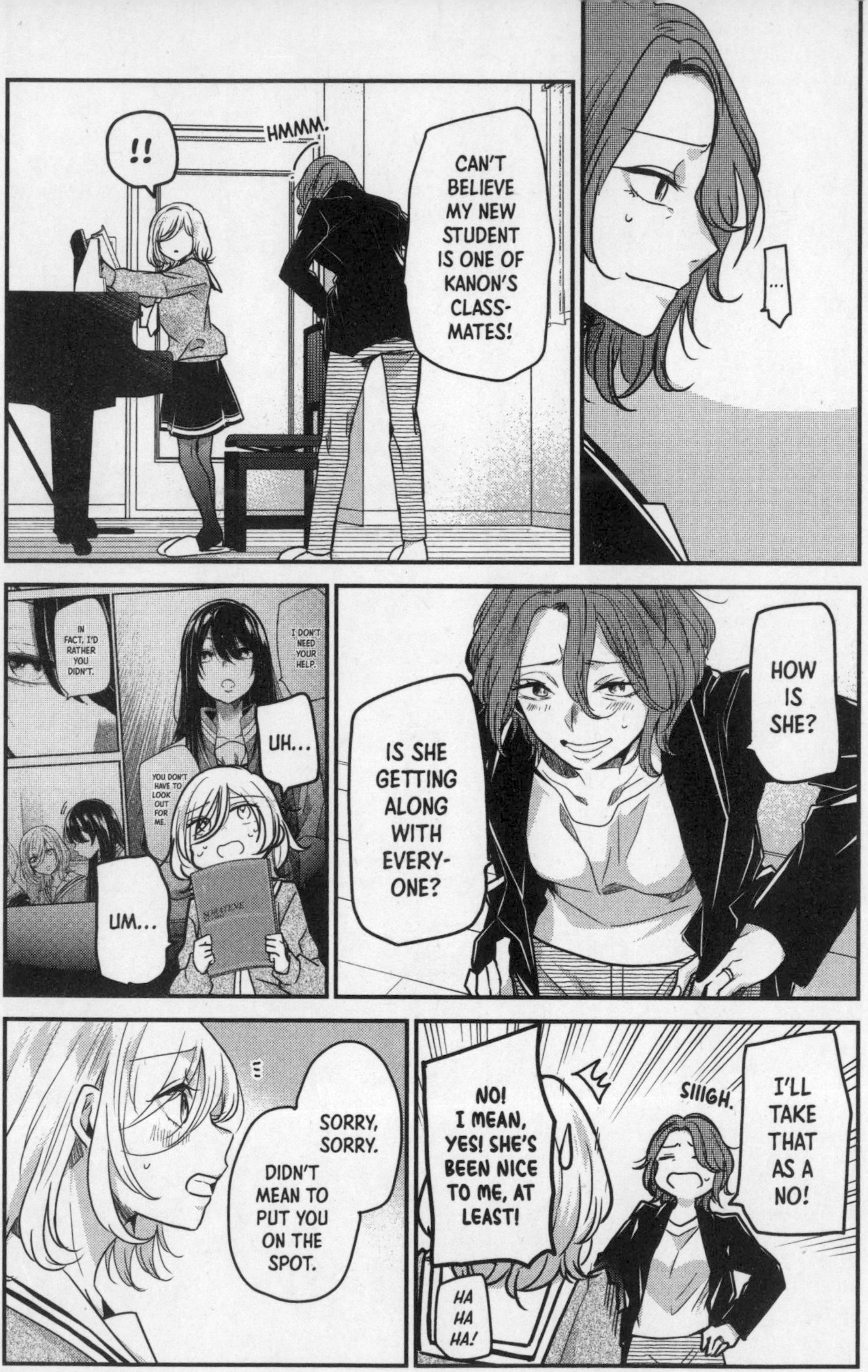
...
CAN'T BELIEVE MY NEW STUDENT IS ONE OF KANON'S CLASS-MATES!
HMMM.
!!
HOW IS SHE?
IS SHE GETTING ALONG WITH EVERY-ONE?
I DON'T NEED YOUR HELP.
IN FACT, I'D RATHER YOU DIDN'T.
UH...
YOU DON'T HAVE TO LOOK OUT FOR ME.
UM...
I'LL TAKE THAT AS A NO!
SIIIGH.
NO! I MEAN, YES! SHE'S BEEN NICE TO ME, AT LEAST!
HA HA HA!
SORRY, SORRY.
DIDN'T MEAN TO PUT YOU ON THE SPOT.

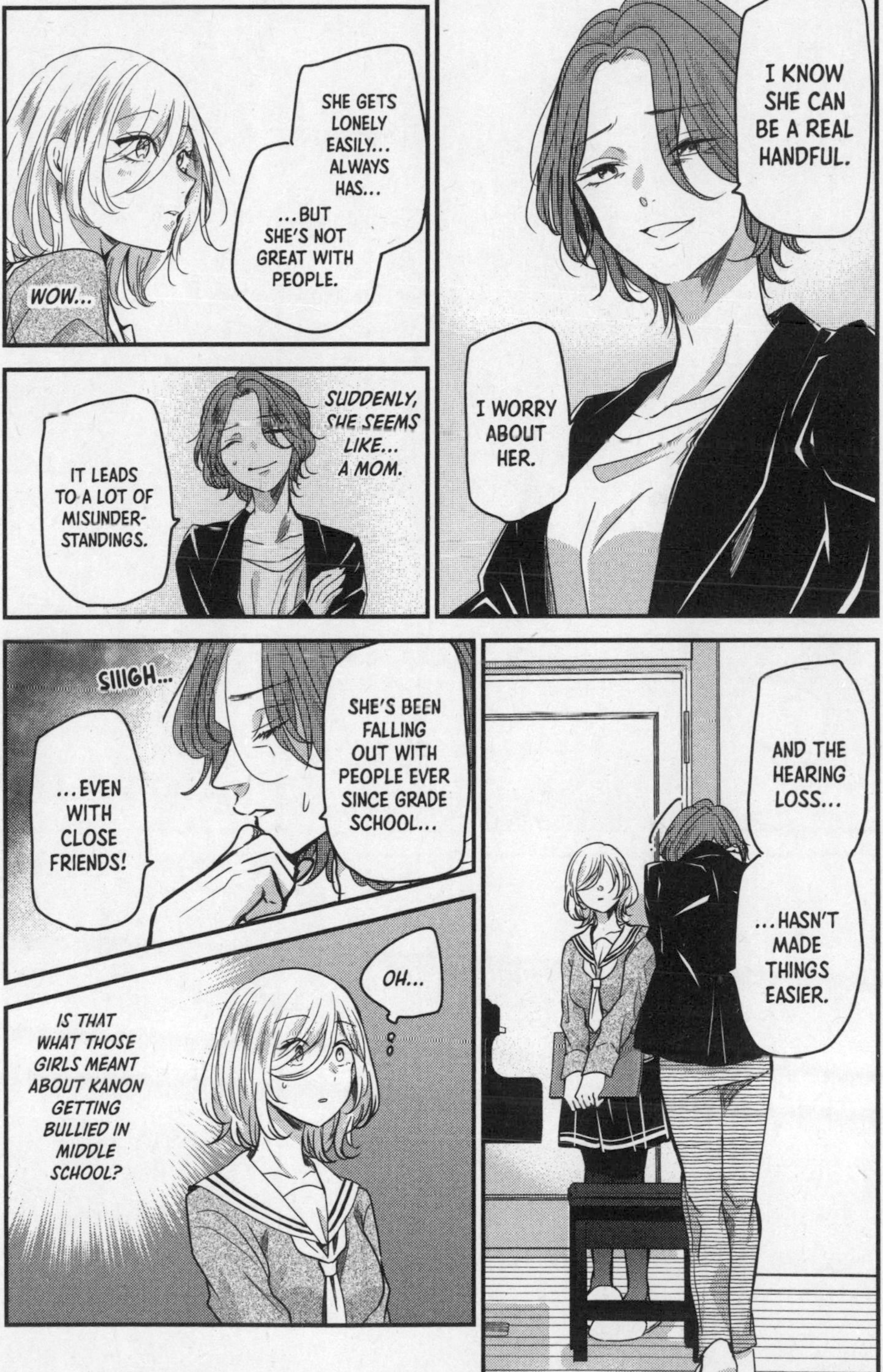
I KNOW SHE CAN BE A REAL HANDFUL.
I WORRY ABOUT HER.
SHE GETS LONELY EASILY... ALWAYS HAS...
...BUT SHE'S NOT GREAT WITH PEOPLE.
WOW...
SUDDENLY, SHE SEEMS LIKE... A MOM.
IT LEADS TO A LOT OF MISUNDER-STANDINGS.
AND THE HEARING LOSS...
...HASN'T MADE THINGS EASIER.
SHE'S BEEN FALLING OUT WITH PEOPLE EVER SINCE GRADE SCHOOL...
SIIIGH...
...EVEN WITH CLOSE FRIENDS!
OH...
IS THAT WHAT THOSE GIRLS MEANT ABOUT KANON GETTING BULLIED IN MIDDLE SCHOOL?

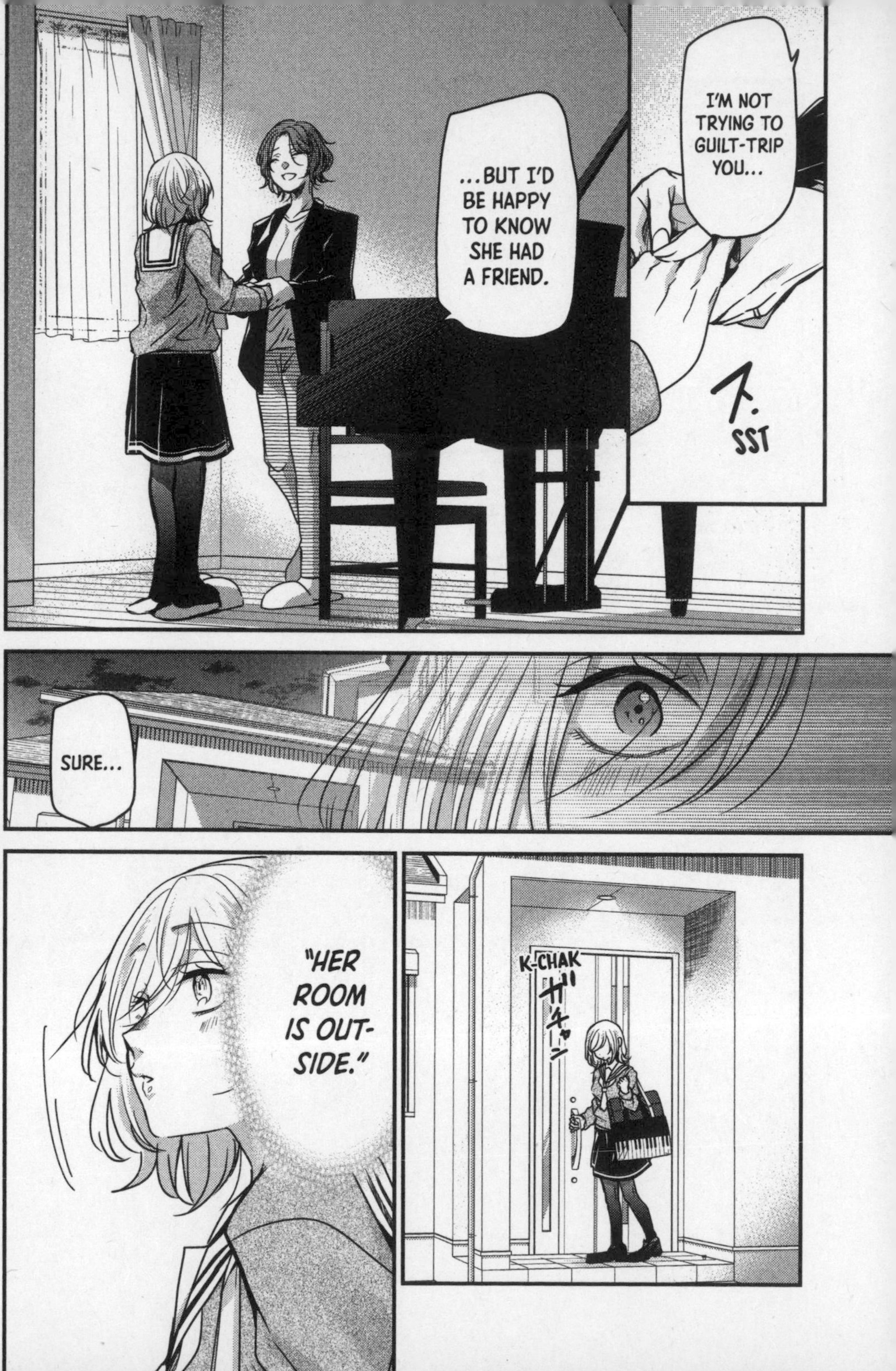
I'M NOT TRYING TO GUILT-TRIP YOU...
ス.
SST
...BUT I'D BE HAPPY TO KNOW SHE HAD A FRIEND.
SURE...
K-CHAK
ガチャン
"HER ROOM IS OUT-SIDE."

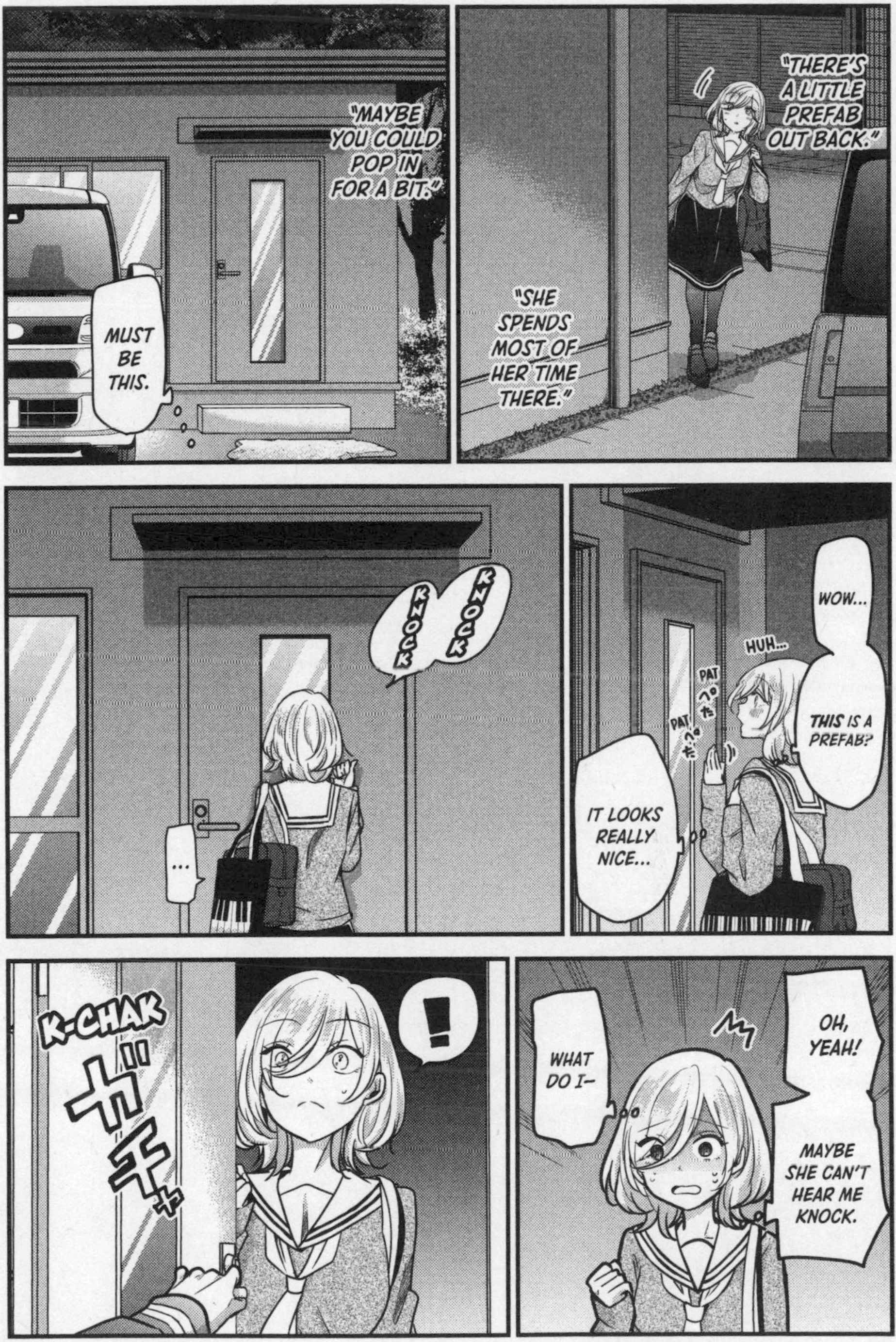
"THERE'S A LITTLE PREFAB OUT BACK."
"SHE SPENDS MOST OF HER TIME THERE."
"MAYBE YOU COULD POP IN FOR A BIT."
MUST BE THIS.
WOW...
HUH...
THIS IS A PREFAB?
PAT
PAT
IT LOOKS REALLY NICE...
KNOCK
KNOCK
...
OH, YEAH!
MAYBE SHE CAN'T HEAR ME KNOCK.
WHAT DO I-
!
K-CHAK

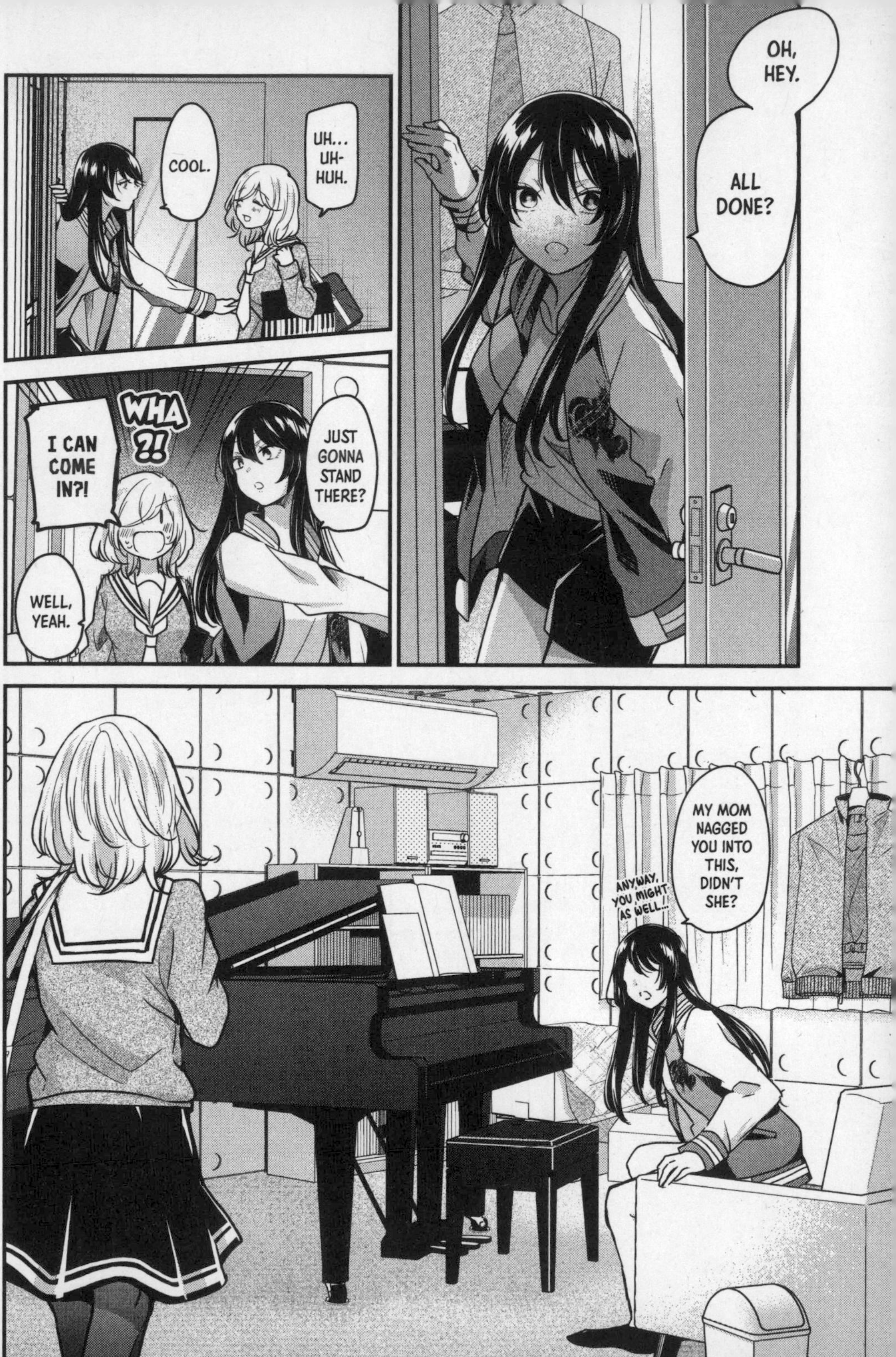
OH, HEY.
ALL DONE?
UH... UH-HUH.
COOL.
JUST GONNA STAND THERE?
WHA ?!
I CAN COME IN?!
WELL, YEAH.
MY MOM NAGGED YOU INTO THIS, DIDN'T SHE?
ANYWAY, YOU MIGHT AS WELL...!

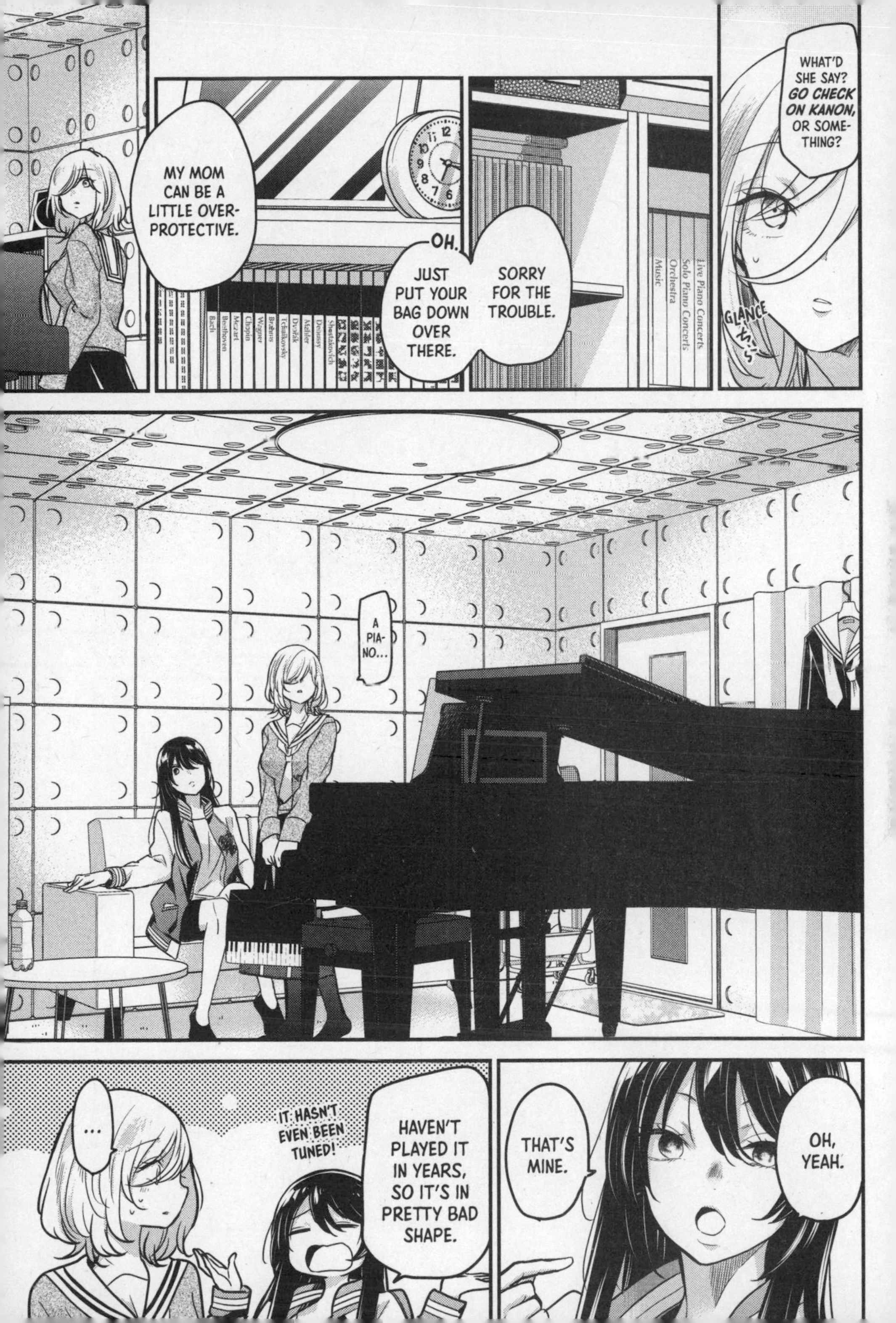
WHAT'D SHE SAY? GO CHECK ON KANON, OR SOMETHING?
GLANCE
SORRY FOR THE TROUBLE.
—OH.
JUST PUT YOUR BAG DOWN OVER THERE.
Live Piano Concerts
Solo Piano Concerts
Orchestra
Music
Bach
Beethoven
Mozart
Chopin
Wagner
Brahms
Tchaikovsky
Dvořák
Mahler
Debussy
Shostakovich
MY MOM CAN BE A LITTLE OVER-PROTECTIVE.
A PIA-NO...
OH, YEAH.
THAT'S MINE.
HAVEN'T PLAYED IT IN YEARS, SO IT'S IN PRETTY BAD SHAPE.
IT HASN'T EVEN BEEN TUNED!
...

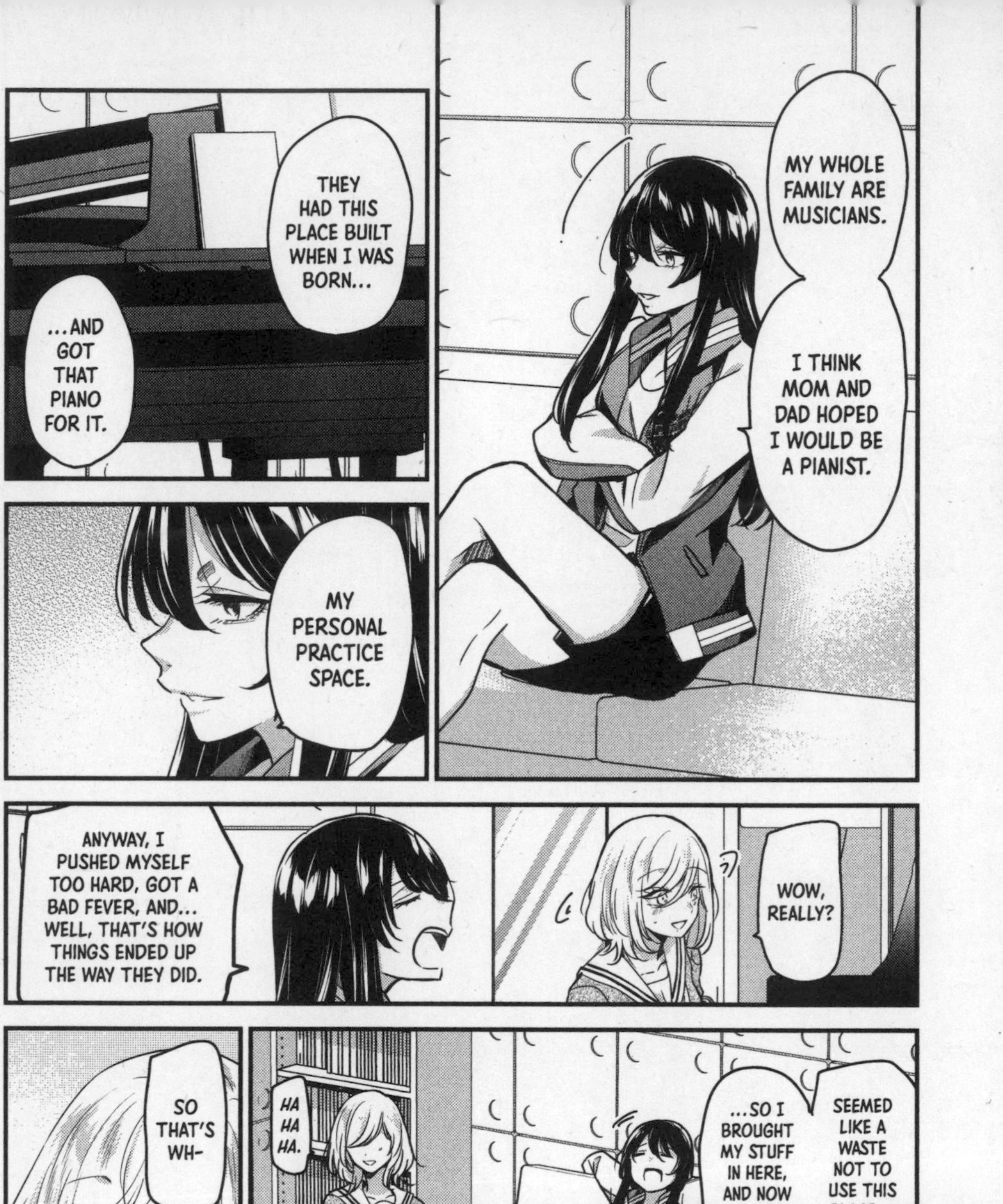
MY WHOLE FAMILY ARE MUSICIANS.
I THINK MOM AND DAD HOPED I WOULD BE A PIANIST.
THEY HAD THIS PLACE BUILT WHEN I WAS BORN...
...AND GOT THAT PIANO FOR IT.
MY PERSONAL PRACTICE SPACE.
WOW, REALLY?
ANYWAY, I PUSHED MYSELF TOO HARD, GOT A BAD FEVER, AND... WELL, THAT'S HOW THINGS ENDED UP THE WAY THEY DID.
SEEMED LIKE A WASTE NOT TO USE THIS PLACE...
...SO I BROUGHT MY STUFF IN HERE, AND NOW IT'S MY HIDEOUT!
HA HA HA.
SO THAT'S WH-
!

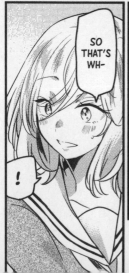

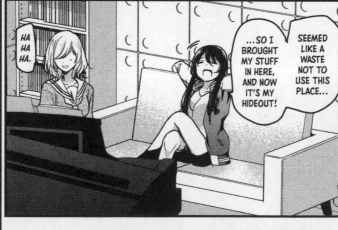

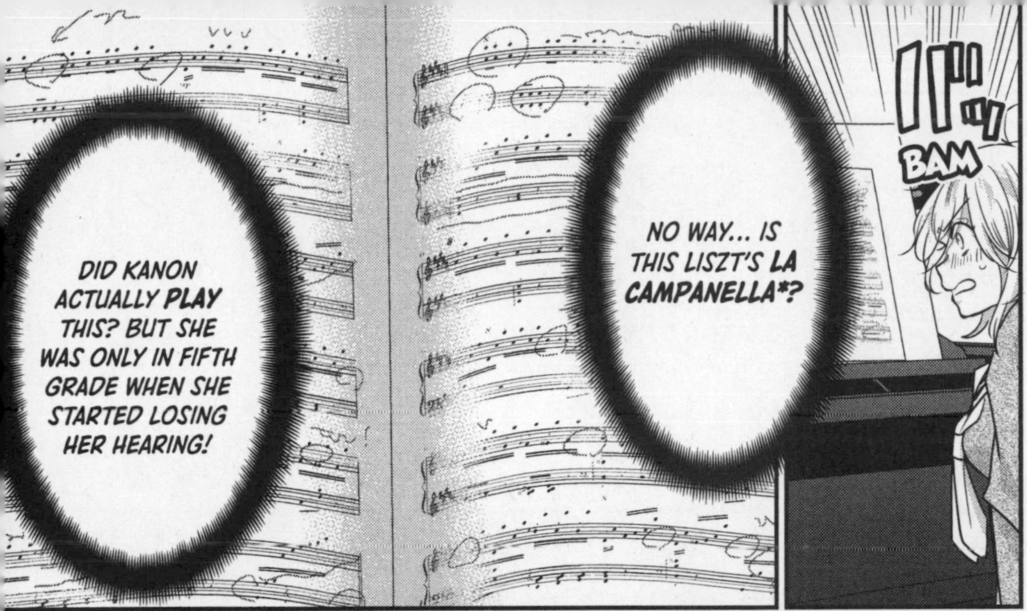
BAM
NO WAY... IS THIS LISZT'S LA CAMPANELLA*?
DID KANON ACTUALLY PLAY THIS? BUT SHE WAS ONLY IN FIFTH GRADE WHEN SHE STARTED LOSING HER HEARING!

*A notoriously difficult piece by Hungarian composer and pianist Franz Liszt (1811-1886).

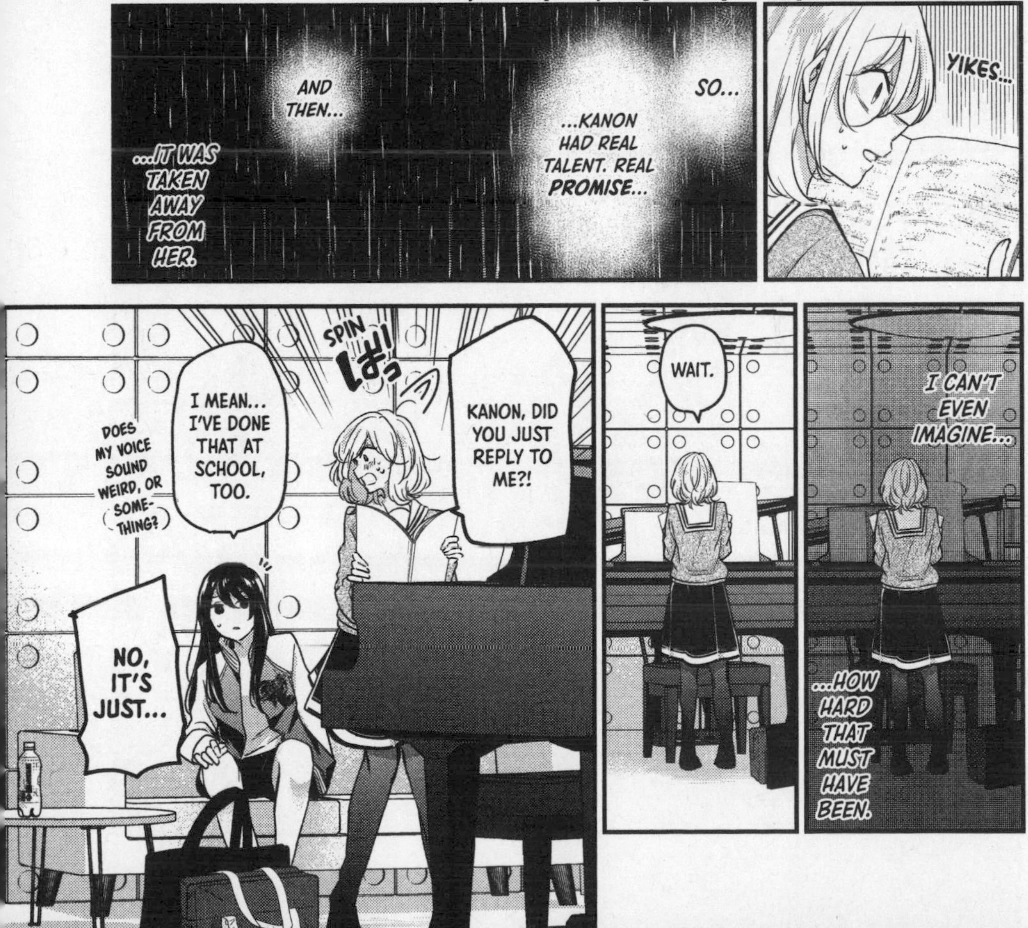
YIKES...
SO...
...KANON HAD REAL TALENT. REAL PROMISE...
AND THEN...
...IT WAS TAKEN AWAY FROM HER.
I CAN'T EVEN IMAGINE...
...HOW HARD THAT MUST HAVE BEEN.
WAIT.
SPIN
KANON, DID YOU JUST REPLY TO ME?!
I MEAN... I'VE DONE THAT AT SCHOOL, TOO.
DOES MY VOICE SOUND WEIRD, OR SOME-THING?
NO, IT'S JUST...

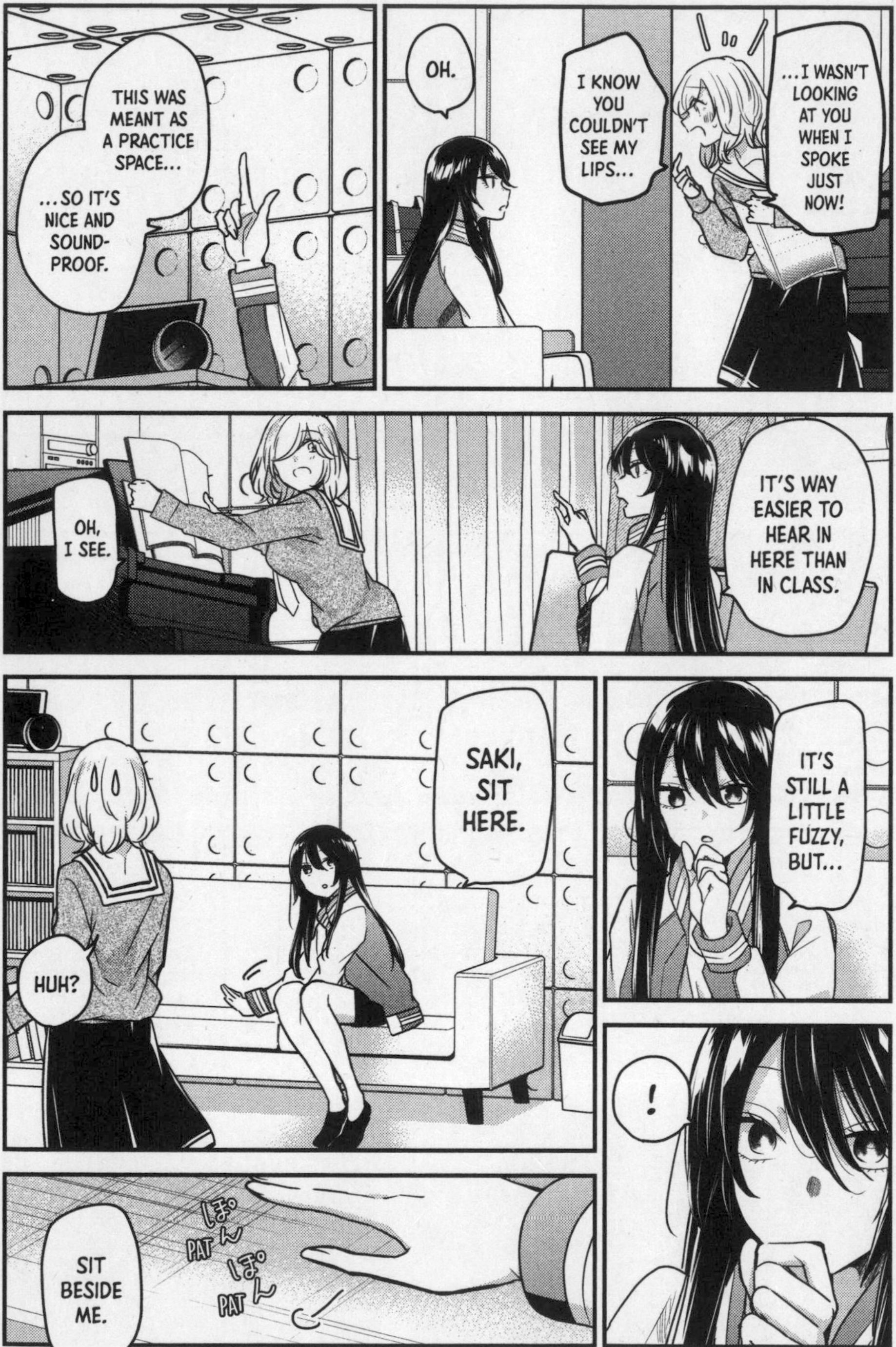
...I WASN'T LOOKING AT YOU WHEN I SPOKE JUST NOW!
I KNOW YOU COULDN'T SEE MY LIPS...
OH.
THIS WAS MEANT AS A PRACTICE SPACE...
...SO IT'S NICE AND SOUND-PROOF.
IT'S WAY EASIER TO HEAR IN HERE THAN IN CLASS.
OH, I SEE.
IT'S STILL A LITTLE FUZZY, BUT...
SAKI, SIT HERE.
HUH?
!
ぽん PAT
ぽん PAT
SIT BESIDE ME.

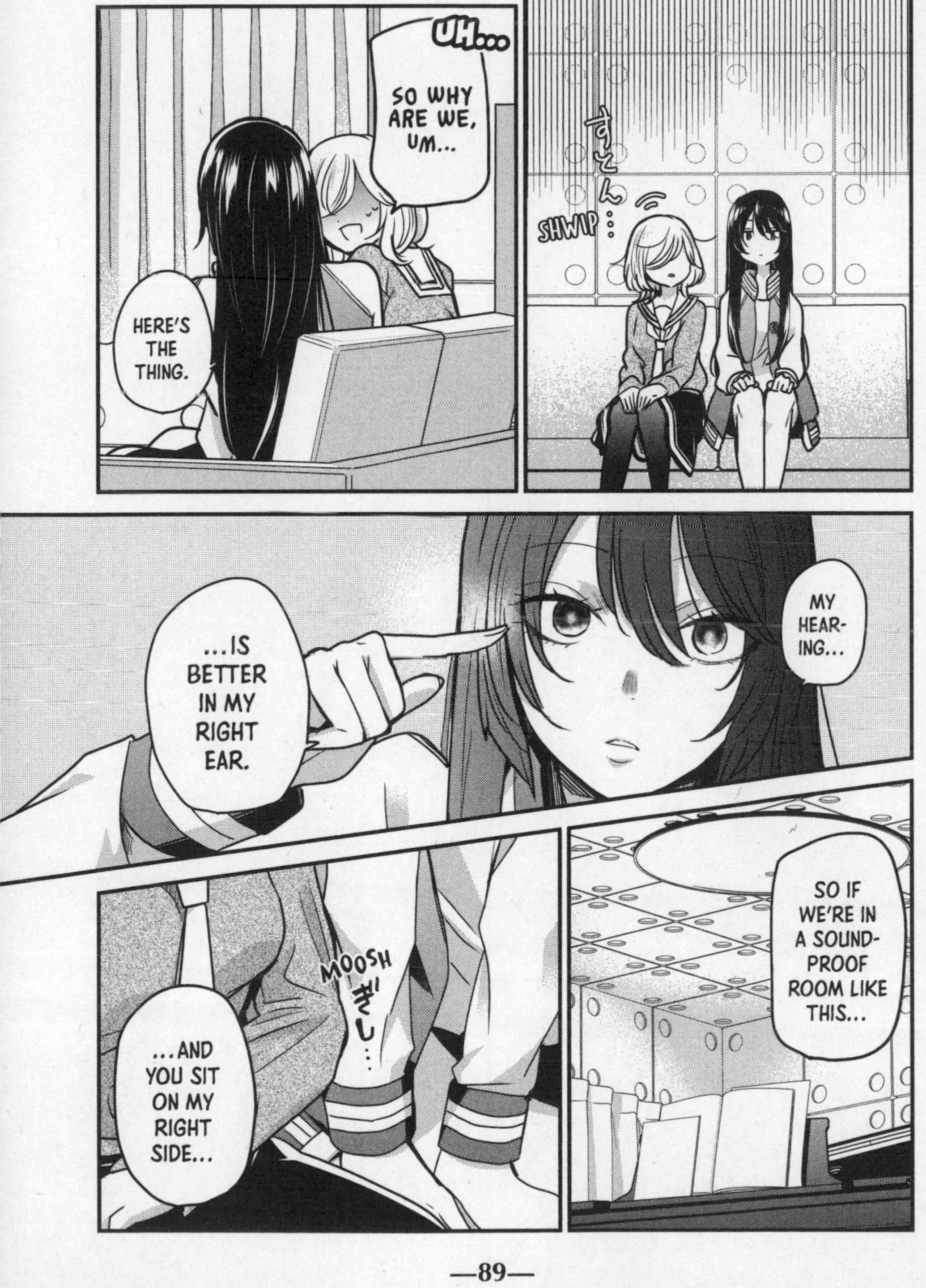

すとん…
SHWIP
UH…
SO WHY ARE WE, UM…
HERE'S THE THING.
MY HEAR-ING…
…IS BETTER IN MY RIGHT EAR.
SO IF WE'RE IN A SOUND-PROOF ROOM LIKE THIS…
MOOSH
ぎし…
…AND YOU SIT ON MY RIGHT SIDE…

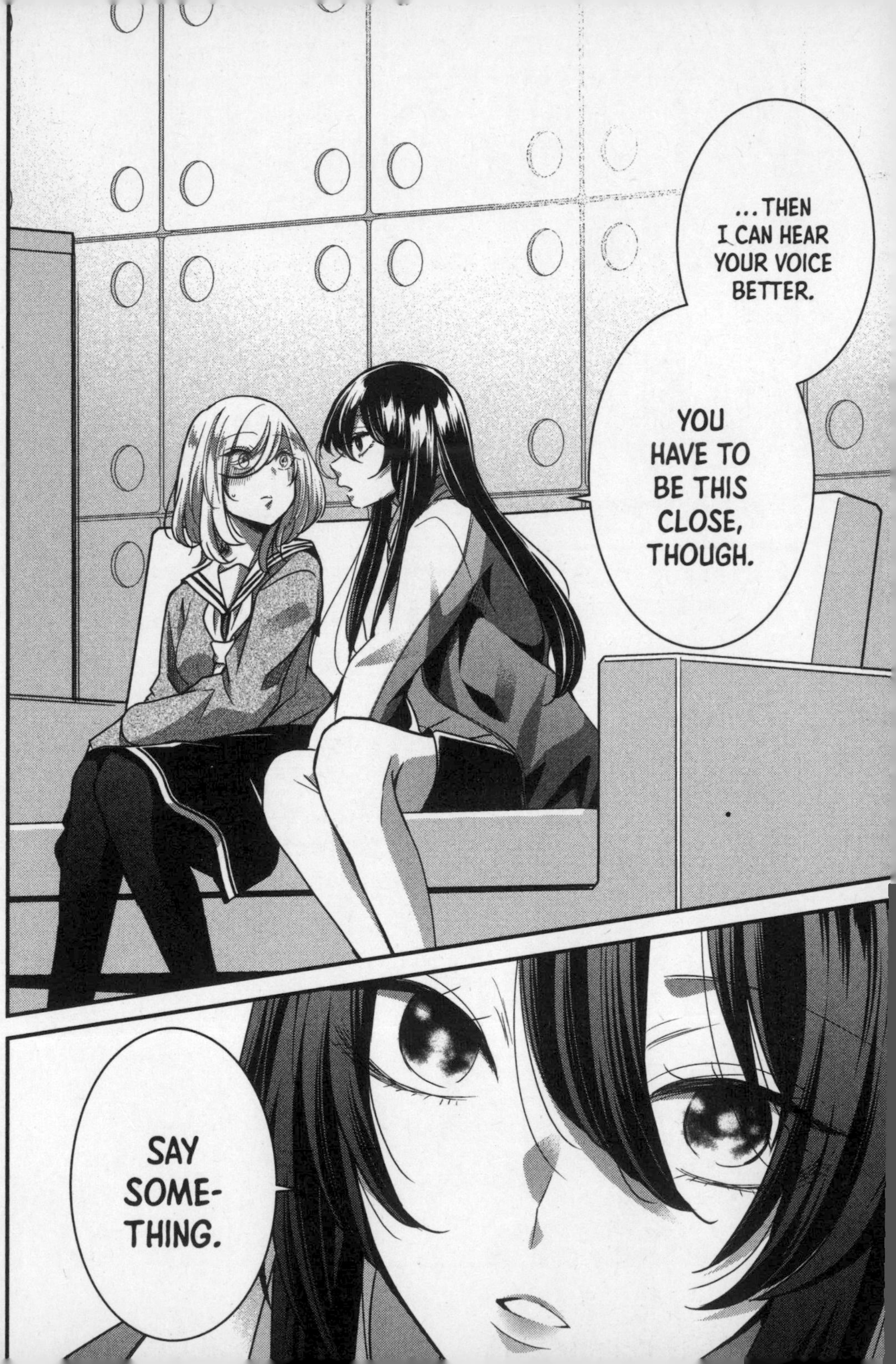
...THEN I CAN HEAR YOUR VOICE BETTER.
YOU HAVE TO BE THIS CLOSE, THOUGH.
SAY SOME-THING.

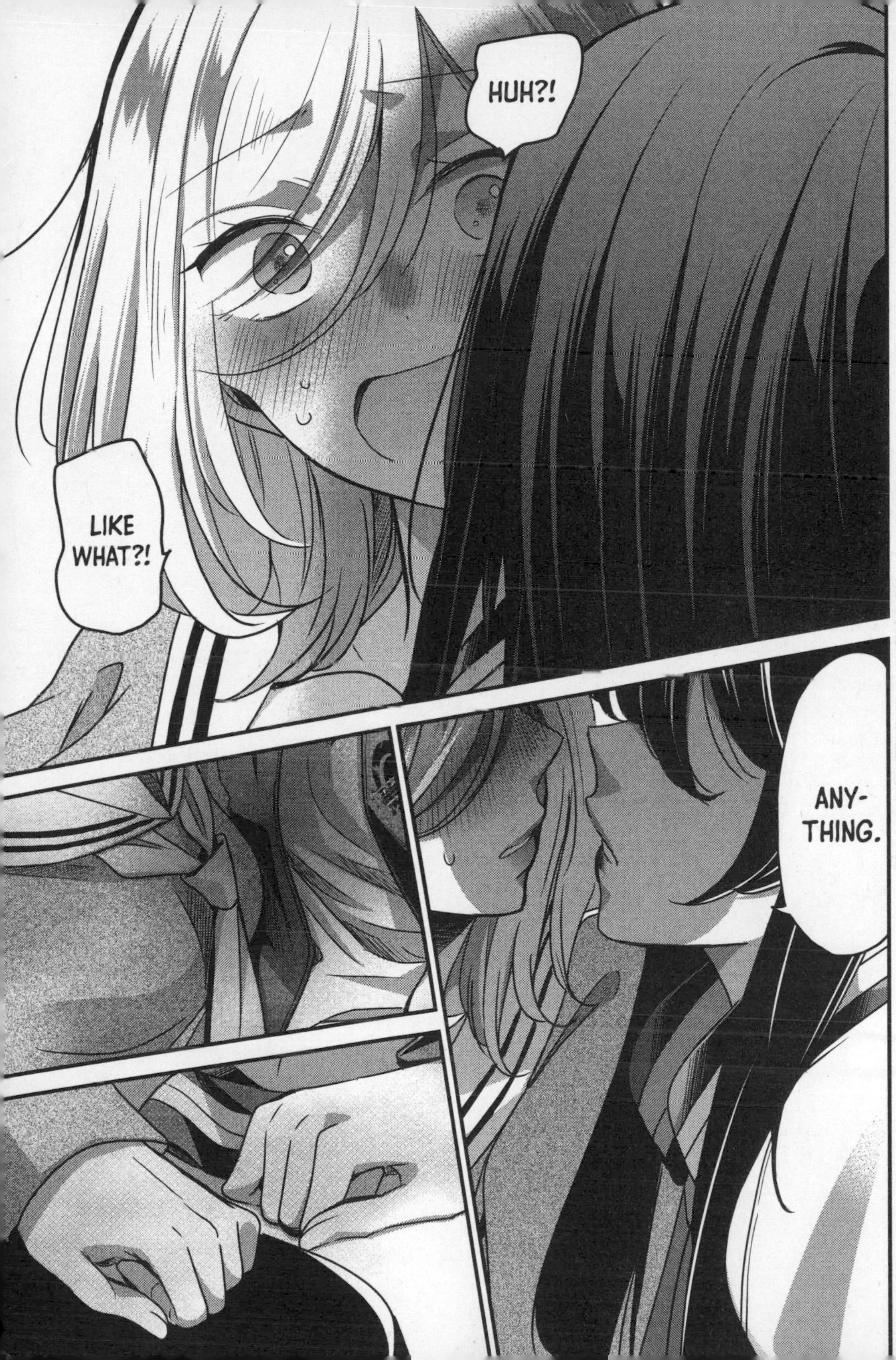
HUH?!
LIKE WHAT?!
ANY-THING.

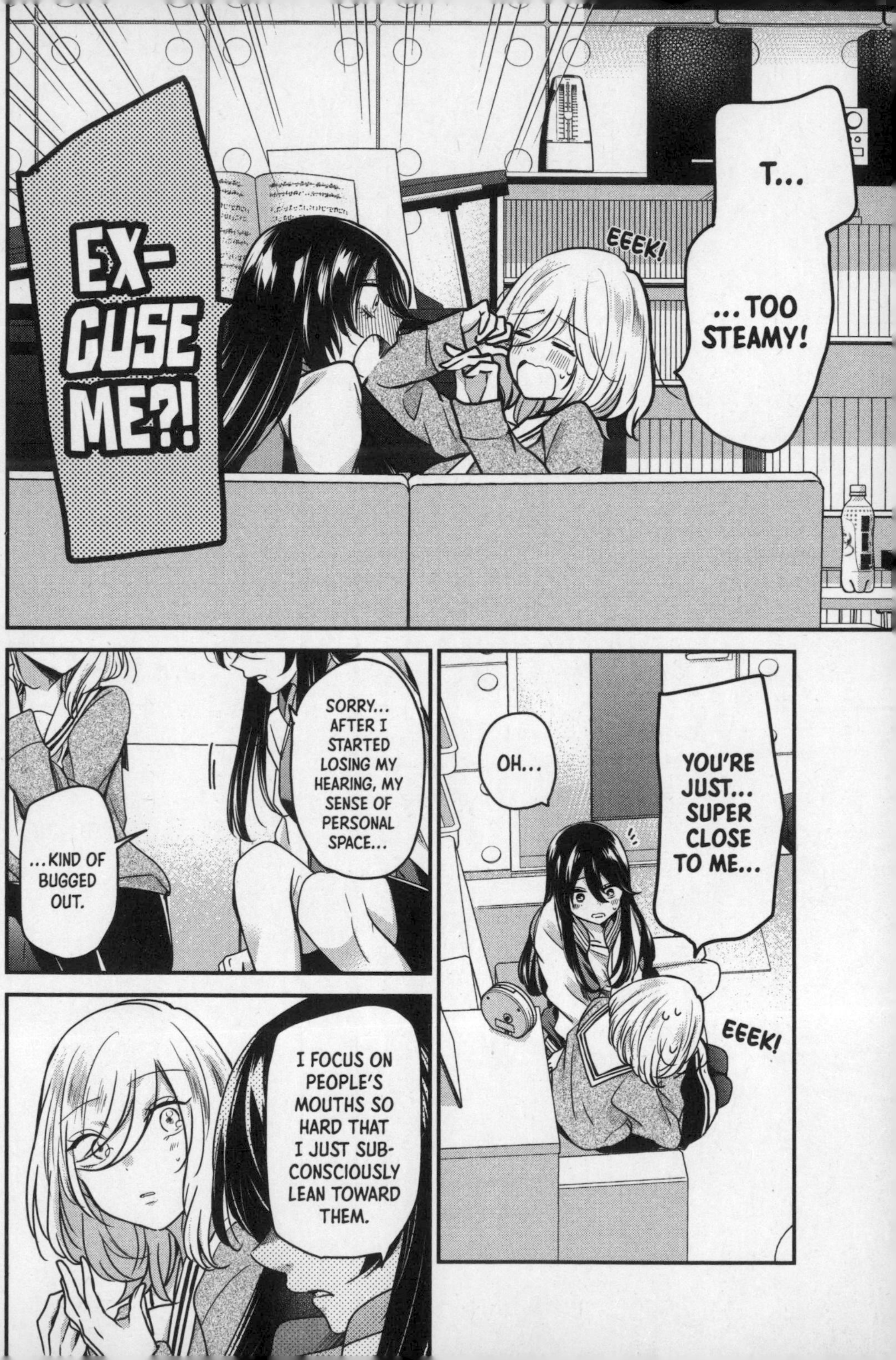
T...
EEEK!
...TOO STEAMY!
EX-CUSE ME?!
YOU'RE JUST... SUPER CLOSE TO ME...
OH...
EEEK!
SORRY... AFTER I STARTED LOSING MY HEARING, MY SENSE OF PERSONAL SPACE...
...KIND OF BUGGED OUT.
I FOCUS ON PEOPLE'S MOUTHS SO HARD THAT I JUST SUB-CONSCIOUSLY LEAN TOWARD THEM.

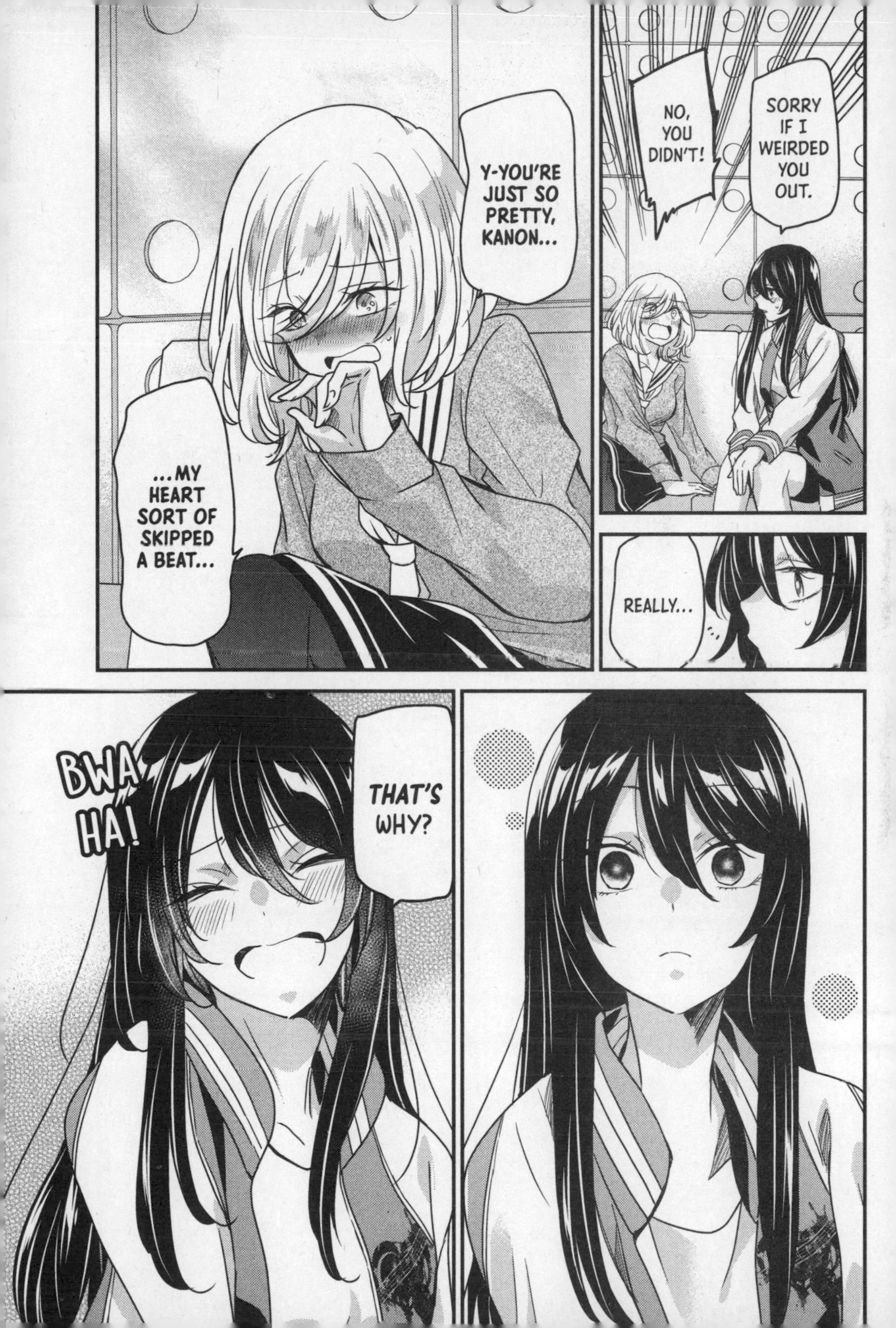
SORRY IF I WEIRDED YOU OUT.
NO, YOU DIDN'T!
REALLY...
Y-YOU'RE JUST SO PRETTY, KANON...
...MY HEART SORT OF SKIPPED A BEAT...
THAT'S WHY?
BWA HA!

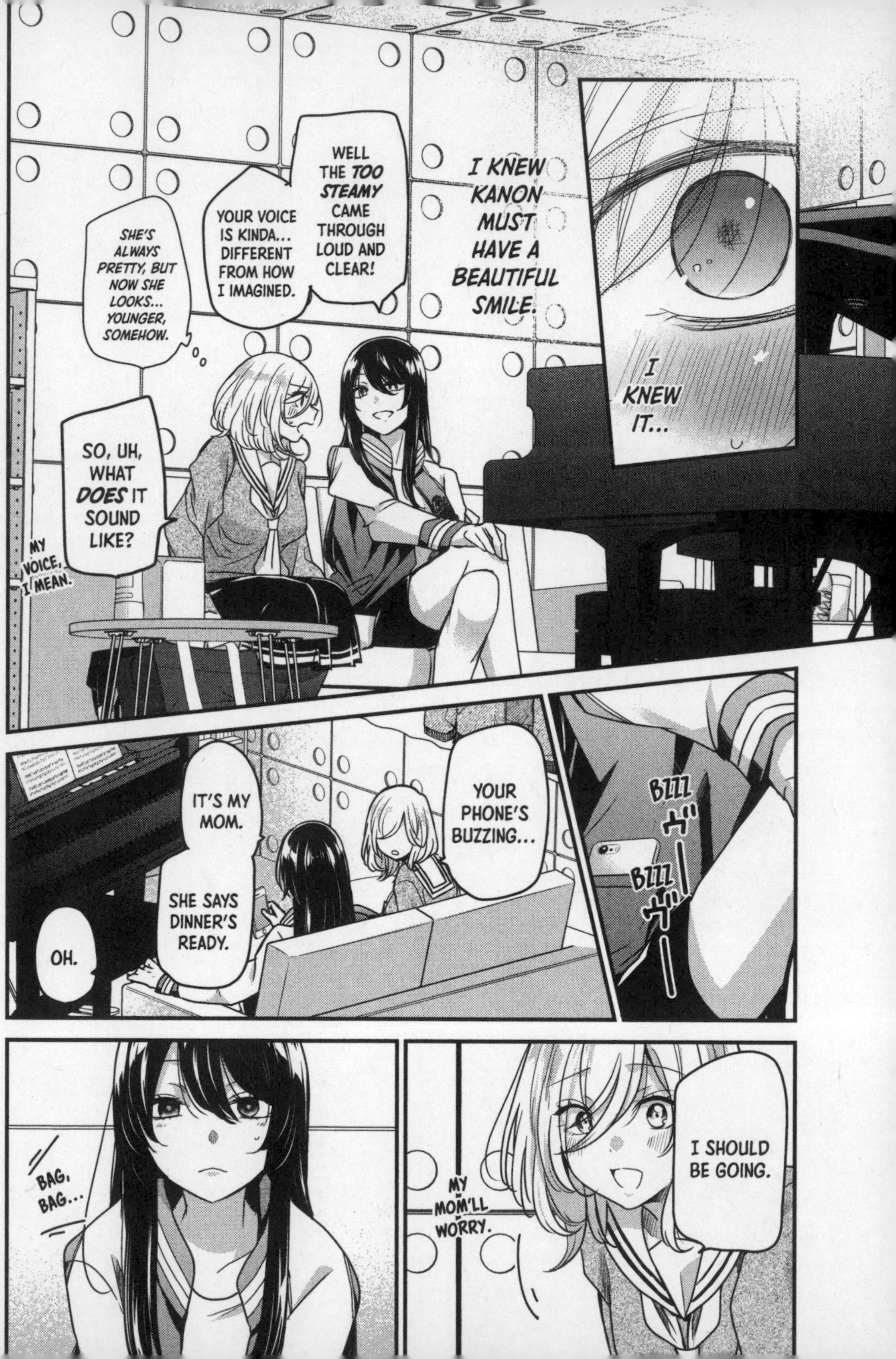
I KNEW KANON MUST HAVE A BEAUTIFUL SMILE.
I KNEW IT...
WELL THE TOO STEAMY CAME THROUGH LOUD AND CLEAR!
YOUR VOICE IS KINDA... DIFFERENT FROM HOW I IMAGINED.
SHE'S ALWAYS PRETTY, BUT NOW SHE LOOKS... YOUNGER, SOMEHOW.
SO, UH, WHAT DOES IT SOUND LIKE?
MY VOICE, I MEAN.
BZZZ
ヴー
BZZZ
ヴー
YOUR PHONE'S BUZZING...
IT'S MY MOM.
SHE SAYS DINNER'S READY.
OH.
I SHOULD BE GOING.
MY MOM'LL WORRY.
BAG, BAG...

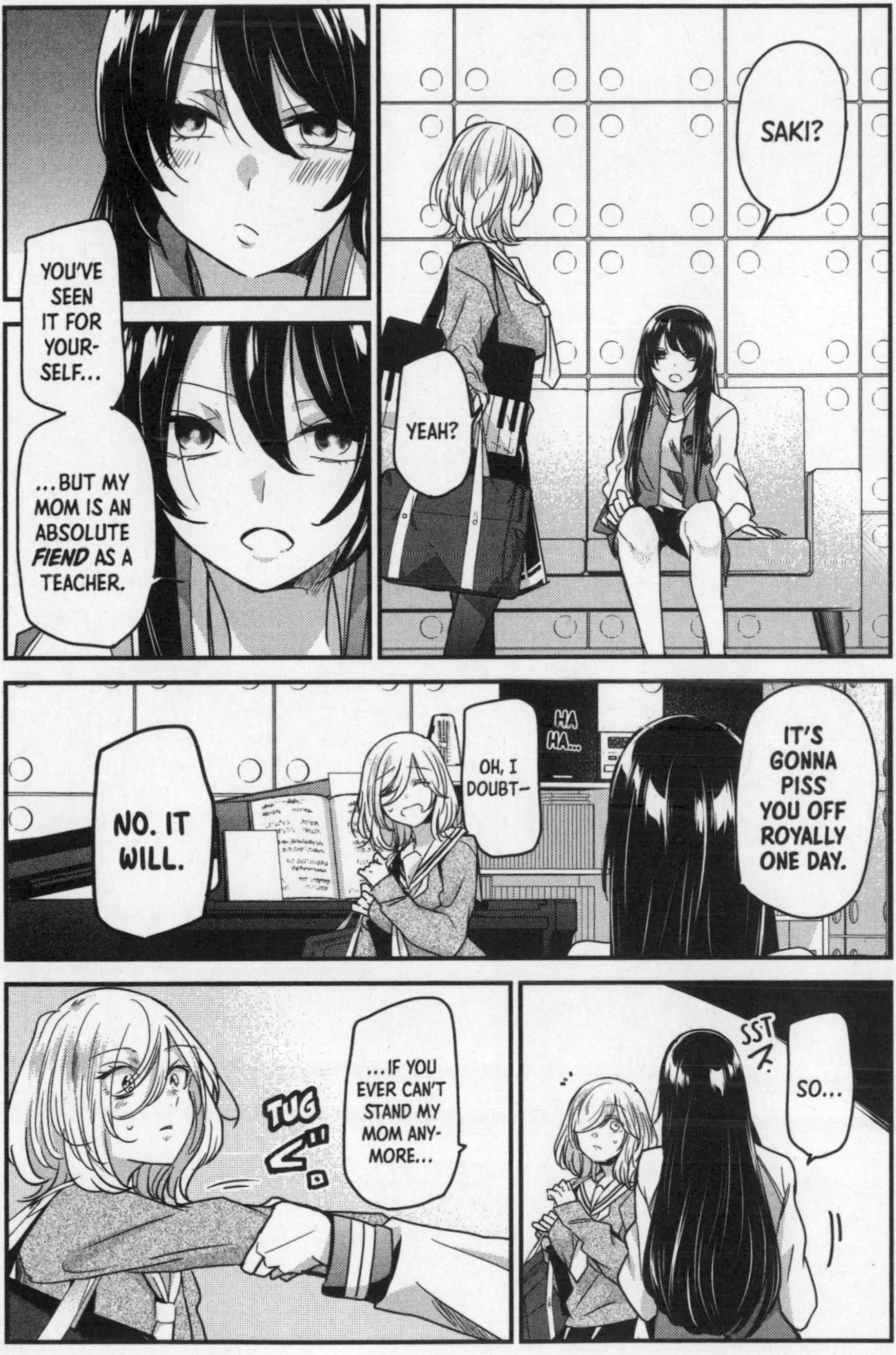
SAKI?
YEAH?
YOU'VE SEEN IT FOR YOURSELF...
...BUT MY MOM IS AN ABSOLUTE *FIEND* AS A TEACHER.
IT'S GONNA PISS YOU OFF ROYALLY ONE DAY.
HA HA...
OH, I DOUBT—
NO. IT WILL.
SST
SO...
TUG
...IF YOU EVER CAN'T STAND MY MOM ANYMORE...

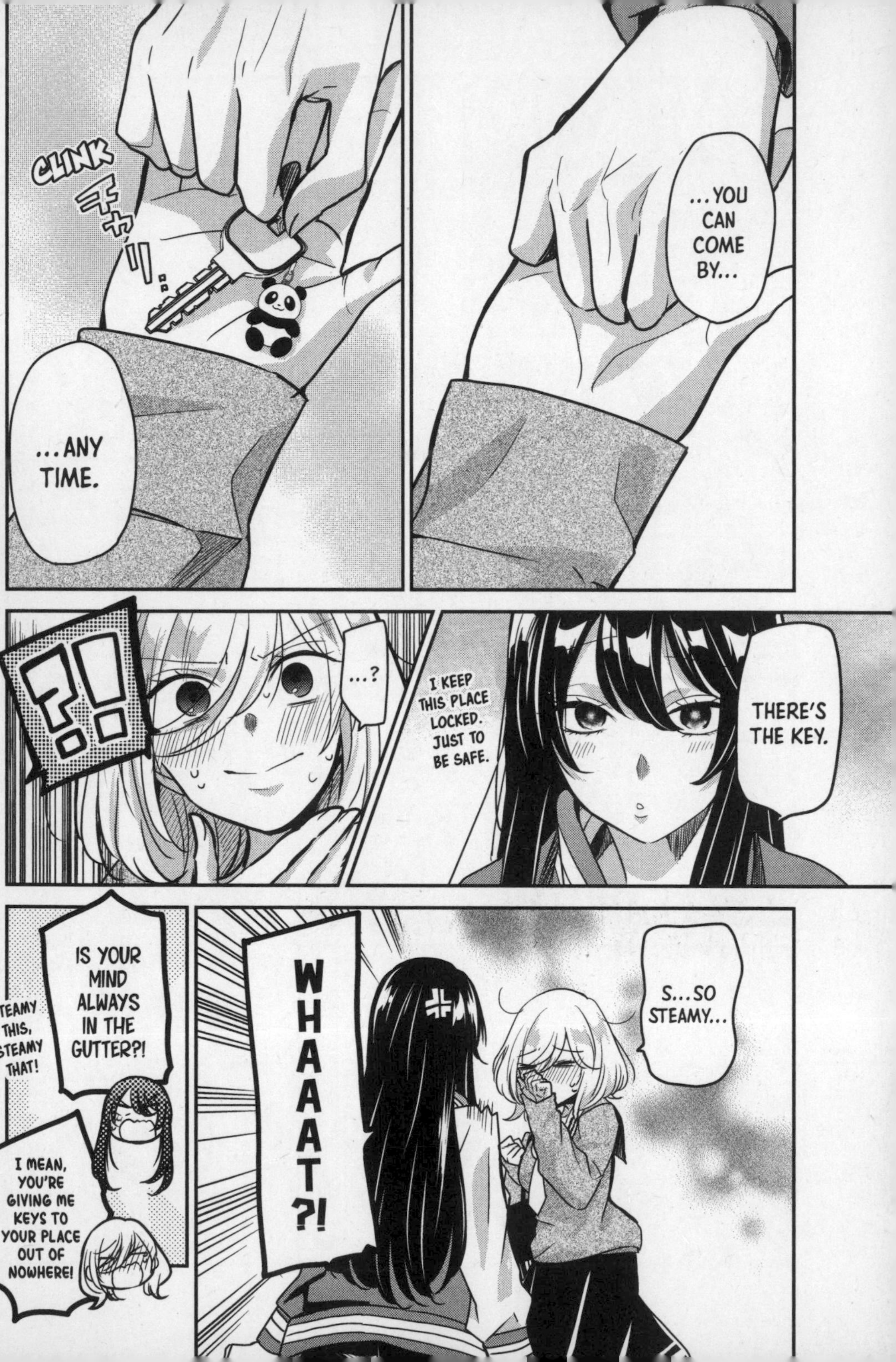
...YOU CAN COME BY...
CLINK
...ANY TIME.
THERE'S THE KEY.
I KEEP THIS PLACE LOCKED. JUST TO BE SAFE.
...?
?!!
S...SO STEAMY...
WHAAAAT?!
IS YOUR MIND ALWAYS IN THE GUTTER?!
STEAMY THIS, STEAMY THAT!
I MEAN, YOU'RE GIVING ME KEYS TO YOUR PLACE OUT OF NOWHERE!

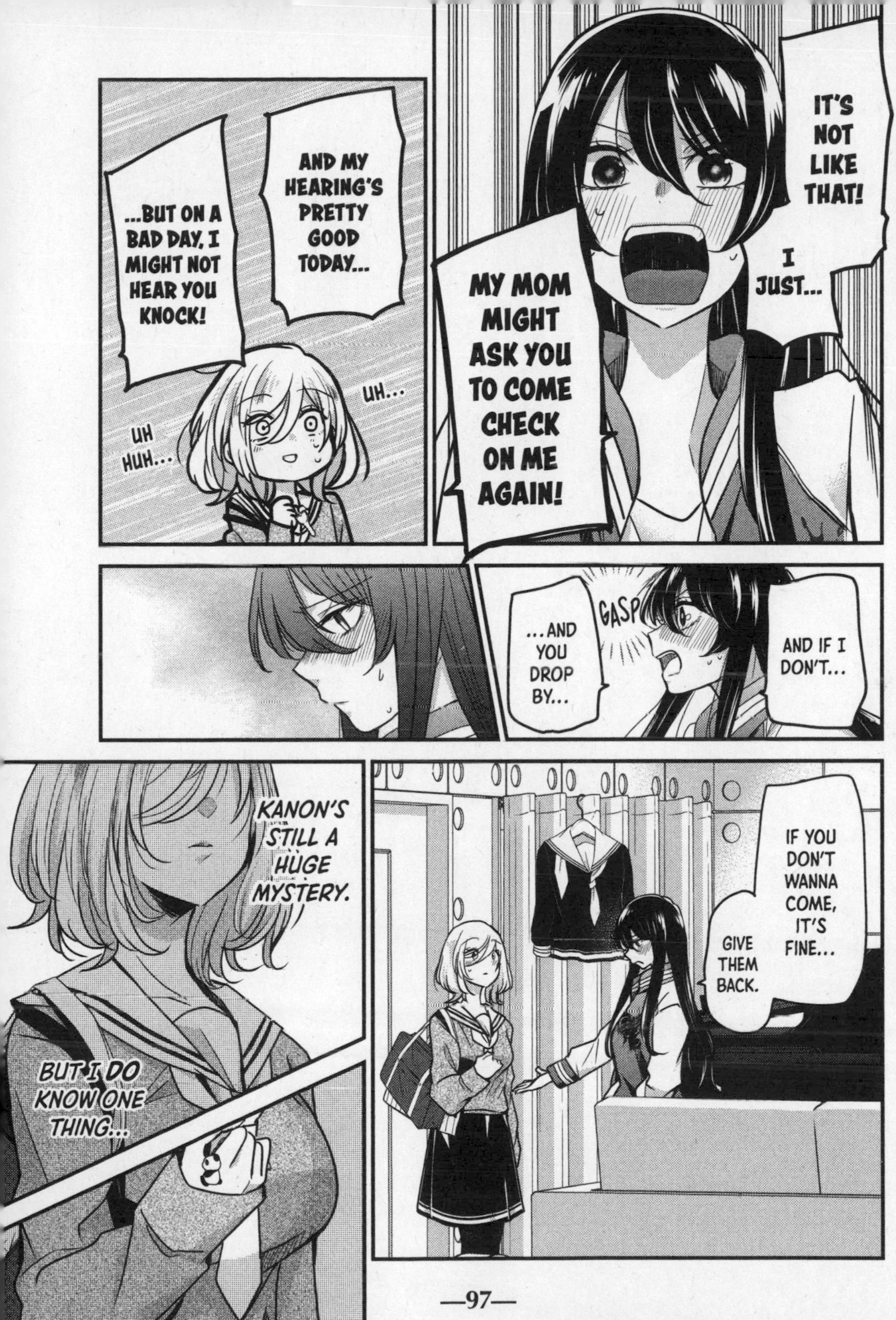
IT'S NOT LIKE THAT!
I JUST...
MY MOM MIGHT ASK YOU TO COME CHECK ON ME AGAIN!
AND MY HEARING'S PRETTY GOOD TODAY...
...BUT ON A BAD DAY, I MIGHT NOT HEAR YOU KNOCK!
UH...
UH HUH...
AND IF I DON'T...
GASP
...AND YOU DROP BY...
IF YOU DON'T WANNA COME, IT'S FINE...
GIVE THEM BACK.
KANON'S STILL A HUGE MYSTERY.
BUT I DO KNOW ONE THING...

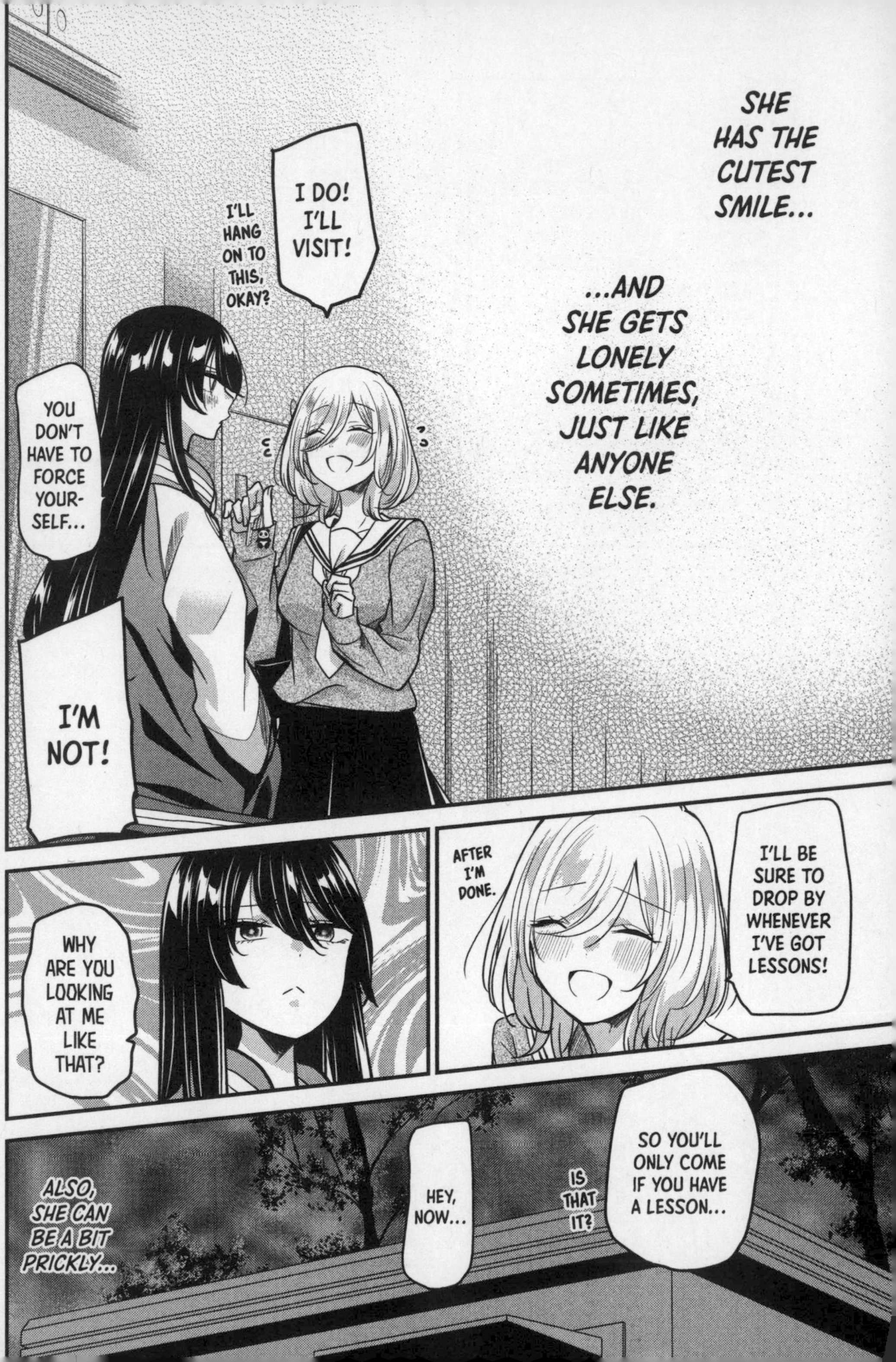
SHE HAS THE CUTEST SMILE...
I DO! I'LL VISIT!
I'LL HANG ON TO THIS, OKAY?
...AND SHE GETS LONELY SOMETIMES, JUST LIKE ANYONE ELSE.
YOU DON'T HAVE TO FORCE YOUR-SELF...
I'M NOT!
I'LL BE SURE TO DROP BY WHENEVER I'VE GOT LESSONS!
AFTER I'M DONE.
WHY ARE YOU LOOKING AT ME LIKE THAT?
SO YOU'LL ONLY COME IF YOU HAVE A LESSON...
IS THAT IT?
HEY, NOW...
ALSO, SHE CAN BE A BIT PRICKLY...

A panda....
Cute!

the moon on a rainy night

Chapter 3: Refuge

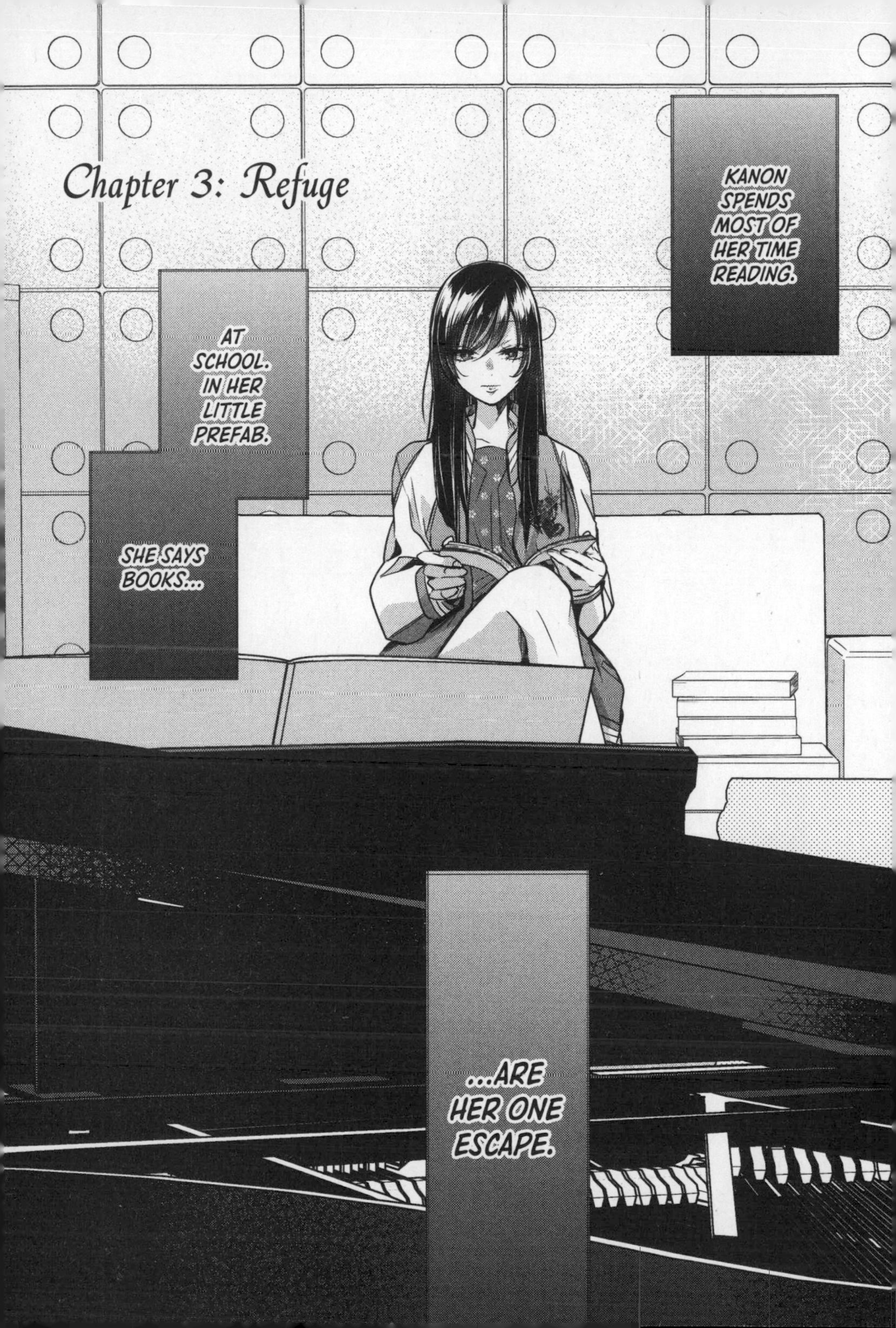
KANON SPENDS MOST OF HER TIME READING.
AT SCHOOL. IN HER LITTLE PREFAB.
SHE SAYS BOOKS...
...ARE HER ONE ESCAPE.

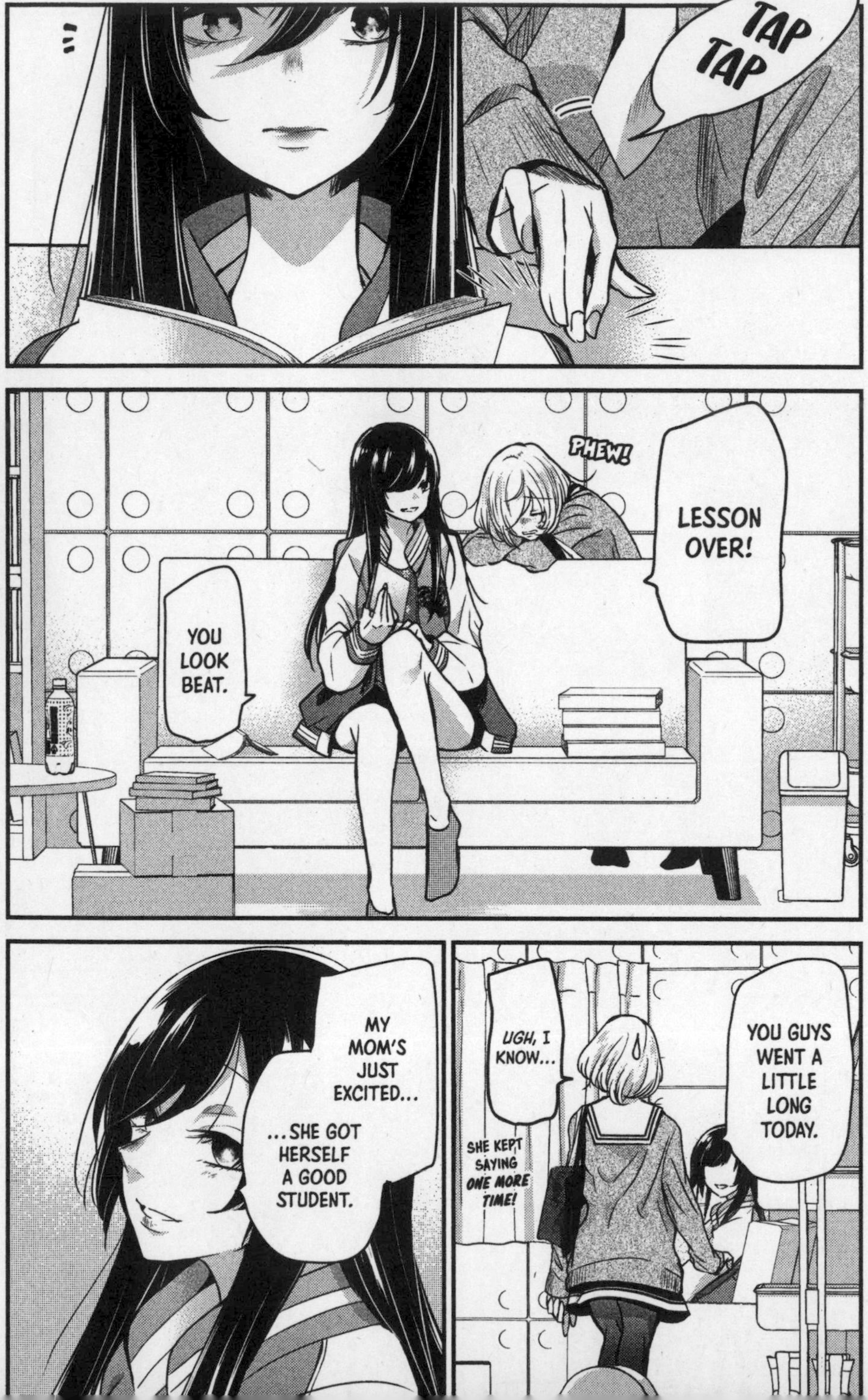
TAP TAP
LESSON OVER!
PHEW!
YOU LOOK BEAT.
YOU GUYS WENT A LITTLE LONG TODAY.
UGH, I KNOW...
SHE KEPT SAYING ONE MORE TIME!
MY MOM'S JUST EXCITED...
...SHE GOT HERSELF A GOOD STUDENT.

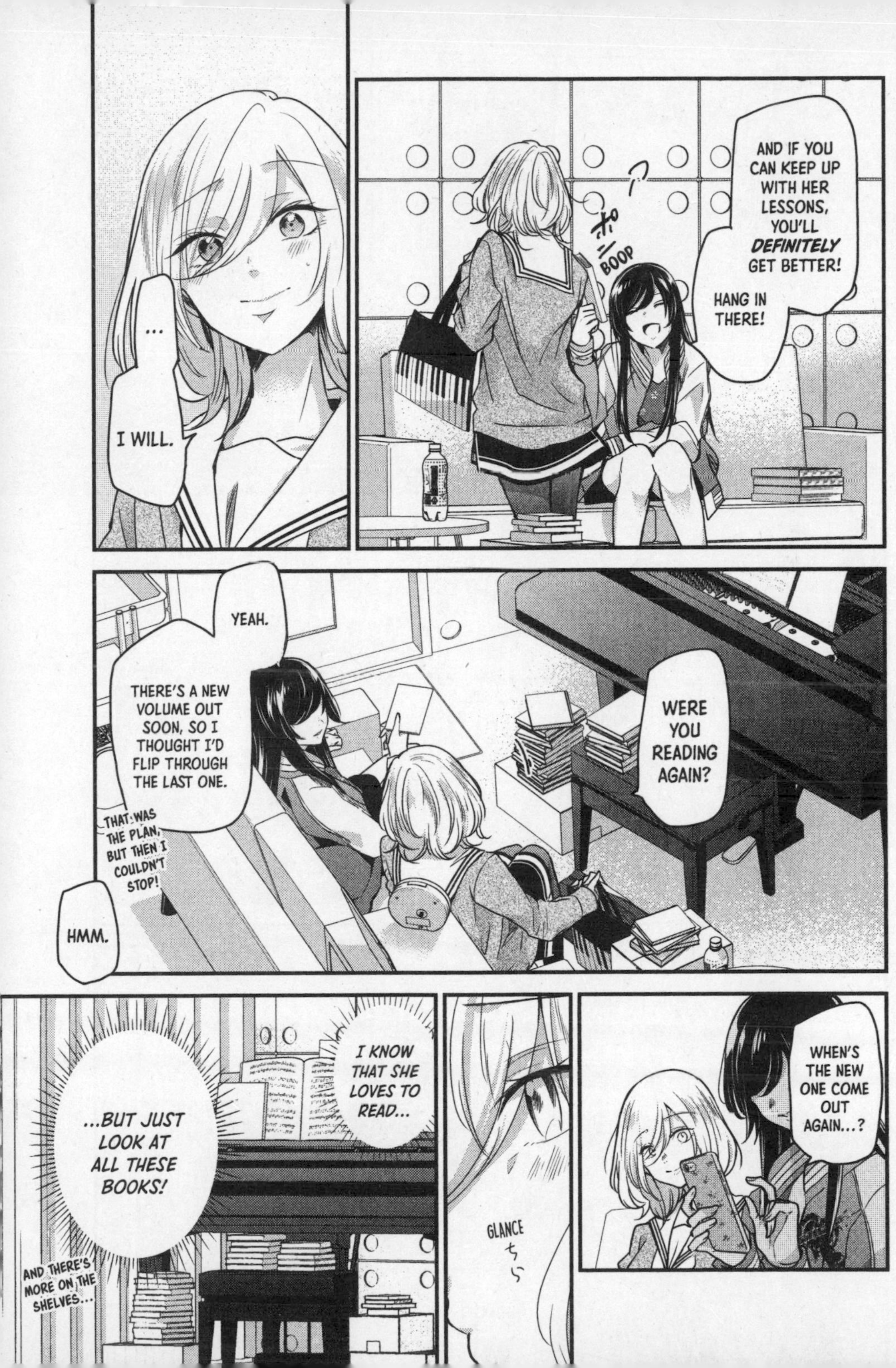
AND IF YOU CAN KEEP UP WITH HER LESSONS, YOU'LL *DEFINITELY* GET BETTER!
HANG IN THERE!
?
ポ BOOP
...
I WILL.
WERE YOU READING AGAIN?
YEAH.
THERE'S A NEW VOLUME OUT SOON, SO I THOUGHT I'D FLIP THROUGH THE LAST ONE.
THAT WAS THE PLAN, BUT THEN I COULDN'T STOP!
HMM.
WHEN'S THE NEW ONE COME OUT AGAIN...?
GLANCE ちら
I KNOW THAT SHE LOVES TO READ...
...BUT JUST LOOK AT ALL THESE BOOKS!
AND THERE'S MORE ON THE SHELVES...

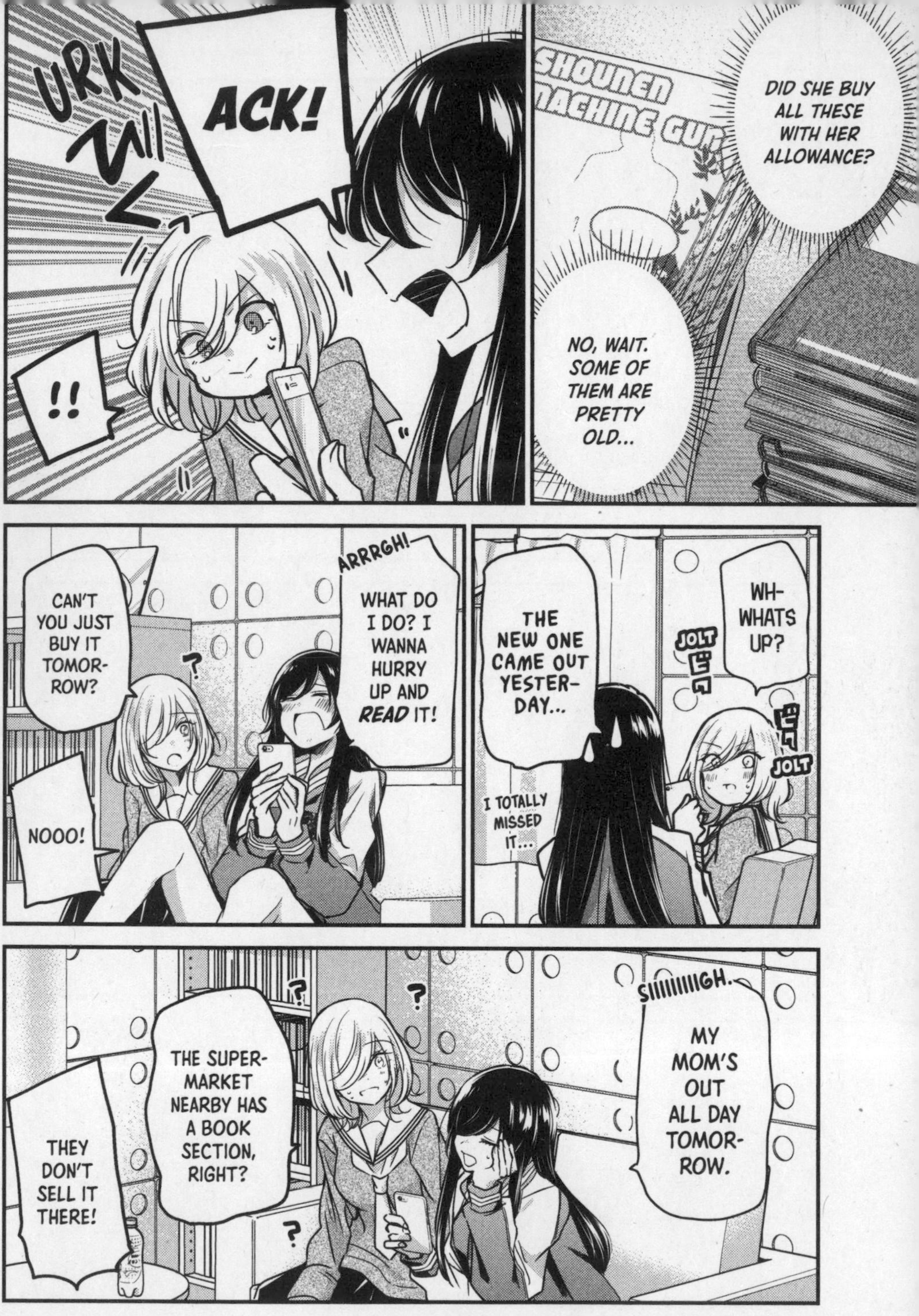
DID SHE BUY ALL THESE WITH HER ALLOWANCE?
SHOUNEN MACHINE GUN
NO, WAIT. SOME OF THEM ARE PRETTY OLD...
URK
ACK!
!!
WH- WHATS UP?
JOLT
JOLT
THE NEW ONE CAME OUT YESTER- DAY...
I TOTALLY MISSED IT...
ARRRGH!
WHAT DO I DO? I WANNA HURRY UP AND READ IT!
CAN'T YOU JUST BUY IT TOMOR- ROW?
NOOO!
SIIIIIIIIGH.
MY MOM'S OUT ALL DAY TOMOR- ROW.
THE SUPER- MARKET NEARBY HAS A BOOK SECTION, RIGHT?
THEY DON'T SELL IT THERE!

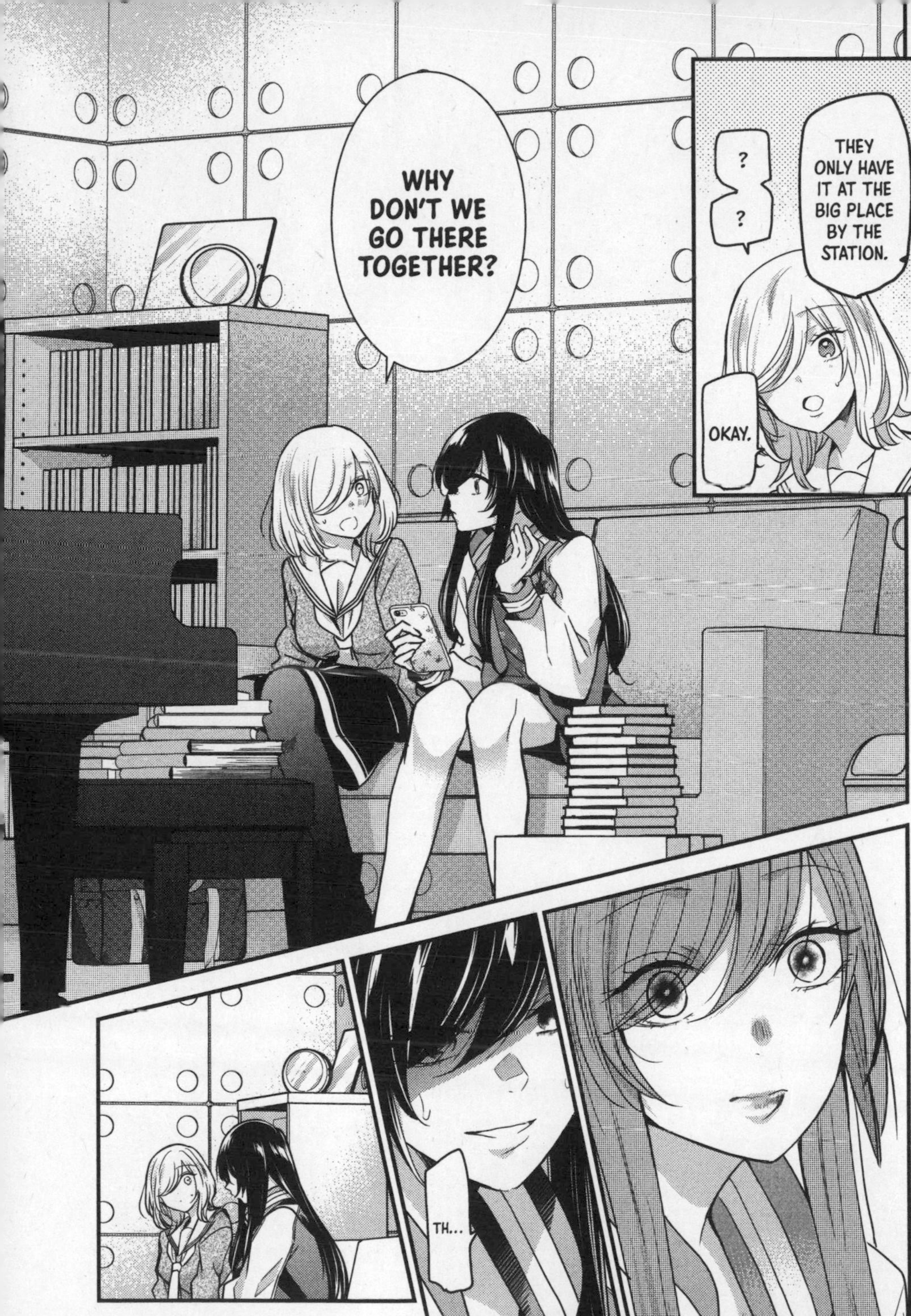
THEY ONLY HAVE IT AT THE BIG PLACE BY THE STATION.
? ?
OKAY.
WHY DON'T WE GO THERE TOGETHER?
TH...

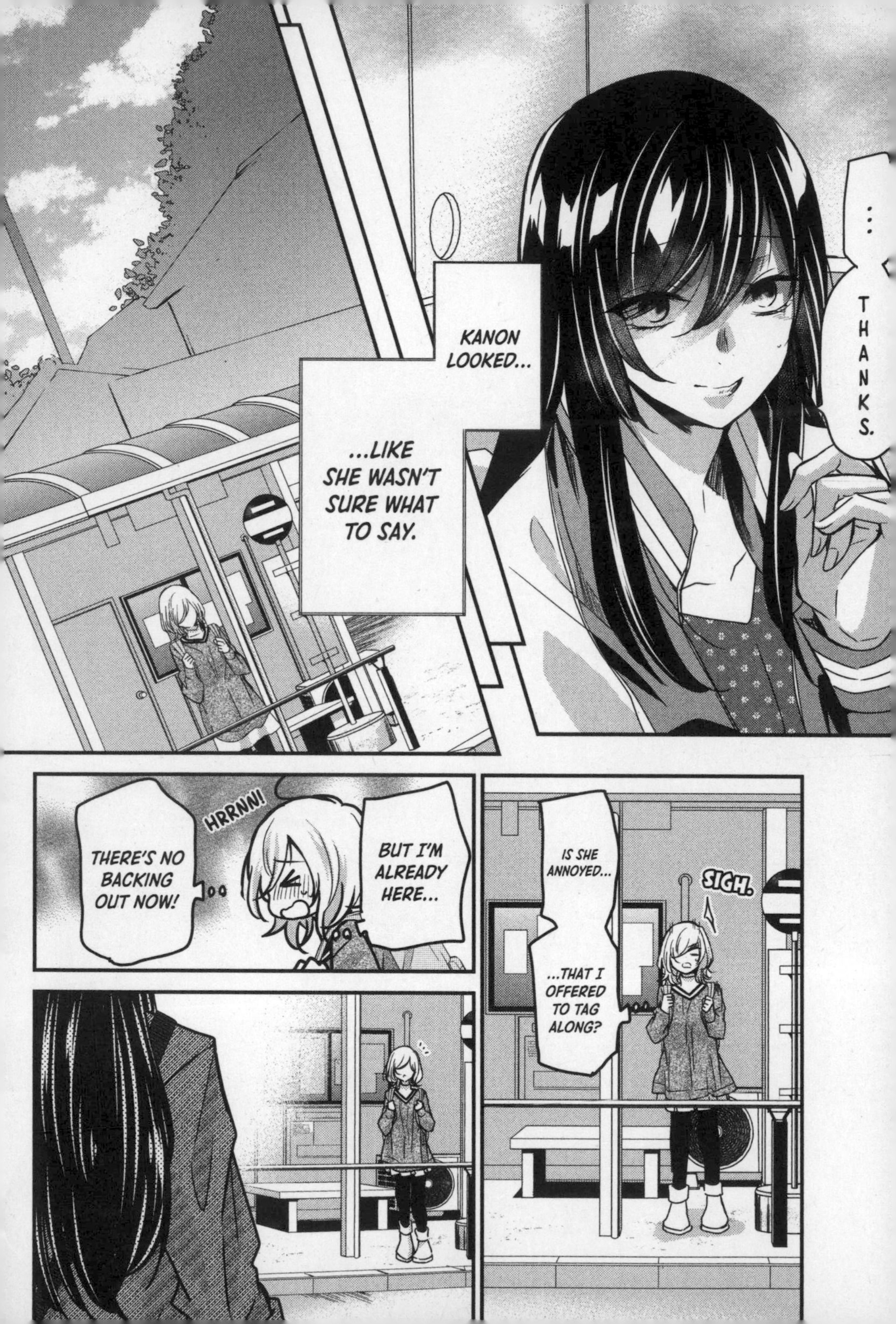
...THANKS.
KANON LOOKED...
...LIKE SHE WASN'T SURE WHAT TO SAY.
IS SHE ANNOYED...
SIGH.
...THAT I OFFERED TO TAG ALONG?
BUT I'M ALREADY HERE...
HRRNN!
THERE'S NO BACKING OUT NOW!

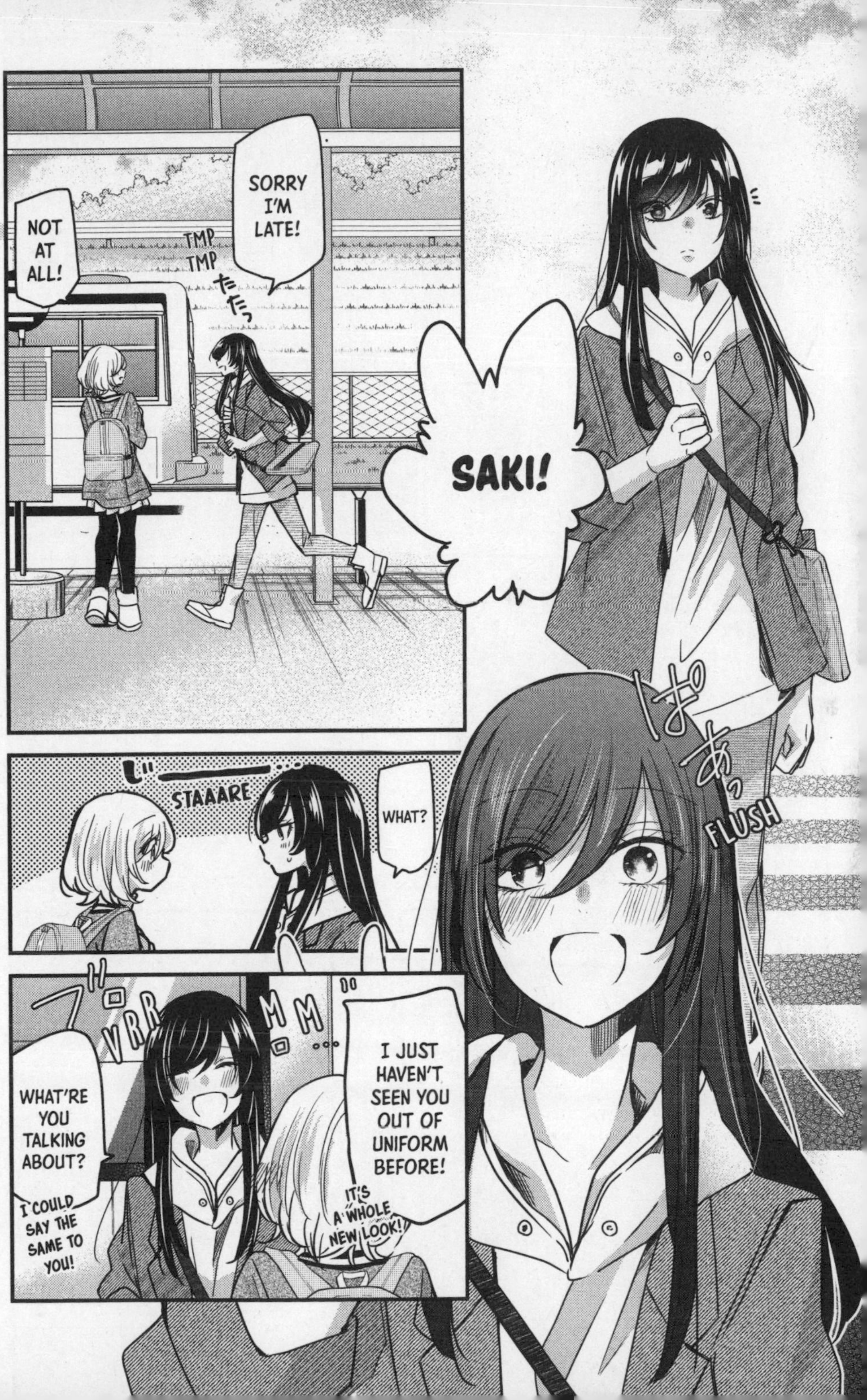
SAKI!
SORRY I'M LATE!
NOT AT ALL!
TMP TMP
たたっ
ぱぁっ
FLUSH
じ——
STAAARE
WHAT?
I JUST HAVEN'T SEEN YOU OUT OF UNIFORM BEFORE!
IT'S A WHOLE NEW LOOK!
ブロロ
VRRMM
WHAT'RE YOU TALKING ABOUT?
I COULD SAY THE SAME TO YOU!

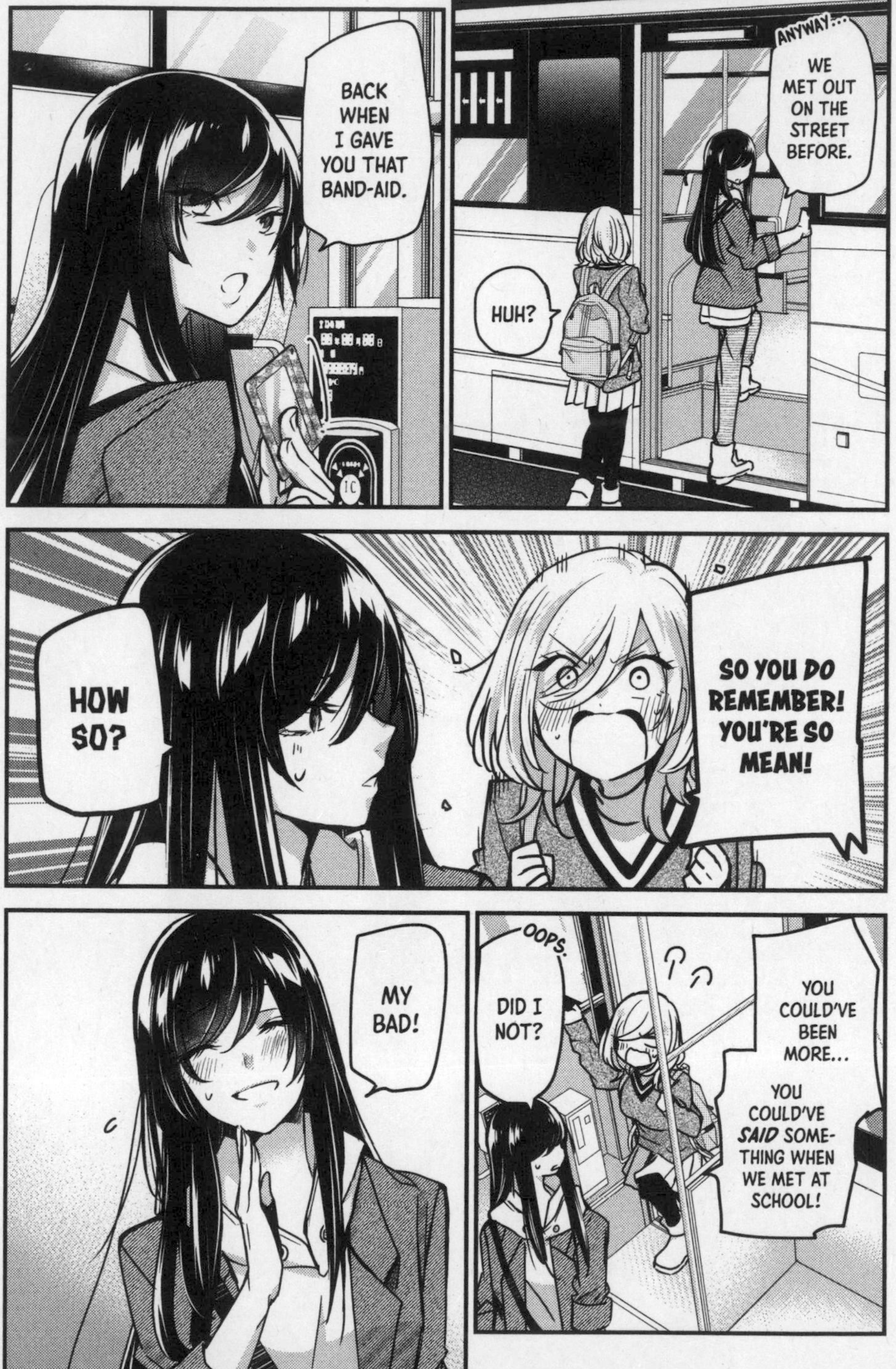
ANYWAY...
WE MET OUT ON THE STREET BEFORE.
HUH?
BACK WHEN I GAVE YOU THAT BAND-AID.
SO YOU DO REMEMBER! YOU'RE SO MEAN!
HOW SO?
YOU COULD'VE BEEN MORE...
YOU COULD'VE SAID SOMETHING WHEN WE MET AT SCHOOL!
OOPS.
DID I NOT?
MY BAD!

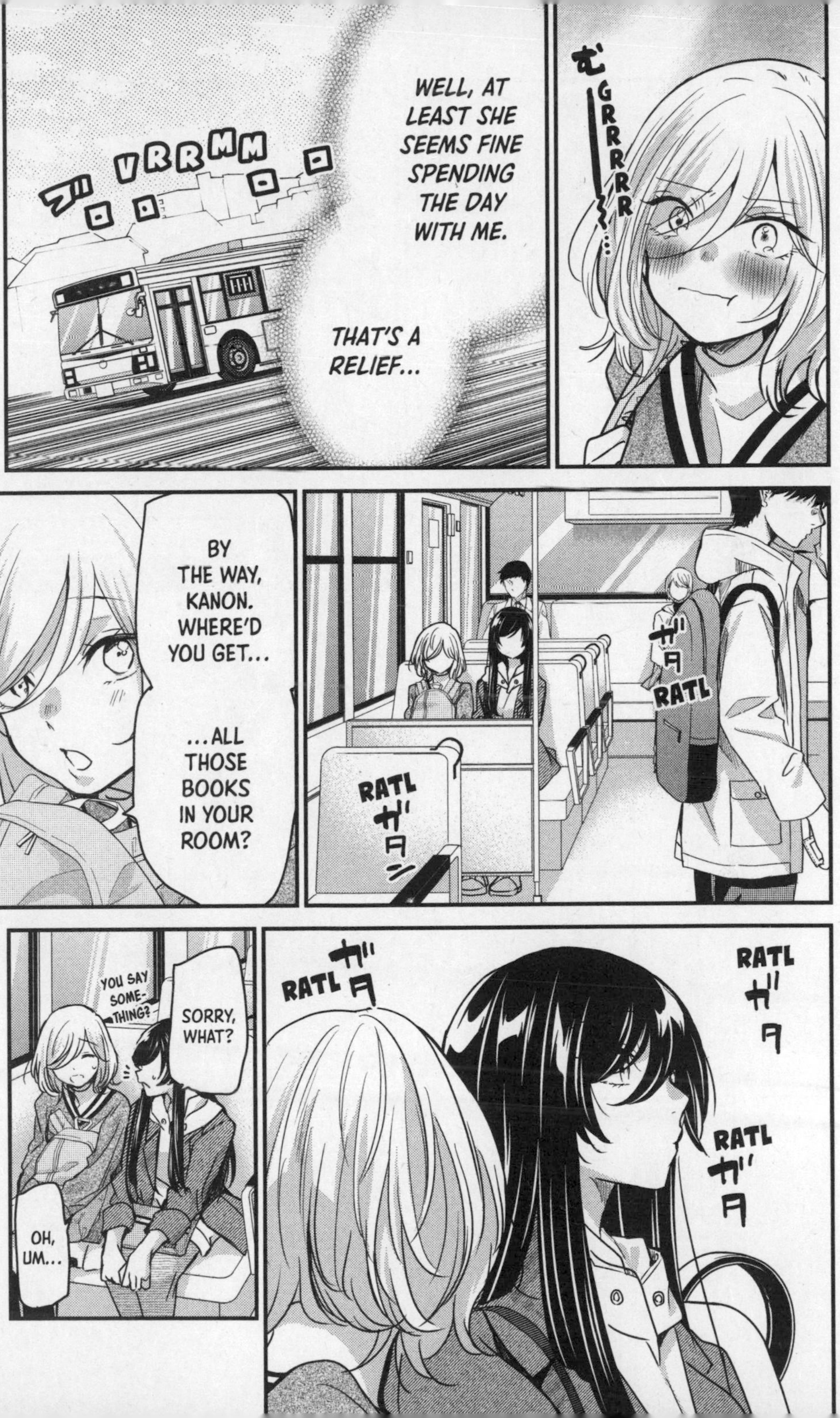
む
GRRRRR...
WELL, AT LEAST SHE SEEMS FINE SPENDING THE DAY WITH ME.
THAT'S A RELIEF...
ブロロロロ
VRRMM
ガタ
RATL
RATL
ガタン
BY THE WAY, KANON. WHERE'D YOU GET...
...ALL THOSE BOOKS IN YOUR ROOM?
RATL
ガタ
RATL
ガタ
RATL
ガタ
SORRY, WHAT?
YOU SAY SOME-THING?
OH, UM...

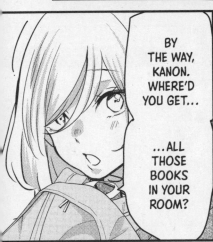

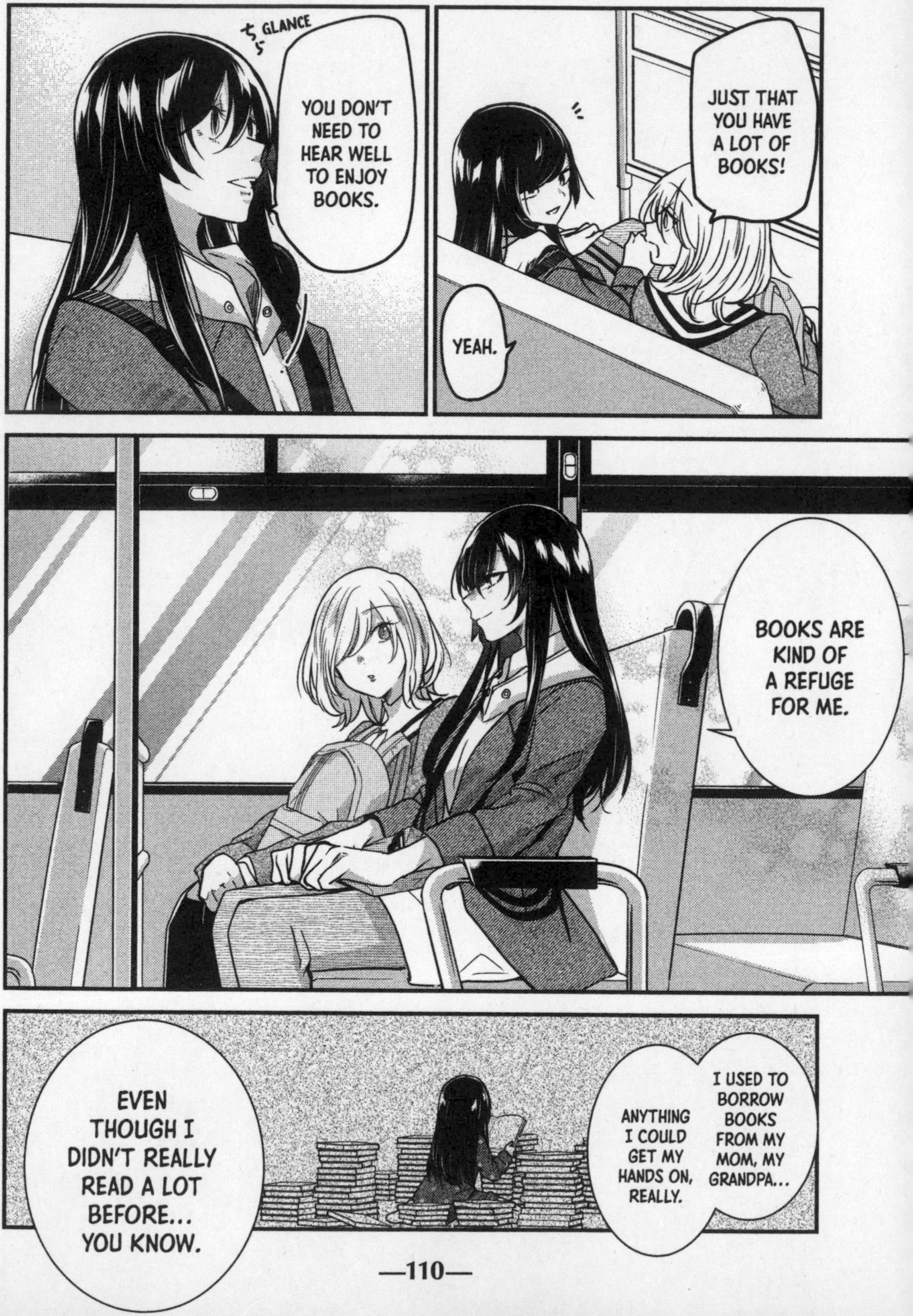
JUST THAT YOU HAVE A LOT OF BOOKS!
YEAH.
GLANCE
YOU DON'T NEED TO HEAR WELL TO ENJOY BOOKS.
BOOKS ARE KIND OF A REFUGE FOR ME.
I USED TO BORROW BOOKS FROM MY MOM, MY GRANDPA...
ANYTHING I COULD GET MY HANDS ON, REALLY.
EVEN THOUGH I DIDN'T REALLY READ A LOT BEFORE... YOU KNOW.

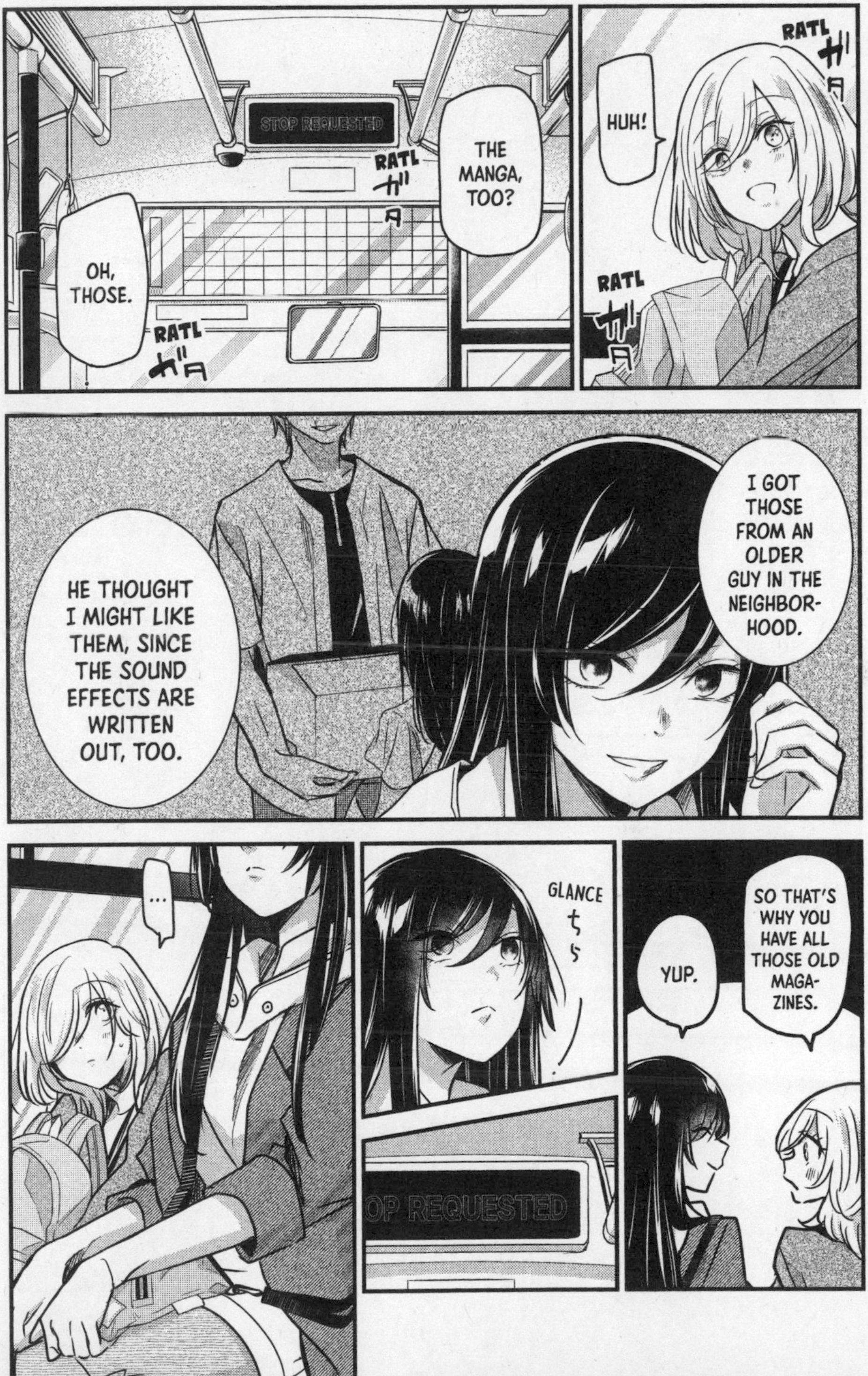
RATL ガタ
HUH!
RATL ガタ
STOP REQUESTED
THE MANGA, TOO?
RATL ガタ
OH, THOSE.
RATL ガタ
I GOT THOSE FROM AN OLDER GUY IN THE NEIGHBOR-HOOD.
HE THOUGHT I MIGHT LIKE THEM, SINCE THE SOUND EFFECTS ARE WRITTEN OUT, TOO.
SO THAT'S WHY YOU HAVE ALL THOSE OLD MAGA-ZINES.
YUP.
OP REQUESTED
GLANCE ちら
...

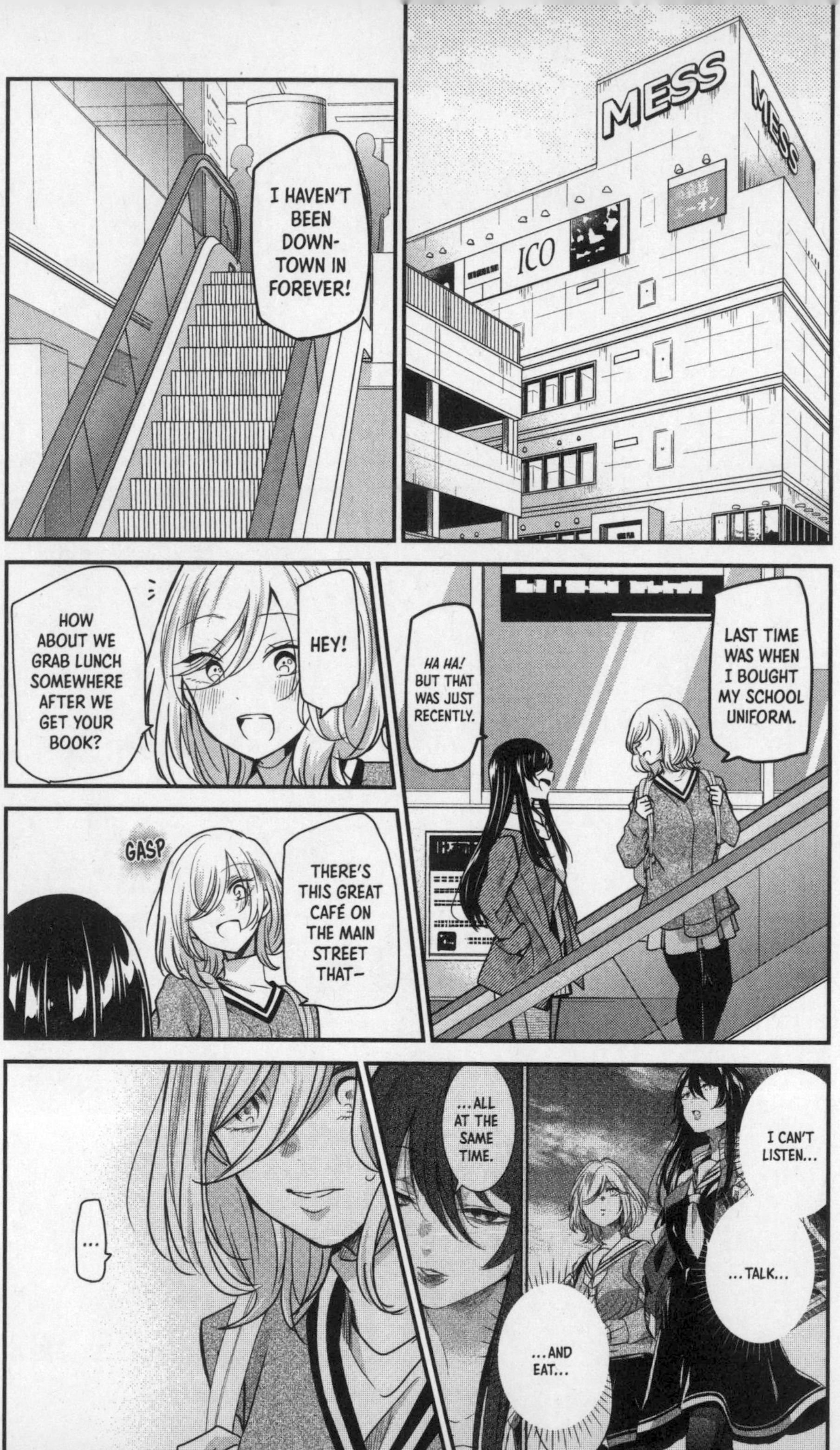
MESS
MESS
ICO
I HAVEN'T BEEN DOWN-TOWN IN FOREVER!
LAST TIME WAS WHEN I BOUGHT MY SCHOOL UNIFORM.
HA HA! BUT THAT WAS JUST RECENTLY.
HEY!
HOW ABOUT WE GRAB LUNCH SOMEWHERE AFTER WE GET YOUR BOOK?
GASP
THERE'S THIS GREAT CAFÉ ON THE MAIN STREET THAT—
I CAN'T LISTEN...
...TALK...
...AND EAT...
...ALL AT THE SAME TIME.
...

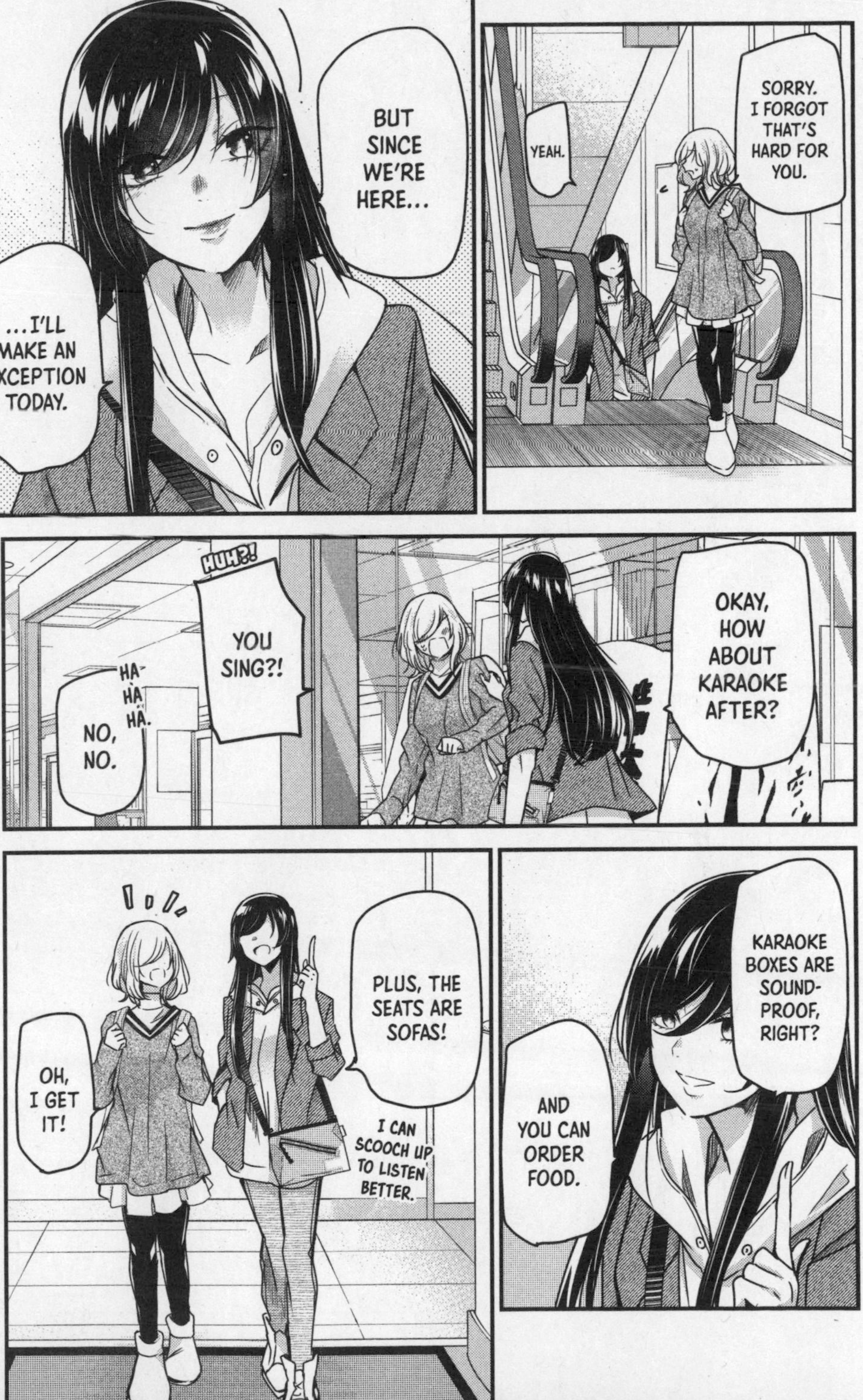
SORRY. I FORGOT THAT'S HARD FOR YOU.
YEAH.
BUT SINCE WE'RE HERE...
...I'LL MAKE AN EXCEPTION TODAY.
OKAY, HOW ABOUT KARAOKE AFTER?
HUH?!
YOU SING?!
HA HA HA.
NO, NO.
KARAOKE BOXES ARE SOUND-PROOF, RIGHT?
AND YOU CAN ORDER FOOD.
PLUS, THE SEATS ARE SOFAS!
I CAN SCOOCH UP TO LISTEN BETTER.
OH, I GET IT!

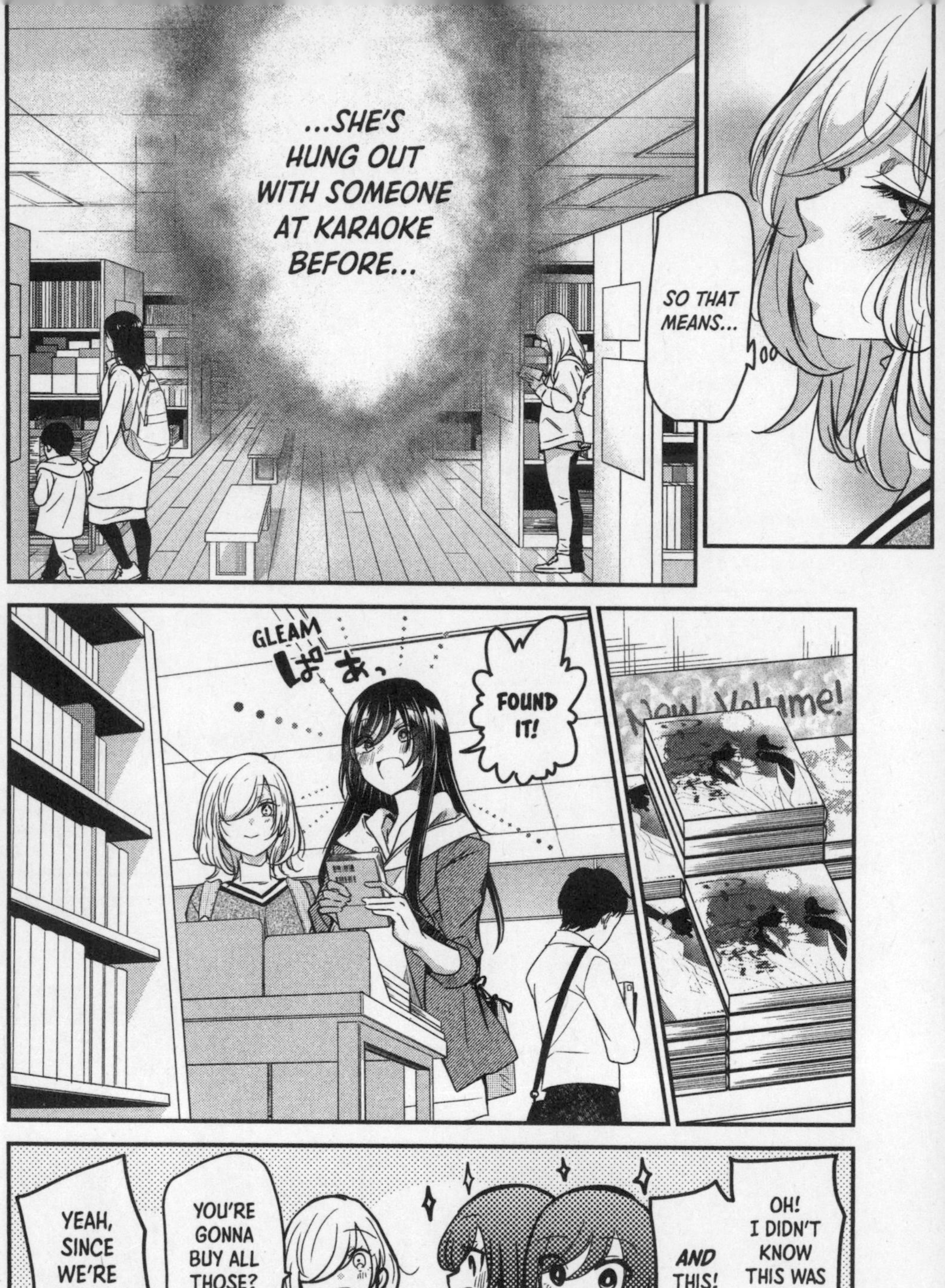
SO THAT MEANS...
...SHE'S HUNG OUT WITH SOMEONE AT KARAOKE BEFORE...
New Volume!
FOUND IT!
GLEAM
ぱあっ
OH! I DIDN'T KNOW THIS WAS OUT!
AND THIS!
YOU'RE GONNA BUY ALL THOSE?
YEAH, SINCE WE'RE HERE!

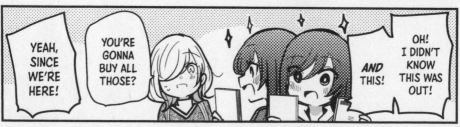

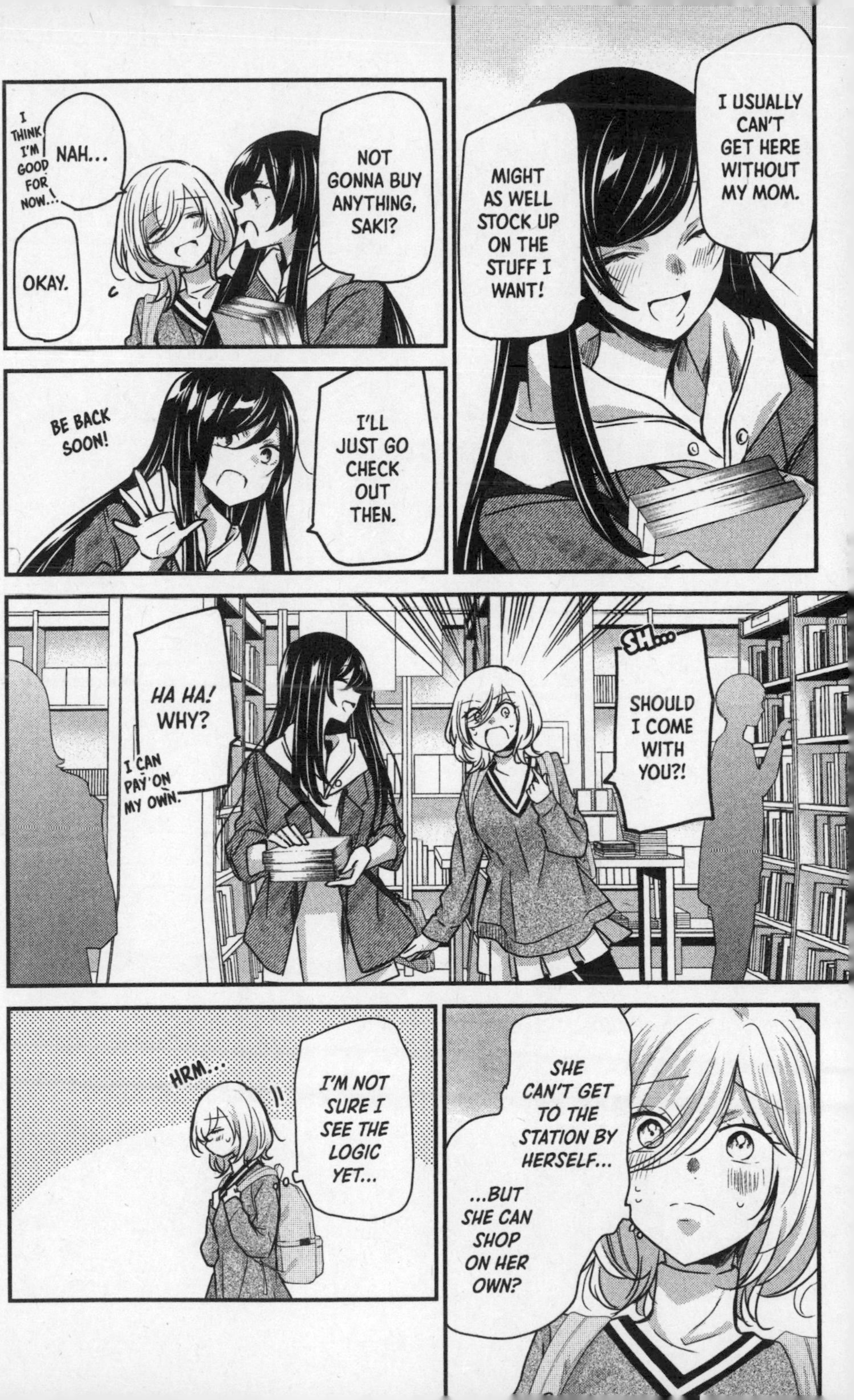
I USUALLY CAN'T GET HERE WITHOUT MY MOM.
MIGHT AS WELL STOCK UP ON THE STUFF I WANT!
NOT GONNA BUY ANYTHING, SAKI?
NAH...
I THINK I'M GOOD FOR NOW...
OKAY.
I'LL JUST GO CHECK OUT THEN.
BE BACK SOON!
SH...
SHOULD I COME WITH YOU?!
HA HA! WHY?
I CAN PAY ON MY OWN.
SHE CAN'T GET TO THE STATION BY HERSELF...
...BUT SHE CAN SHOP ON HER OWN?
HRM...
I'M NOT SURE I SEE THE LOGIC YET...

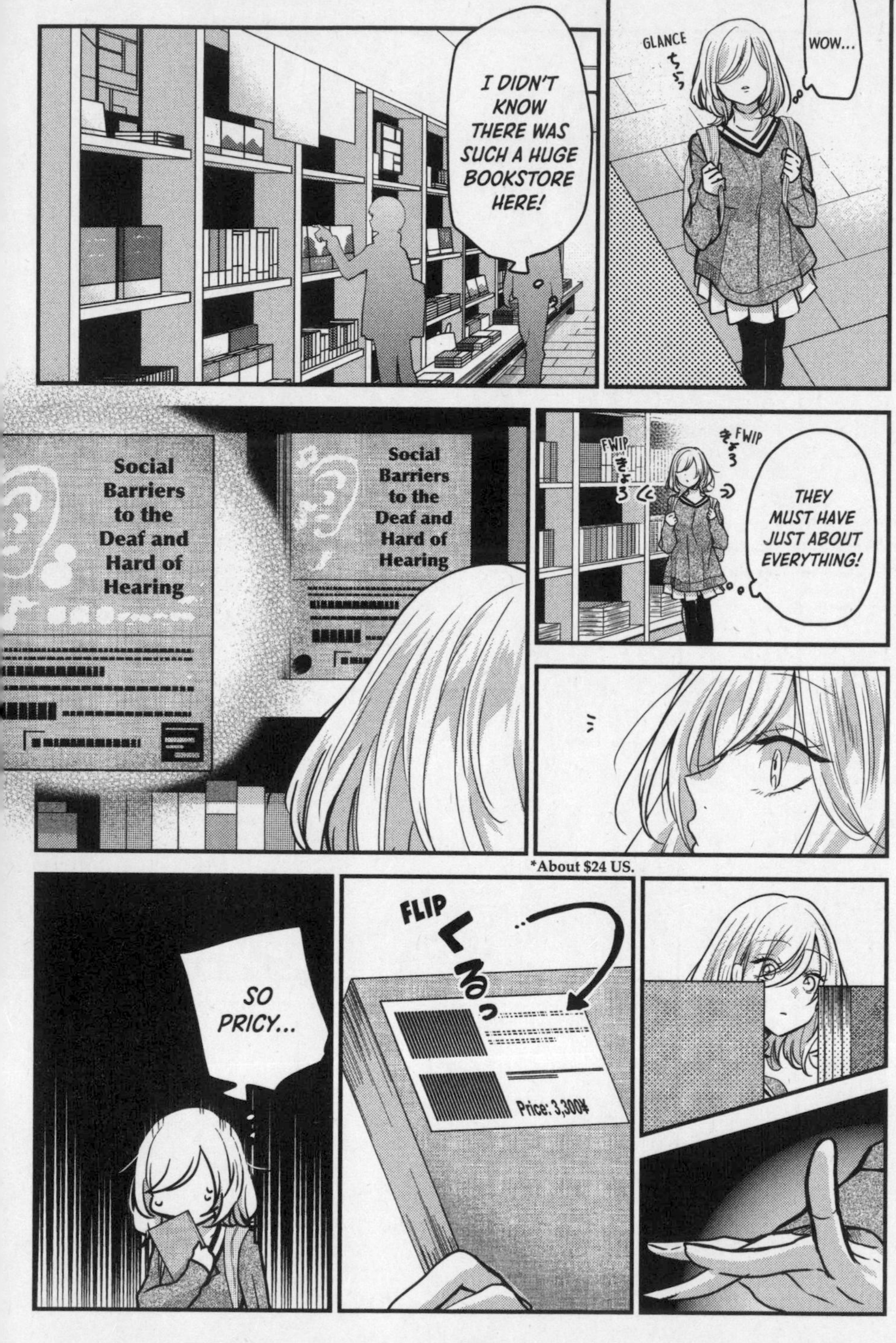
GLANCE
ちらっ
WOW...
I DIDN'T KNOW THERE WAS SUCH A HUGE BOOKSTORE HERE!
FWIP
きょろ
FWIP
きょろ
THEY MUST HAVE JUST ABOUT EVERYTHING!
Social Barriers to the Deaf and Hard of Hearing
Social Barriers to the Deaf and Hard of Hearing
FLIP
Price: 3,300¥
SO PRICY...

*About $24 US.

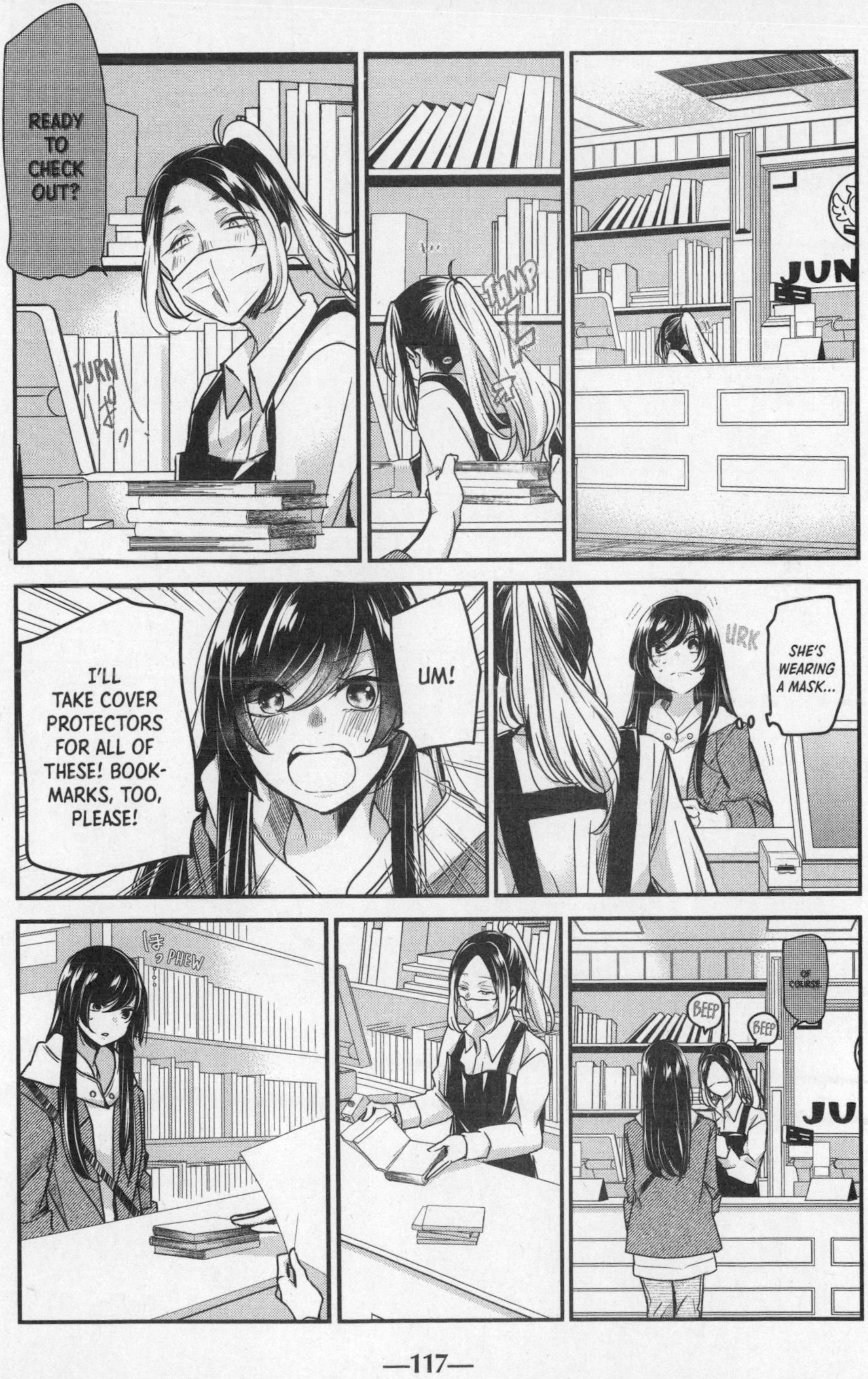
JUN
...
THMP
READY TO CHECK OUT?
TURN
URK
SHE'S WEARING A MASK...
UM!
I'LL TAKE COVER PROTECTORS FOR ALL OF THESE! BOOK-MARKS, TOO, PLEASE!
OF COURSE
BEEP
BEEP
JU
PHEW

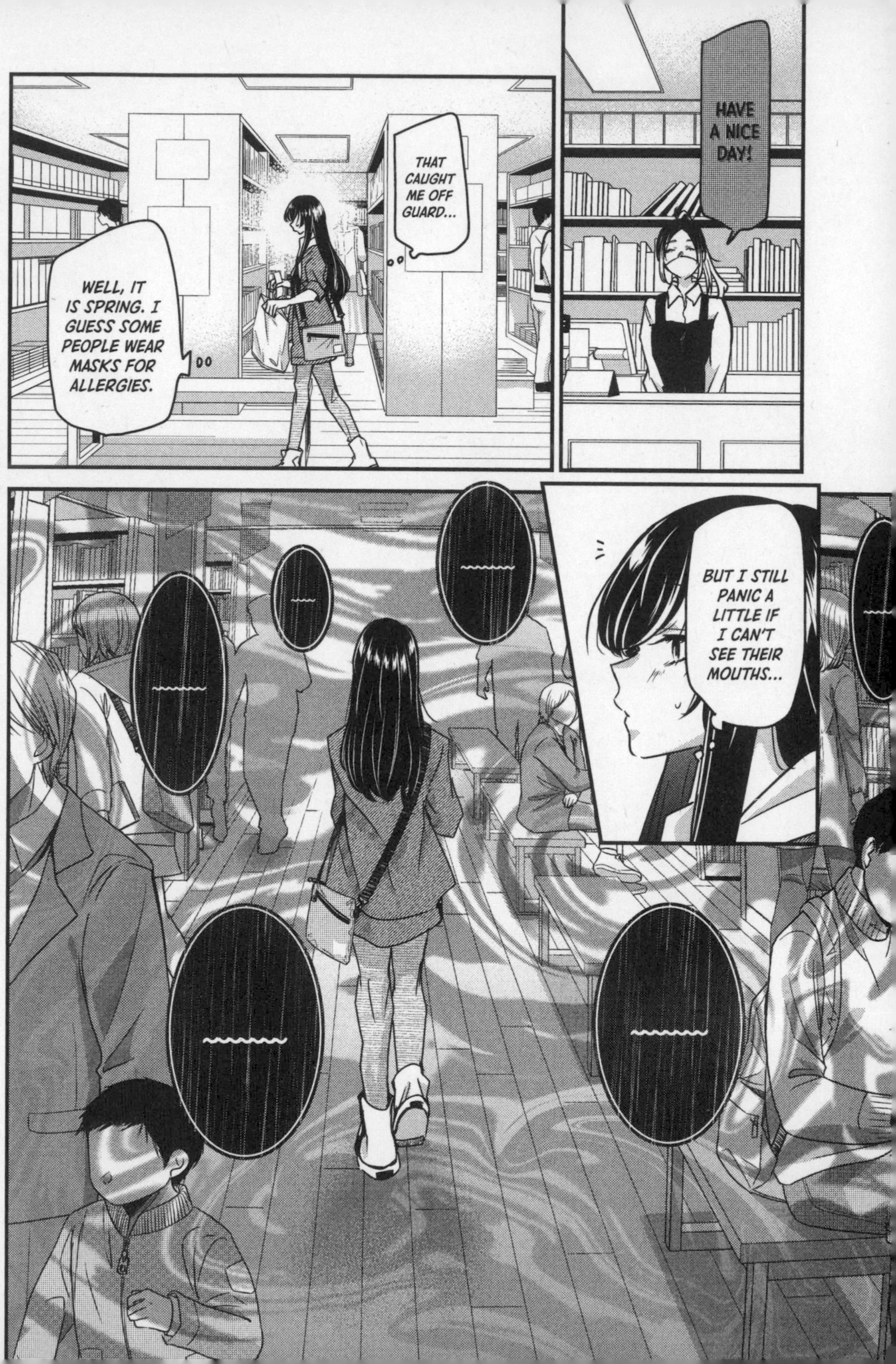
HAVE A NICE DAY!
THAT CAUGHT ME OFF GUARD...
WELL, IT IS SPRING. I GUESS SOME PEOPLE WEAR MASKS FOR ALLERGIES.
BUT I STILL PANIC A LITTLE IF I CAN'T SEE THEIR MOUTHS...

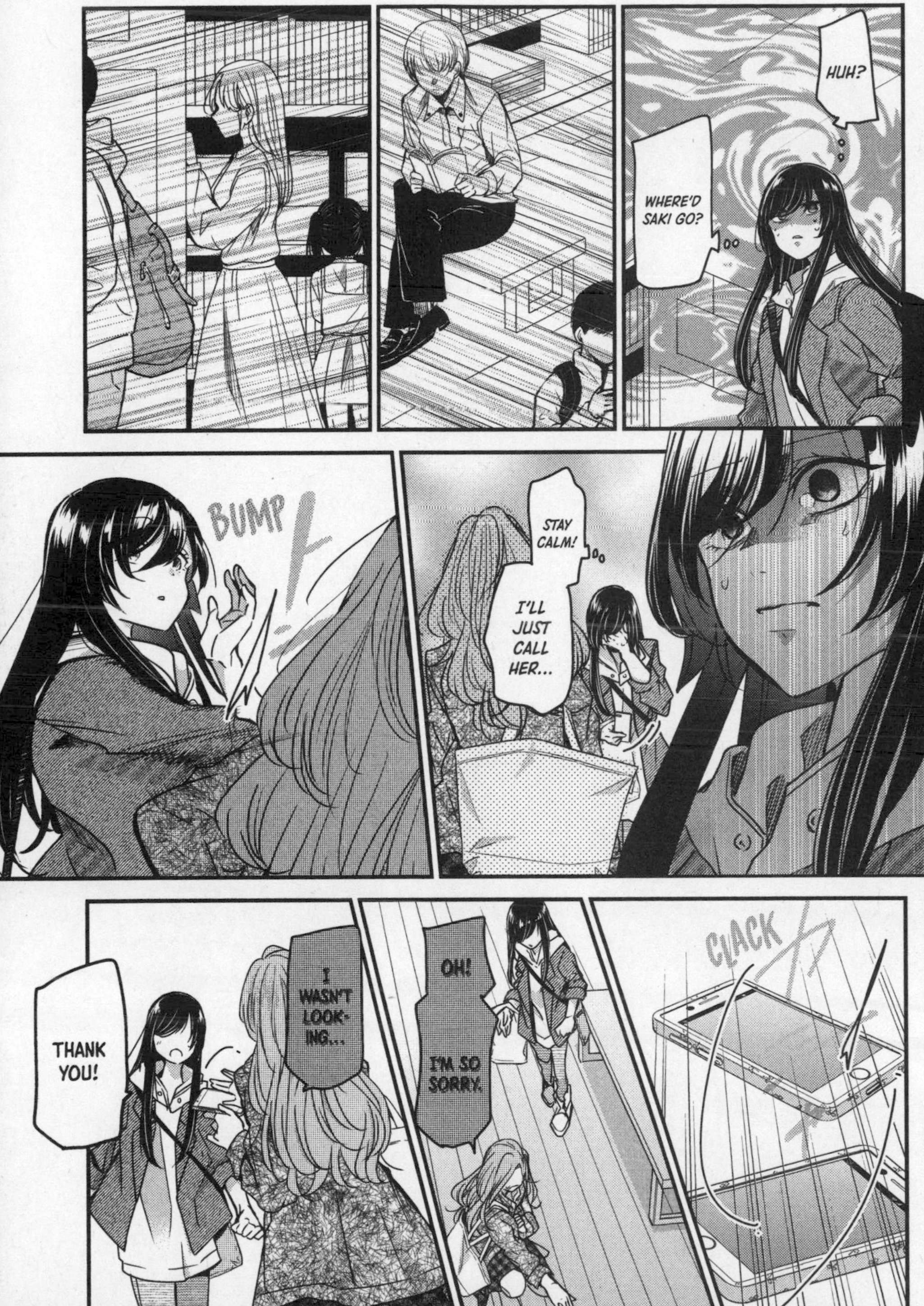
HUH?
WHERE'D SAKI GO?
STAY CALM!
I'LL JUST CALL HER...
BUMP
CLACK
OH!
I'M SO SORRY.
I WASN'T LOOK-ING...
THANK YOU!

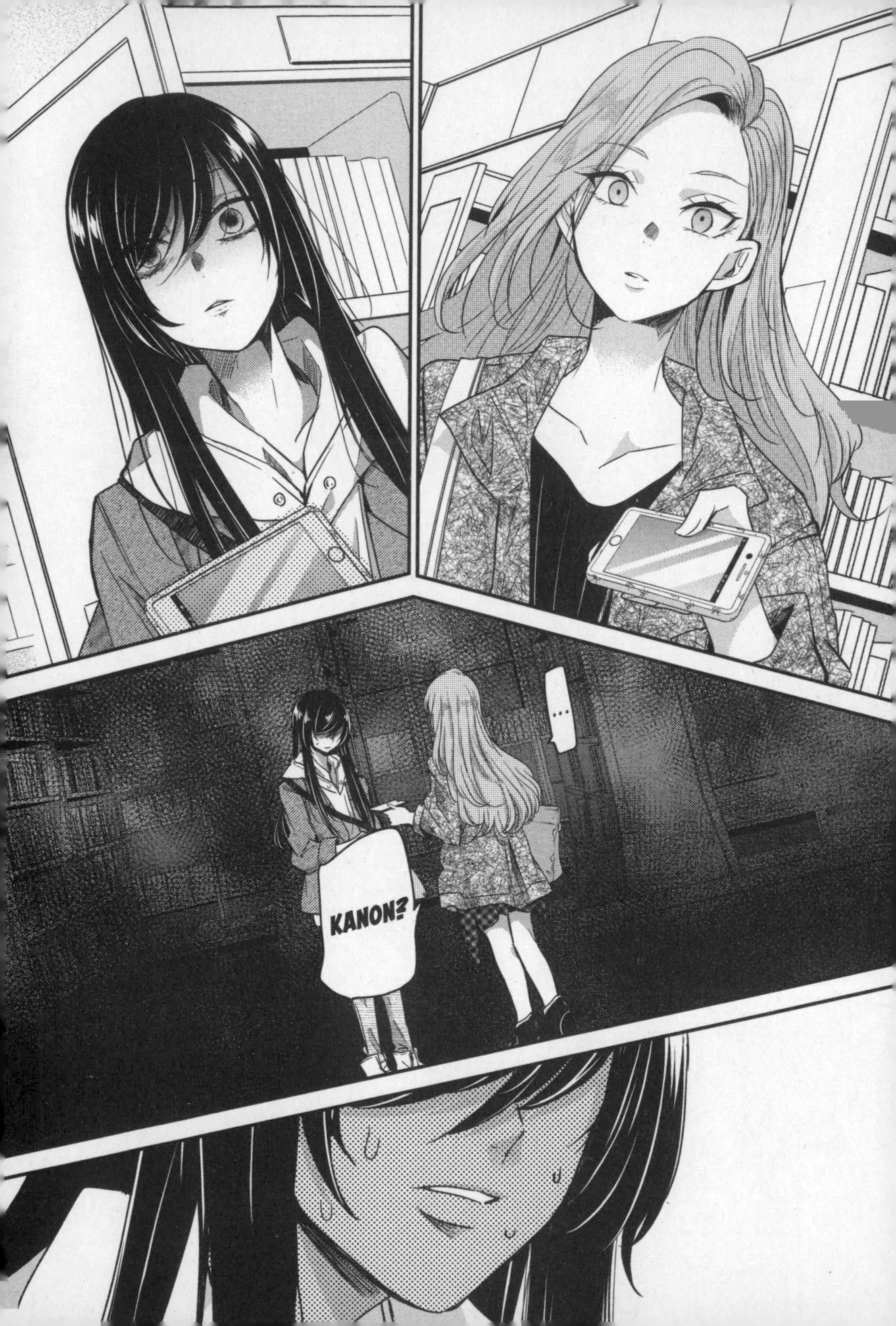
...
KANON?

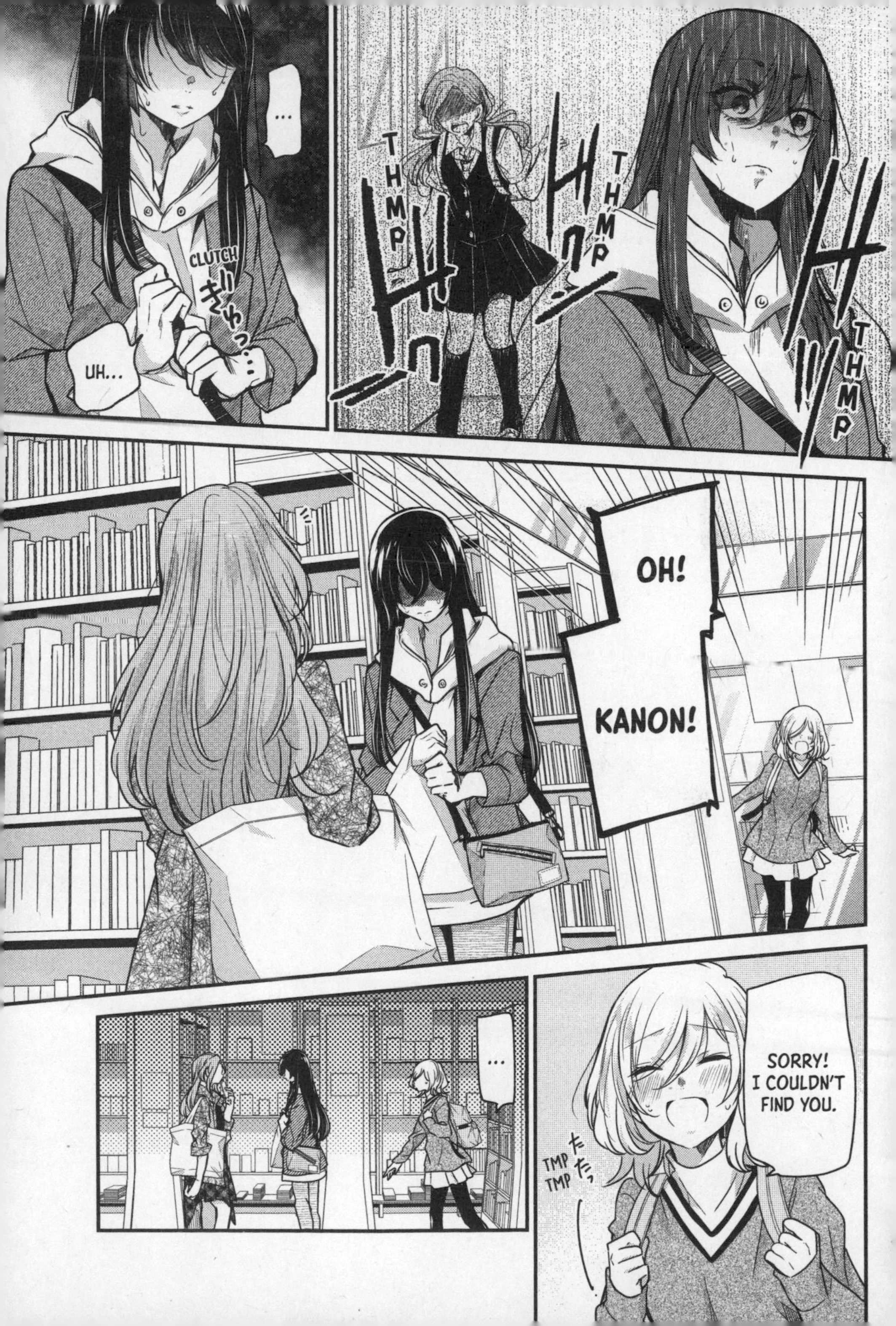
THMP
THMP
THMP
...
CLUTCH
UH...
OH!
KANON!
SORRY! I COULDN'T FIND YOU.
TMP TMP
たたっ
...

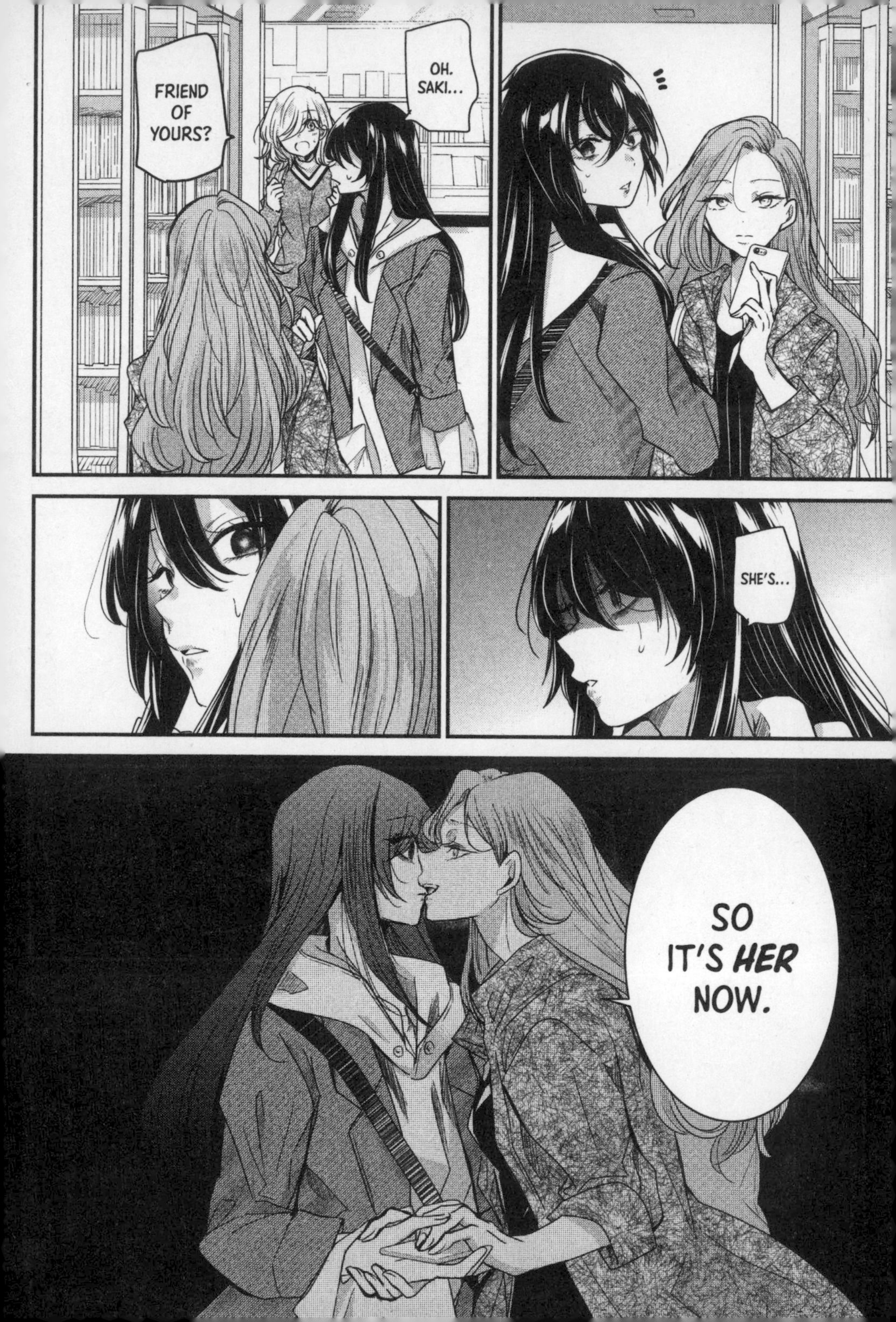
OH. SAKI...
FRIEND OF YOURS?
SHE'S...
SO IT'S **HER** NOW.

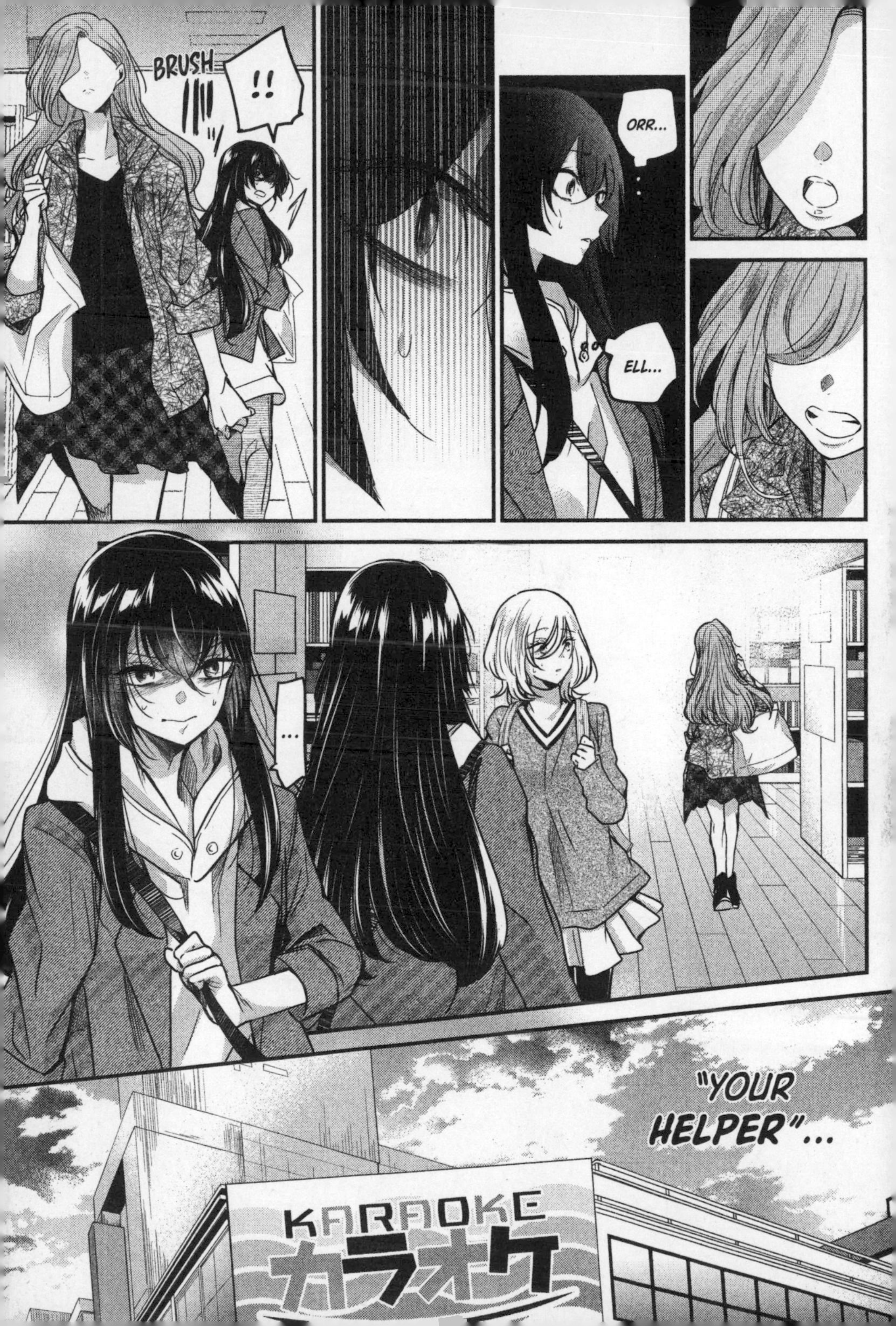
ORR...
ELL...
!!
BRUSH
...
"YOUR HELPER"...
KARAOKE
カラオケ

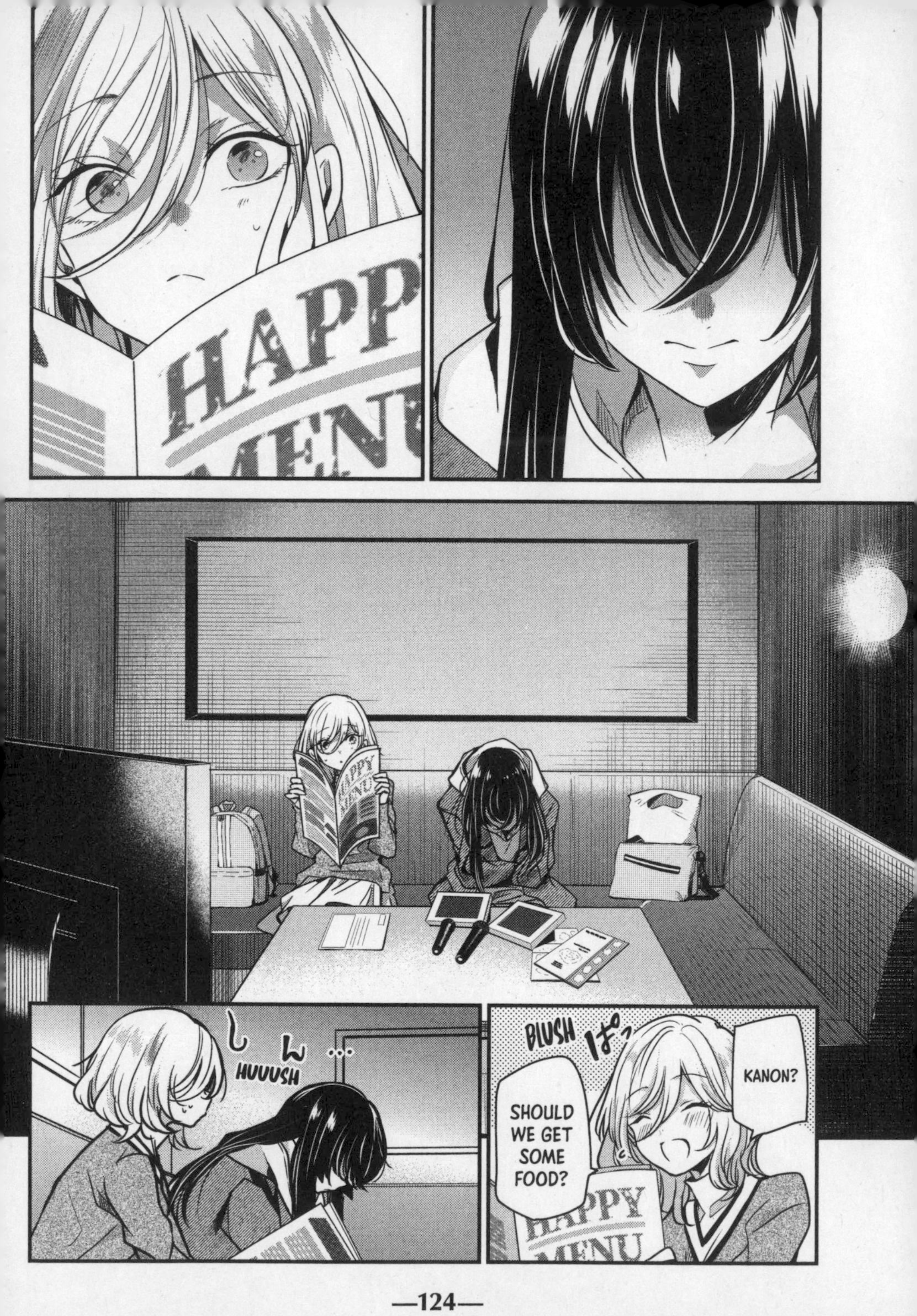
KANON?
BLUSH
ぽっ
SHOULD WE GET SOME FOOD?
HAPPY MENU
しん…
HUUUSH

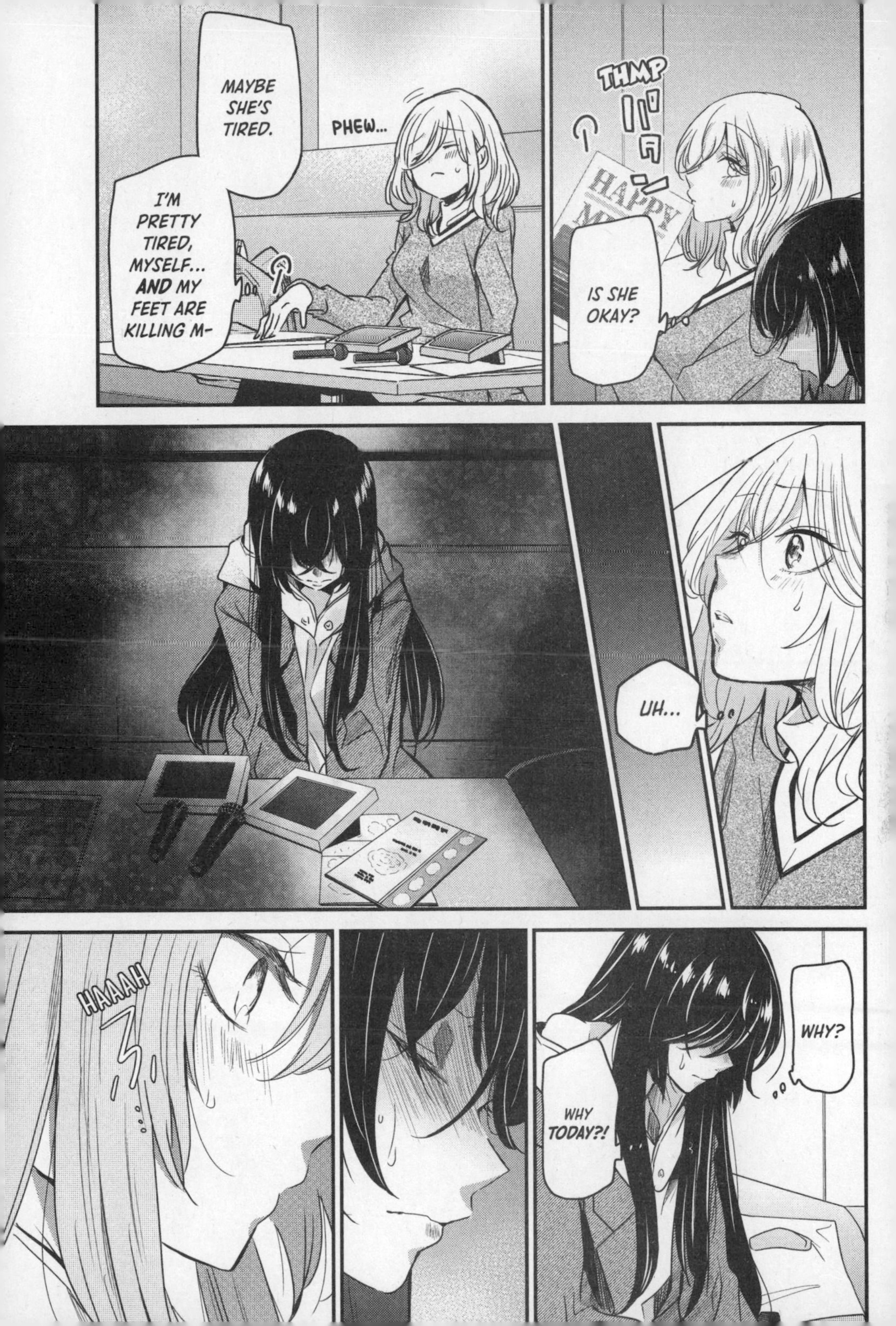
THMP
IS SHE OKAY?
PHEW...
MAYBE SHE'S TIRED.
I'M PRETTY TIRED, MYSELF... AND MY FEET ARE KILLING M-
UH...
WHY?
WHY TODAY?!
HAAAH

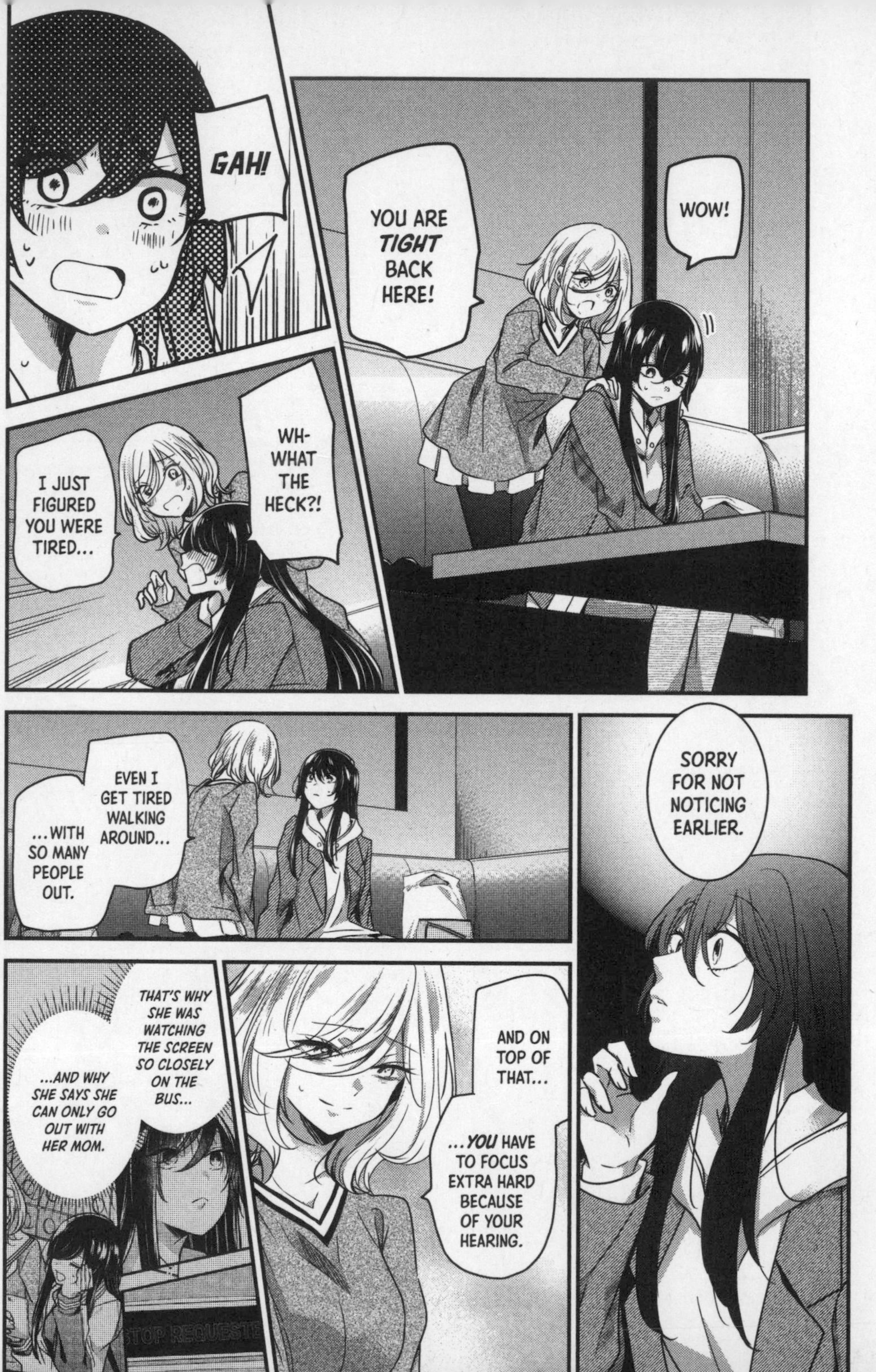
WOW!
YOU ARE TIGHT BACK HERE!
GAH!
WH- WHAT THE HECK?!
I JUST FIGURED YOU WERE TIRED...
SORRY FOR NOT NOTICING EARLIER.
EVEN I GET TIRED WALKING AROUND...
...WITH SO MANY PEOPLE OUT.
AND ON TOP OF THAT...
...YOU HAVE TO FOCUS EXTRA HARD BECAUSE OF YOUR HEARING.
THAT'S WHY SHE WAS WATCHING THE SCREEN SO CLOSELY ON THE BUS...
...AND WHY SHE SAYS SHE CAN ONLY GO OUT WITH HER MOM.
STOP REQUESTE

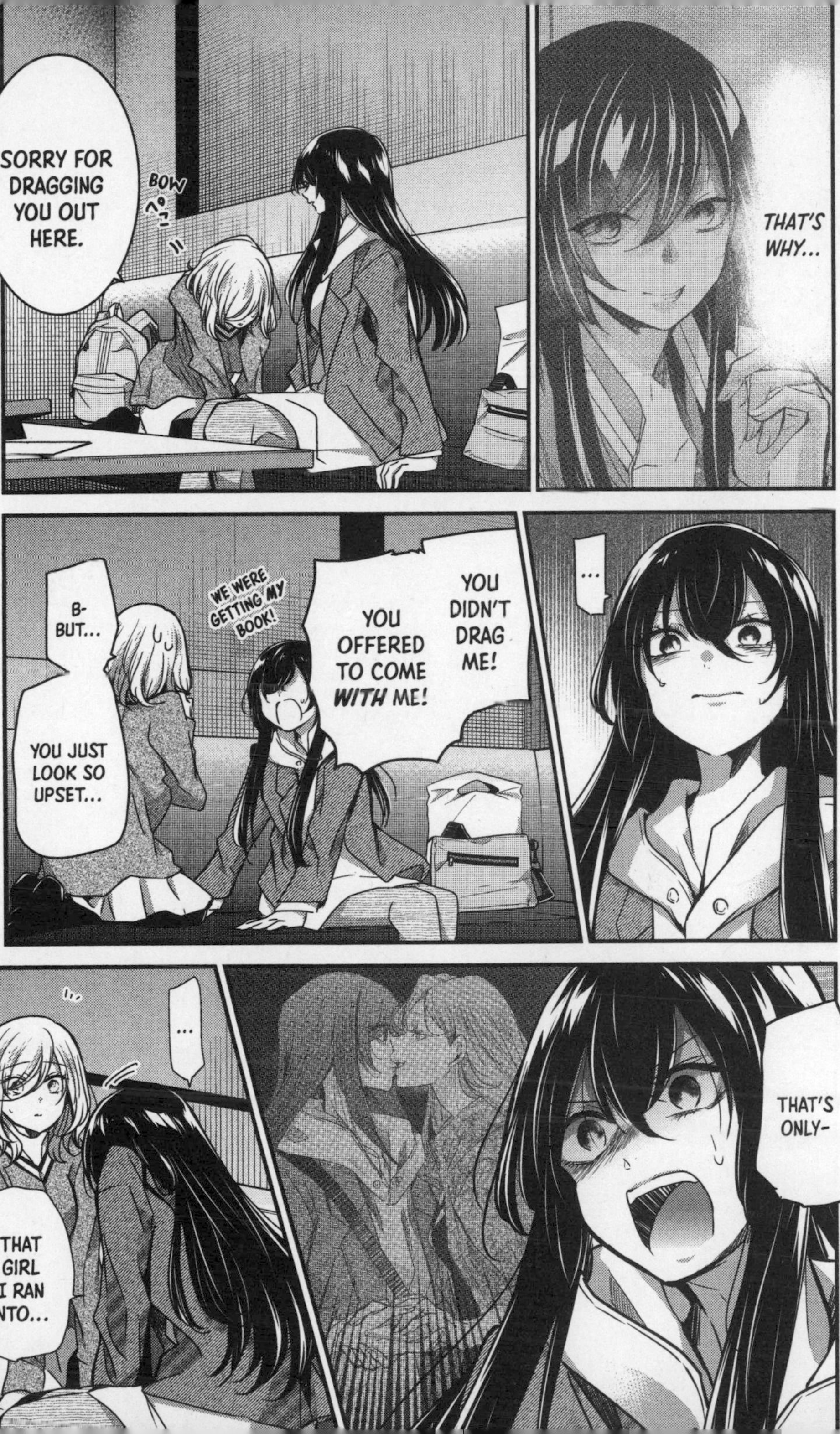
THAT'S WHY...
SORRY FOR DRAGGING YOU OUT HERE.
BOW
...
YOU DIDN'T DRAG ME!
YOU OFFERED TO COME WITH ME!
WE WERE GETTING MY BOOK!
B-BUT...
YOU JUST LOOK SO UPSET...
THAT'S ONLY-
...
THAT GIRL I RAN INTO...

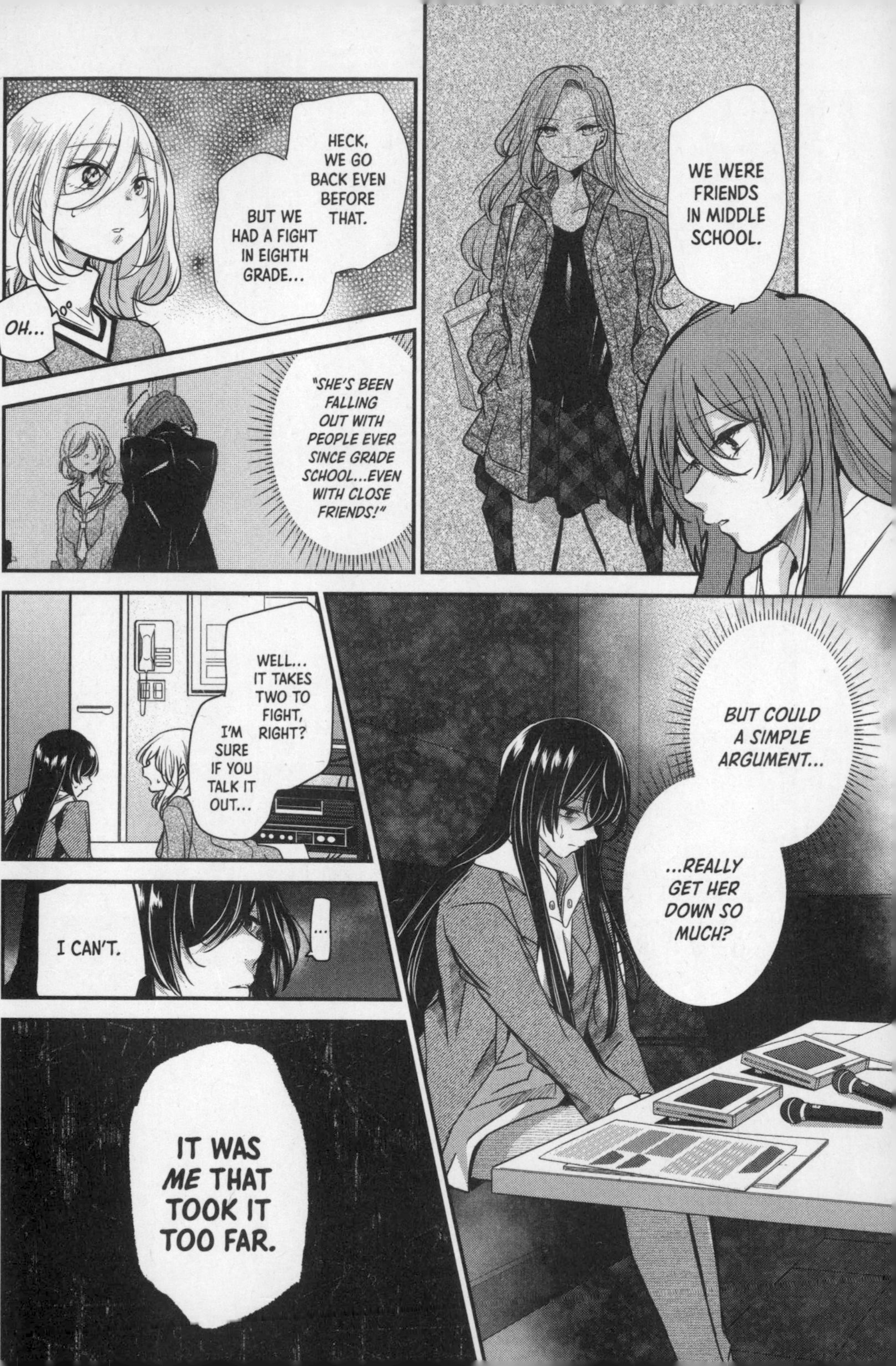
WE WERE FRIENDS IN MIDDLE SCHOOL.
HECK, WE GO BACK EVEN BEFORE THAT.
BUT WE HAD A FIGHT IN EIGHTH GRADE...
OH...
"SHE'S BEEN FALLING OUT WITH PEOPLE EVER SINCE GRADE SCHOOL...EVEN WITH CLOSE FRIENDS!"
BUT COULD A SIMPLE ARGUMENT...
...REALLY GET HER DOWN SO MUCH?
WELL... IT TAKES TWO TO FIGHT, RIGHT?
I'M SURE IF YOU TALK IT OUT...
...
I CAN'T.
IT WAS *ME* THAT TOOK IT TOO FAR.

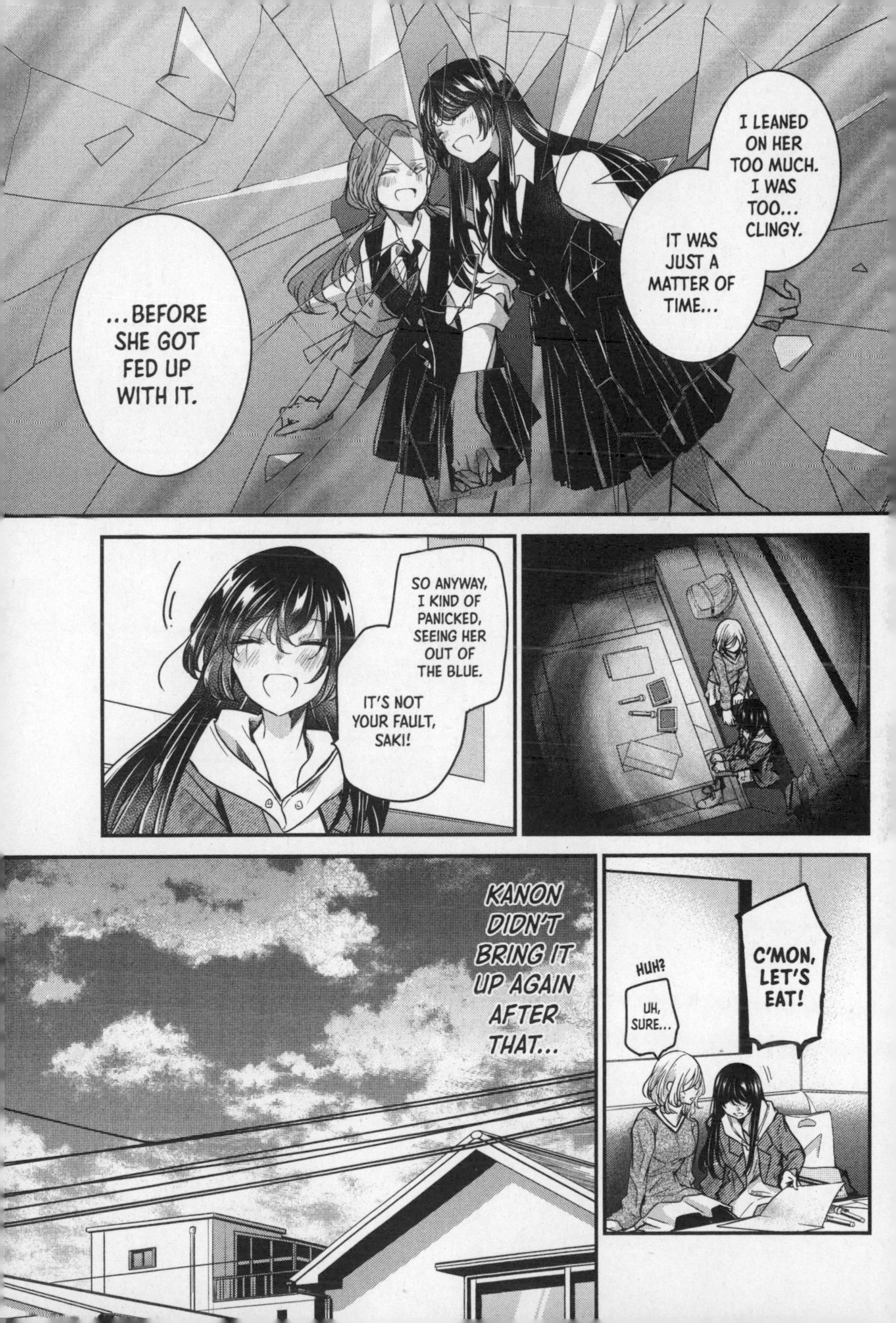
I LEANED ON HER TOO MUCH. I WAS TOO... CLINGY.
IT WAS JUST A MATTER OF TIME...
...BEFORE SHE GOT FED UP WITH IT.
SO ANYWAY, I KIND OF PANICKED, SEEING HER OUT OF THE BLUE.
IT'S NOT YOUR FAULT, SAKI!
C'MON, LET'S EAT!
HUH?
UH, SURE...
KANON DIDN'T BRING IT UP AGAIN AFTER THAT...

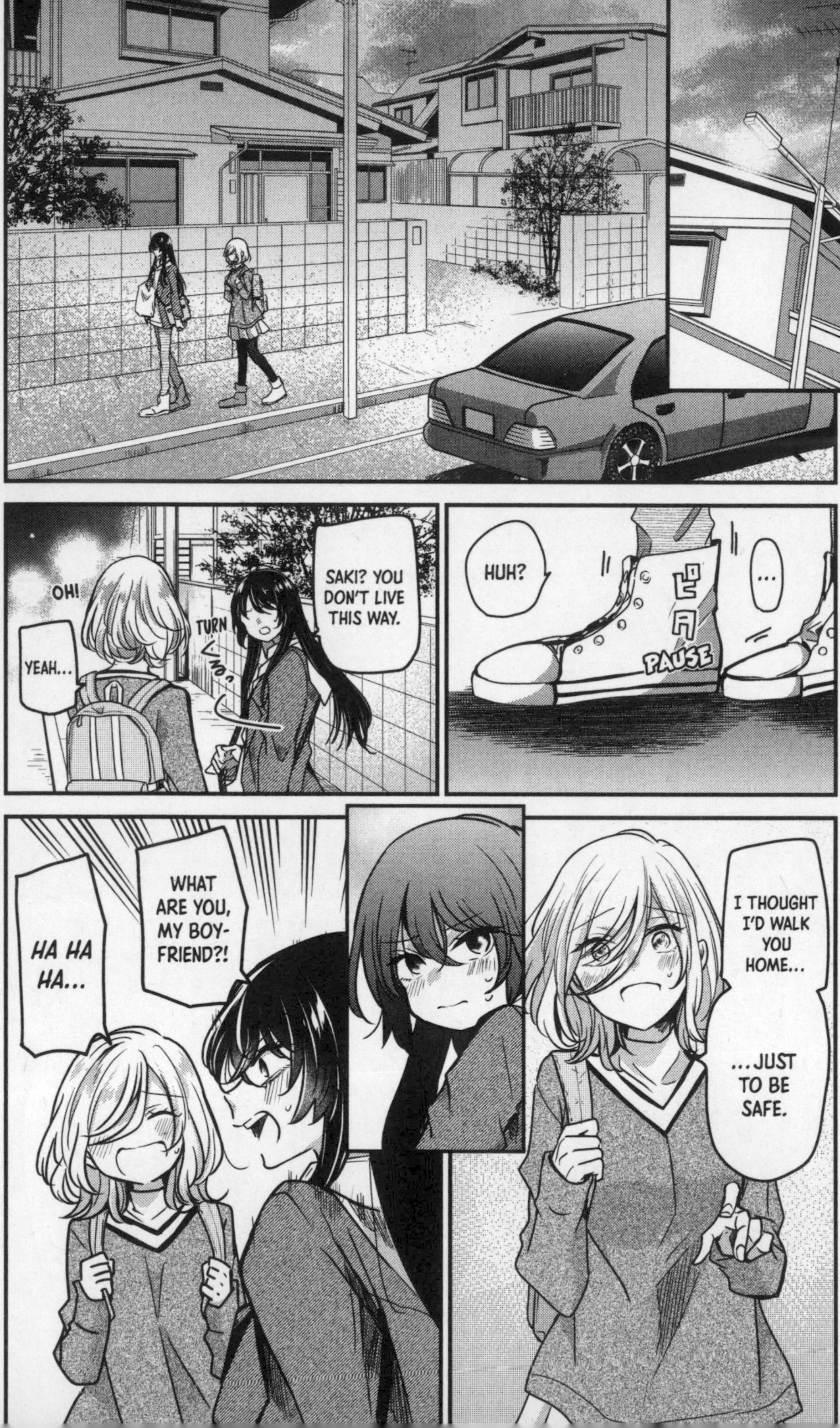
...
HUH?
PAUSE
SAKI? YOU DON'T LIVE THIS WAY.
TURN
OH!
YEAH...
I THOUGHT I'D WALK YOU HOME...
...JUST TO BE SAFE.
WHAT ARE YOU, MY BOY-FRIEND?!
HA HA HA...

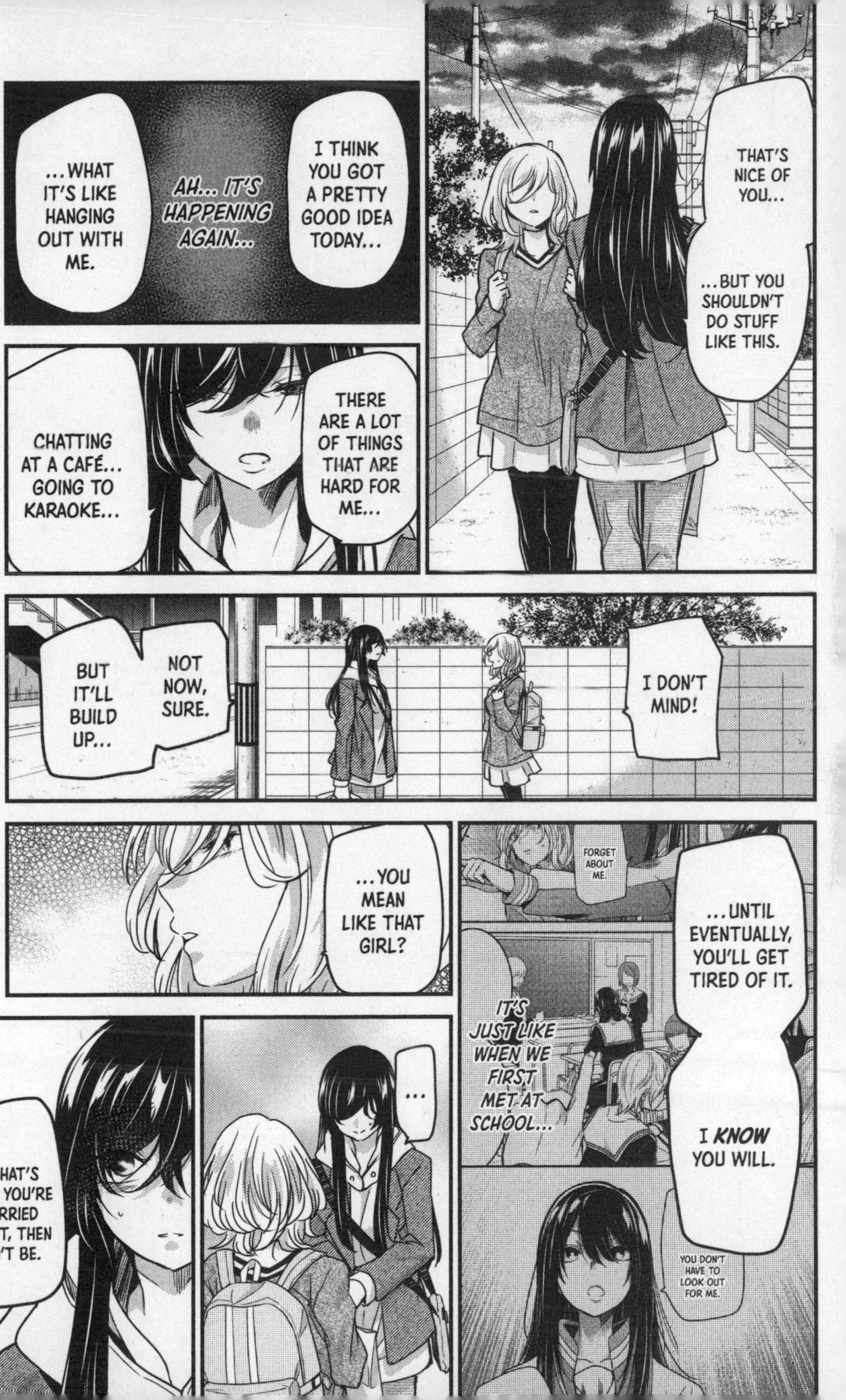
THAT'S NICE OF YOU...
...BUT YOU SHOULDN'T DO STUFF LIKE THIS.
I THINK YOU GOT A PRETTY GOOD IDEA TODAY...
AH... IT'S HAPPENING AGAIN...
...WHAT IT'S LIKE HANGING OUT WITH ME.
THERE ARE A LOT OF THINGS THAT ARE HARD FOR ME...
CHATTING AT A CAFÉ... GOING TO KARAOKE...
I DON'T MIND!
NOT NOW, SURE.
BUT IT'LL BUILD UP...
FORGET ABOUT ME.
...UNTIL EVENTUALLY, YOU'LL GET TIRED OF IT.
IT'S JUST LIKE WHEN WE FIRST MET AT SCHOOL...
I *KNOW* YOU WILL.
YOU DON'T HAVE TO LOOK OUT FOR ME.
...YOU MEAN LIKE THAT GIRL?
...
IF THAT'S WHAT YOU'RE WORRIED ABOUT, THEN DON'T BE.

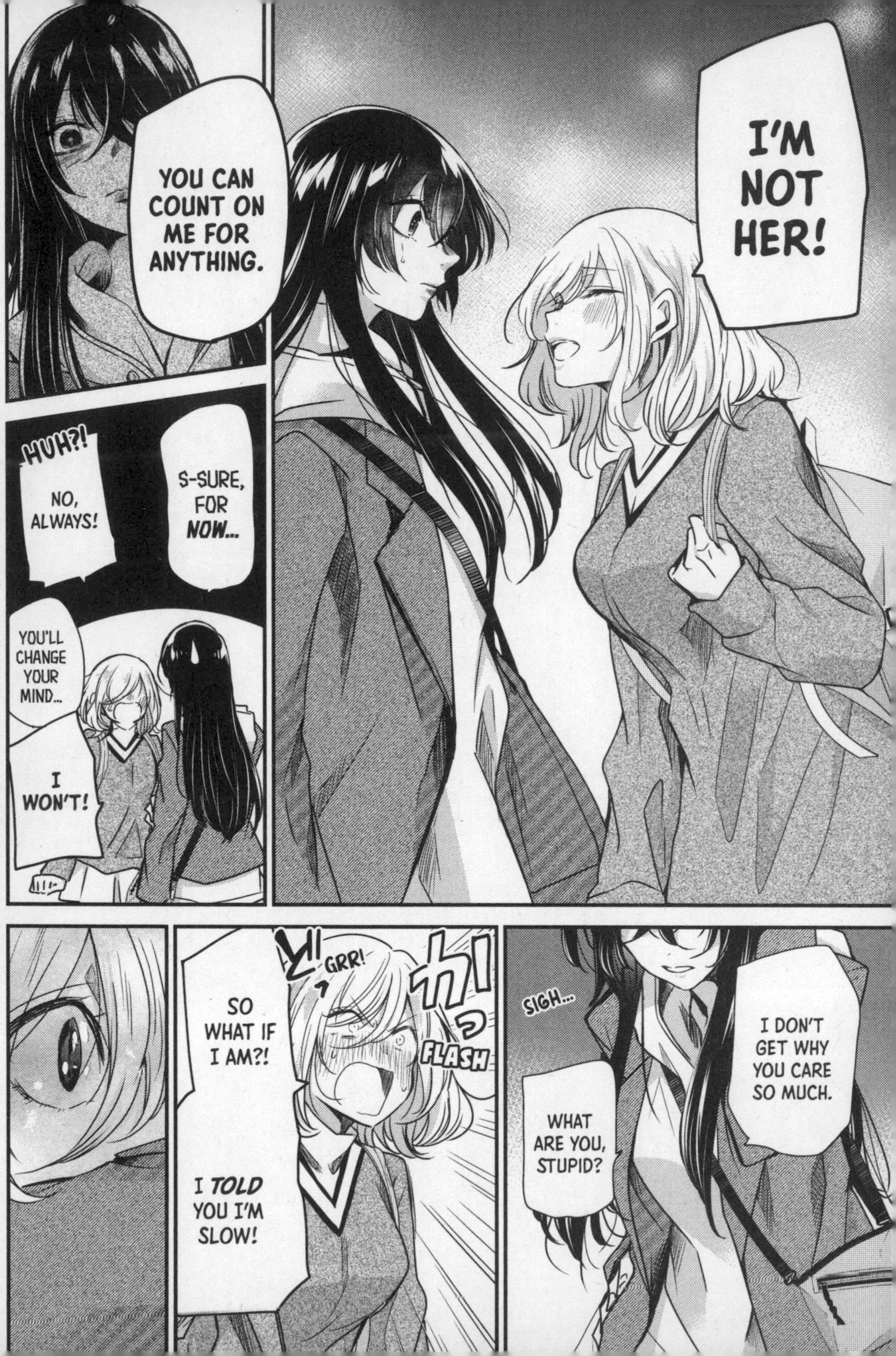
I'M NOT HER!
YOU CAN COUNT ON ME FOR ANYTHING.
S-SURE, FOR NOW...
HUH?!
NO, ALWAYS!
YOU'LL CHANGE YOUR MIND...
I WON'T!
SIGH...
I DON'T GET WHY YOU CARE SO MUCH.
WHAT ARE YOU, STUPID?
GRR!
カッ
FLASH
SO WHAT IF I AM?!
I TOLD YOU I'M SLOW!

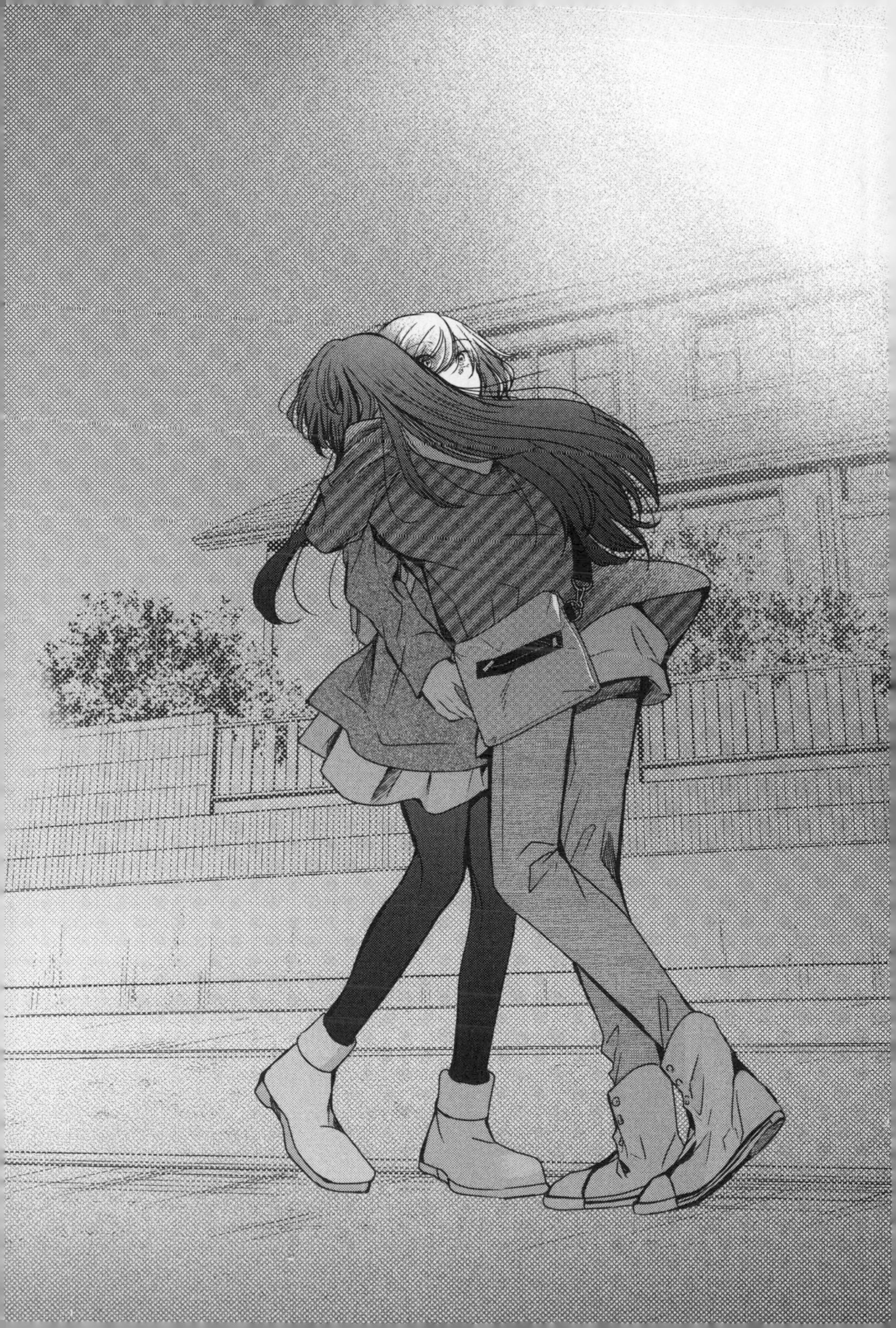

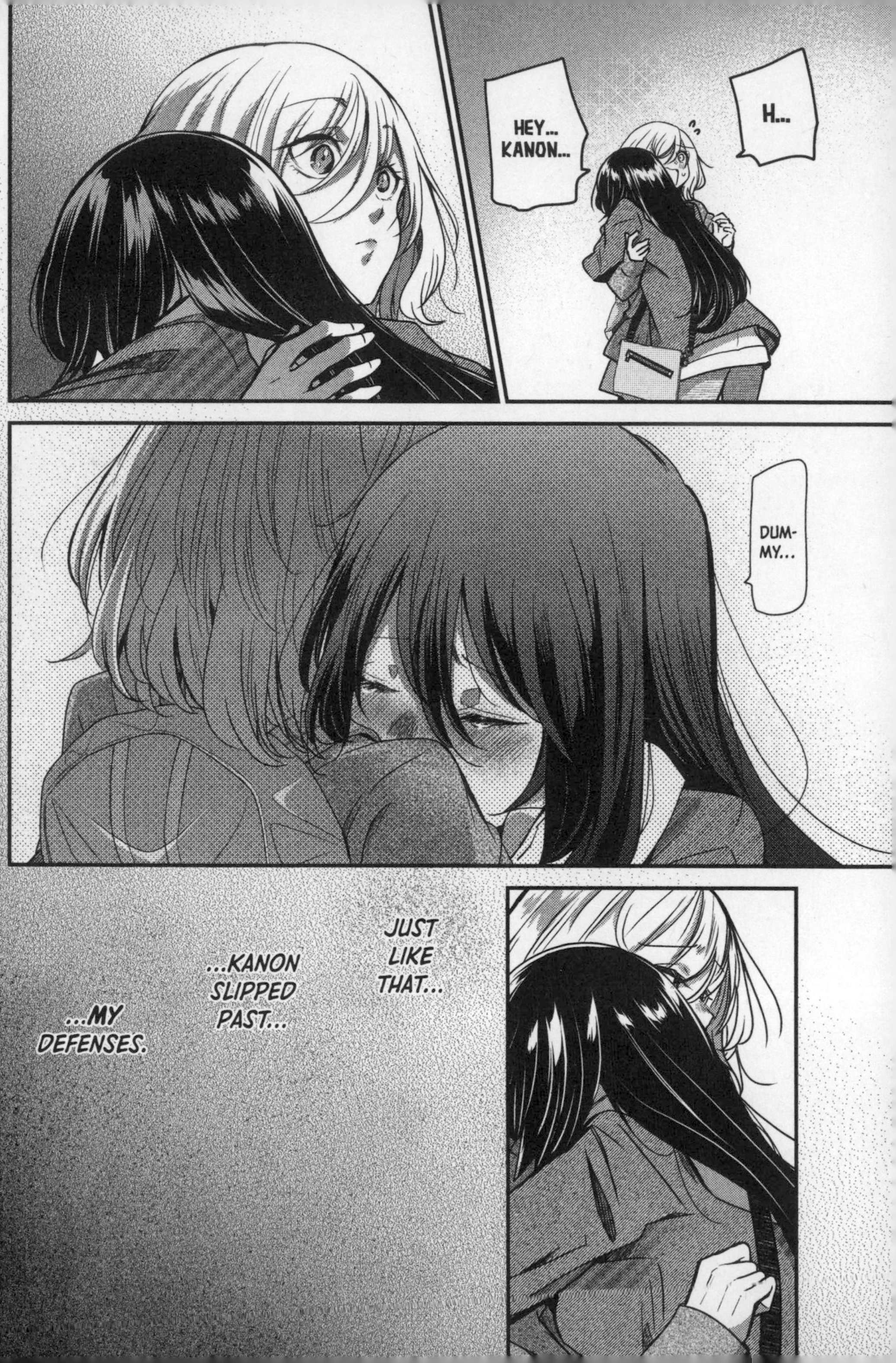
H...
HEY... KANON...
DUM-MY...
JUST LIKE THAT...
...KANON SLIPPED PAST...
...MY DEFENSES.

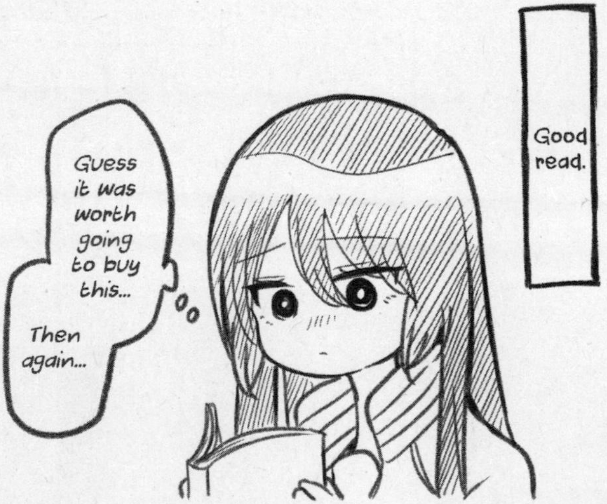
Good read.
Guess it was worth going to buy this...
Then again...

the moon on a rainy night

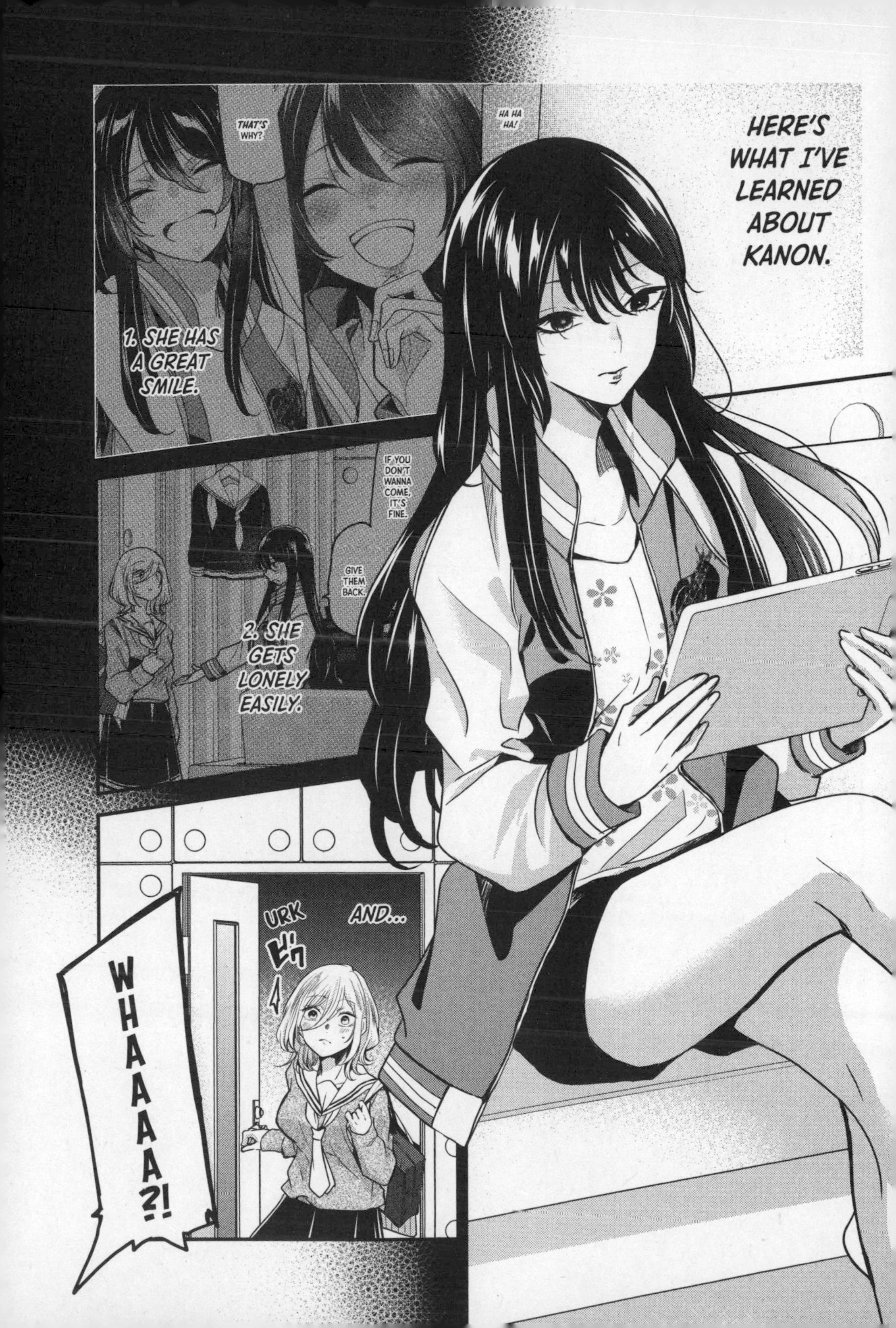
HERE'S WHAT I'VE LEARNED ABOUT KANON.
HA HA HA!
THAT'S WHY?
1. SHE HAS A GREAT SMILE.
IF YOU DON'T WANNA COME, IT'S FINE.
GIVE THEM BACK.
2. SHE GETS LONELY EASILY.
AND...
URK
ビク
WHAAAAA?!

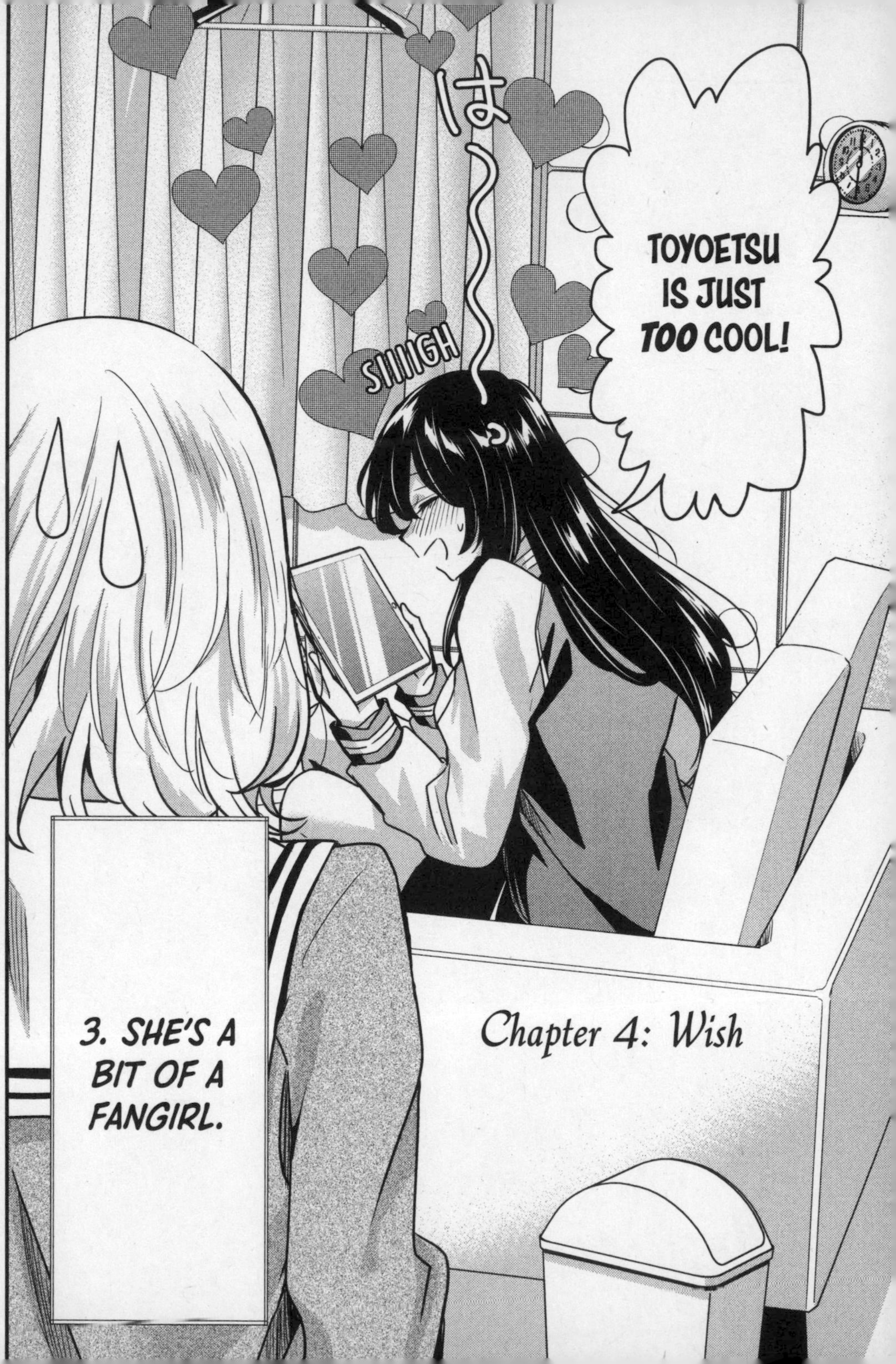
TOYOETSU IS JUST TOO COOL!
は〜
SIIIGH
Chapter 4: Wish
3. SHE'S A BIT OF A FANGIRL.

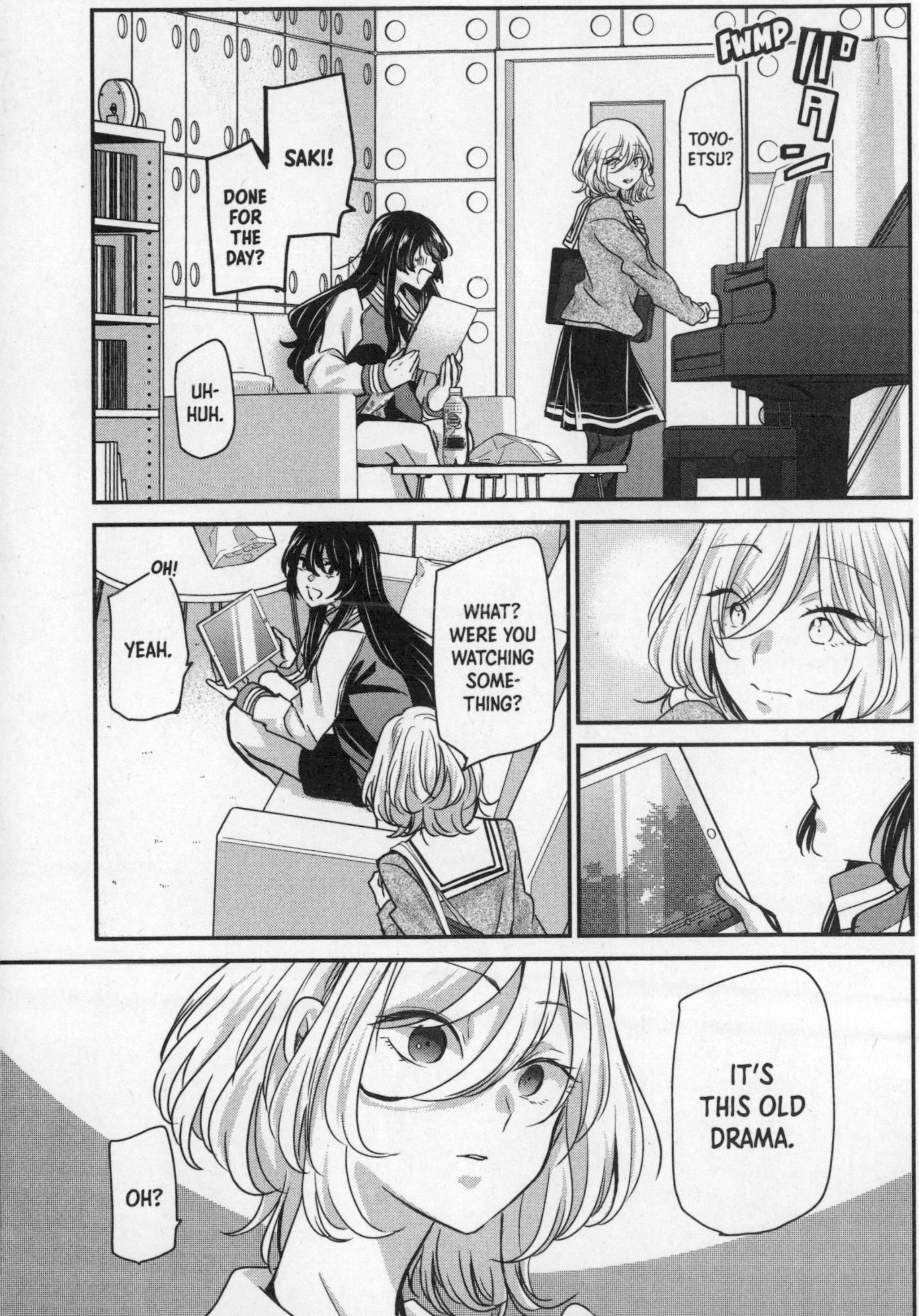
FWMP
TOYO-ETSU?
SAKI! DONE FOR THE DAY?
UH-HUH.
WHAT? WERE YOU WATCHING SOME-THING?
OH! YEAH.
IT'S THIS OLD DRAMA.
OH?

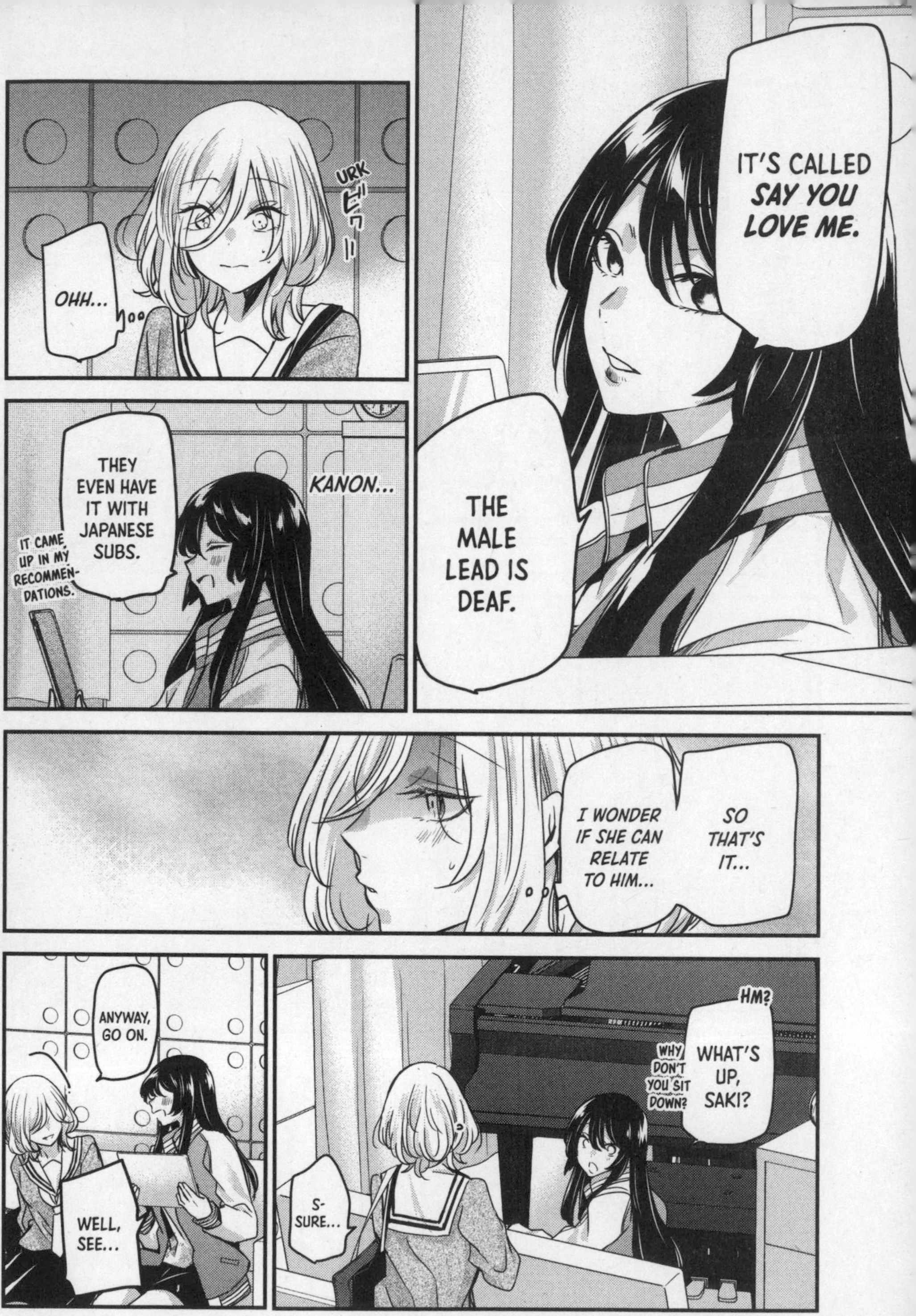
IT'S CALLED SAY YOU LOVE ME.
THE MALE LEAD IS DEAF.
URK
OHH...
KANON...
THEY EVEN HAVE IT WITH JAPANESE SUBS.
IT CAME UP IN MY RECOMMEN-DATIONS.
SO THAT'S IT...
I WONDER IF SHE CAN RELATE TO HIM...
HM?
WHAT'S UP, SAKI?
WHY DON'T YOU SIT DOWN?
S-SURE...
ANYWAY, GO ON.
WELL, SEE...

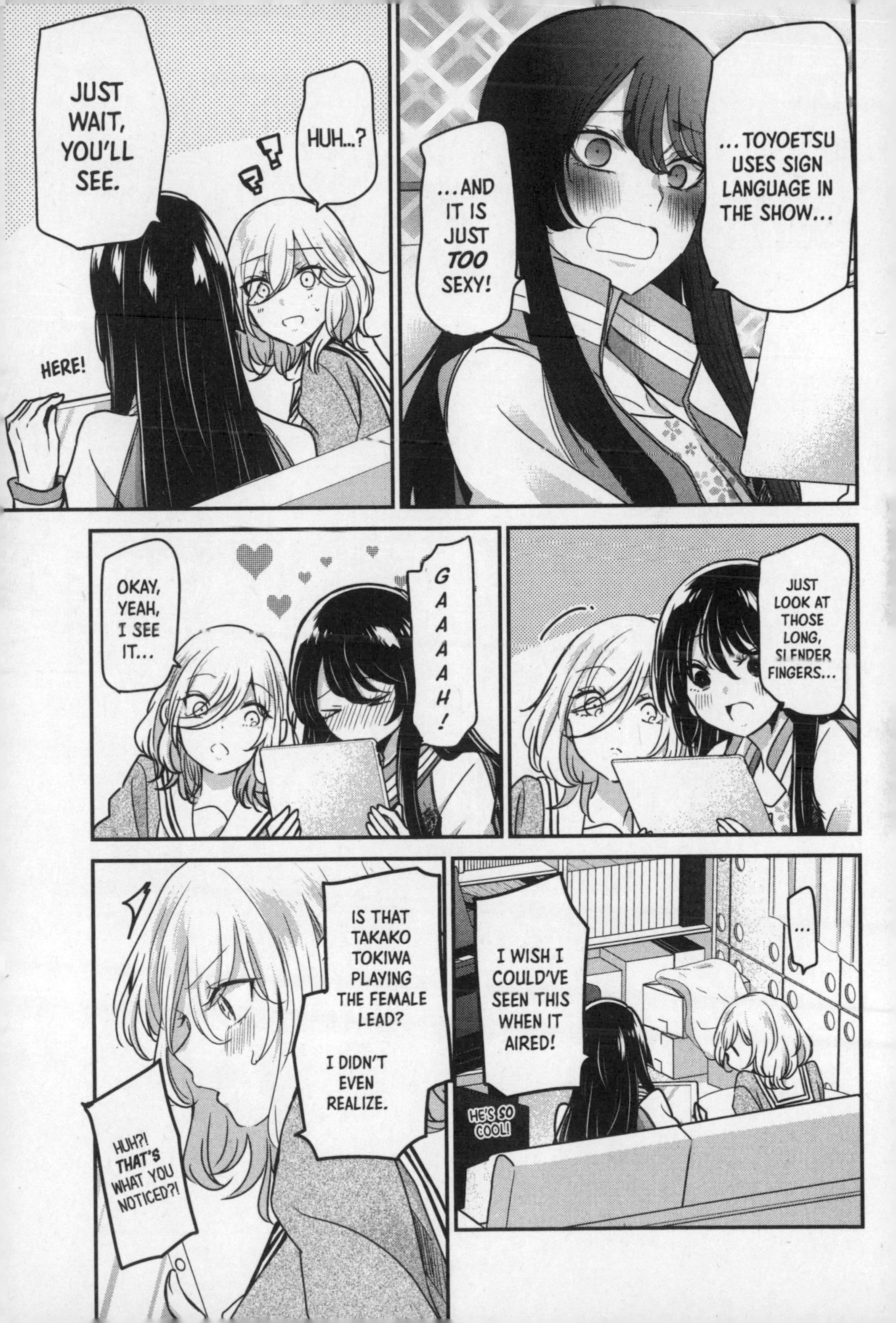
...TOYOETSU USES SIGN LANGUAGE IN THE SHOW...
...AND IT IS JUST *TOO* SEXY!
JUST WAIT, YOU'LL SEE.
HUH...?
HERE!
JUST LOOK AT THOSE LONG, SLENDER FINGERS...
GAAAAAH!
OKAY, YEAH, I SEE IT...
...
I WISH I COULD'VE SEEN THIS WHEN IT AIRED!
HE'S SO COOL!
IS THAT TAKAKO TOKIWA PLAYING THE FEMALE LEAD?
I DIDN'T EVEN REALIZE.
HUH?! THAT'S WHAT YOU NOTICED?!

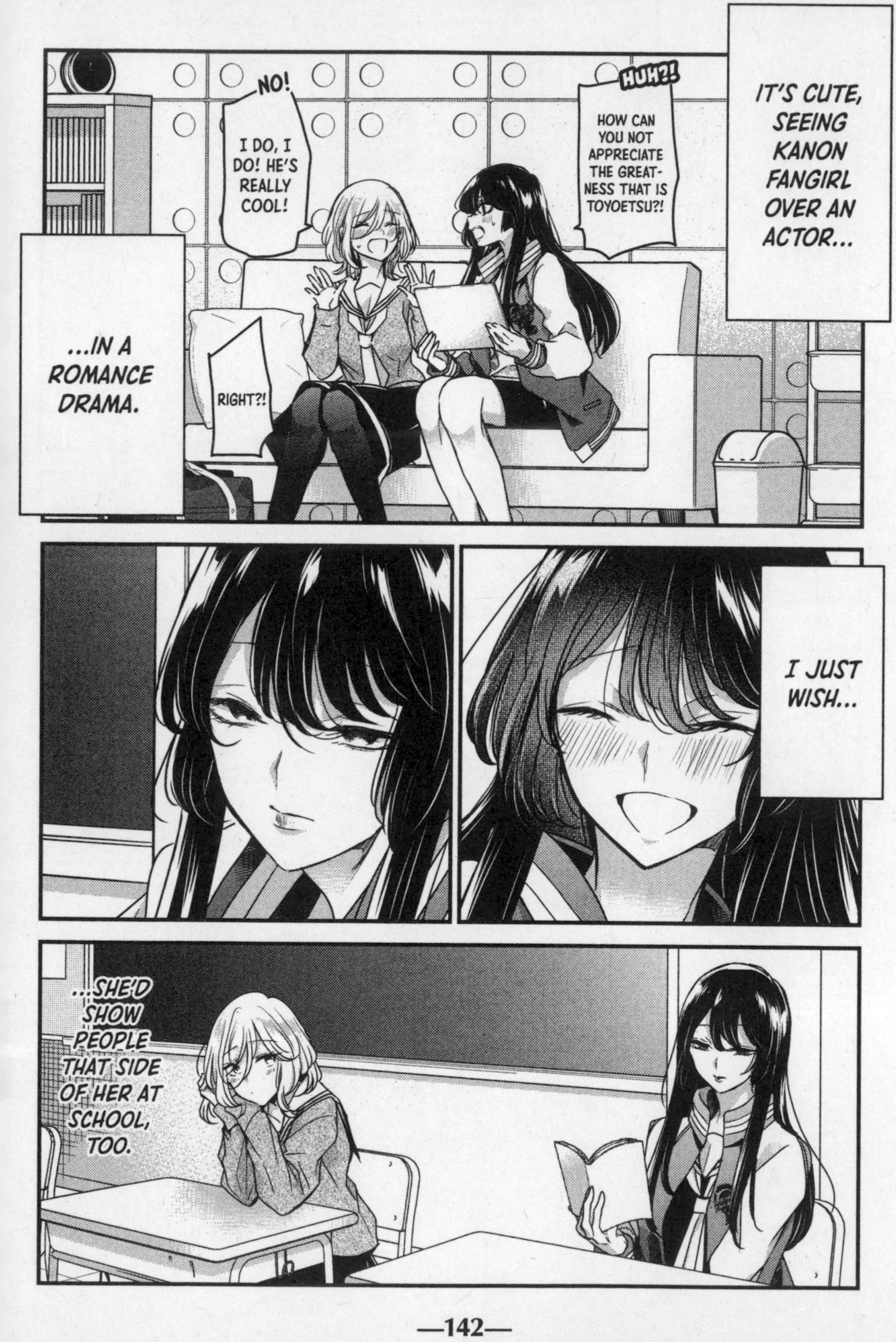
IT'S CUTE, SEEING KANON FANGIRL OVER AN ACTOR...
HUH?!
HOW CAN YOU NOT APPRECIATE THE GREATNESS THAT IS TOYOETSU?!
NO!
I DO, I DO! HE'S REALLY COOL!
RIGHT?!
...IN A ROMANCE DRAMA.
I JUST WISH...
...SHE'D SHOW PEOPLE THAT SIDE OF HER AT SCHOOL, TOO.

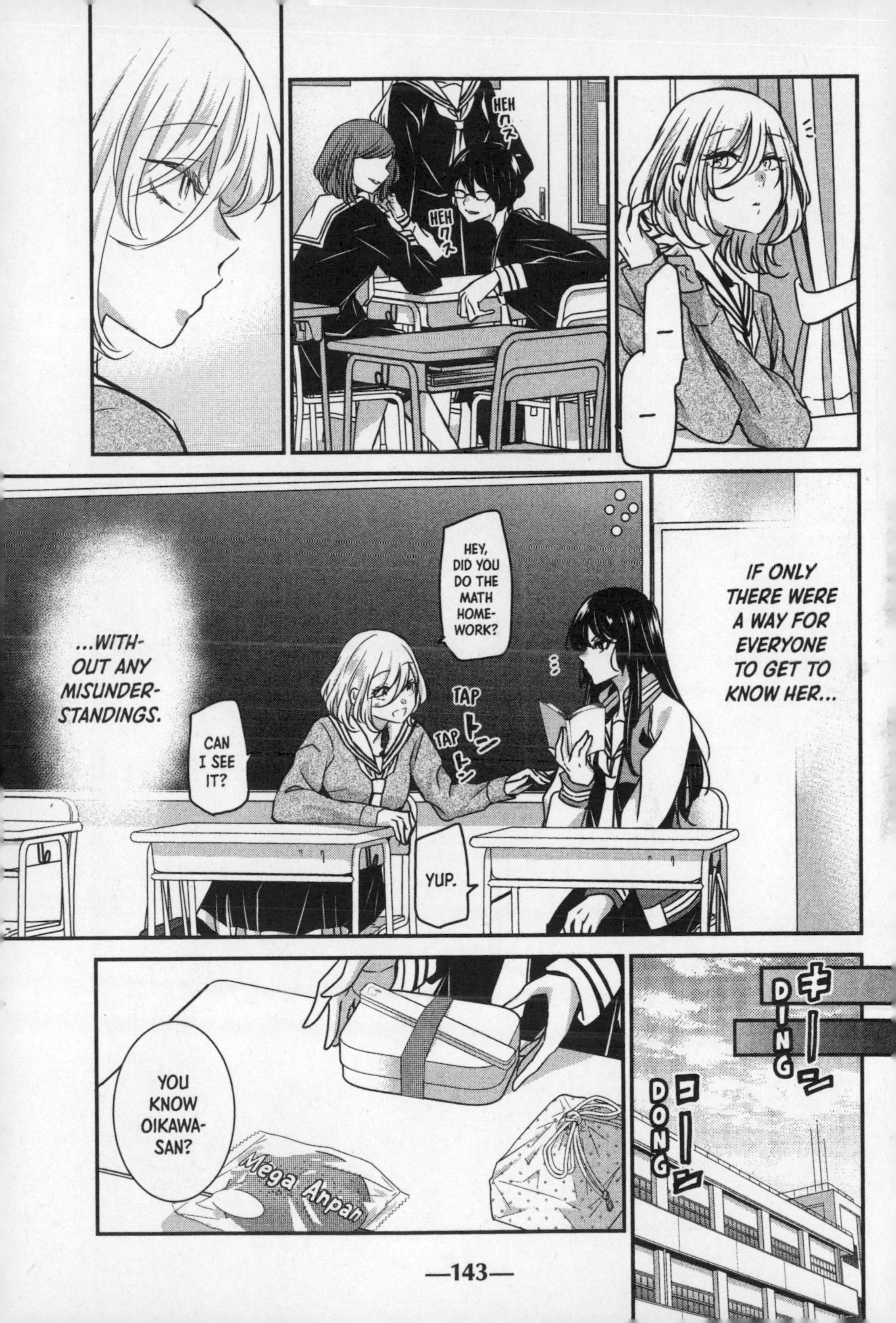
HEH
HEH
IF ONLY THERE WERE A WAY FOR EVERYONE TO GET TO KNOW HER...
HEY, DID YOU DO THE MATH HOME-WORK?
TAP
TAP
CAN I SEE IT?
YUP.
...WITH-OUT ANY MISUNDER-STANDINGS.
DING
DONG
YOU KNOW OIKAWA-SAN?
Mega Anpan

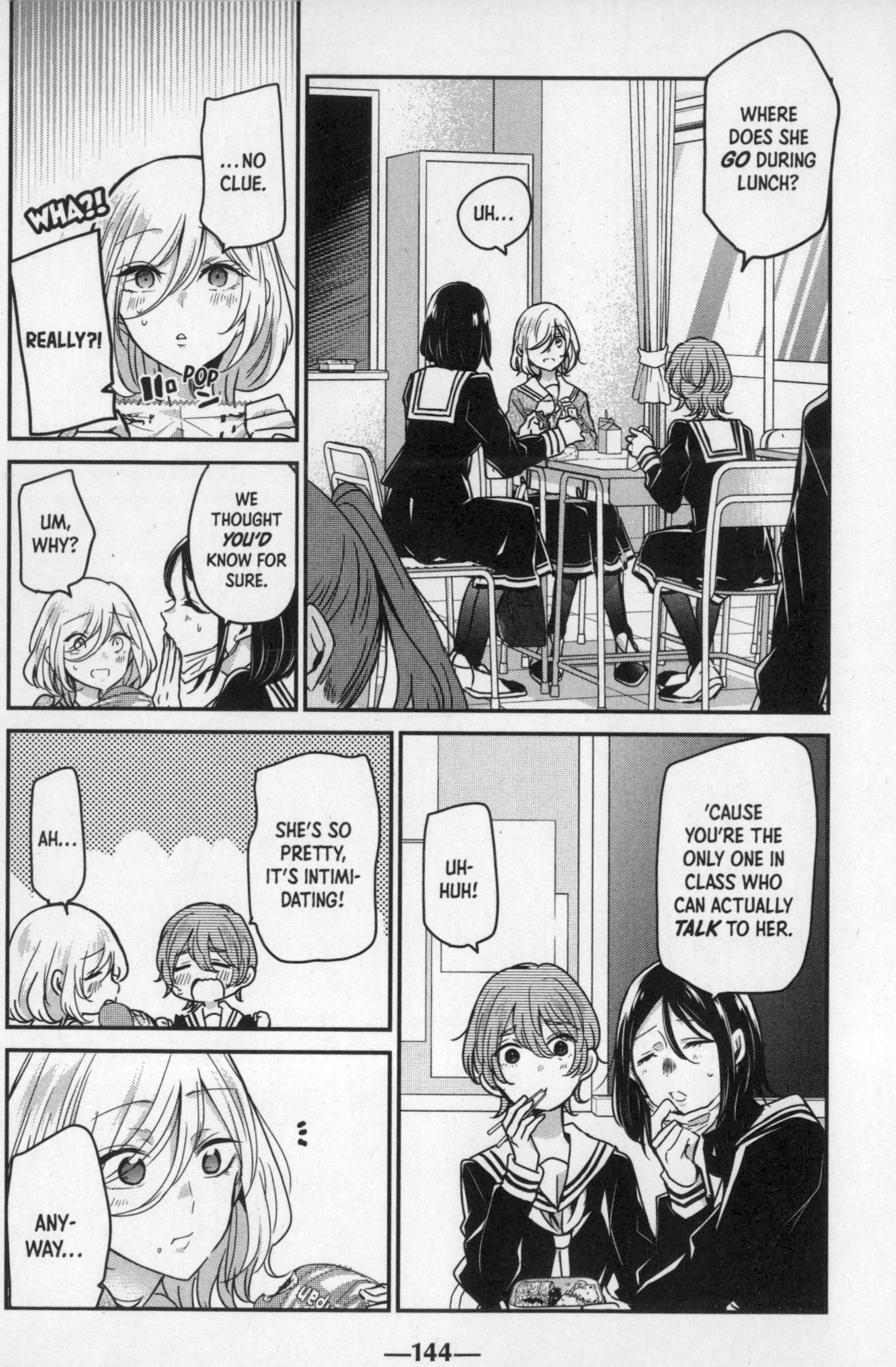
WHERE DOES SHE GO DURING LUNCH?
UH...
...NO CLUE.
WHA?!
REALLY?!
POP
WE THOUGHT YOU'D KNOW FOR SURE.
UM, WHY?
'CAUSE YOU'RE THE ONLY ONE IN CLASS WHO CAN ACTUALLY TALK TO HER.
UH-HUH!
SHE'S SO PRETTY, IT'S INTIMI-DATING!
AH...
...
ANY-WAY...

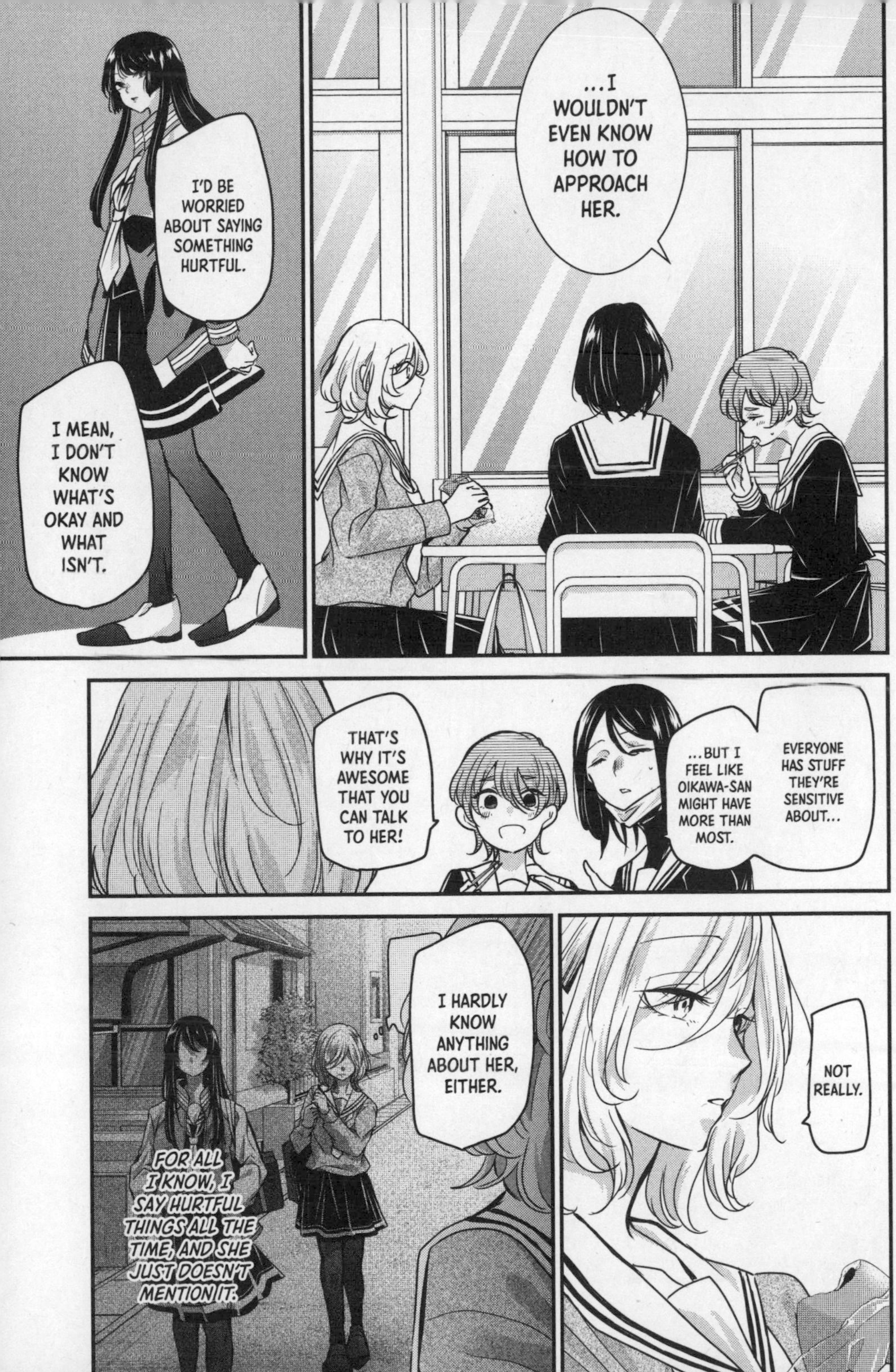
...I WOULDN'T EVEN KNOW HOW TO APPROACH HER.
I'D BE WORRIED ABOUT SAYING SOMETHING HURTFUL.
I MEAN, I DON'T KNOW WHAT'S OKAY AND WHAT ISN'T.
EVERYONE HAS STUFF THEY'RE SENSITIVE ABOUT...
...BUT I FEEL LIKE OIKAWA-SAN MIGHT HAVE MORE THAN MOST.
THAT'S WHY IT'S AWESOME THAT YOU CAN TALK TO HER!
NOT REALLY.
I HARDLY KNOW ANYTHING ABOUT HER, EITHER.
FOR ALL I KNOW, I SAY HURTFUL THINGS ALL THE TIME, AND SHE JUST DOESN'T MENTION IT.

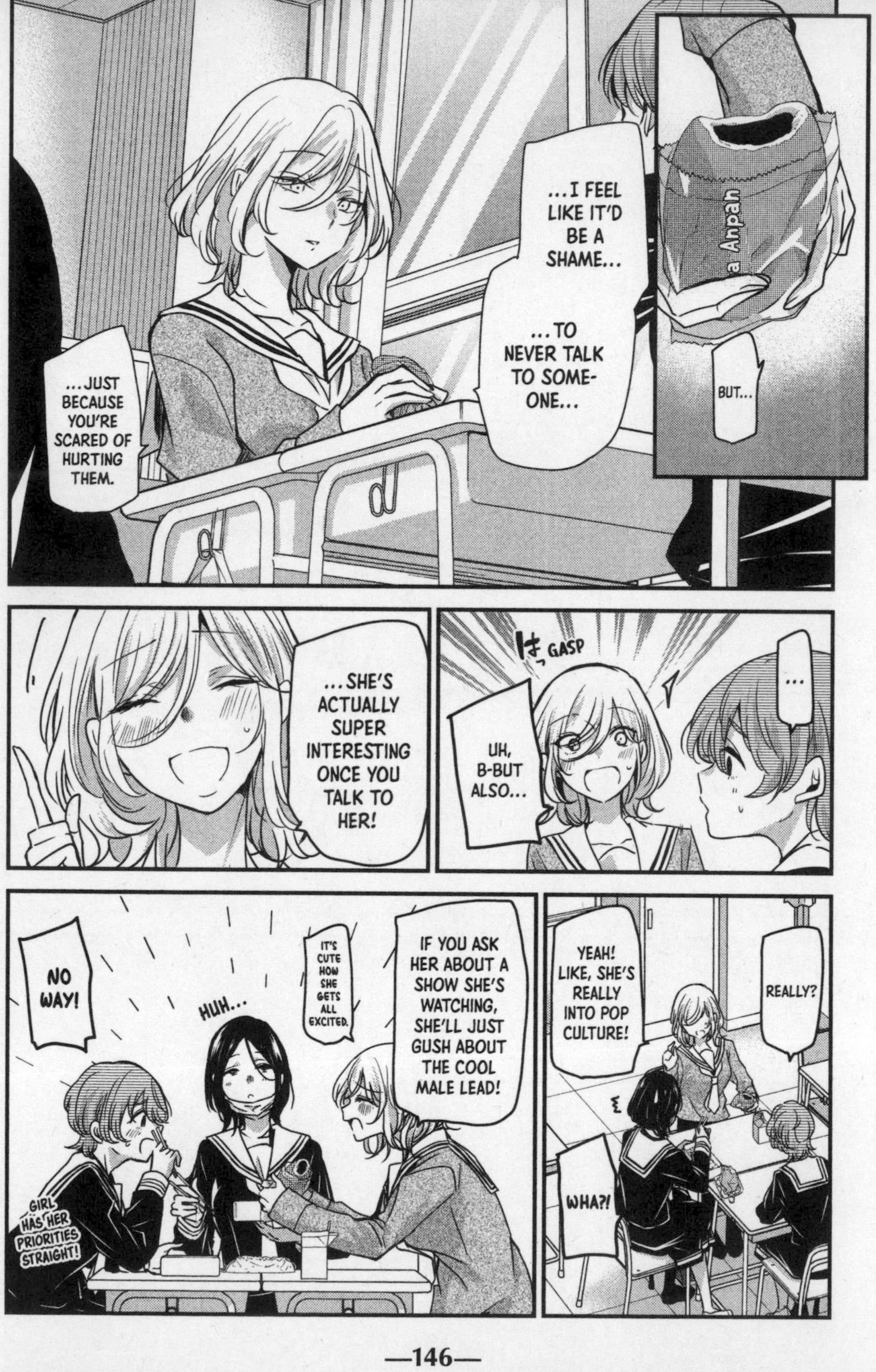
a Anpah
BUT...
...I FEEL LIKE IT'D BE A SHAME...
...TO NEVER TALK TO SOME-ONE...
...JUST BECAUSE YOU'RE SCARED OF HURTING THEM.
は GASP
...
UH, B-BUT ALSO...
...SHE'S ACTUALLY SUPER INTERESTING ONCE YOU TALK TO HER!
REALLY?
YEAH! LIKE, SHE'S REALLY INTO POP CULTURE!
WHA?!
IF YOU ASK HER ABOUT A SHOW SHE'S WATCHING, SHE'LL JUST GUSH ABOUT THE COOL MALE LEAD!
IT'S CUTE HOW SHE GETS ALL EXCITED.
HUH...
NO WAY!
GIRL HAS HER PRIORITIES STRAIGHT!

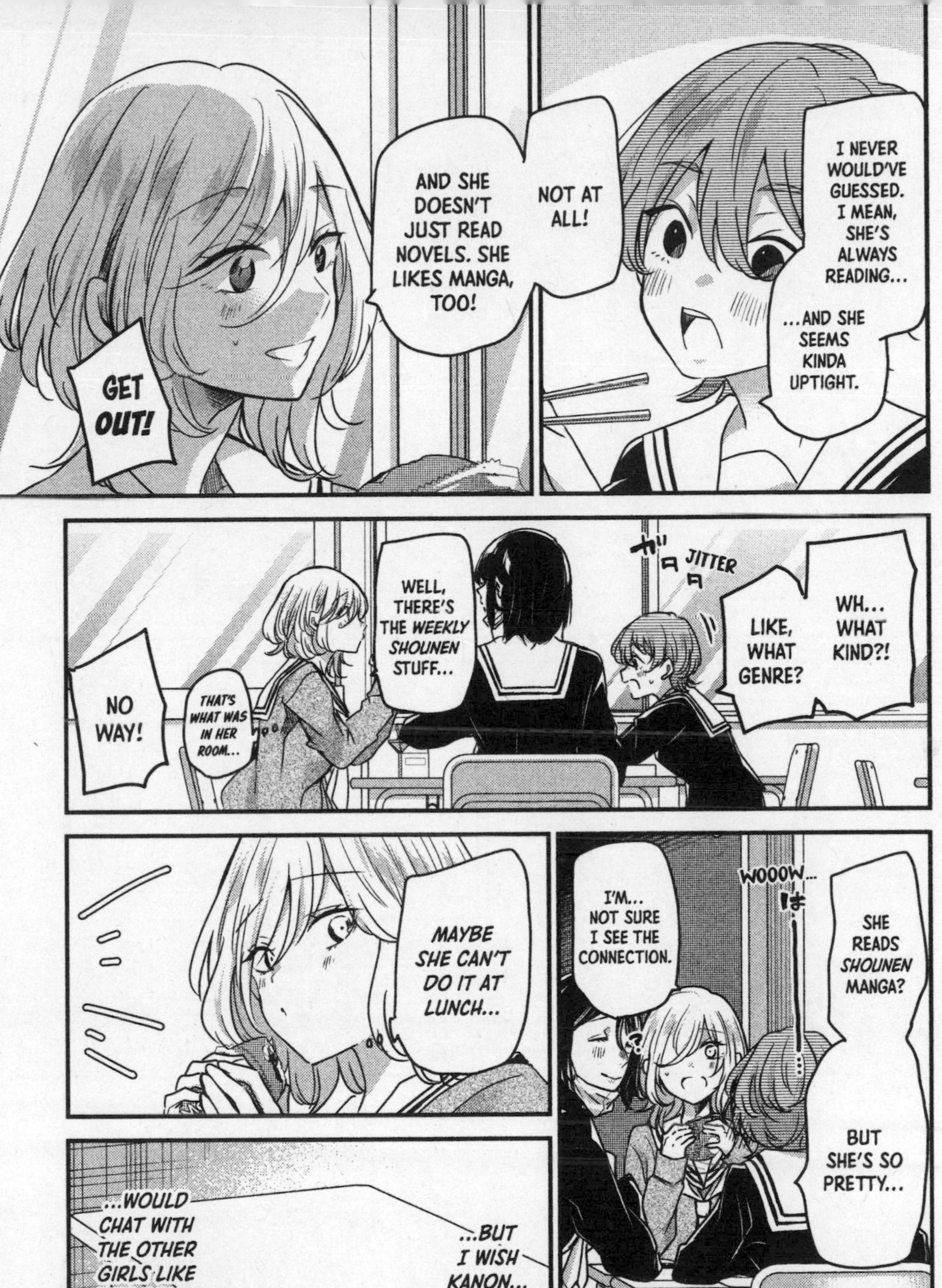
I NEVER WOULD'VE GUESSED. I MEAN, SHE'S ALWAYS READING...
...AND SHE SEEMS KINDA UPTIGHT.
NOT AT ALL!
AND SHE DOESN'T JUST READ NOVELS. SHE LIKES MANGA, TOO!
GET OUT!
WH... WHAT KIND?!
LIKE, WHAT GENRE?
JITTER
WELL, THERE'S THE *WEEKLY SHOUNEN* STUFF...
THAT'S WHAT WAS IN HER ROOM...
NO WAY!
WOOOW...
SHE READS *SHOUNEN* MANGA?
BUT SHE'S SO PRETTY...
I'M... NOT SURE I SEE THE CONNECTION.
MAYBE SHE CAN'T DO IT AT LUNCH...
...BUT I WISH KANON...
...WOULD CHAT WITH THE OTHER GIRLS LIKE THIS SOMETIMES...

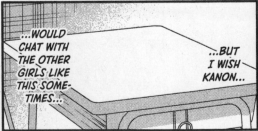

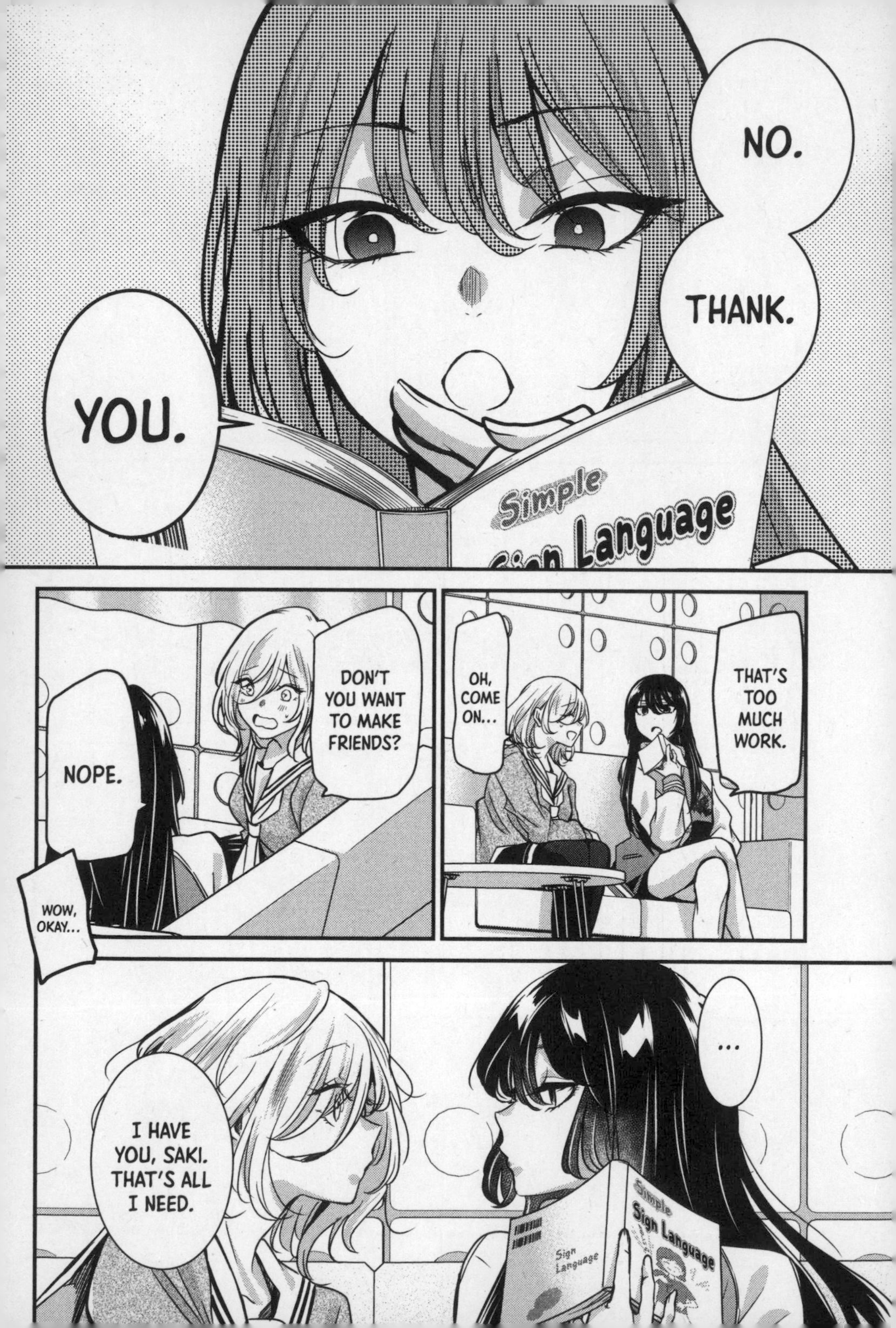
NO.
THANK.
YOU.
Simple Sign Language
THAT'S TOO MUCH WORK.
OH, COME ON...
DON'T YOU WANT TO MAKE FRIENDS?
NOPE.
WOW, OKAY...
...
I HAVE YOU, SAKI. THAT'S ALL I NEED.
Simple Sign Language
Sign Language

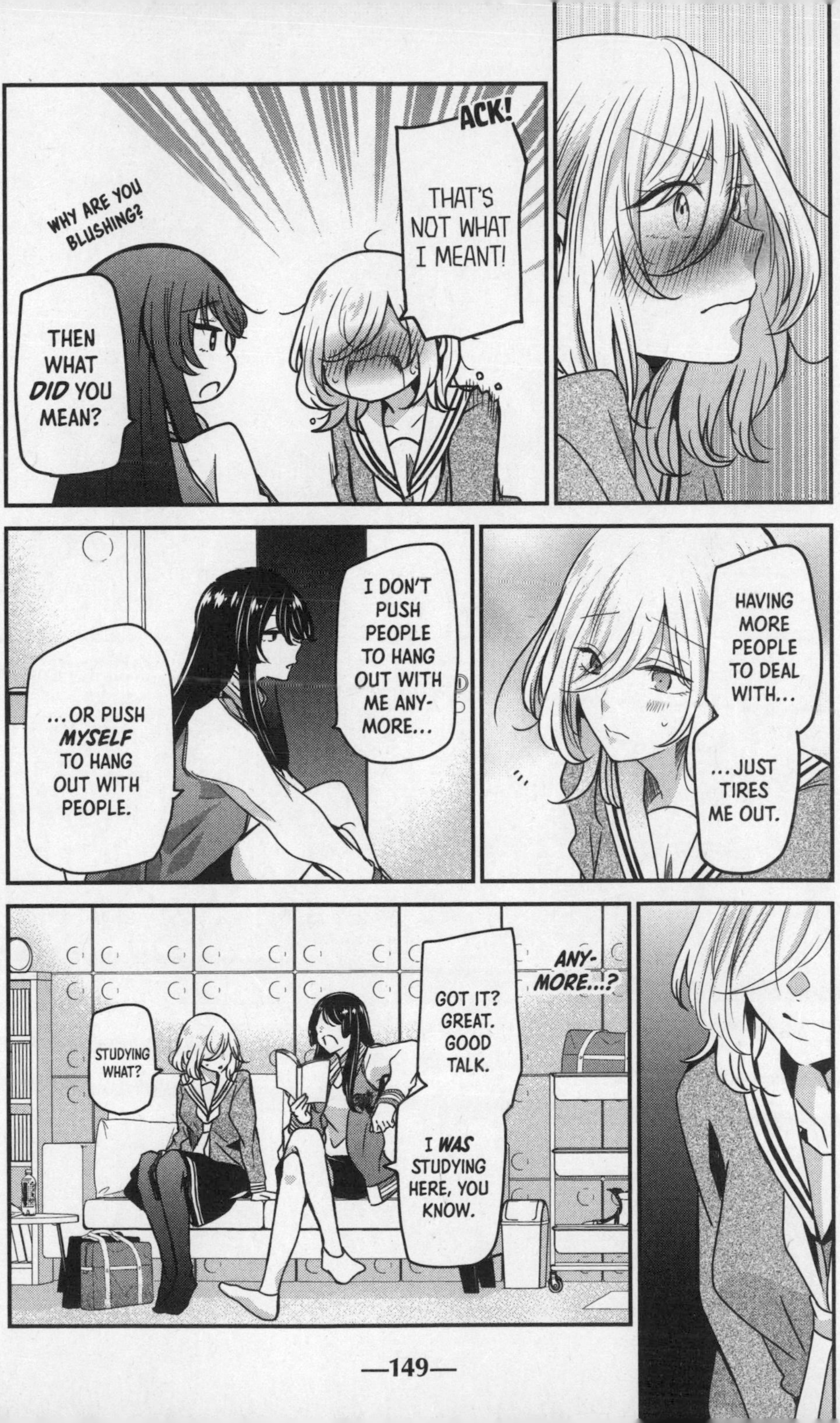
ACK!
THAT'S NOT WHAT I MEANT!
WHY ARE YOU BLUSHING?
THEN WHAT DID YOU MEAN?
HAVING MORE PEOPLE TO DEAL WITH...
...JUST TIRES ME OUT.
I DON'T PUSH PEOPLE TO HANG OUT WITH ME ANY-MORE...
...OR PUSH MYSELF TO HANG OUT WITH PEOPLE.
ANY-MORE...?
GOT IT? GREAT. GOOD TALK.
I WAS STUDYING HERE, YOU KNOW.
STUDYING WHAT?

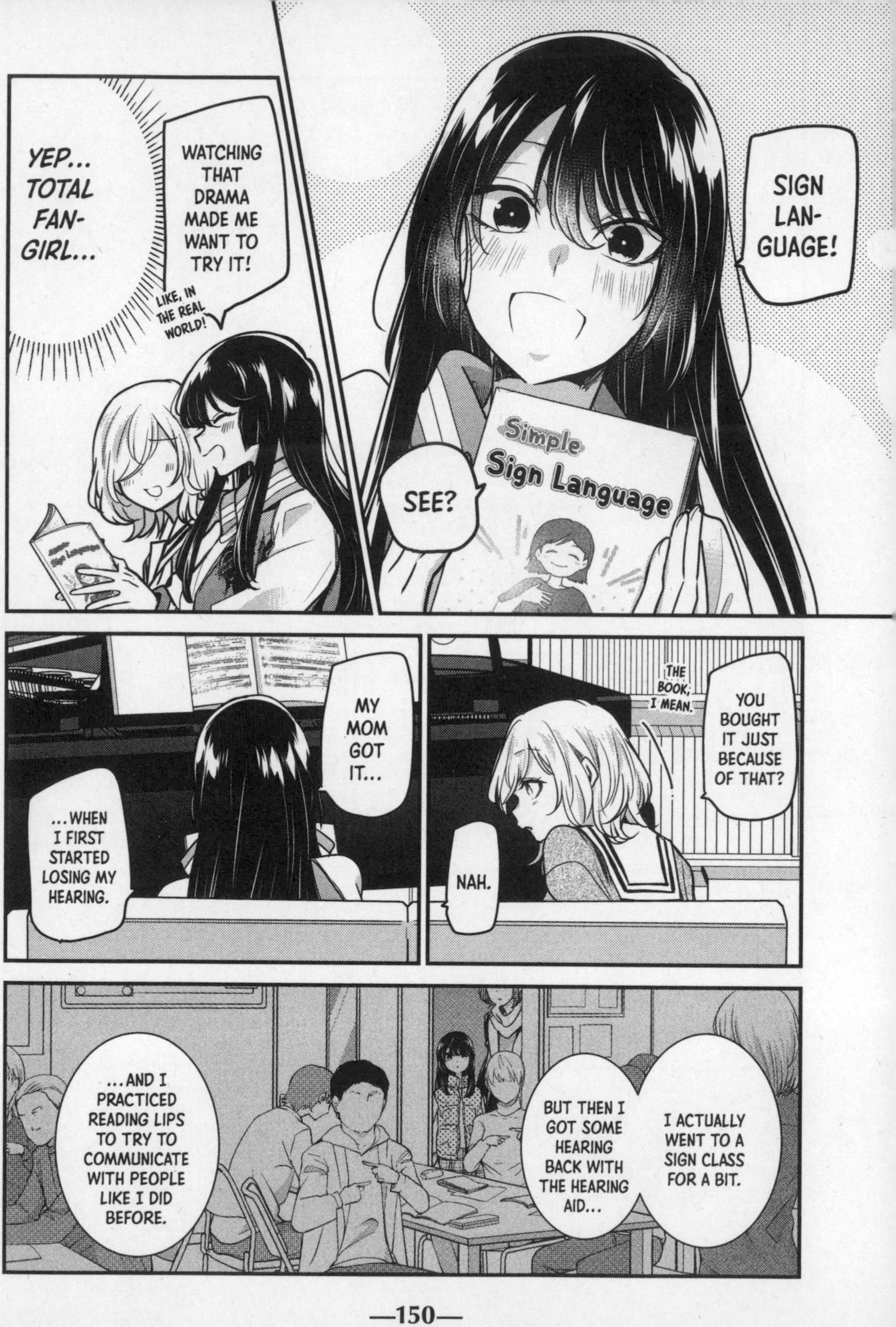
SIGN LAN-GUAGE!
SEE?
Simple Sign Language
WATCHING THAT DRAMA MADE ME WANT TO TRY IT!
LIKE, IN THE REAL WORLD!
YEP... TOTAL FAN-GIRL...
YOU BOUGHT IT JUST BECAUSE OF THAT?
THE BOOK, I MEAN.
NAH.
MY MOM GOT IT...
...WHEN I FIRST STARTED LOSING MY HEARING.
I ACTUALLY WENT TO A SIGN CLASS FOR A BIT.
BUT THEN I GOT SOME HEARING BACK WITH THE HEARING AID...
...AND I PRACTICED READING LIPS TO TRY TO COMMUNICATE WITH PEOPLE LIKE I DID BEFORE.

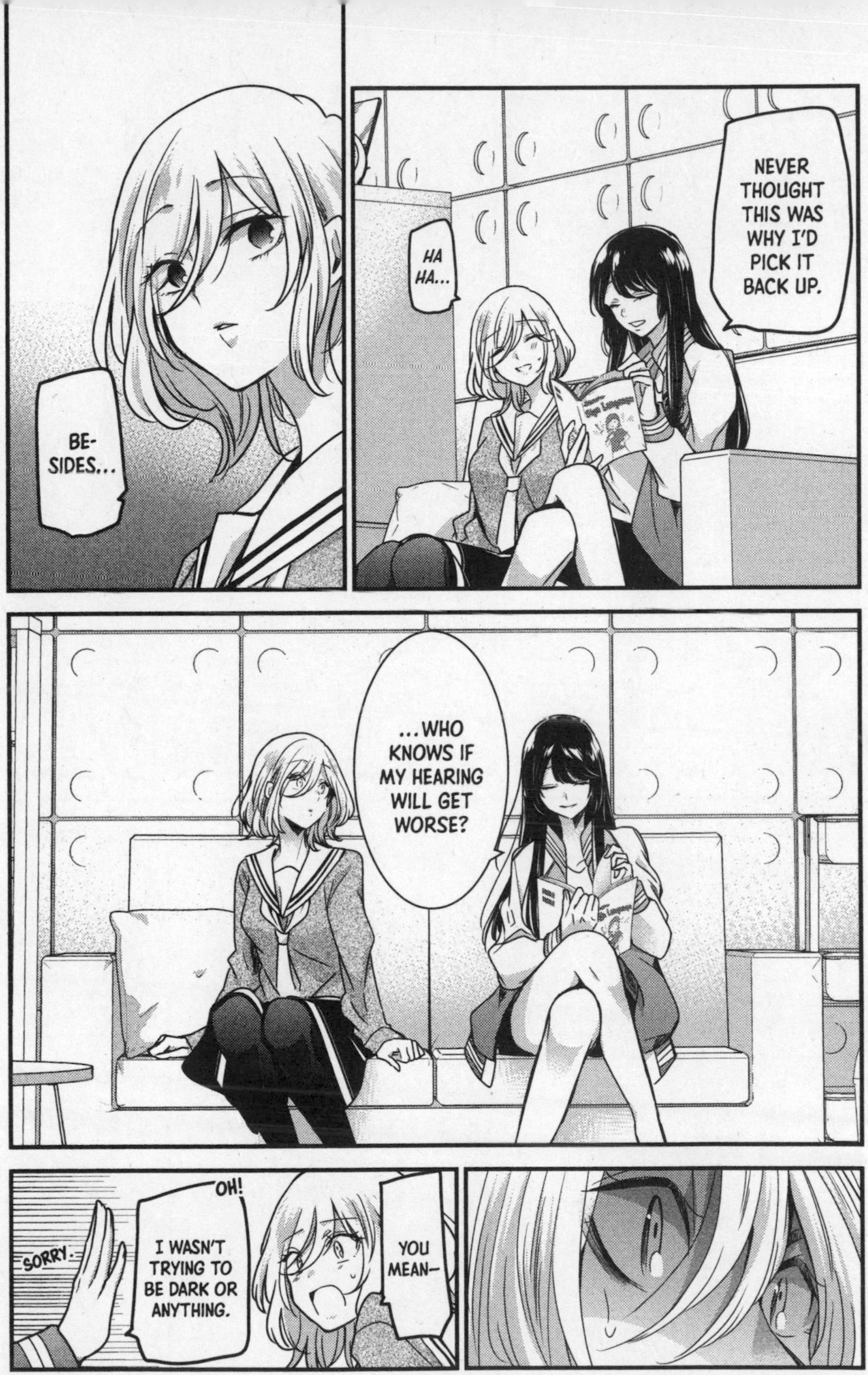
NEVER THOUGHT THIS WAS WHY I'D PICK IT BACK UP.
HA HA...
BE-SIDES...
...WHO KNOWS IF MY HEARING WILL GET WORSE?
YOU MEAN—
OH!
I WASN'T TRYING TO BE DARK OR ANYTHING.
SORRY.

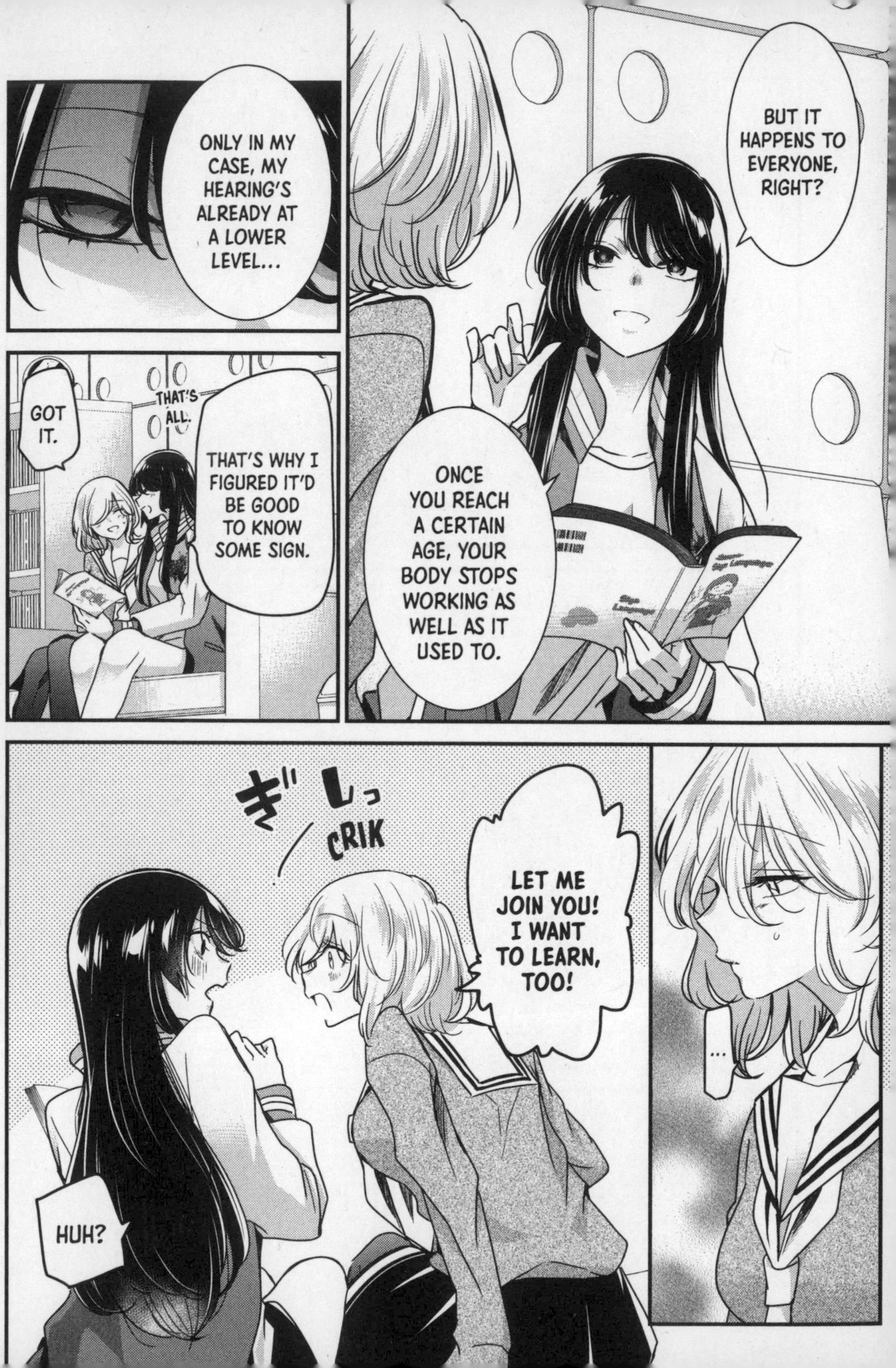
BUT IT HAPPENS TO EVERYONE, RIGHT?
ONCE YOU REACH A CERTAIN AGE, YOUR BODY STOPS WORKING AS WELL AS IT USED TO.
ONLY IN MY CASE, MY HEARING'S ALREADY AT A LOWER LEVEL...
THAT'S WHY I FIGURED IT'D BE GOOD TO KNOW SOME SIGN.
THAT'S ALL.
GOT IT.
...
ぎしっ
CRIK
LET ME JOIN YOU! I WANT TO LEARN, TOO!
HUH?

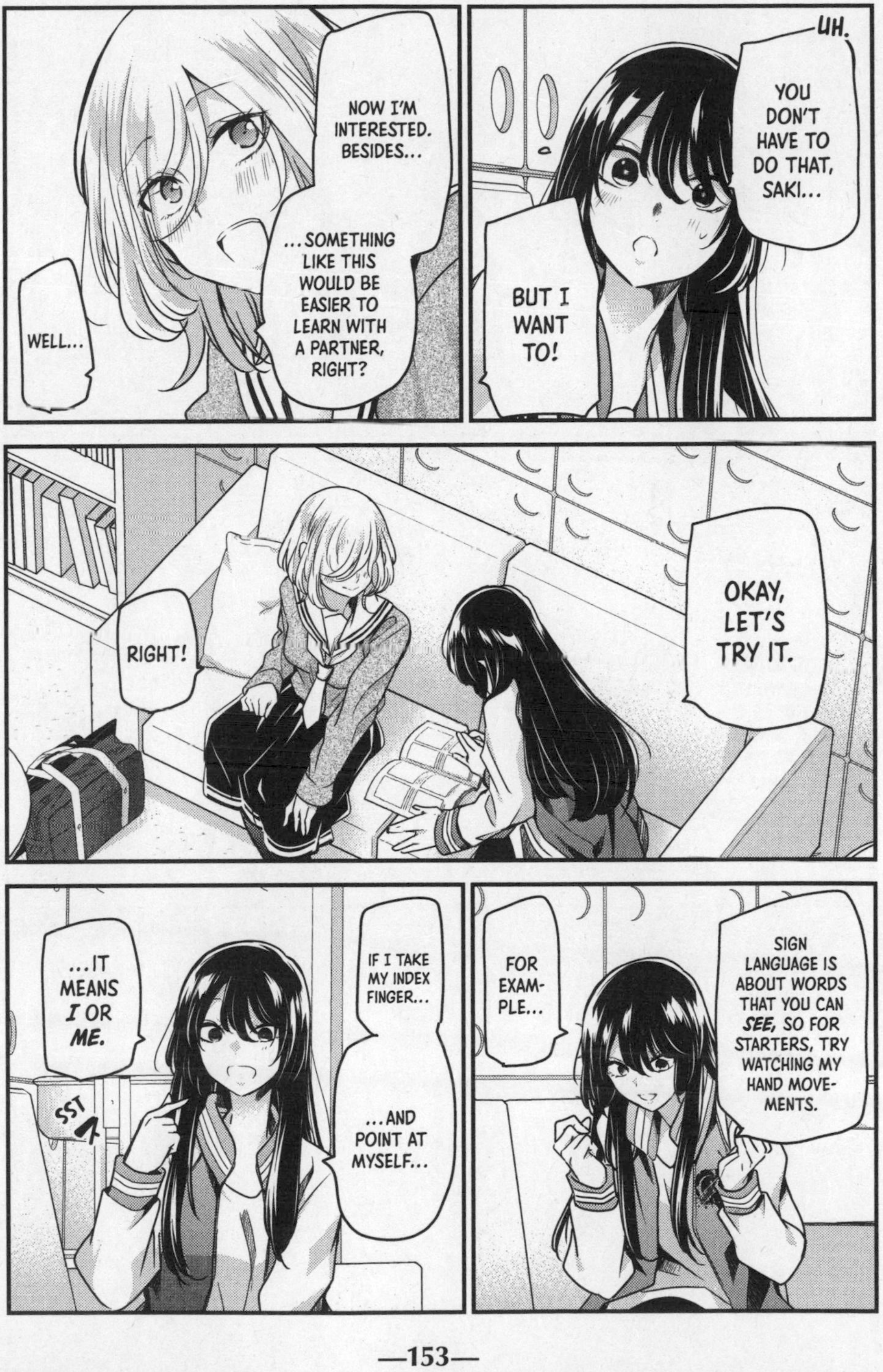
UH.
YOU DON'T HAVE TO DO THAT, SAKI...
BUT I WANT TO!
NOW I'M INTERESTED. BESIDES...
...SOMETHING LIKE THIS WOULD BE EASIER TO LEARN WITH A PARTNER, RIGHT?
WELL...
OKAY, LET'S TRY IT.
RIGHT!
SIGN LANGUAGE IS ABOUT WORDS THAT YOU CAN *SEE,* SO FOR STARTERS, TRY WATCHING MY HAND MOVE-MENTS.
FOR EXAM-PLE...
IF I TAKE MY INDEX FINGER...
...AND POINT AT MYSELF...
...IT MEANS *I* OR *ME.*
SST

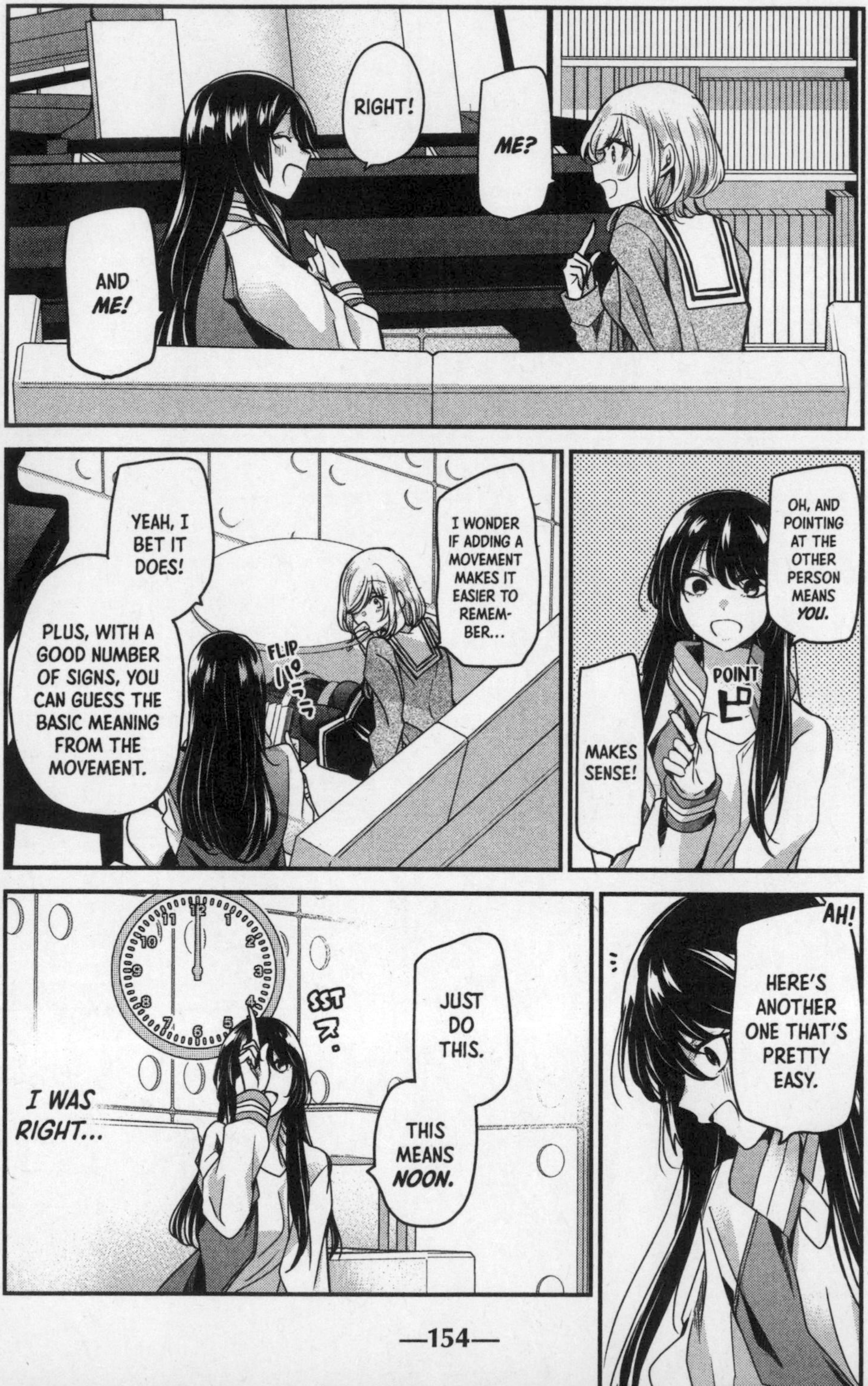
ME?
RIGHT!
AND ME!
OH, AND POINTING AT THE OTHER PERSON MEANS YOU.
POINT
MAKES SENSE!
I WONDER IF ADDING A MOVEMENT MAKES IT EASIER TO REMEMBER...
FLIP
YEAH, I BET IT DOES!
PLUS, WITH A GOOD NUMBER OF SIGNS, YOU CAN GUESS THE BASIC MEANING FROM THE MOVEMENT.
AH!
HERE'S ANOTHER ONE THAT'S PRETTY EASY.
JUST DO THIS.
SST
THIS MEANS NOON.
I WAS RIGHT...

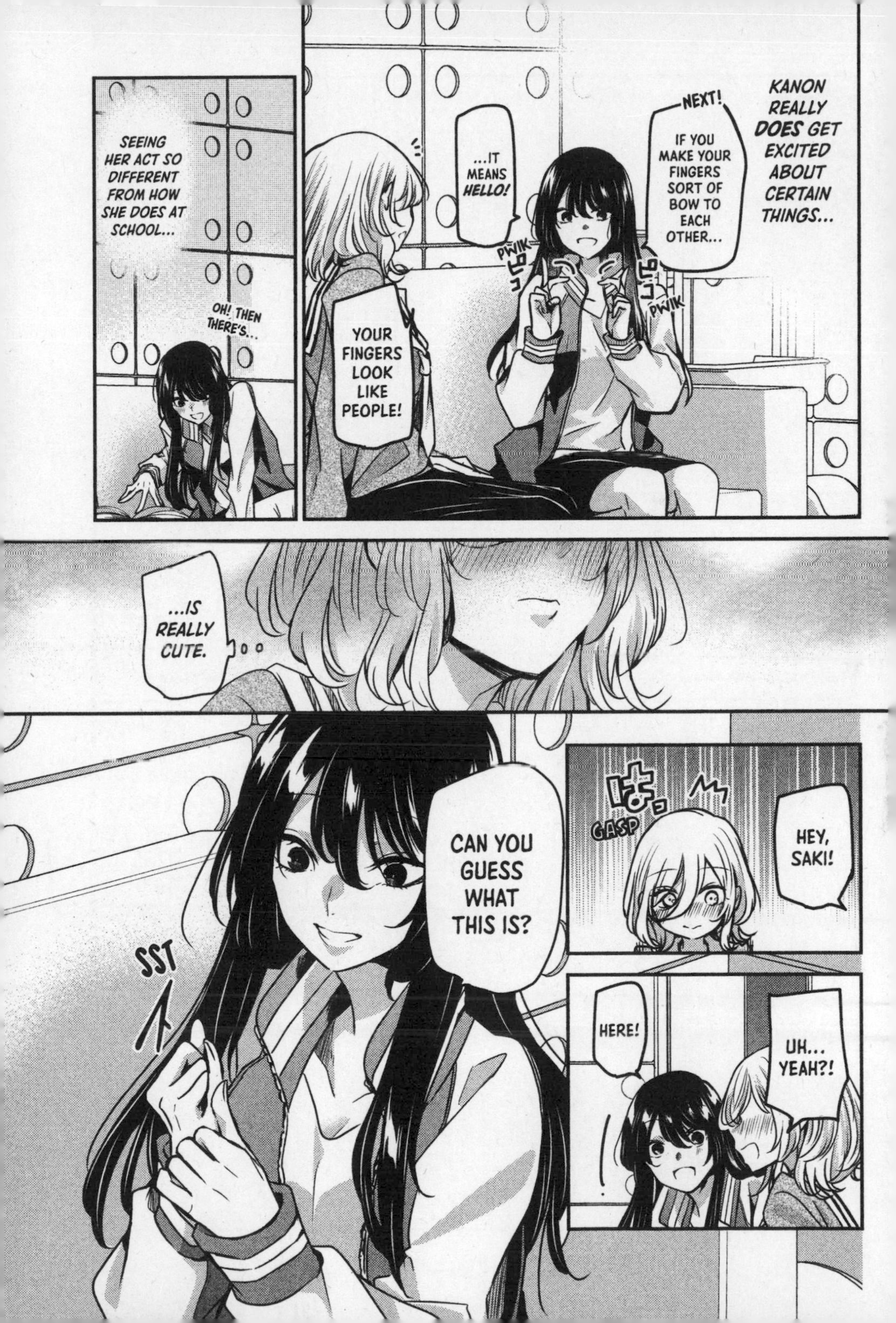
KANON REALLY DOES GET EXCITED ABOUT CERTAIN THINGS...
NEXT!
IF YOU MAKE YOUR FINGERS SORT OF BOW TO EACH OTHER...
PWIK
PWIK
...IT MEANS HELLO!
YOUR FINGERS LOOK LIKE PEOPLE!
SEEING HER ACT SO DIFFERENT FROM HOW SHE DOES AT SCHOOL...
OH! THEN THERE'S...
...IS REALLY CUTE.
HEY, SAKI!
GASP
UH... YEAH?!
HERE!
CAN YOU GUESS WHAT THIS IS?
SST

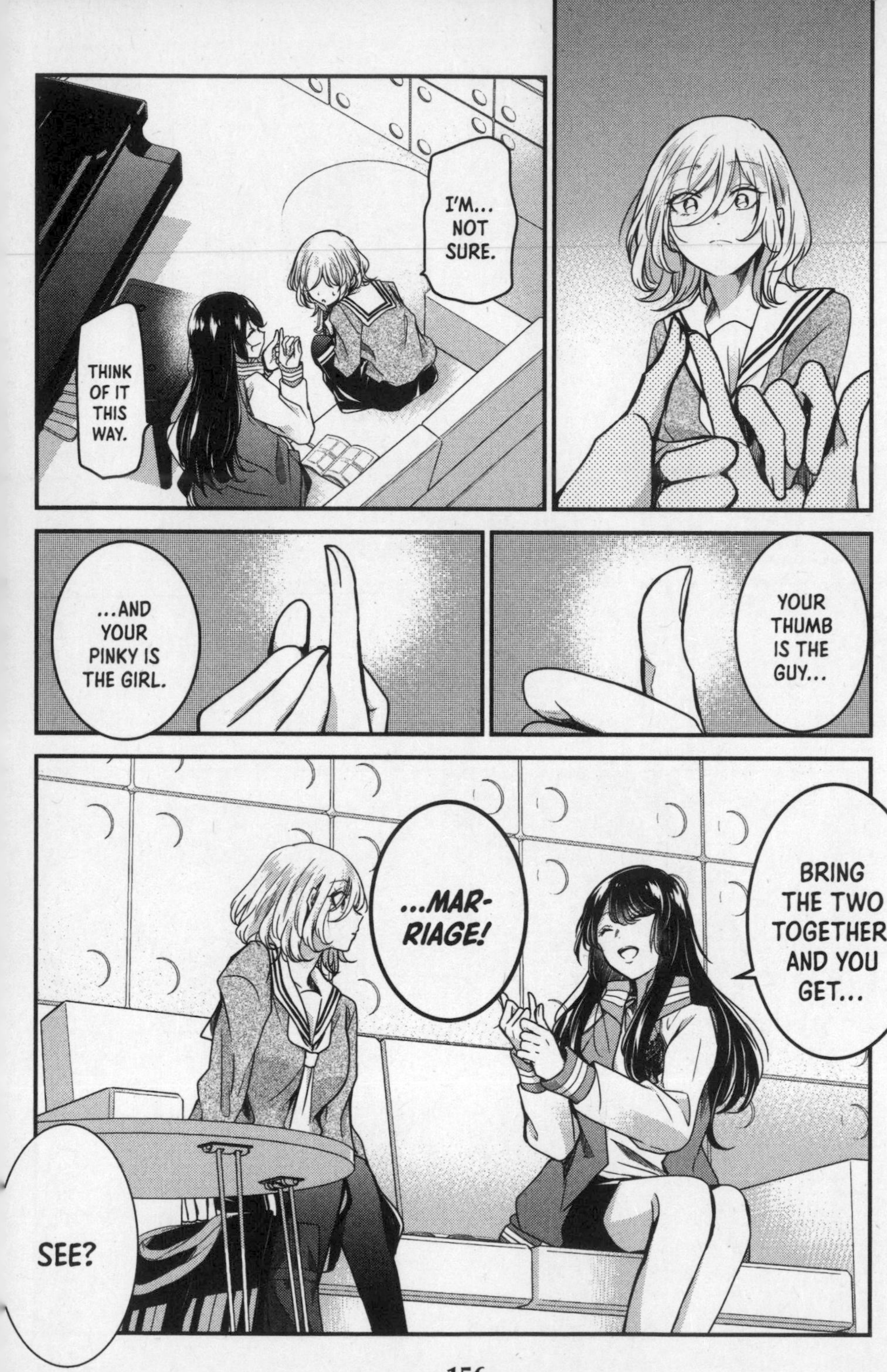
I'M... NOT SURE.
THINK OF IT THIS WAY.
YOUR THUMB IS THE GUY...
...AND YOUR PINKY IS THE GIRL.
BRING THE TWO TOGETHER, AND YOU GET...
...MAR-RIAGE!
SEE?

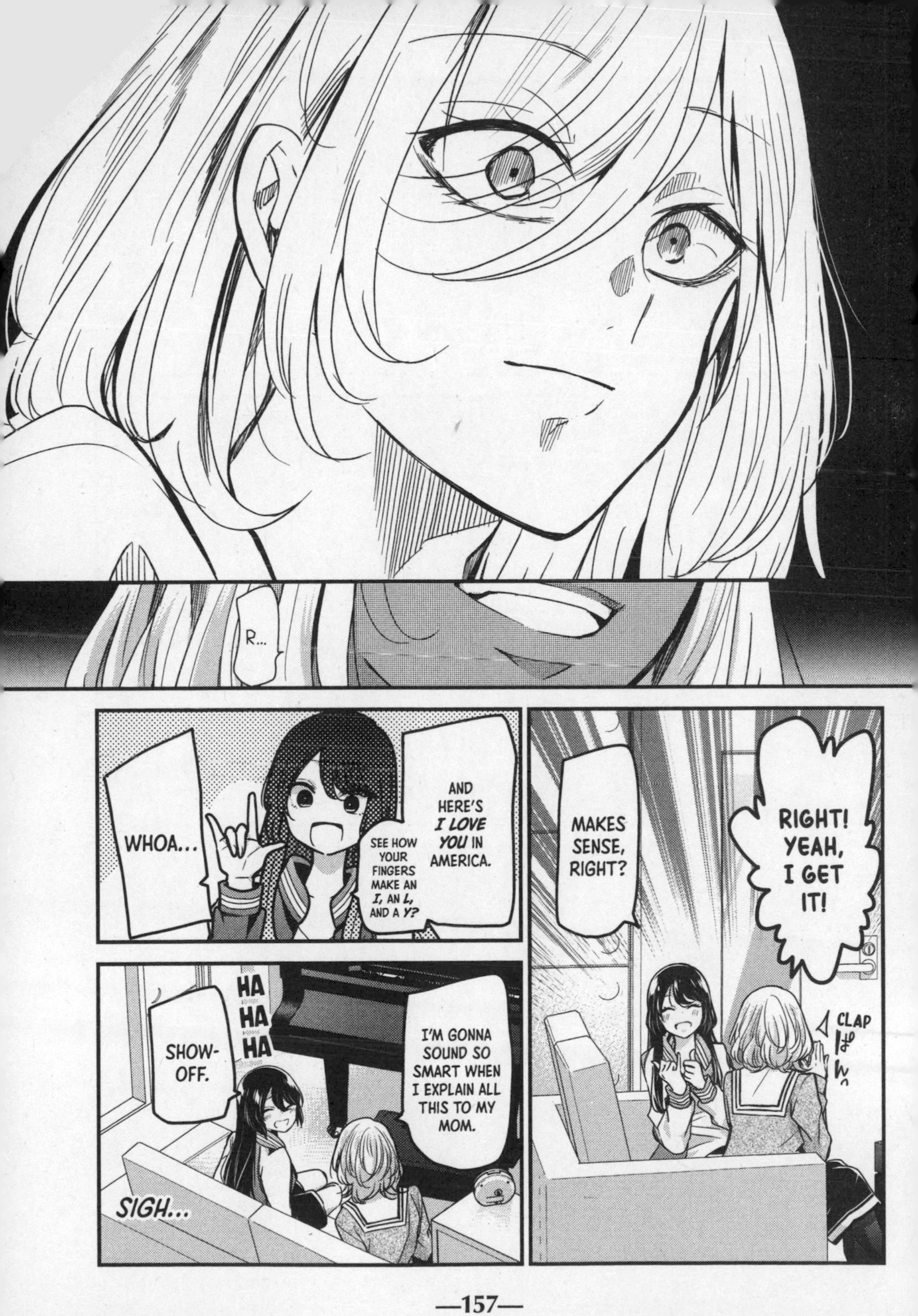
R...
RIGHT! YEAH, I GET IT!
MAKES SENSE, RIGHT?
CLAP
ぱん
AND HERE'S I LOVE YOU IN AMERICA.
SEE HOW YOUR FINGERS MAKE AN I, AN L, AND A Y?
WHOA...
I'M GONNA SOUND SO SMART WHEN I EXPLAIN ALL THIS TO MY MOM.
HA HA HA
SHOW-OFF.
SIGH...

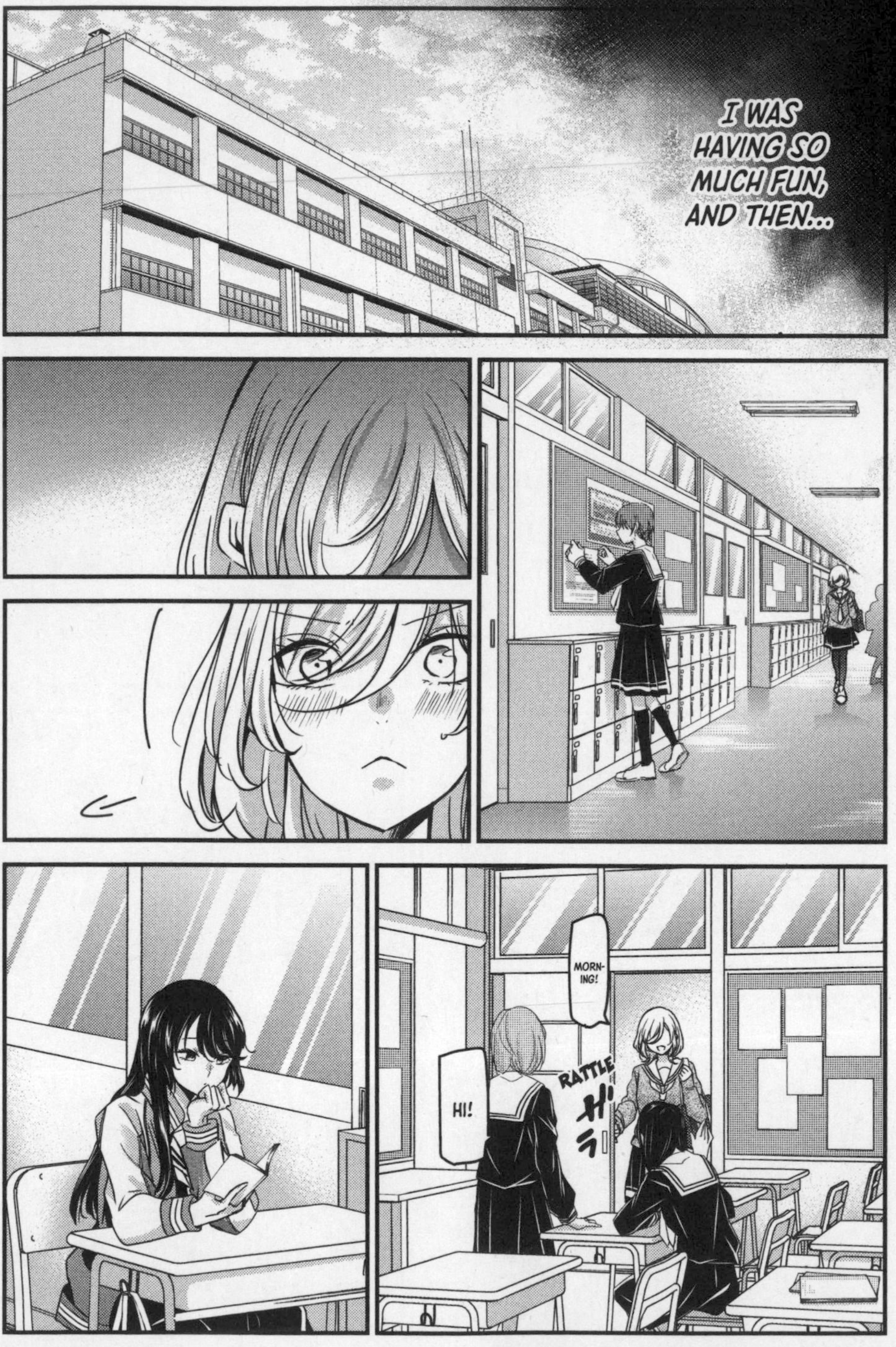
I WAS HAVING SO MUCH FUN, AND THEN...
MORN-ING!
RATTLE
ガラ
HI!

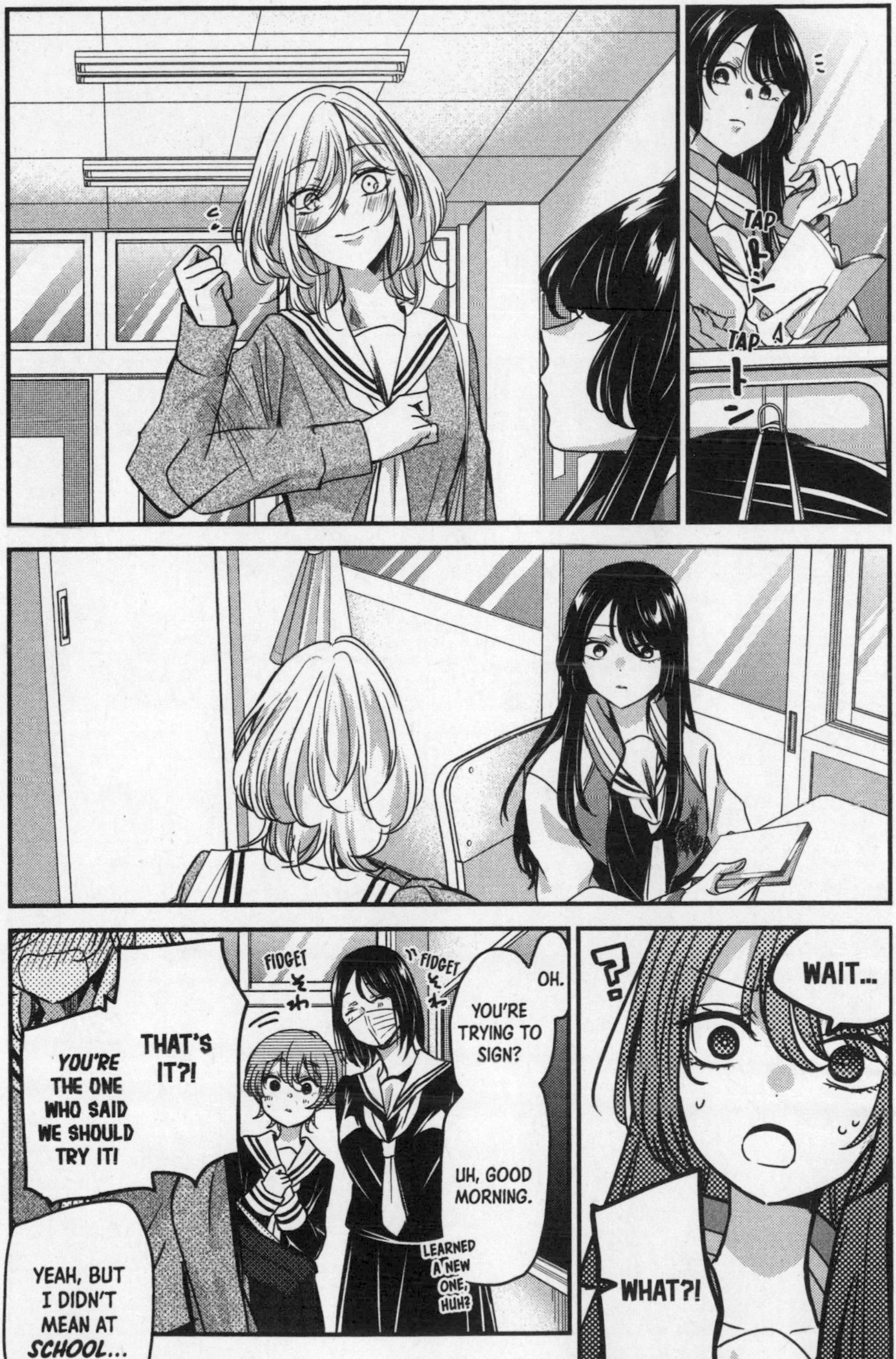
TAP
TAP
WAIT...
WHAT?!
OH.
YOU'RE TRYING TO SIGN?
UH, GOOD MORNING.
FIDGET
FIDGET
LEARNED A NEW ONE, HUH?
THAT'S IT?!
YOU'RE THE ONE WHO SAID WE SHOULD TRY IT!
YEAH, BUT I DIDN'T MEAN AT *SCHOOL*...

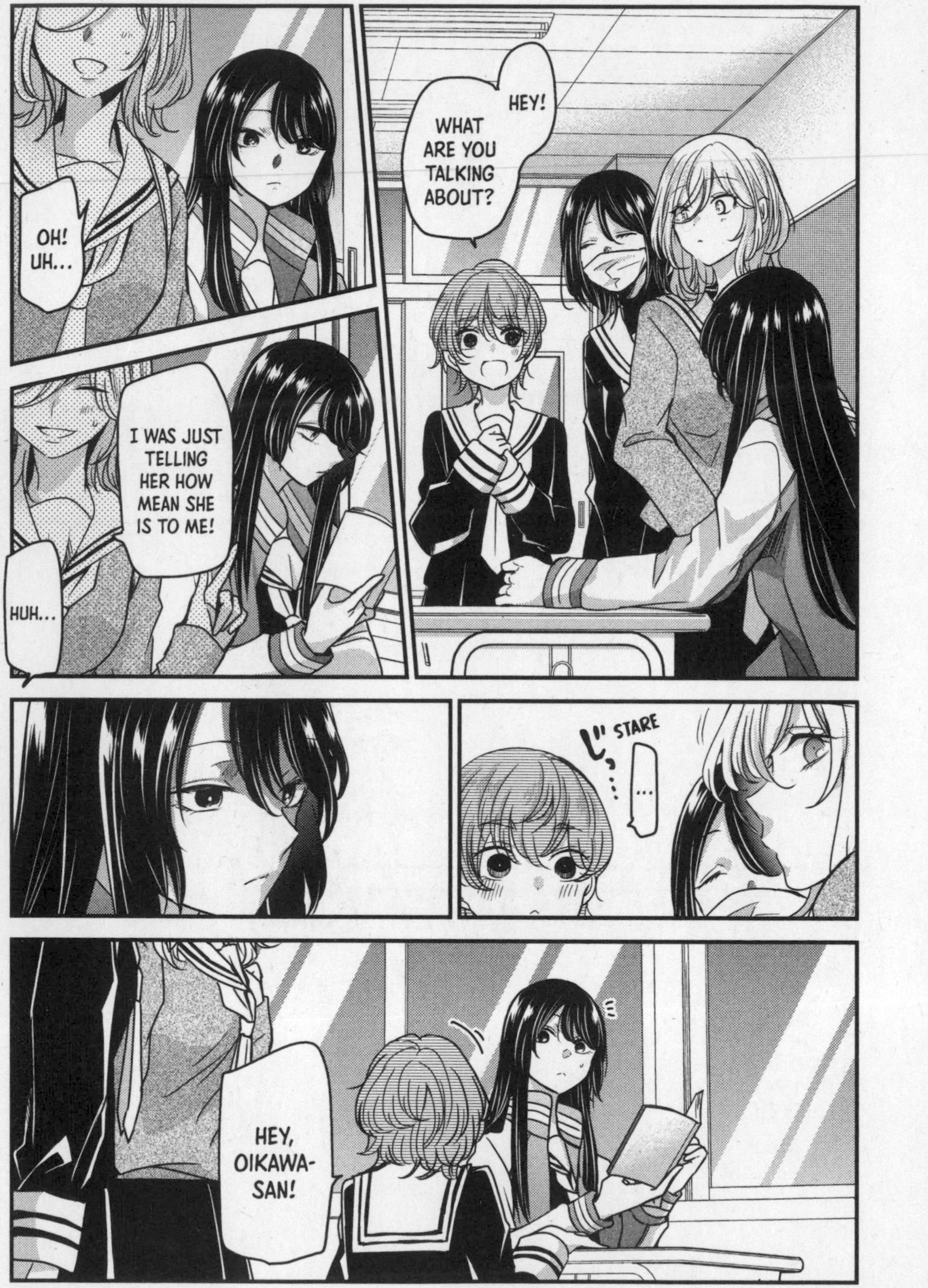
HEY!
WHAT ARE YOU TALKING ABOUT?
OH! UH...
I WAS JUST TELLING HER HOW MEAN SHE IS TO ME!
HUH...
STARE
...
HEY, OIKAWA-SAN!

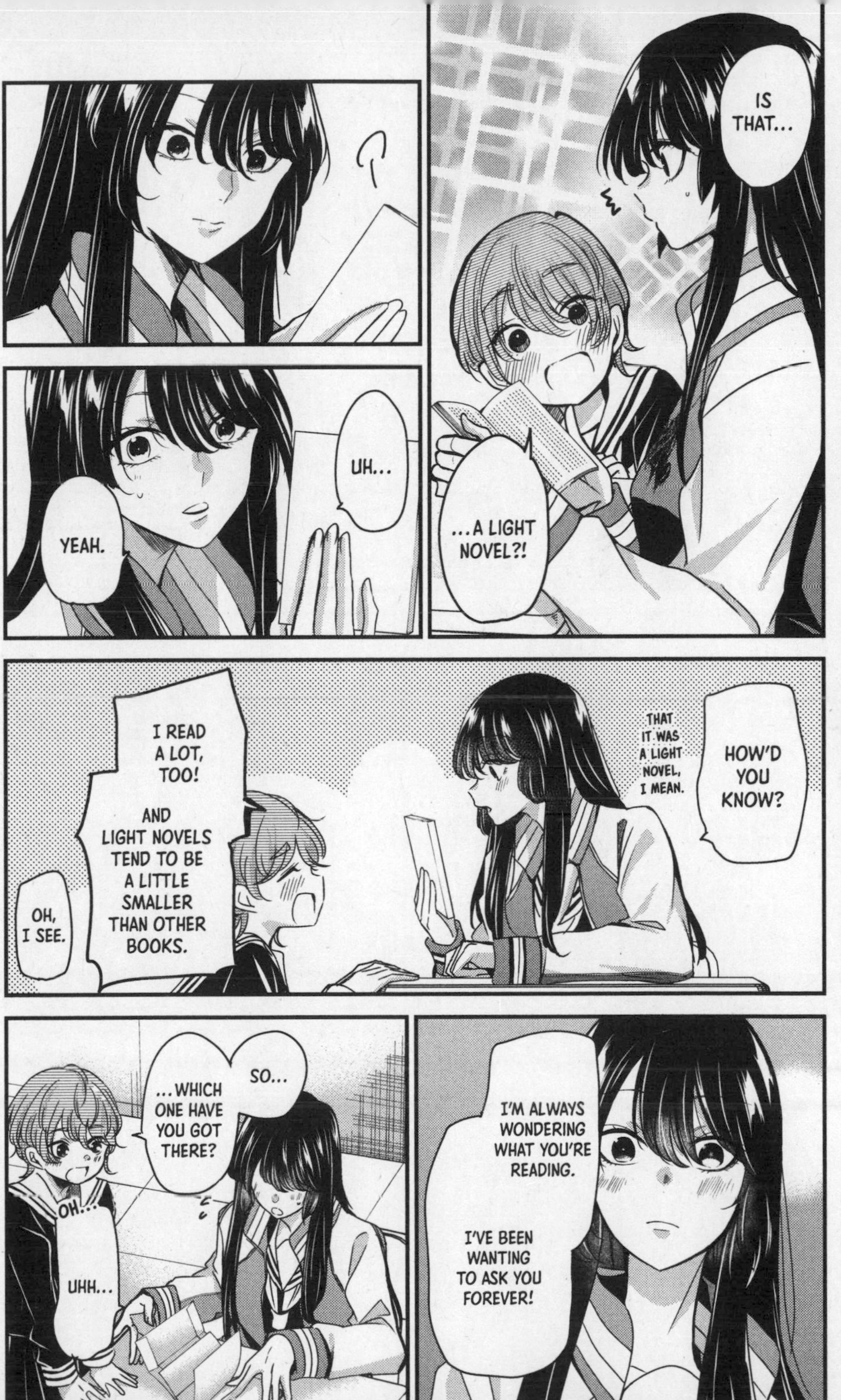
IS THAT...
...A LIGHT NOVEL?!
UH...
YEAH.
HOW'D YOU KNOW?
THAT IT WAS A LIGHT NOVEL, I MEAN.
I READ A LOT, TOO!
AND LIGHT NOVELS TEND TO BE A LITTLE SMALLER THAN OTHER BOOKS.
OH, I SEE.
I'M ALWAYS WONDERING WHAT YOU'RE READING.
I'VE BEEN WANTING TO ASK YOU FOREVER!
SO...
...WHICH ONE HAVE YOU GOT THERE?
OH...
UHH...

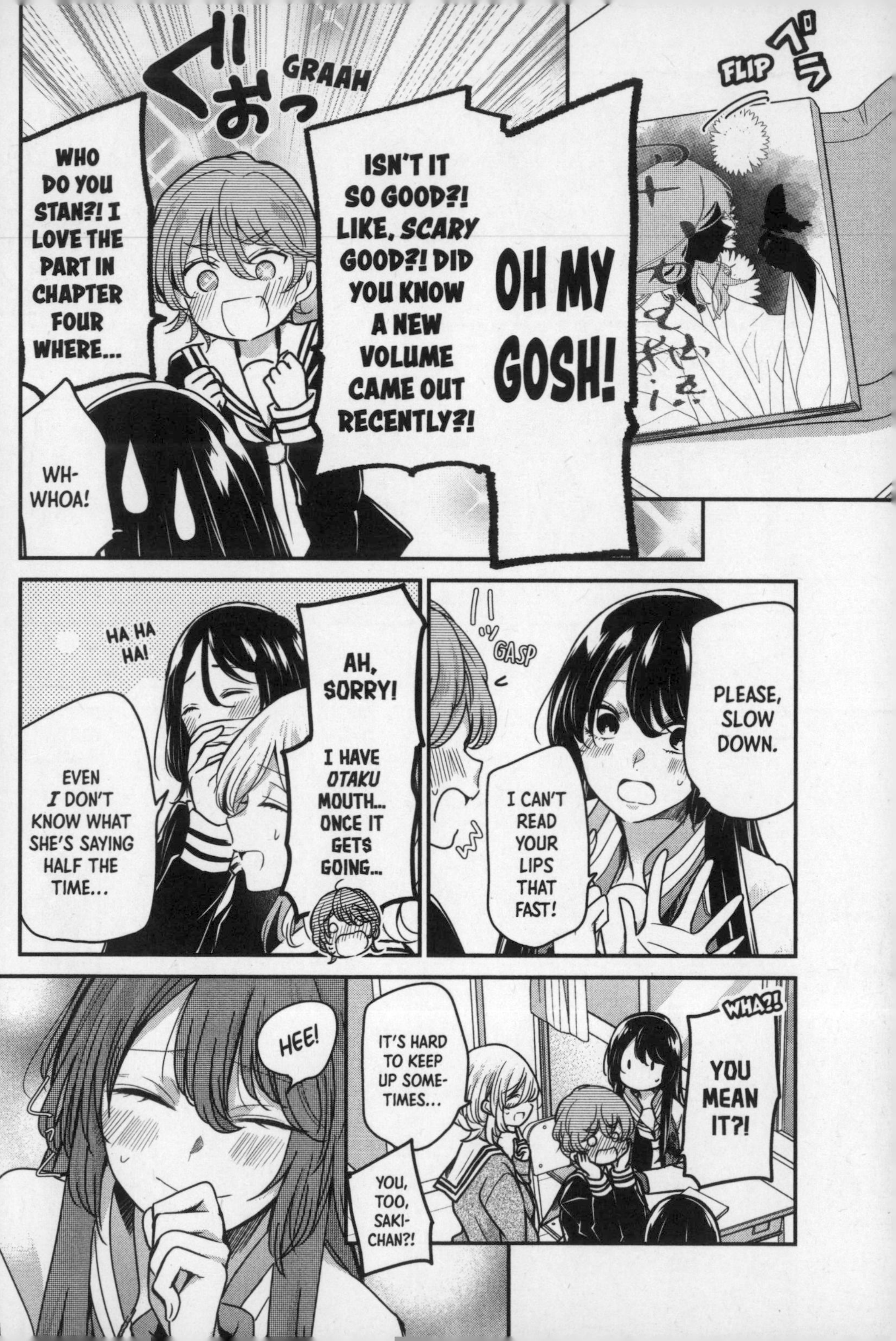
FLIP
プラ
OH MY GOSH!
ISN'T IT SO GOOD?! LIKE, *SCARY* GOOD?! DID YOU KNOW A NEW VOLUME CAME OUT RECENTLY?!
GRAAH
ぐおっ
WHO DO YOU STAN?! I LOVE THE PART IN CHAPTER FOUR WHERE...
WH- WHOA!
GASP
PLEASE, SLOW DOWN.
I CAN'T READ YOUR LIPS THAT FAST!
AH, SORRY!
I HAVE *OTAKU* MOUTH... ONCE IT GETS GOING...
HA HA HA!
EVEN *I* DON'T KNOW WHAT SHE'S SAYING HALF THE TIME...
WHA?!
YOU MEAN IT?!
IT'S HARD TO KEEP UP SOME- TIMES...
YOU, TOO, SAKI- CHAN?!
HEE!

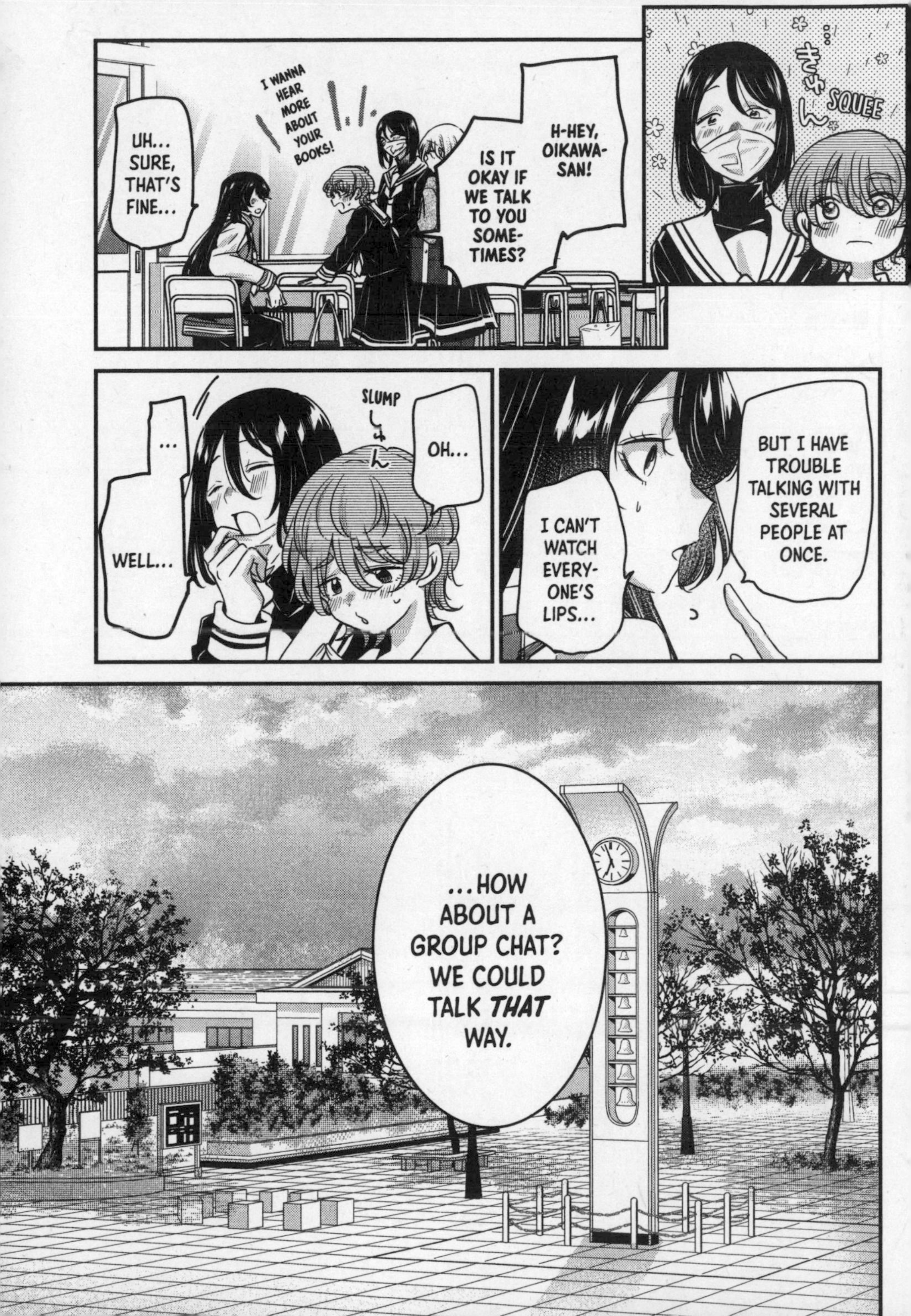
きゅん…
SQUEE
H-HEY, OIKAWA-SAN!
IS IT OKAY IF WE TALK TO YOU SOMETIMES?
I WANNA HEAR MORE ABOUT YOUR BOOKS!
UH... SURE, THAT'S FINE...
BUT I HAVE TROUBLE TALKING WITH SEVERAL PEOPLE AT ONCE.
I CAN'T WATCH EVERYONE'S LIPS...
OH...
SLUMP
しゅん
...
WELL...
...HOW ABOUT A GROUP CHAT? WE COULD TALK *THAT* WAY.

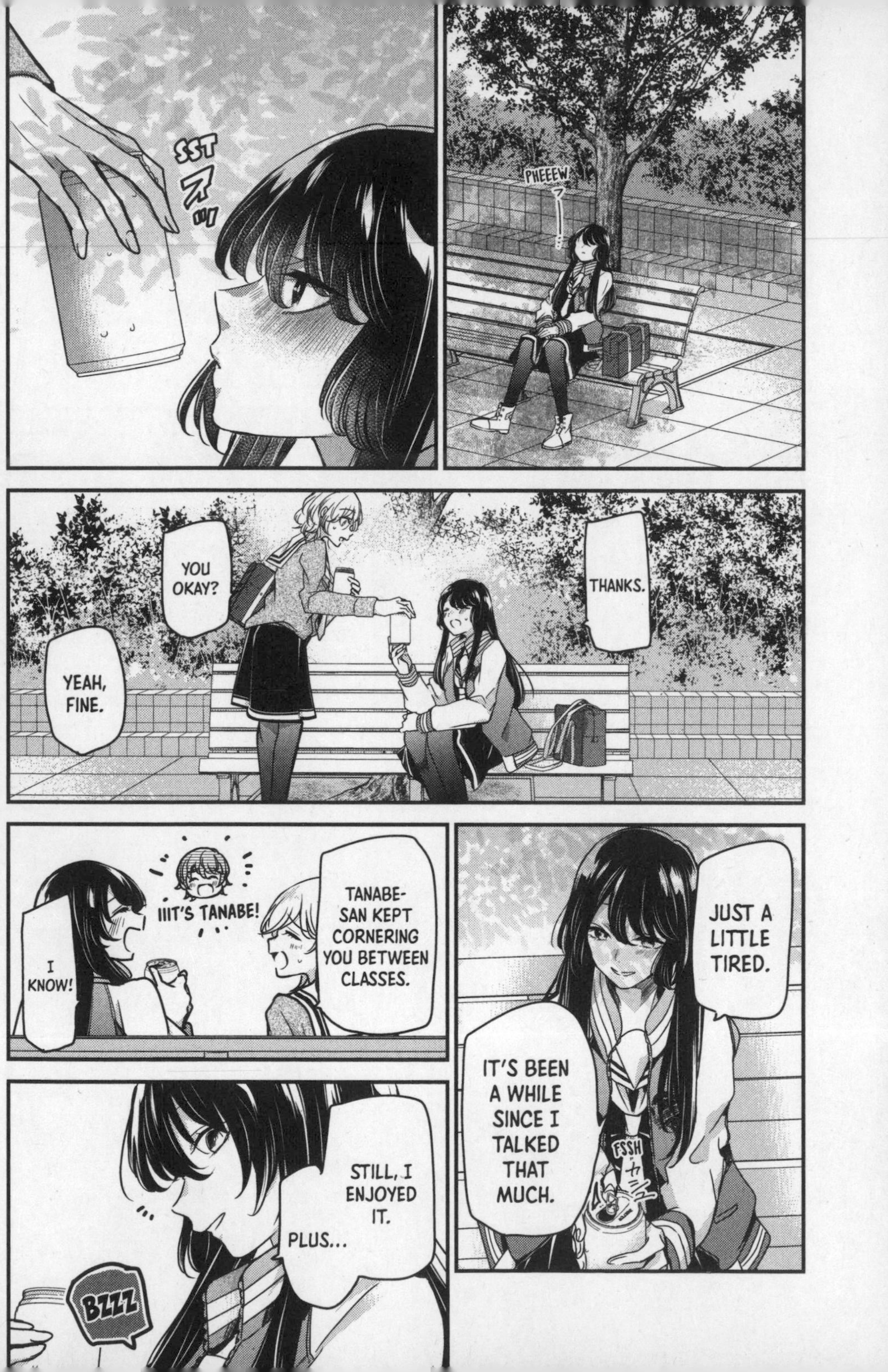
PHEEEW
SST
YOU OKAY?
THANKS.
YEAH, FINE.
JUST A LITTLE TIRED.
IT'S BEEN A WHILE SINCE I TALKED THAT MUCH.
FSSH
TANABE-SAN KEPT CORNERING YOU BETWEEN CLASSES.
IIIT'S TANABE!
I KNOW!
STILL, I ENJOYED IT.
PLUS...
BZZZ

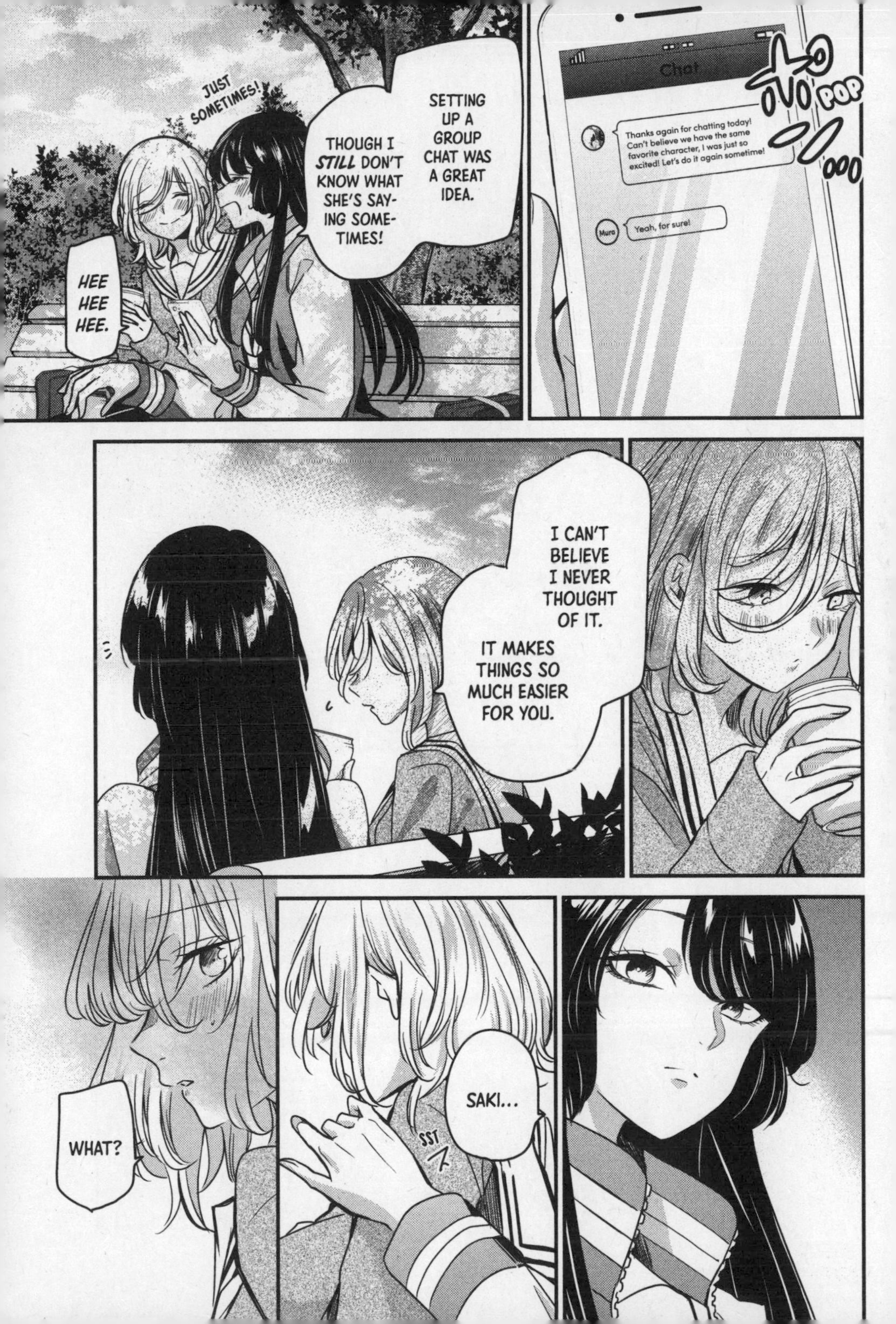
POP
Chat
Thanks again for chatting today! Can't believe we have the same favorite character, I was just so excited! Let's do it again sometime!
Muro
Yeah, for sure!
SETTING UP A GROUP CHAT WAS A GREAT IDEA.
THOUGH I STILL DON'T KNOW WHAT SHE'S SAYING SOMETIMES!
JUST SOMETIMES!
HEE HEE HEE.
I CAN'T BELIEVE I NEVER THOUGHT OF IT.
IT MAKES THINGS SO MUCH EASIER FOR YOU.
SAKI...
SST
WHAT?

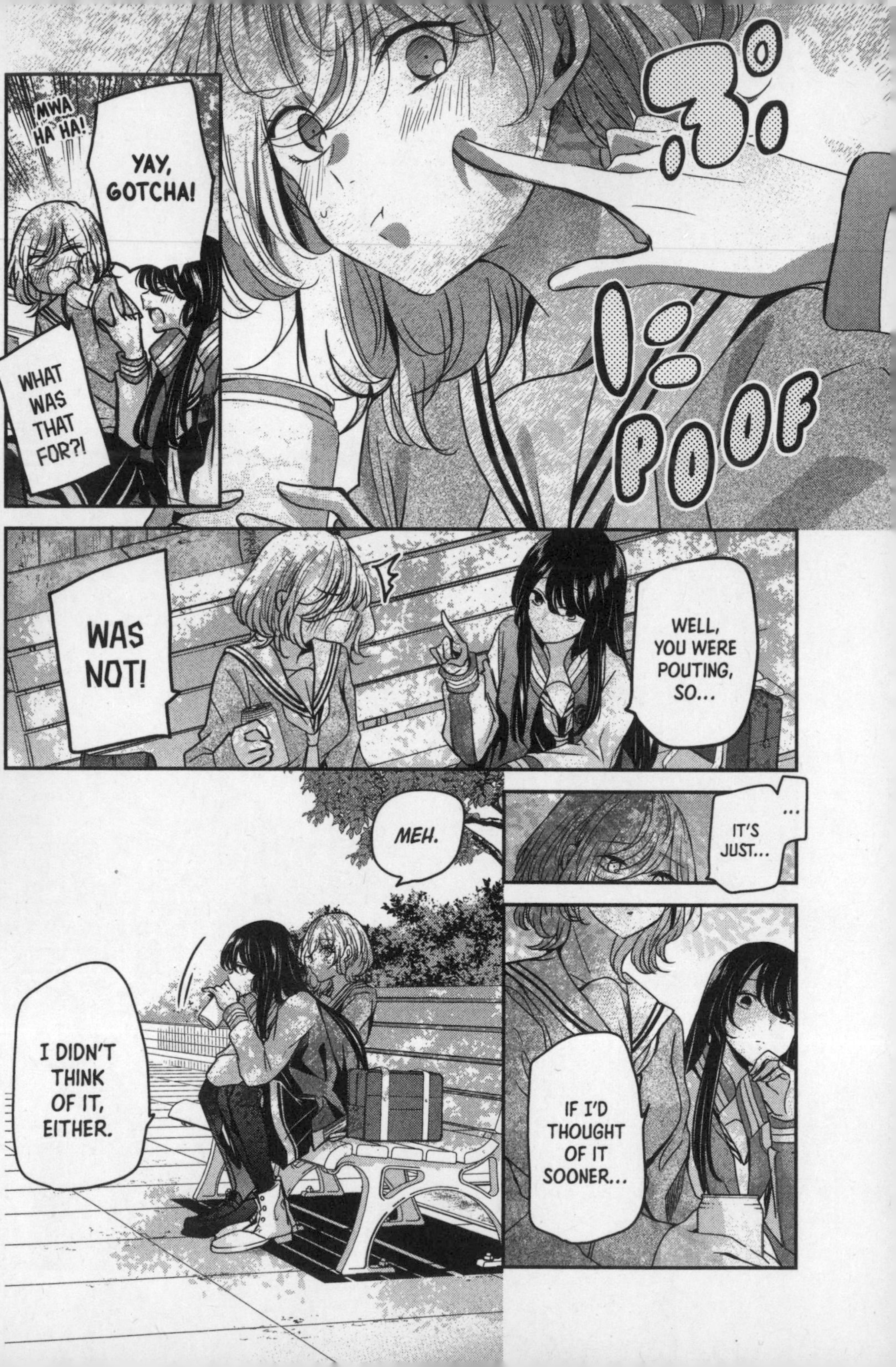
ぷ
POOF
YAY, GOTCHA!
MWA HA HA!
WHAT WAS THAT FOR?!
WELL, YOU WERE POUTING, SO...
WAS NOT!
... IT'S JUST...
IF I'D THOUGHT OF IT SOONER...
MEH.
I DIDN'T THINK OF IT, EITHER.

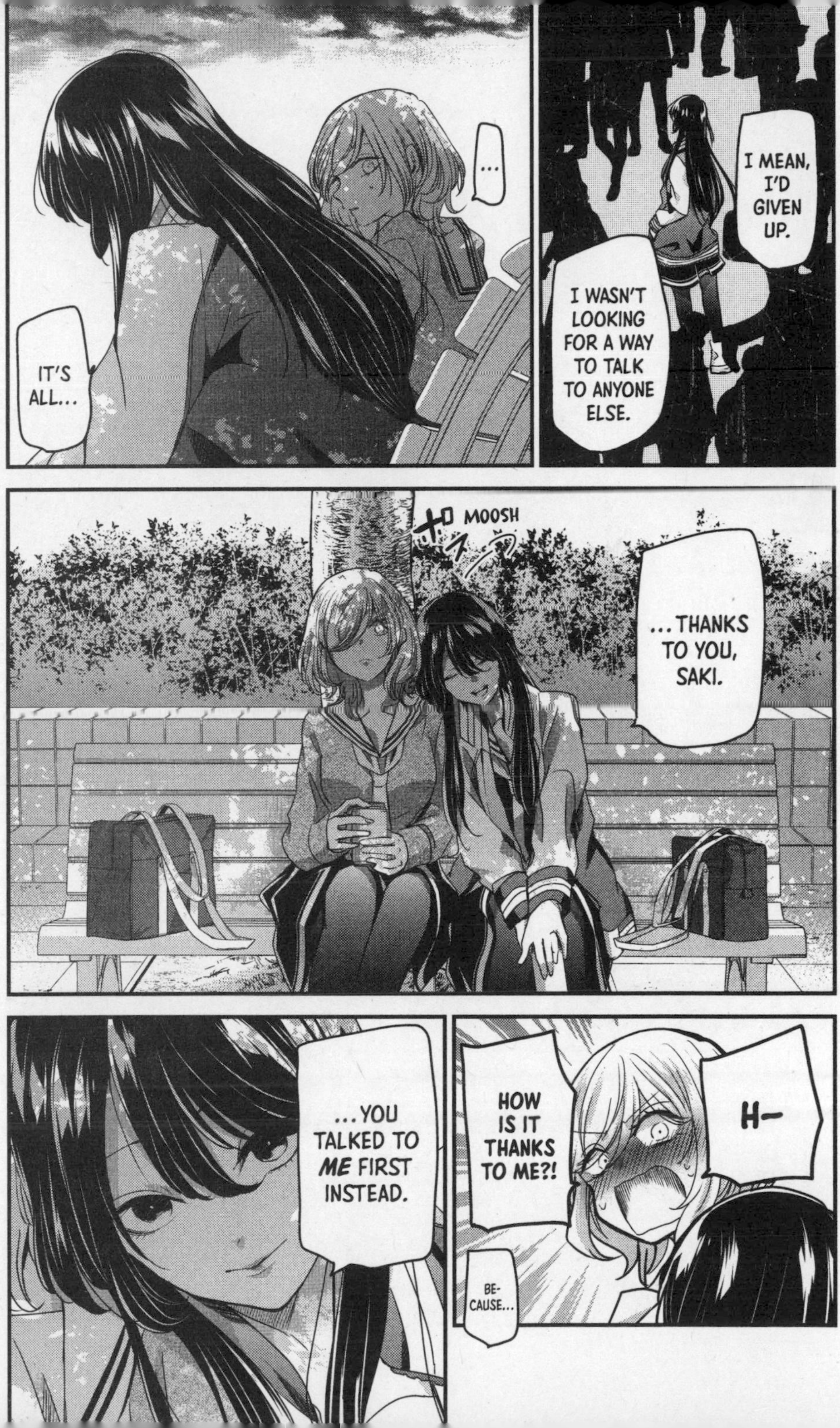
I MEAN, I'D GIVEN UP.
I WASN'T LOOKING FOR A WAY TO TALK TO ANYONE ELSE.
...
IT'S ALL...
MOOSH
...THANKS TO YOU, SAKI.
H—
HOW IS IT THANKS TO ME?!
BE-CAUSE...
...YOU TALKED TO *ME* FIRST INSTEAD.

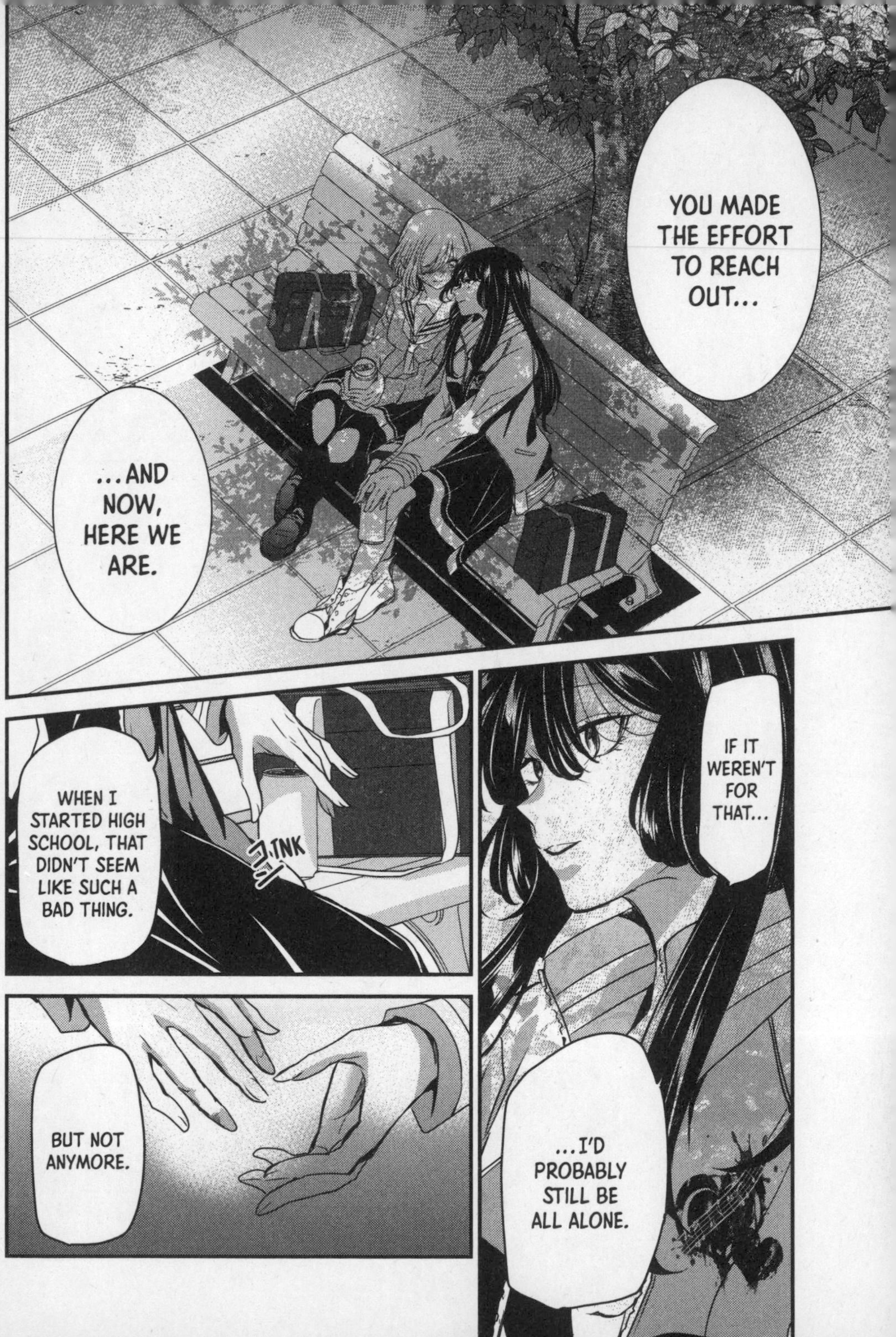
YOU MADE THE EFFORT TO REACH OUT...
...AND NOW, HERE WE ARE.
IF IT WEREN'T FOR THAT...
...I'D PROBABLY STILL BE ALL ALONE.
WHEN I STARTED HIGH SCHOOL, THAT DIDN'T SEEM LIKE SUCH A BAD THING.
INK
BUT NOT ANYMORE.

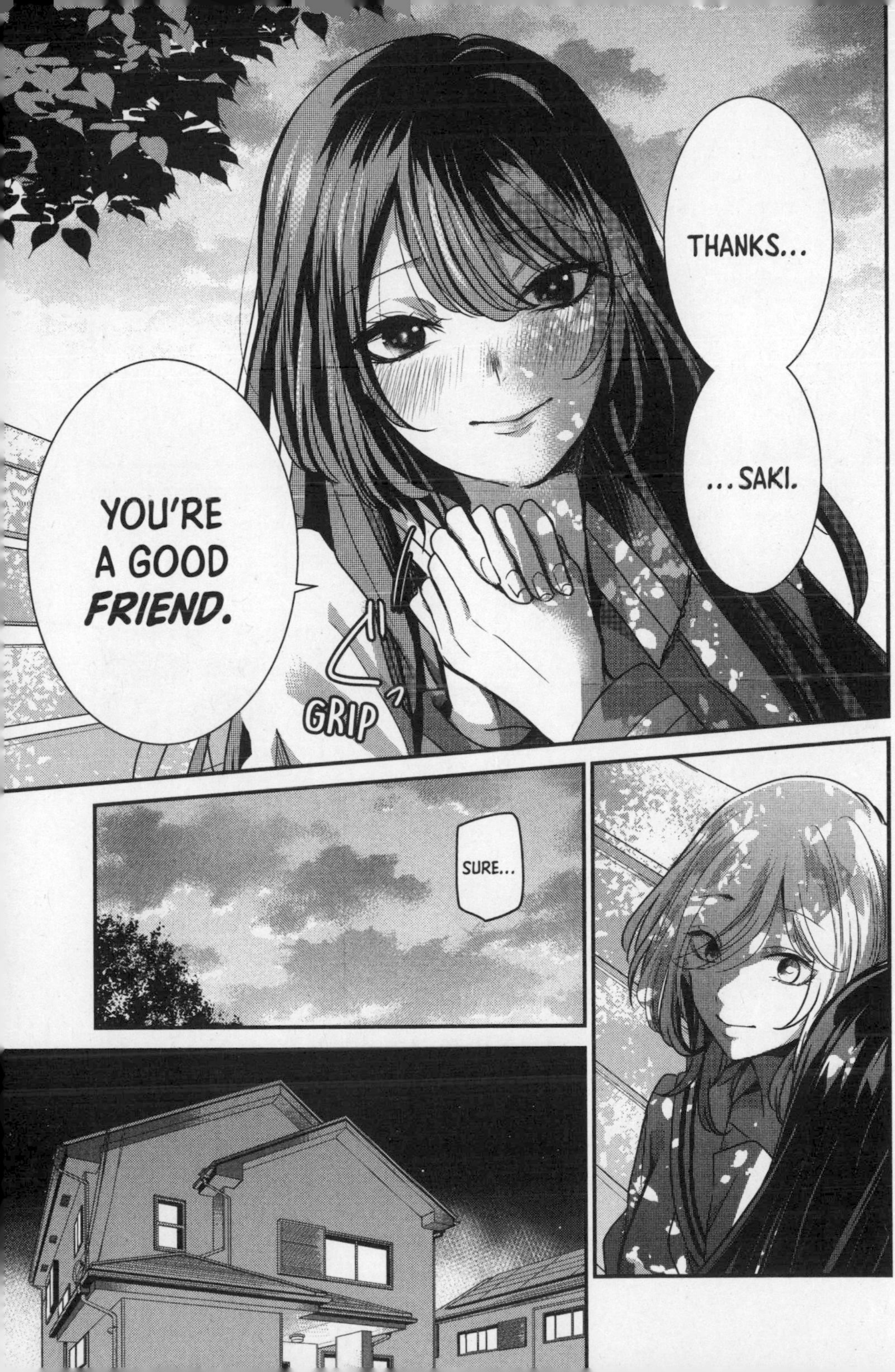
THANKS...
...SAKI.
YOU'RE A GOOD FRIEND.
GRIP
SURE...

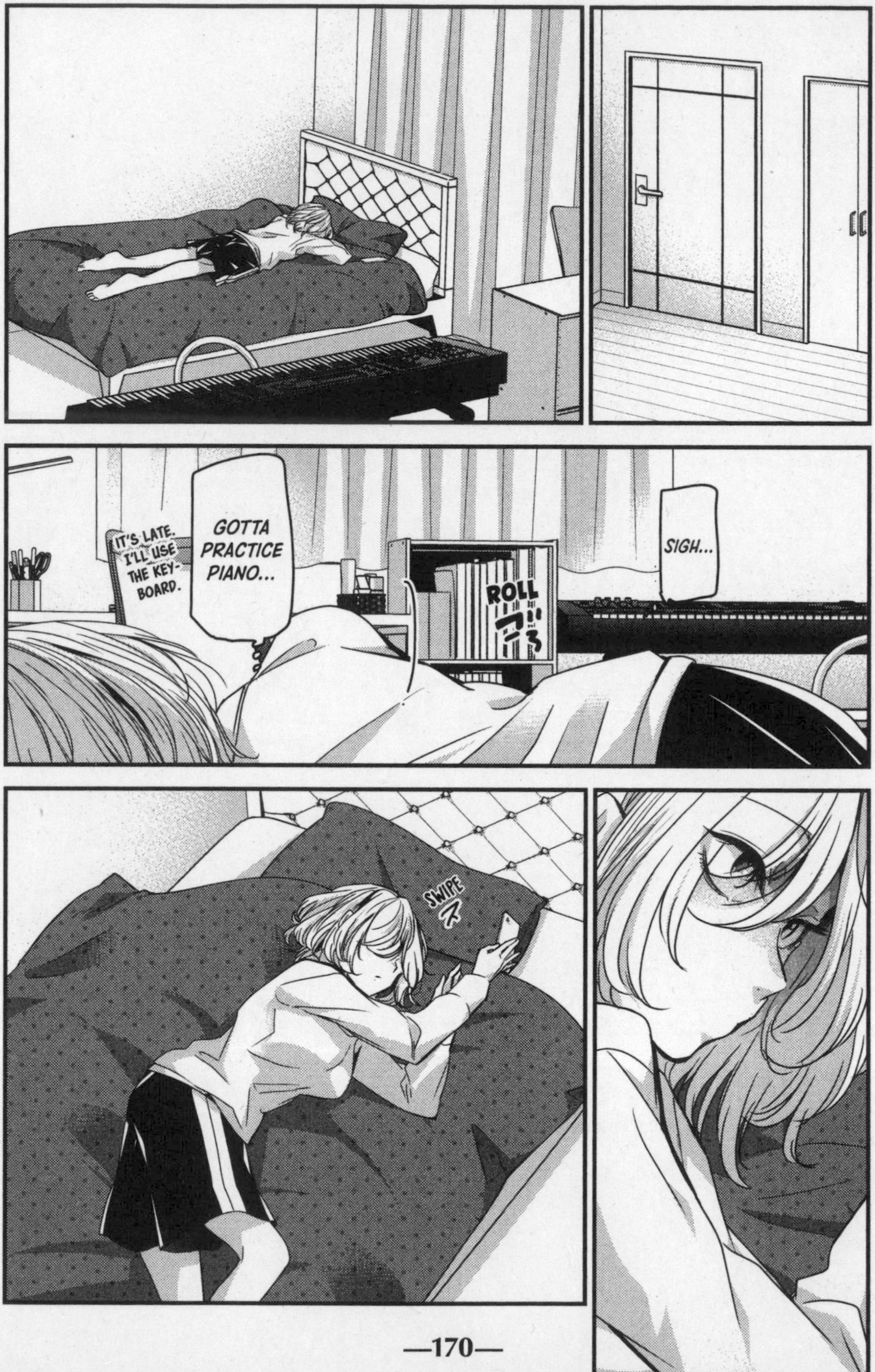
SIGH...
ROLL
GOTTA PRACTICE PIANO...
IT'S LATE. I'LL USE THE KEY-BOARD.
SWIPE

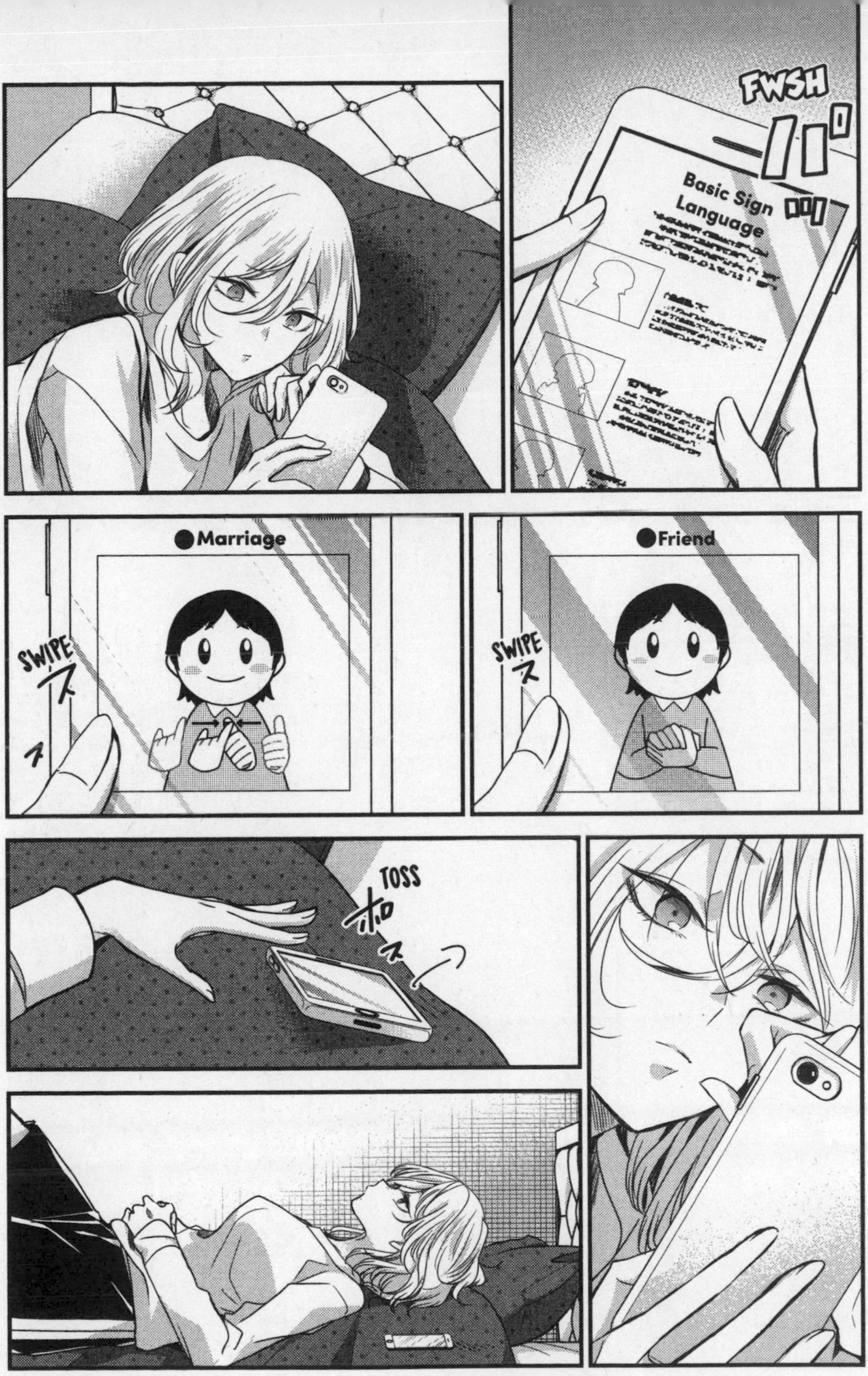
FWSH
Basic Sign Language
Friend
SWIPE
Marriage
SWIPE
TOSS

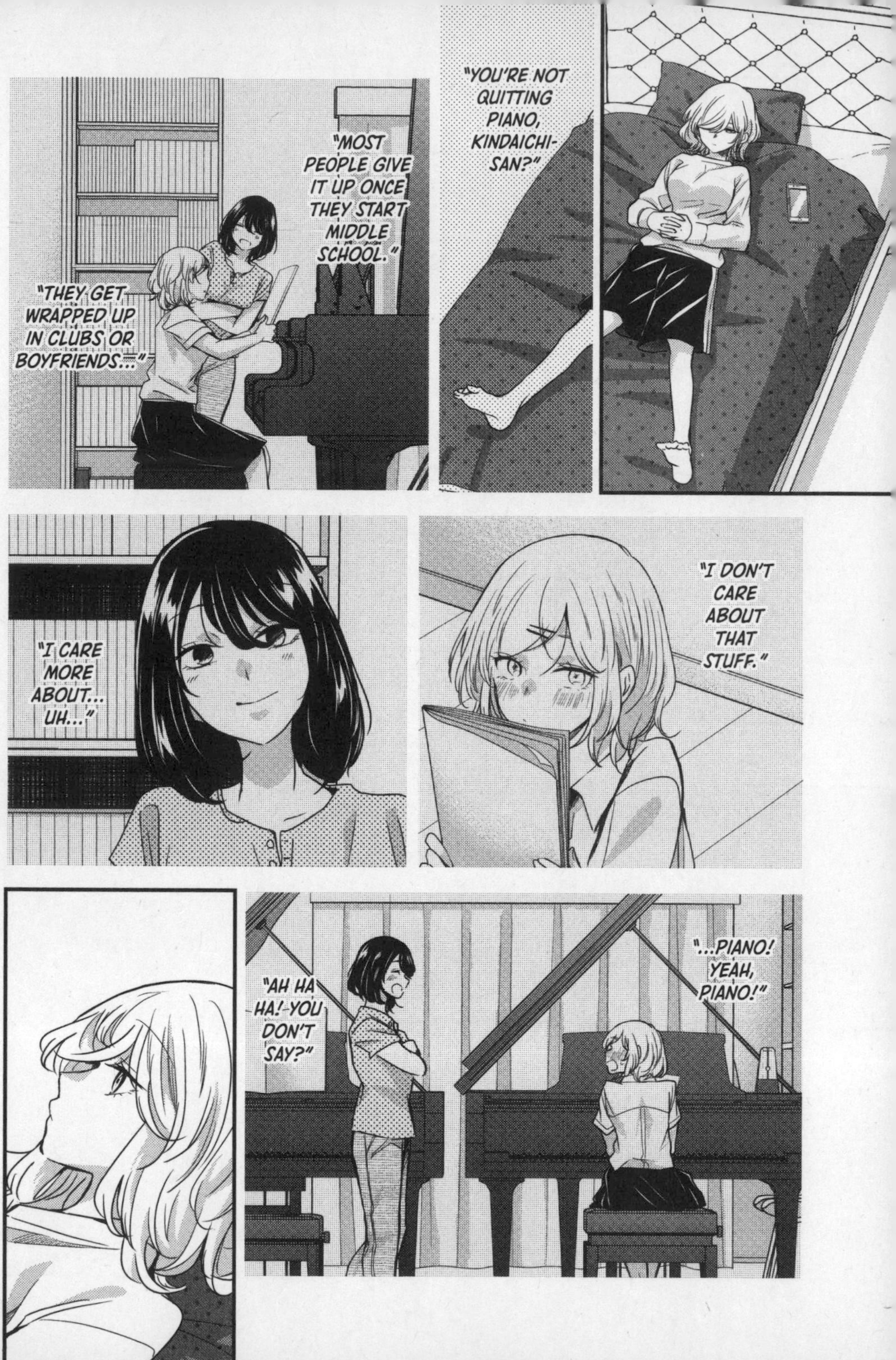
"YOU'RE NOT QUITTING PIANO, KINDAICHI-SAN?"
"MOST PEOPLE GIVE IT UP ONCE THEY START MIDDLE SCHOOL."
"THEY GET WRAPPED UP IN CLUBS OR BOYFRIENDS..."
"I DON'T CARE ABOUT THAT STUFF."
"I CARE MORE ABOUT... UH..."
"...PIANO! YEAH, PIANO!"
"AH HA HA! YOU DON'T SAY?"

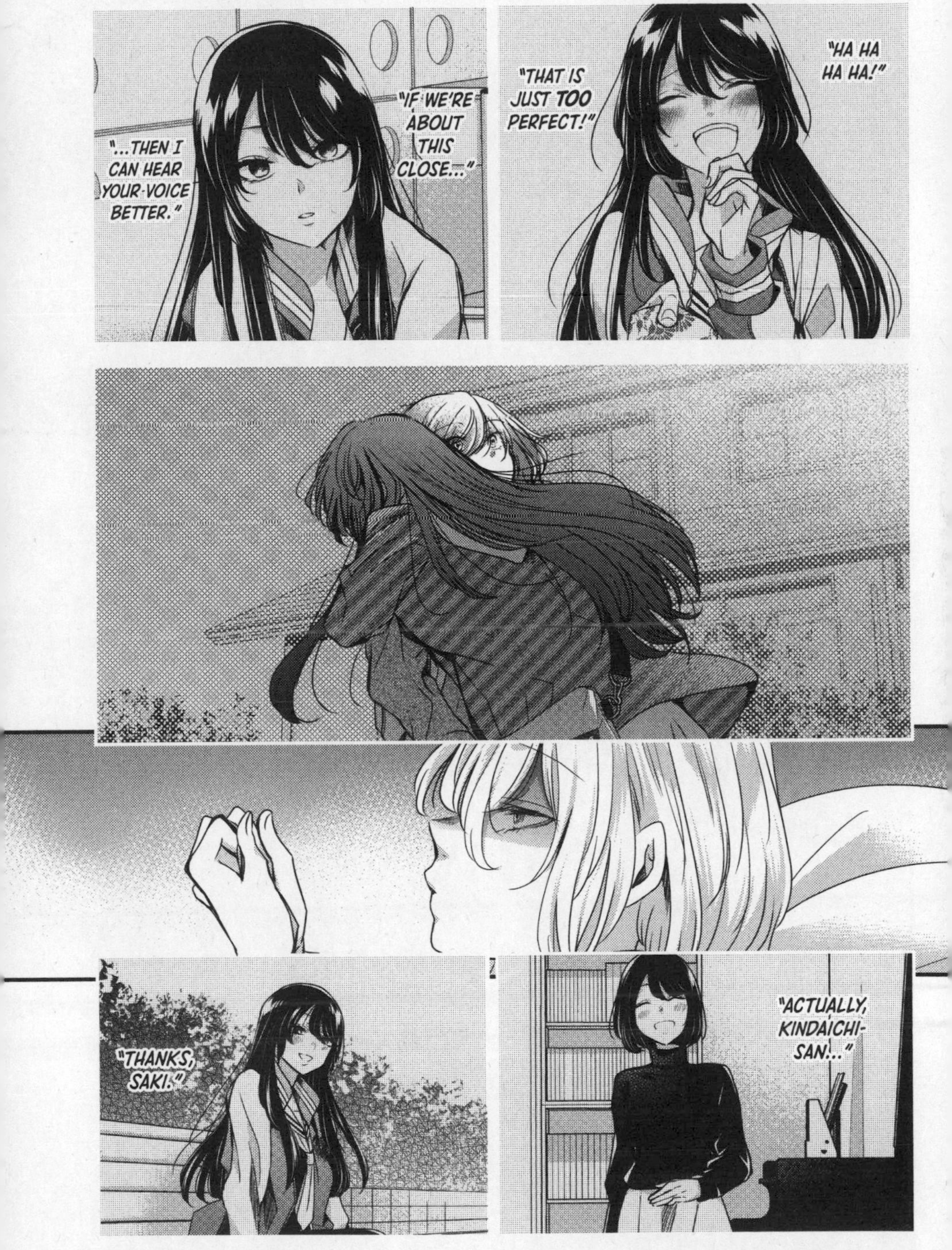
"HA HA HA HA!"
"THAT IS JUST TOO PERFECT!"
"IF WE'RE ABOUT THIS CLOSE..."
"...THEN I CAN HEAR YOUR VOICE BETTER."
"ACTUALLY, KINDAICHI-SAN..."
"THANKS, SAKI."

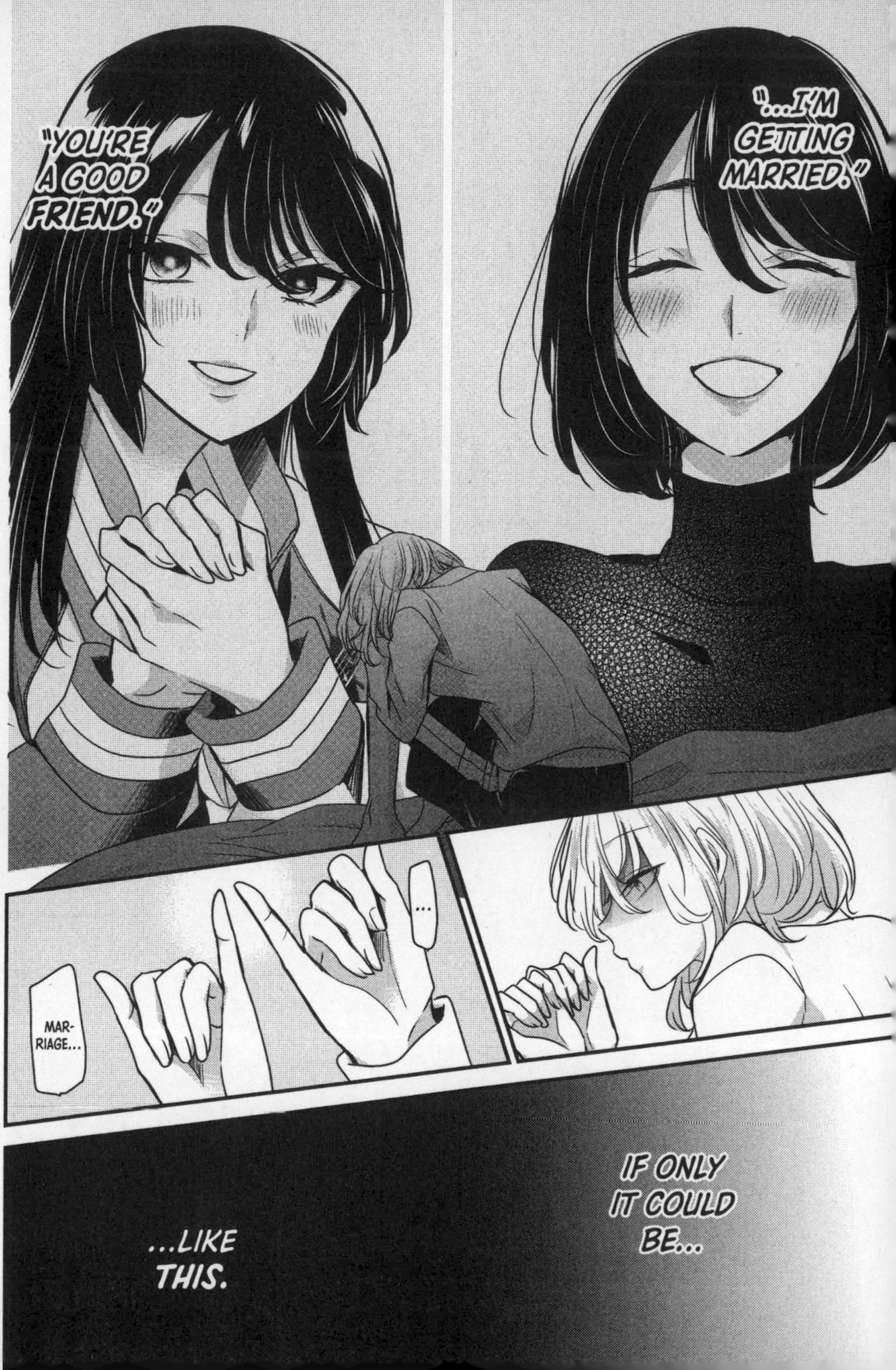
"...I'M GETTING MARRIED."
"YOU'RE A GOOD FRIEND."
...
MAR-RIAGE...
IF ONLY IT COULD BE...
...LIKE THIS.

Works Consulted

Haga, Yuuko and Karin Matsumori, eds., with manga by Sayo Takeshima. *Yuuko to Karin no baria furii komyunikeishon* (Yuko's and Karin's Barrier-Free Communication). Shogakukan Inc.

Organization for Psychological Issues of the Hard of Hearing, ed. *Nanchousha to chuuto shicchousha no shinrigaku: kikoenikusa wo kakaete ikiru* (Psychology of the Late-Deafened and Hard of Hearing: Living with Hearing Loss). Kamogawa Shuppan Inc.

Outani, Kunio. *Mimi no kikoenai hito, omoroi yan! to omowazu icchau hon* (A Book That Will Leave You Thinking, "Deaf People Are So Interesting!"). Seikosha Inc.

Shirai, Kazuo, Teruo Koami, and Yayoi Satou, eds. *Nanchouji/seito rikai handobukku: tsuujou no gakkyuu de oshieru sensei he* (Understanding Children and Students with Hearing Loss: A Handbook for Teachers in Regular Education). Gakuensha Inc.

Wakinaka, Kiyoko. *Choukaku-shougaisha kyouiku: kore made to kore kara. Komyunikeishon ronsou/kyuusai no kabe/shougai ninshiki wo chuushin ni* (Education for the Deaf and Hard of Hearing: Past and Present. With a Focus on Communications Theory, the "Age-Nine Barrier," and Disability Awareness). Kitaohji Shobo Inc.

Yamaguchi, Toshikatsu. *Chuuto shicchousha to nanchousha no sekai: mikake wa kenjousha, kizukarenai shougaisha* (The World of the Late-Deafened and Hard of Hearing: Outward Normalcy, Hidden Disability). Hitotsubashi Shuppan Inc.

Research Assistance

Yurika Wagatsuma (01familia, Ltd.)

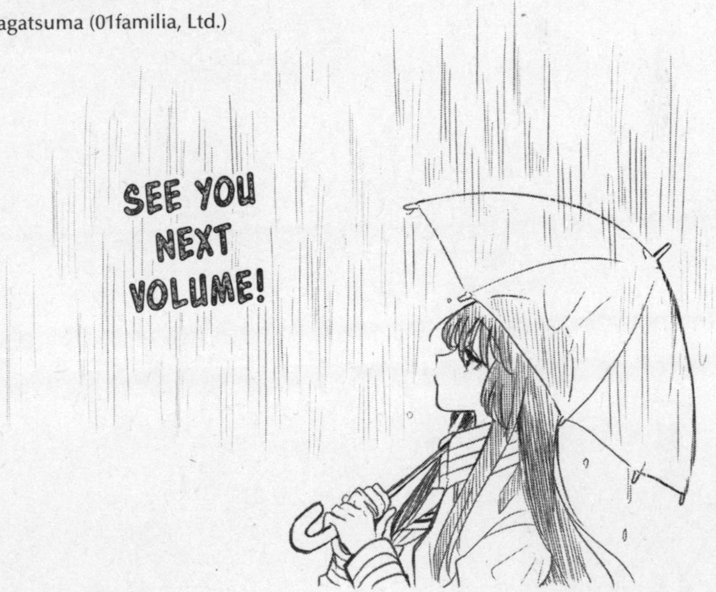

SEE YOU NEXT VOLUME!

Author's Notes

[1]From the Japanese Ministry of Health, Labour, and Welfare's *Heisei juuhachinendo shintai shougaiji/sha jittai chousa kekka no choukaku shougaisha no komyunikei-shon shudan no joukyou* (Current Communication Methods of the Deaf and Hard of Hearing, as reported in the *2006 Survey on Children and Individuals with Disabilities*). In addition to sign language, survey respondents also reported using lip reading, written communication, hearing aids, and cochlear implants.

[2]Hearing loss may present as: conductive hearing loss (due to damage to the outer or middle ear); sensorineural hearing loss (due to damage to the inner ear or the nerves further in); or mixed hearing loss, a combination of the two. Each type of hearing loss features a range of different symptoms.

[3]When hearing people are confronted with a host of different sounds or voices, their brains automatically filter out noise that is irrelevant to them; this phenomenon is known as "the cocktail party effect." Some people with hearing loss are unable to filter out background noise in this manner.

Translation Notes

Iwate, p. 6
Located south of Aomori and east of Akita, Iwate is the second largest prefecture in Japan and one of the northernmost prefectures on the main island of Honshu. As is the case with other regions of Japan that receive heavy snowfall, Iwate may sometimes be referred to as *yukiguni* (雪国, "snow country").

Kanon and Saki, p. 8
Like in many anime and manga, Kanon's and Saki's names may echo their respective roles in the story. The kanji in 奏音 (Kanon) can mean "to perform music" or "to play sound," while the kanji in 咲希 (Saki) can mean "rare blossom" or "blossom of hope."

Terminology, p. 24-25
Every effort has been made to use the closest English equivalents when translating terms referring to deafness or hearing loss. However, Japanese may offer a broader selection of terminology in this respect. For example, on page 24, Kanon's teacher describes Kanon as *mimi ga fujiyuu* (耳が不自由, "[one's] ears are not free/[one's] hearing is limited"), while on the next page, Kanon refers to the deaf and hard of hearing as *choukaku shougaisha* (聴覚障害者, "people with an impaired sense of hearing"). Other terms may be used depending on the context. The Tokyo Federation for the Deaf (TFD) notes that the term *rousha* (ろう者, "deaf person") can refer to those who are unable to hear even with a hearing aid, or who communicate primarily through sign language; while the term *nanchousha* (難聴者, "people with difficulty hearing") can refer to those who have some hearing and communicate primarily through spoken language.

Terminology can also take on different meanings in a social context. For example, Kanon indirectly cites a study from the Japanese Ministry of Health, Labour, and Welfare when lecturing her classmates on the deaf or hard of hearing. In this study, the ministry defines *choukaku shougaisha* as those who hold a government-issued disability card or who meet government criteria for disability.

Whether in Japan or outside of it, the choice of terminology can include an element of self-identification. The National Association of the Deaf (NAD) notes that deaf or hard of hearing people in the United States may identify with different labels depending on a range of factors, including age of onset, cultural identity, and level of hearing.

Shounen Machine Gun, p. 104
The name of this fictional magazine appears to be a play on *Shuukan Shounen Magajin* (*Weekly Shounen Magazine*), a long-running Kodansha publication in Japan.

Say You Love Me, p. 140
Aishiteiru to itte kure (愛していると言ってくれ, "Say You Love Me") is a popular 1995 J-drama starring Toyokawa Etsushi (a.k.a. Toyoetsu) and Tokiwa Takako. The show revolves around the budding romance between a painter named Koji (Toyokawa) who lost his hearing at the age of seven and a young actress named Hiroko (Tokiwa). Hiroko eventually begins learning sign language to communicate better with Koji.

Mega Anpan, p. 143
Anpan (あんぱん, "red bean paste bread") is a bun filled with sweet red bean paste.

Translation Notes (continued)

Shounen manga, p. 147

As the name implies, *shounen* manga (少年漫画, "young boys' manga") were originally marketed toward pre-teen and teenaged boys. *Shounen* can include everything from sports to slice-of-life stories, but is perhaps best known for action and adventure stories. Given *shounen's* image, Tanabe appears surprised that someone as pretty and "feminine" as Kanon would gravitate toward it.

"I love you," p. 157

In previous scenes, Kanon is shown using *nihon shuwa* (日本手話, "Japanese sign language/JSL"). However, in this panel, Kanon uses the American Sign Language (ASL) sign for "I love you." The "I love you" or "ILY" sign is commonly used in the American deaf community as a nonromantic greeting or parting, or as an informal expression of gratitude, goodwill, and friendship. The sign may be well known in Japan, particularly in the deaf community, due to the influence of American culture.

A SMART, NEW ROMANTIC COMEDY FOR FANS OF *SHORTCAKE CAKE* AND *TERRACE HOUSE*!

Living-Room Matsunaga-san © Keiko Iwashita / Kodansha Ltd

A romance manga starring high school girl Meeko, who learns to live on her own in a boarding house whose living room is home to the odd (but handsome) Matsunaga-san. She begins to adjust to her new life away from her parents, but Meeko soon learns that no matter how far away from home she is, she's still a young girl at heart — especially when she finds herself falling for Matsunaga-san.

Young characters and steampunk setting, like *Howl's Moving Castle* and *Battle Angel Alita*

Beyond the Clouds © 2018 Nicke / Ki-oon

A boy with a talent for machines and a mysterious girl whose wings he's fixed will take you beyond the clouds! In the tradition of the high-flying, resonant adventure stories of Studio Ghibli comes a gorgeous tale about the longing of young hearts for adventure and friendship!

CUTE ANIMALS AND LIFE LESSONS, PERFECT FOR ASPIRING PET VETS OF ALL AGES!

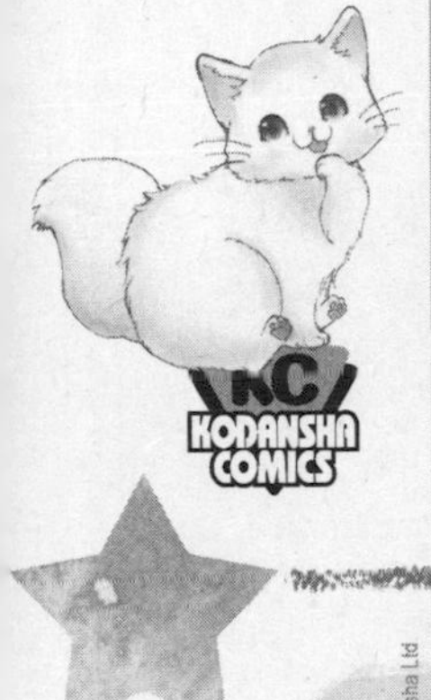

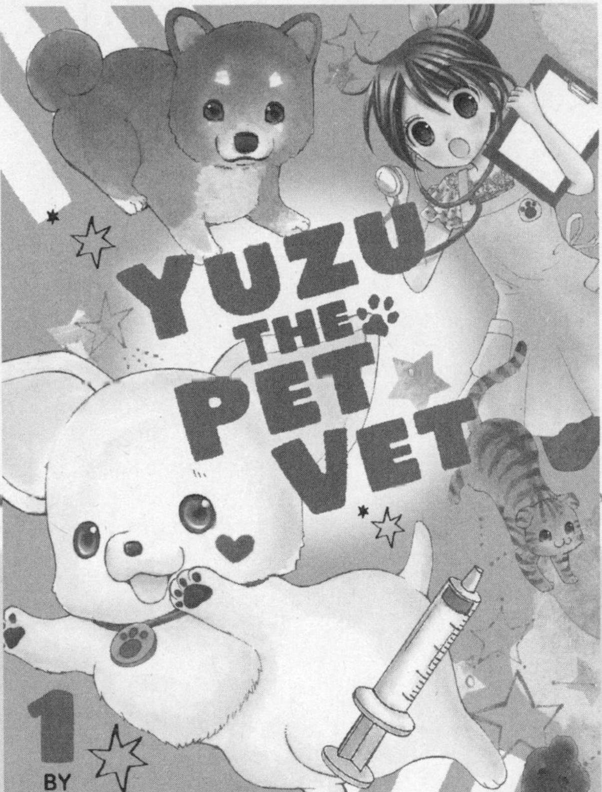
YUZU THE PET VET
1
BY
MINGO ITO
In collaboration with
NIPPON COLUMBIA CO., LTD.

KODANSHA COMICS

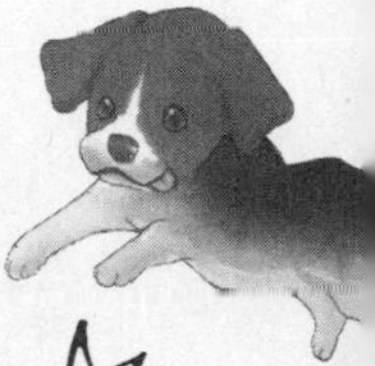

For an 11-year-old, Yuzu has a lot on her plate. When her mom gets sick and has to be hospitalized, Yuzu goes to live with her uncle who runs the local veterinary clinic. Yuzu's always been scared of animals, but she tries to help out. Through all the tough moments in her life, Yuzu realizes that she can help make things all right with a little help from her animal pals, peers, and kind grown-ups.

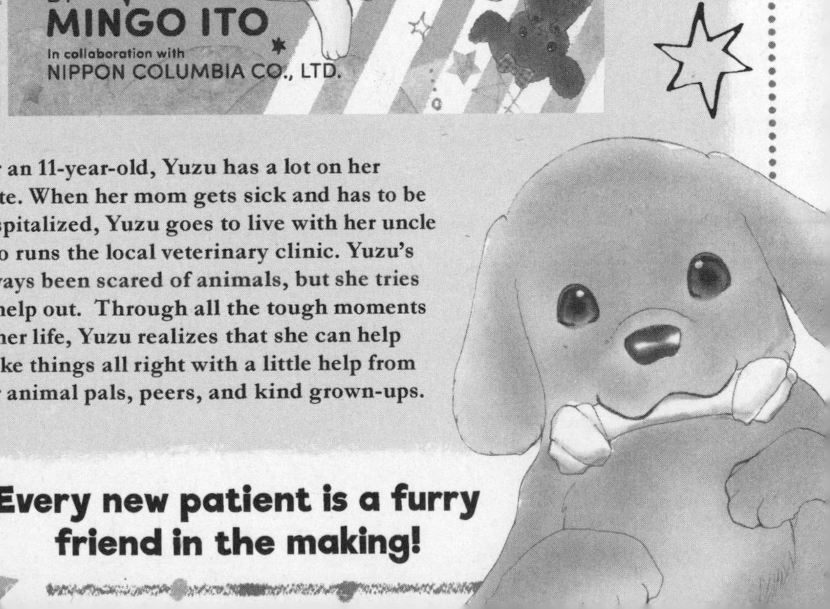

Every new patient is a furry friend in the making!

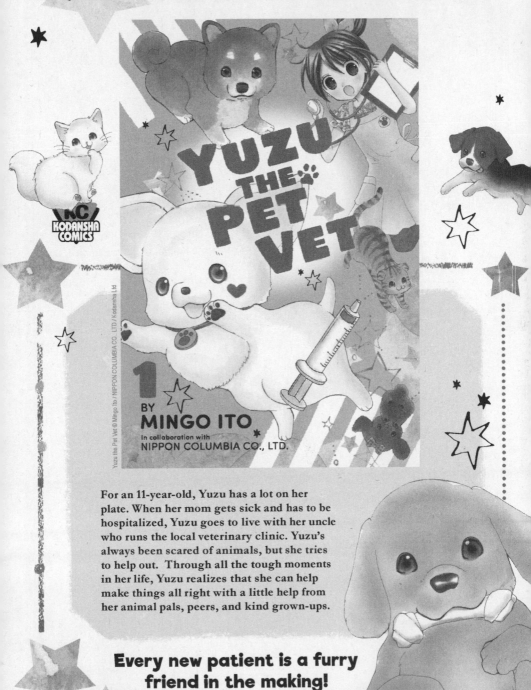

1 PERFECT WORLD

Rie Aruga

A TOUCHING NEW SERIES ABOUT LOVE AND COPING WITH DISABILITY

An office party reunites Tsugumi with her high school crush Itsuki. He's realized his dream of becoming an architect, but along the way, he experienced a spinal injury that put him in a wheelchair. Now Tsugumi's rekindled feelings will butt up against prejudices she never considered — and Itsuki will have to decide if he's ready to let someone into his heart...

"Depicts with great delicacy and courage the difficulties some with disabilities experience getting involved in romantic relationships... Rie Aruga refuses to romanticize, pushing her heroine to face the reality of disability. She invites her readers to the same tasks of empathy, knowledge and recognition."
—Slate.fr

"An important entry [in manga romance]... The emotional core of both plot and characters indicates thoughtfulness... [Aruga's] research is readily apparent in the text and artwork, making this feel like a real story."
—Anime News Network

The boys are back, in 400-page hardcovers that are as pretty and badass as they are!

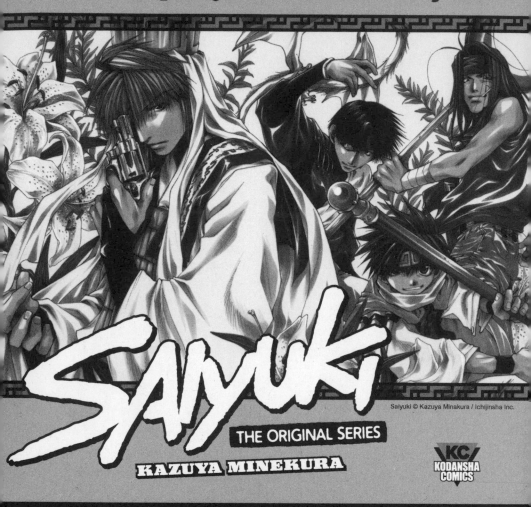

Saiyuki © Kazuya Minakura / Ichijinsha Inc.

SAIYUKI

THE ORIGINAL SERIES

KAZUYA MINEKURA

KC
KODANSHA
COMICS

"AN EDGY COMIC LOOK AT AN ANCIENT CHINESE TALE." —YALSA

Genjo Sanzo is a Buddhist priest in the city of Togenkyo, which is being ravaged by yokai spirits that have fallen out of balance with the natural order. His superiors send him on a journey far to the west to discover why this is happening and how to stop it. His companions are three yokai with human souls. But this is no day trip — the four will encounter many discoveries and horrors on the way.

FEATURES NEW TRANSLATION, COLOR PAGES, AND BEAUTIFUL WRAPAROUND COVER ART!

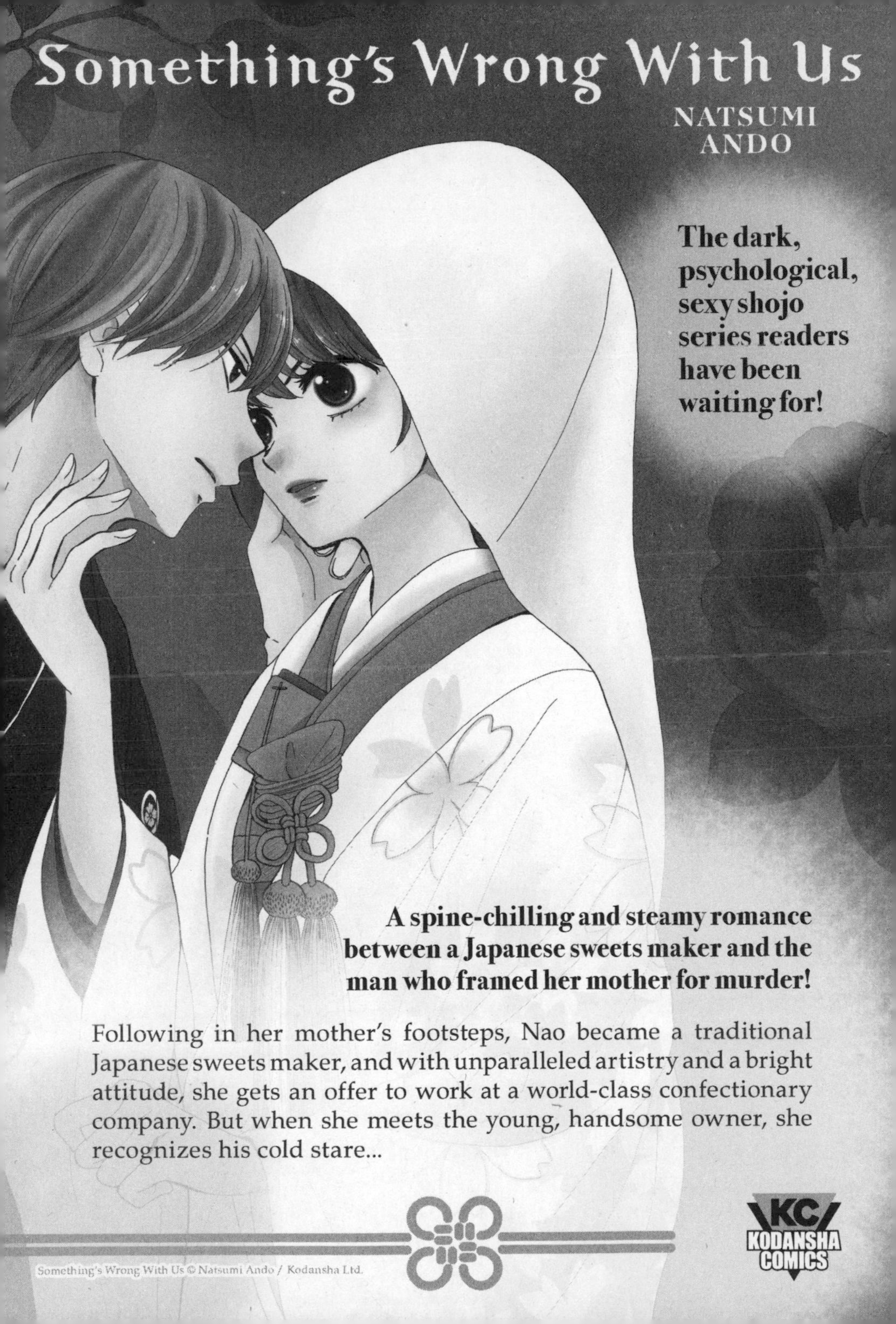
Something's Wrong With Us
NATSUMI ANDO
The dark, psychological, sexy shojo series readers have been waiting for!
A spine-chilling and steamy romance between a Japanese sweets maker and the man who framed her mother for murder!
Following in her mother's footsteps, Nao became a traditional Japanese sweets maker, and with unparalleled artistry and a bright attitude, she gets an offer to work at a world-class confectionary company. But when she meets the young, handsome owner, she recognizes his cold stare...
KC KODANSHA COMICS
Something's Wrong With Us © Natsumi Ando / Kodansha Ltd.

THE SWEET SCENT OF LOVE IS IN THE AIR! FOR FANS OF OFFBEAT ROMANCES LIKE *WOTAKOI*

Sweat and Soap © Kintetsu Yamada / Kodansha Ltd.

In an office romance, there's a fine line between sexy and awkward... and that line is where Asako — a woman who sweats copiously — meets Koutarou — a perfume developer who can't get enough of Asako's, er, scent. Don't miss a romcom manga like no other!

The art-deco cyberpunk classic from the creators of *xxxHOLiC* and *Cardcaptor Sakura!*

CLAMP

CLOVER

—— COLLECTOR'S EDITION ——

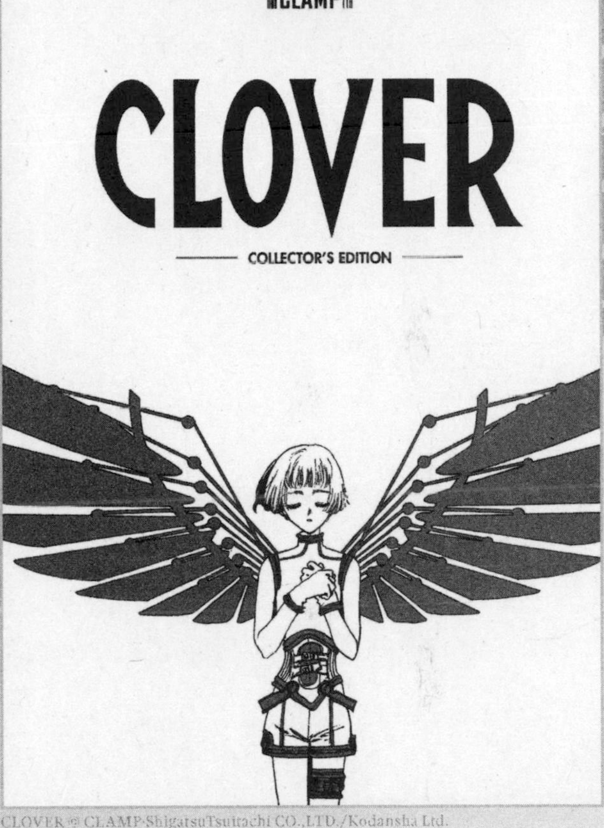

CLOVER © CLAMP·ShigatsuTsuitachi CO.,LTD./Kodansha Ltd.

Su was born into a bleak future, where the government keeps tight control over children with magical powers—codenamed "Clovers." With Su being the only "four-leaf" Clover in the world, she has been kept isolated nearly her whole life. Can ex-military agent Kazuhiko deliver her to the happiness she seeks? Experience the complete series in this hardcover edition, which also includes over twenty pages of ravishing color art!

KC
KODANSHA COMICS

One of CLAMP's biggest hits returns in this definitive, premium, hardcover 20th anniversary collector's edition!

CLAMP

Chobits 1

20TH ANNIVERSARY EDITION

"A wonderfully entertaining story that would be a great installment in anybody's manga collection."
— Anime News Network

"CLAMP is an all-female manga-creating team whose feminine touch shows in this entertaining, sci-fi soap opera."
— Publishers Weekly

Poor college student Hideki is down on his luck. All he wants is a good job, a girlfriend, and his very own "persocom"—the latest and greatest in humanoid computer technology. Hideki's luck changes one night when he finds Chi—a persocom thrown out in a pile of trash. But Hideki soon discovers that there's much more to his cute new persocom than meets the eye.

KC
KODANSHA
COMICS

MAGIC ● KNIGHT RAYEARTH

25TH ANNIVERSARY EDITION

CLAMP

A BELOVED CLASSIC MAKES ITS STUNNING RETURN IN THIS GORGEOUS, LIMITED EDITION BOX SET!

This tale of three Tokyo teenagers who cross through a magical portal and become the champions of another world is a modern manga classic. The box set includes three volumes of manga covering the entire first series of *Magic Knight Rayearth*, plus the series's super-rare full-color art book companion, all printed at a larger size than ever before on premium paper, featuring a newly-revised translation and lettering, and exquisite foil-stamped covers.

A strictly limited edition, this will be gone in a flash!

KC
KODANSHA
COMICS

The beloved characters from *Cardcaptor Sakura* return in a brand new, reimagined fantasy adventure!

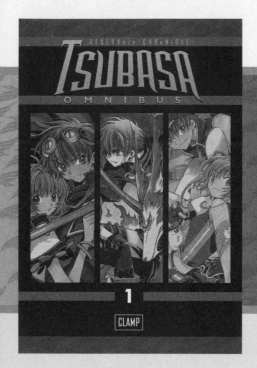

"[*Tsubasa*] takes readers on a fantastic ride that only gets more exhilarating with each successive chapter." —Anime News Network

In the Kingdom of Clow, an archaeological dig unleashes an incredible power, causing Princess Sakura to lose her memories. To save her, her childhood friend Syaoran must follow the orders of the Dimension Witch and travel alongside Kurogane, an unrivaled warrior; Fai, a powerful magician; and Mokona, a curiously strange creature, to retrieve Sakura's dispersed memories!